DHARMA FLOWER SUTRA

Hsüan-hua

THE WONDERFUL DHARMA LOTUS FLOWER SUTRA

Translated into Chinese by
Tripitaka Master Kumarajiva of Yao Ch'in

Volume 4: Chapter 3: A Parable

with the commentary of

Tripitaka Master Hua

Translated into English by
The Buddhist Text Translation Society
San Francisco
1979

Translated by the Buddhist Text Translation Society

Primary translation: Bhikshuni Heng Yin
Reviewed by: Bhikshuni Heng Ch'ih
Edited by: Upasika Kuo-lin Lethcoe

Certified by: The Venerable Master Hua

Printed in the United States of America

First Printing--1979

For information address:

Sino American Buddhist Association
Gold Mountain Monastery
1731 15th Street
San Francisco, California 94103
U.S.A
(415) 621-5202
(415) 861-9672

ISBN 0-917512-62-6

Acknowledgements:
Cover: Shramanerika Heng-chieh
Index: Shramanerika Heng-ming
Proofreading and other: Upasikas Kuo-ts'an, Kuo-chu, Kuo-li
Chinese Calligraphy: Shramanerika Heng-wen
English Calligraphy: Jerri-jo Idarius
Photo of the Master: Kuo-ying Brevoort
Graphic: Kuo-ling

TABLE OF CONTENTS

The Venerable Master Hua

TRANSLATOR'S INTRODUCTION

After setting the stage for the speaking of *The Dharma Flower Sutra* in Chapter One, the Buddha opens the provisional to reveal the real. In Chapter Two he speaks the Dharma directly, setting forth the doctrine of universal salvation by means of the One Buddha Vehicle. In Chapter Two he speaks for those of superior roots and sharp wisdom. Those of average and inferior roots were unable to resolve their doubts.

In his great compassion, the Buddha then speaks a parable to lead those of average roots to understanding. That is Chapter Three: "A Parable," the present volume. It is one of the most important chapters in the Sutra. For this reason, the Venerable Master Hua commented on it at length and in great detail.

In the analogy there is a great elder who left his children at home and went on a journey. As he was returning, he saw that his house had caught fire. He called to the children to come out, but they were so absorbed in their play that they paid no attention to him. The elder then used an expedient device. "Come out," he said. "I have some fine toys for you right outside the door. I have sheep carts, deer carts, and ox carts. Come out and take them!" Hearing this, the children ran from the house to safety and demanded the carts. Instead of the three carts he had promised, he gave them each a great white ox cart, wonderful far beyond their original hopes.

The great elder is, of course, the Buddha. His children are those of the Three Vehicles and also all living beings. Playing in the burning house of the three realms, living beings continue to amuse themselves, ignoring the Buddha's warnings and unaware of the danger. The Buddha expediently offers the teachings of the Three Vehicles, but gives us instead the One Buddha Vehicle, the Great White Ox Cart.

Those who study this volume will find it a treasury of lists, stories, and detailed explanations of doctrine. Studying it, we should endeavor to put its principles into practice, and thereby escape the burning house of birth and death in the three realms.

For there's only One Vehicle
   in the worlds great and small--
The Lotus of Dharma which blooms in us all.
There's only One Vehicle,
   not two or three.
Rejoice, now, for one day Buddha's we'll be.

Bhikshuni Heng-yin
Buddhist Text Translation Society
City of Ten Thousand Buddhas
July 1979

REVIEWER'S PREFACE

It is said that the Buddhadharma is also the dharma of living beings and the dharma of the mind. The three are not different but are one-in-the-same.

The Wonderful Dharma Lotus Flower Sutra reveals without provision, beyond a doubt, the actuality of this principle of three-in-one. Who can accept it? Everyone, potentially. Yet in Chapter Two, after three requests, when Shakyamuni Buddha finally reveals that all living beings have the Buddhanature and can become Buddhas, five thousand people leave the assembly because their arrogance obstructs them. Even now in Chapter Three, Shariputra, who had insistently requested the Buddha to speak, at once is delighted to hear the Great Vehicle Dharma, but he still has to admit his initial doubt that perhaps he was being deluded by a demon in the guise of a Buddha.

Arrogance in some, doubt in others, greed, hatred, and stupidity to varying degrees in all, are afflictions of the mind that prevent us from accepting the revelation of truth. Living beings, when told they have the pure and perfect Buddhanature inherent within them, and that the capacity of their minds is as vast as emptiness and encompasses all existence, cannot believe it. Unable to transcend the massive net of afflictions they have created they are prevents, indeed they prevent themselves, from realizing their own potential.

Knowing very well the ways in which living beings are obstructed, Shakyamuni Buddha first assures them that all living beings *can* become Buddhas by giving Shariputra a detailed prediction of Buddhahood. Because he represents those who have not yet been able to fathom the Great Vehicle Buddhadharma or ther own mind's capacity to experience ultimate awakening--Nirvana Without Residue--Shariputra is easy for us to identify with, that is, we, too, could receive such a prediction!

To help convince us of the unlimited extent of our inherent worth, the Buddha speaks a parable, simple and entertaining, to open gently and explain the principle so that we may awaken to and enter it. The layers of meaning multiply as the parable is meshed with the actual teaching in the masterful description of the great white ox cart. The initial and ultimate unity of Buddhas, living beings, and the mind is confirmed again and again in the extended analogy.

All the intricate aspects of the parable are elaborated upon in the precise commentary of the Venerable Master Hua with such finesse that the shedding of afflictions and realization of our potential becomes a sheer irresistable force.

May it be so for you.

Bhikshuni Heng-ch'ih
Buddhist Text Translation Society
City of Ten Thousand Buddhas
July 12, 1979
Anniversary of Kuan-yin Bodhisattva's
Leaving the home-life

CHAPTER THREE: OUTLINE

F2. Shariputra is led to understanding. (text page 515)
  G1. Editor's preface. (515)
  G2. Shariputra explains himself. (516)
    H1. Prose. (516)
      I1. Telling of the three kinds of rejoicing. (516)
      I2. Explanation. (517)
      I3. Conclusion. (520)
        J1. Conclusion proper. (520)
        J2. Realization. (522)
    H2. Verse. (522)
      I1. Announcing the verse. (522)
      I2. Setting forth the verse. (523)
        J1. The wisdom was not lost. (523)
        J2. The wisdom formerly lost. (525)
      I3. Conclusion. (529)
        J1. Conclusion itself. (529)
          K1. Conclusion proper. (529)
          K2. Narrating the doubts. (530)
          K3. Narrating his presently being led to understanding. (531)
        J2. Final statement. (533)
F3. The Thus Come One tells of Shariputra's realization. (535)
  G1. Shariputra was taught the Great Vehicle in the past. (535)
  G2. Halfway through he forgot it and grasped the Small Vehicle. (537)
  G3. Once again he is taught the Great Vehicle. (537)
F4. Shariputra is given a prediction. (538)
  G1. Prose. (538)
    H1. Time. (538)
    H2. Causal practice. (538)

Shakyamuni Buddha

Shariputra (cover detail)

PART ONE: SHARIPUTRA'S PREDICAMENT

Sutra: T.262,10b29

CHAPTER THREE: A PARABLE

THEREUPON, SHARIPUTRA, WITH JOYFUL ENTHUSIASM, ROSE, JOINED HIS PALMS TOGETHER, AND GAZED REVERENTLY AT THE HONORED ONE'S FACE...

Outline:

F2. Shariputra is led to understanding.
G1. Editor's preface.

Commentary:

In this, the third chapter of *The Wonderful Dharma Lotus Flower Sutra*, A PARABLE is used because the doctrine is so profound that, if it were spoken outright, no one would understand it. In this way, those of average roots can be led to understanding.

THEREUPON, right after the second chapter, "Expedient Devices" had been spoken and the entire assembly had received predictions of Buddhahood, SHARIPUTRA, the Disciple foremost in wisdom, WITH JOYFUL ENTHUSIASM,

ROSE, JOINED HIS PALMS TOGETHER AND GAZED REVERENTLY AT THE HONORED ONE'S FACE...Pure in the three karmas of body, mouth, and mind, Shariputra spoke to the Buddha.

Sutra: T.10c1

...AND SAID TO THE BUDDHA, "NOW, HAVING HEARD THIS SOUND OF DHARMA FROM THE WORLD HONORED ONE, MY HEART REJOICES AND I HAVE OBTAINED WHAT I NEVER HAD BEFORE."

Outline:

G2. Shariputra explains himself.
H1. Prose.
I1. Telling of the three kinds of rejoicing.

Commentary:

...AND SAID TO THE BUDDHA, "NOW, HAVING HEARD THIS SOUND OF DHARMA FROM THE WORLD HONORED ONE, having heard *The Wonderful Dharma Lotus Flower Sutra*, MY HEART REJOICES AND I HAVE OBTAINED WHAT I NEVER HAD BEFORE. Previously, in the Vaipulya and Prajna assemblies, I never heard a wonderful Dharma as subtle and miraculous as this."

Sutra: T.10c2

"WHAT IS THE REASON? IN THE PAST, I HEARD A DHARMA SUCH AS THIS FROM THE BUDDHA, AND SAW THE BODHISATTVAS RECEIVE PREDICTIONS OF BUDDHAHOOD, BUT WE HAD NO PART IN THIS MATTER. I WAS DEEPLY HURT THAT I HAD LOST THE LIMITLESS KNOWLEDGE AND VISION OF THE THUS COME ONE.

"WORLD HONORED ONE, WHEN I USED TO DWELL ALONE IN MOUNTAIN FORESTS AT THE FOOT OF TREES, WHETHER SITTING OR WALKING I CONTINUALLY HAD

THIS THOUGHT: 'WE ALL IDENTICALLY ENTER INTO THE DHARMA NATURE. WHY HAS THE THUS COME ONE SHOWN US DELIVERANCE BY MEANS OF THE SMALL VEHICLE DHARMA? IT IS OUR FAULT, NOT THE WORLD HONORED ONE'S.'"

Outline:

I2. Explanation

Commentary:

"WHAT IS THE REASON? IN THE PAST, I HEARD DHARMA SUCH AS THIS FROM THE BUDDHA, AND SAW THE BODHISATTVAS RECEIVE PREDICTIONS OF BUDDHAHOOD. The Buddha conferred upon them predictions of their future Buddhahood. BUT WE HAD NO PART IN THIS MATTER. Although the Bodhisattvas had received predictions, we of the Small Vehicle did not have the status to take part in this supreme affair. We did not obtain a prediction from the Buddha because we didn't have the standing. I WAS DEEPLY HURT THAT I HAD LOST THE LIMITLESS KNOWLEDGE AND VISION OF THE THUS COME ONE. I was extremely pained because I had not obtained a prediction from the Thus Come One. I had not been favored with the Buddha's compassion and I thought I had lost out on the limitless knowledge and the limitless good roots.

"WORLD HONORED ONE, WHEN I USED TO DWELL ALONE IN MOUNTAIN FORESTS AT THE FOOT OF TREES, WHETHER SITTING OR WALKING I CONTINUALLY HAD THIS THOUGHT: 'WE ALL IDENTICALLY ENTER INTO THE DHARMA NATURE. I used to live alone in the mountains, beneath the trees, because such places are very clean and quiet. They are appropriate for cultivation. I may have been sitting in meditation for several days at a stretch without moving. Then, when I got tired, I would get up and take exercise by walking around the tree or just walking through the glen. In any case, I always thought that we of the Small Vehicle and the Bodhisattvas identically possess the Dharma nature. Together we obtain the Dharma spoken by the Buddha, the nourishing moisture of the Dharma rain. WHY HAS THE THUS COME ONE SHOWN US DELIVERANCE BY MEANS OF THE SMALL VEHICLE DHARMA? Why not use the Great Vehicle Dharma? Why did he use the Small Vehicle Dharma to save us? Was the Thus Come One prejudiced? Did the Buddha not care for the Small Vehicle people? Was he not compassionate?"

Those were Shariputra's false thoughts.

"IT IS OUR FAULT, NOT THE WORLD HONORED ONE'S.'" Shariputra false thought back and forth, around and around, until he finally returned the light and reversed the illumination. "It's our fault.We of the Small Vehicle have dispositions which are shallow and thin. Our wisdom is non-existent; we're quite stupid, actually. So if the Buddha had spoken the Great Vehicle Dharma to us, we would have been unable to accept it. It's our own fault. It has nothing to do with the World Honored One. It's not a question of his being prejudiced or not being compassionate. And it's not that he doesn't care for us. Our own base, lowly dispositions, our own bad natures were such that, although the Buddha may have wished to speak the Great Vehicle Dharma, we could not have accepted it."

Sutra: T.10c7

"WHAT IS THE REASON? IF WE HAD WAITED FOR THE LECTURE ON THE CAUSE OF REALIZING ANUTTARASAMYAKSAMBODHI, WE SHOULD CERTAINLY HAVE BEEN DELIVERED BY MEANS OF THE GREAT VEHICLE. BUT WE DID NOT UNDERSTAND THAT EXPEDIENT DEVICES WERE SPOKEN IN ACCORD WITH WHAT WAS APPROPRIATE. THEREFORE, WHEN WE FIRST HEARD THE BUDDHADHARMA, UPON ENCOUNTERING IT WE IMMEDIATELY BELIEVED AND ACCEPTED IT, CONSIDERED IT, AND TOOK CERTIFICATION."

Commentary:

"WHAT IS THE REASON? Why is it our fault and not a case of the World Honored One being unfair? IF WE HAD WAITED FOR THE LECTURE ON THE CAUSE OF REALIZING ANUTTARASAMYAKSAMBODHI, WE SHOULD CERTAINLY HAVE BEEN DELIVERED BY MEANS OF THE GREAT VEHICLE. If we had waited a bit, thought it over, and then realized the unsurpassed, proper-equal and right enlightenment, we would certainly have been saved by means of the Great Vehicle. We would have relied on the Great Vehicle in our cultivation and in that way obtained salvation.

Anuttarasamyaksambodhi is the highest enlightenment of the Buddha. It is said to be "right" enlightenment to differentiate it from the state of common people. Common people are not enlightened. The things that common people do are crazy and mixed-up because they are not awake. Right enlightenment doesn't signify the state of enlightening others. Those of the Two Vehicles have obtained right enlightenment, but they have not attained proper-equal enlightenment. The Buddha's proper-equal enlightenment distinguishes him from those of the Two Vehicles. Proper-equal enlightenment is the enlightenment of the Great Vehicle Bodhisattvas, the Equal Enlightenment Bodhisattvas who enlighten themselves and enlighten others. They are properly equal with the Buddha, but still off by just a little bit. Equal Enlightenment Bodhisattvas still have one share of production mark ignorance[1] which they haven't destroyed. When they destroy it, they realize Wonderful Enlightenment, the enlightenment which is unsurpassed. This is the unsurpassed proper-equal and right enlightenment, the position of Buddhahood.

At the level of Wonderful Enlightenment one is called an "unsurpassed hero."[2] Before reaching that level, the Bodhisattvas are called "surpassed heroes,"[3] because the Buddha is still above them. The Buddha is the unsurpassed hero, having realized the fruit of Buddhahood, the unsurpassed proper-equal and right enlightenment.

If you wish to certify to the fruit of Buddhahood, you must rely upon the Dharma of the Great Vehicle Bodhisattva.

"BUT WE DID NOT UNDERSTAND THAT EXPEDIENT DEVICES WERE SPOKEN IN ACCORD WITH WHAT WAS APPROPRIATE. We didn't understand that when the Buddha spoke the Dharma

---

1 生相無明-*sheng hsiang wu ming.*

2 無上士-*wu shang shih.*

3 有上士-*yu shang shih.*

he was using expedient devices to teach and transform us. He regards the potentials of beings and dispenses the teaching appropriate to the person. He prescribes the medicine according to the illness. He bestows the teaching according to the needs of the person being taught. Thus, he speaks in accord with what is appropriate.

"THEREFORE, WHEN WE FIRST HEARD THE BUDDHADHARMA, UPON ENCOUNTERING IT WE IMMEDIATELY BELIEVED AND ACCEPTED IT...When we heard the Buddha speak the dharmas of the Four Truths, the Twelve Causes and Conditions, we believed them. CONSIDERED IT, AND TOOK CERTIFICATION. We applied effort, cultivated, considered it, and certified to the fruit of Arhatship.

Sutra: T.10c10

"WORLD HONORED ONE, FROM OF OLD I HAVE, DAY AND NIGHT, CONTINUALLY REPROACHED MYSELF. NOW, FROM THE BUDDHA, I HAVE HEARD WHAT I NEVER HEARD BEFORE, THIS DHARMA WHICH HAS NEVER BEEN BEFORE, AND ALL MY DOUBTS HAVE BEEN SEVERED. MY BODY AND MIND ARE BLISSFULL AND I AM AT PEACE."

Outline:

I3. Conclusion
J1. Conclusion proper.

Commentary:

"WORLD HONORED ONE, FROM OF OLD, I HAVE, DAY AND NIGHT, CONTINUALLY REPROACHED MYSELF. From the time of the Vaipulya Teachings until the present, from morning until night, from night until dawn, I have scolded myself." What is meant by "day and night?" Before one is enlightened, it is as if it were night. After enlightenment, it is as if the sun had risen. Those of the Two Vehicles who had certified to the fruit of Arhatship could be spoken of as being in the daylight. But if you compare them to the Bodhisattvas, they are still in the dark, and the Bodhisattvas are in the daylight.

"Reproach" means to restrain oneself. In Confucianism they speak of it as "restraining oneself and returning to propriety."[1] Yen-yüan asked Confucius, "How does one obtain humaneness?" Confucius replied, "Restrain yourself and return to propriety. That's humaneness."

"But what is meant by 'restrain yourself and return to propriety?'"Yen-yüan continued.

Confucius said," If it's not in accord with propriety, don't look at it. If it's not in accord with propriety, don't say it. If it's not in accord with propriety, don't do it."

He said, "If it's not in accord with propriety, don't look at it. Not only should you not look at it, you shouldn't even listen to it. For example, if people are gossiping, don't listen to them. If it's not in accord with principle, you shouldn't say it. If it's not in accord with principle, you shouldn't do it. In looking, listening, speaking, and acting, you must restrain yourself and return to propriety."

Shariputra constantly restrained and reproached himself. He watched over himself. He followed the rules. He always kept track of himself and didn't relax. For example, he didn't let himself eat good things everyday. If you like to be lazy and sleep, but restrain yourself from doing so, saying, "Hey, don't sleep so much. Do a little more work," that's just restraining yourself. If you don't like to study the Buddhadharma, but think, "I will certainly be vigorous in my studies of the Dharma," you are restraining yourself. Don't fear difficulty. People who succeed are for the greater part those who have skill at self-restraint. Without it, they wouldn't have succeeded.

"NOW, FROM THE BUDDHA, I HAVE HEARD WHAT I NEVER HEARD BEFORE, THIS DHARMA WHICH HAS NEVER BEEN BEFORE, AND ALL MY DOUBTS ARE SEVERED." Shariputra says, "I have studied the Buddhadharma and heard *The Wonderful Dharma Lotus Flower Sutra*, and I have gotten rid of all my doubts. "MY BODY AND MIND ARE BLISSFUL AND I AM AT PEACE." What is meant by "blissful?" It means extremely pure, serene happy, and comfortable. Shariputra is happy in body and in mind. He has attained a state of peace which is quite inconceivable.

---

1 克己復禮-*k'o chi fu li.*

Sutra: T.10c13

"TODAY, INDEED, I KNOW THAT I AM A TRUE DISCIPLE OF THE BUDDHA, BORN FROM THE BUDDHA'S MOUTH, TRANSFORMED FROM THE DHARMA; I HAVE OBTAINED A SHARE OF THE BUDDHADHARMA."

Outline:

J2. Realization.

Commentary:

"TODAY, INDEED, I KNOW THAT I AM A TRUE DISCIPLE OF THE BUDDHA. I know that I am really the Buddha's disciple and that in the future I shall become a Buddha. I am BORN FROM THE BUDDHA'S MOUTH, TRANSFORMED FROM THE DHARMA. I have been born by transformation from out of the Buddhadharma. I HAVE OBTAINED A SHARE OF THE BUDDHA-DHARMA. I have obtained the Buddha nature in its entirety. You might say that I have entered the stream of the Dharma nature."

Sutra: T.10c14

AT THAT TIME SHARIPUTRA, WISHING TO RESTATE THIS MEANING, SPOKE VERSES, SAYING:

HEARING THIS DHARMA SOUND,
I GAIN WHAT I NEVER HAD;
MY HEART IS FILLED WITH GREAT JOY,
THE NET OF DOUBTS HAS BEEN CAST ASIDE.

Outline:

H2. Verse.
I1. Announcing the verse.

Commentary:

AT THAT TIME SHARIPUTRA, WISHING TO RESTATE THIS MEANING, SPOKE VERSES, SAYING...He wanted to express himself even more clearly, so he used verses to speak to the Buddha, saying, "HEARING THIS DHARMA SOUND/ the miraculous sound of *The Wonderful Dharma Lotus Flower Sutra*,

I GAIN WHAT I NEVER HAD/ I have never before heard such a wonderful Dharma. MY HEART IS FILLED WITH GREAT JOY/ Within my heart, happiness arises. The three karmas of body, mouth, and mind are happy. THE NET OF DOUBTS HAS BEEN CAST ASIDE/ The net of doubts and misgivings that had covered my heart has been cast aside."

Sutra: T.10c18

FROM OF OLD, FAVORED WITH THE
BUDDHA'S TEACHING,
I HAD NEVER LOST THE GREATER VEHICLE.
THE BUDDHA'S SOUND IS EXTREMELY RARE,
AND CAN RID BEINGS OF THEIR WOES.
I'VE ALREADY ATTAINED TO THE END OF OUTFLOWS,
YET HEARING IT MY WOES ALSO ARE DISPELLED.

Outline:

I2. Setting forth the verse.
J1. The wisdom was not lost.

Commentary:

FROM OF OLD, FAVORED WITH THE BUDDHA'S TEACHING/ From the long distant past right up until now, I have received the Buddha's teachings. I HAD NEVER LOST THE GREATER VEHICLE/ In this way my Great Vehicle seeds were tended and nourished. In this present life, they have ripened.

THE BUDDHA'S SOUND IS EXTREMELY RARE/ The clear, pure, profound, far-reaching sound of the Buddha's voice is the most rare sound in all the world. AND CAN RID BEINGS OF THEIR WOES/ If they hear the Buddha's clear, pure voice, living beings can be freed of all their afflictions.

I'VE ALREADY ATTAINED TO THE END OF OUTFLOWS/ I have already certified to the Fourth Stage of Arhatship and obtained the Penetration of No Outflows. YET HEARING IT MY WOES ALSO ARE DISPELLED/ I had no worries to begin with, but my state was that of the Small Vehicle. Therefore, I had no genuine understanding of the doctrine of Bodhisattvahood. Hearing *The Wonderful Dharma Lotus Flower Sutra,* however, all my worries have been cleared away.

Sutra: T.10c21

AS I DWELT IN THE MOUNTAIN VALLEYS,
SOMETIMES AT THE FOOT OF TREES,
WHETHER SITTING OR WALKING,
I CONSTANTLY THOUGHT UPON THIS TOPIC:
"AH," I CRIED IN BITTER SELF-REPROACH,
"WHY HAVE I DECEIVED MYSELF?
WE, TOO, ARE THE BUDDHA'S DISCIPLES,
AND EQUALLY ENTER THE NON-OUTFLOW DHARMA;
YET IN THE FUTURE WE SHALL NOT BE ABLE
TO PROCLAIM THE UNSURPASSED PATH.
THE GOLDEN COLOR, THE THIRTY-TWO,
THE TEN POWERS AND ALL THE LIBERATIONS,
ARE TOGETHER IN A SINGLE DHARMA,
BUT I HAVE NOT OBTAINED THESE THINGS.
THE EIGHTY WONDROUS EXCELLENCES,
THE EIGHTEEN UNSHARED DHARMAS,
SUCH QUALITIES OF VIRTUE,
I HAVE MISSED THEM, EVERY ONE.
WHEN I USED TO WALK ALONE
I WOULD SEE THE BUDDHA IN THE GREAT ASSEMBLY,
HIS FAME FILLING THE TEN DIRECTIONS,
VASTLY BENEFITTING ALL BEINGS.
I FELT I'D LOST THIS BENEFIT,
AND HAD BUT CHEATED MYSELF.
CONSTANTLY, BOTH DAY AND NIGHT,
I THOUGHT UPON THIS MATTER,
AND WISHED TO ASK THE WORLD HONORED ONE
WHETHER OR NOT I HAD LOST IT.
I OFTEN SAW THE WORLD HONORED ONE
PRAISING ALL THE BODHISATTVAS,
AND SO IT WAS, BY DAY AND NIGHT,

I PONDERED ON MATTERS SUCH AS THESE.
NOW I HEAR THE BUDDHA'S SOUND,
OPPORTUNELY SPEAKING THAT DHARMA
WHICH IS WITHOUT OUTFLOWS--
HARD TO CONCEIVE OF--
AND LEADS LIVING BEINGS TO THE BODHIMANDA.
ONCE I WAS ATTACHED TO DEVIANT VIEWS,
AND WAS A TEACHER OF THE BRAHMINS.
THE WORLD HONORED ONE KNEW MY HEART,
PULLED OUT THE DEVIANT, TAUGHT ME NIRVANA.
I RID MYSELF OF DEVIANT VIEWS,
CERTIFIED TO THE DHARMA OF EMPTINESS.
THEN I SAID TO MYSELF
THAT I'D ARRIVED AT EXTINCTION.

Outline:

J2. Wisdom formerly lost

Commentary:

AS I DWELT IN THE MOUNTAIN VALLEYS/ Mountain valleys are clean and pure places for cultivation. When I lived there SOMETIMES AT THE FOOT OF TREES/ Sometimes I stayed in the groves, but WHETHER SITTING OR WALKING/ I may have been sitting there in meditation or I may have been walking around. I CONSTANTLY THOUGHT UPON THIS TOPIC/ What topic? "AH," I CRIED IN BITTER SELF-REPROACH/ I sighed in regret."WHY HAVE I DECEIVED MYSELF/ How could I have cheated myself? WE, TOO, ARE THE BUDDHA'S DISCIPLES/ AND EQUALLY ENTER THE NON-OUTFLOW DHARMA/ We all have attained to the dharma of no outflows, that is, the position of Fourth Stage Arhatship, the attainment of the Penetration of No Outflows. The attainment of no outflows means the complete absence of sexual desire. If you have sexual desire, you have not attained to the state of no outflows. This is not to say that when there are no external stimuli you have no sexual desire, but that even when you see it, you have no thoughts of desire regarding that state. When such a state appears before you, you have no thoughts of desire. That's the no outflow dharma.

YET IN THE FUTURE WE SHALL NOT BE ABLE/ TO PROCLAIM

THE UNSURPASSED PATH/ to teach the supreme, most wonderful Buddhadharma. That's what Shariputra was thinking to himself.

THE GOLDEN COLOR, THE THIRTY-TWO/ The Buddha's body is the color of gold and is endowed with the thirty-two marks of a great man. They are:

1. Level feet.
2. Thousand-spoke wheel sign on feet.
3. Long, slender fingers.
4. Pliant hands and feet.
5. Toes and fingers finely webbed.
6. Full-sized heels.
7. Arched insteps.
8. Thighs like a royal stag.
9. Hands reaching below the knees.
10. Well-retracted male organ.
11. Height and stretch of arms equal.
12. Every hair root dark colored.
13. Body hair graceful and curly.
14. Golden-hued body.
15. A ten foot aura around him.
16. Soft, smooth skin.
17. Two soles, two palms, two shoulders, and crown well rounded.
18. Below the armpits well filled.
19. Lion-shaped body.
20. Body erect and upright.
21. Full, round shoulders.
22. Forty teeth.
23. Teeth white, even and close.
24. Four canine teeth pure white.
25. Lion-jawed.
26. Saliva improving the taste of all food.
27. Tongue long and broad.
28. Voice deep and resonant.
29. Eyes deep blue.
30. Eyelashes like a royal bull.
31. A white urna or curl between the eyebrows emitting light.
32. A fleshy protuberance on the crown.

THE TEN POWERS AND ALL THE LIBERATIONS/ The Ten Powers have been discussed. The liberations refer to the Eight Liberations, also called the Eight Castings off the Back.[1] ARE TOGETHER IN A SINGLE DHARMA/ They are

---

[1]For these two lists, see *The Dharma Flower Sutra, Vol. III*, BTTS, 1979 pages 437-9, and 437-8 respectively.

all within the Dharma nature, BUT I HAVE NOT OBTAINED THESE THINGS/ Being of the Small Vehicle, I lacked the merit and virtue necessary to receive a prediction of Buddhahood from the Buddha.

THE EIGHTY WONDROUS EXCELLENCES/ The Buddha's body also is adorned with eighty minor characteristics. THE EIGHTEEN UNSHARED DHARMAS/ What is meant by "unshared?" It means that these eighteen dharmas are not shared by those of the Two Vehicles, the Sound Hearers and the Conditioned Enlightened Ones. They are not shared by the Three Vehicles, the Sound Hearers, the Conditioned Enlightened Ones, and the Bodhisattvas. They are not shared by them on the path of cultivation because these are dharmas possessed only by the Buddha. Thus, they are unshared by others. The Eighteen Unshared Dharmas--and you should know them--are:

The Thus Come One is:

1. Faultless in body.
2. Faultless in speech.
3. Faultless in mindfulness.
4. Has no perception of difference.
5. Has no unconcentrated thoughts.
6. There is nothing he does not know that has not already been cast aside.
7. His zeal never decreases.
8. His vigor never decreases.
9. His concentration never decreases.
10. His wisdom never decreases.
11. His liberation never decreases.
12. His knowledge and vision of liberation never decreases.
13. All his bodily karma accords with the practice of wisdom.
14. All his karma of speech accords with the practice of wisdom.
15. All his karma of mind accords with the practice of wisdom.
16. With his wisdom he has unhindered knowledge of the past.
17. With his wisdom he has unhindered knowledge of the future.
18. With his wisdom he has unhindered knowledge of the present.

These are the Eighteen Unshared Dharmas. Only the Buddha has these eighteen.

SUCH QUALITIES OF VIRTUE/ as previously mentioned, the thirty-two marks, the eighty minor characteristics, the Ten Powers, the Eight Liberations, and all the rest, all this merit and virtue, I HAVE MISSED THEM, EVERY ONE/ I Shariputra, one of the Small Vehicle, have lost out on this merit and virtue.

WHEN I USED TO WALK ALONE/ When I was by myself, meditating or perhaps walking around, I WOULD SEE THE BUDDHA IN THE GREAT ASSEMBLY/ HIS FAME FILLING THE TEN DIRECTIONS/ The Buddha's name is known to all living beings in the ten directions. VASTLY BENEFITTING ALL BEINGS/ The Buddha broadly benefits all living beings. All beings receive benefit. None do not. I FELT I'D LOST THIS BENEFIT/ I felt that I had lost this advantage. AND HAD BUT CHEATED MYSELF/ Really, I never did lose the benefit, but I was cheating myself and CONSTANTLY, BOTH DAY AND NIGHT/ in this six periods of the day and night, I THOUGHT UPON THIS MATTER/ AND WISHED TO ASK THE WORLD HONORED ONE/ WHETHER OR NOT I HAD LOST IT/ Have I lost the benefit or not?

I OFTEN SAW THE WORLD HONORED ONE/ the Buddha, PRAISING ALL THE BODHISATTVAS/ The Buddha continually extolled the virtues of the great Bodhisattvas. AND SO IT WAS, BY DAY AND NIGHT/ all day and all night I PONDERED ON MATTERS SUCH AS THESE/ I thought it over and over.

NOW I HEAR THE BUDDHA'S SOUND/ OPPORTUNELY SPEAKING THAT DHARMA/ He proclaims the wonderful Dharma in accord with the potentials of the living beings to be taught. WHICH IS WITHOUT OUTFLOWS--HARD TO CONCEIVE OF--/ AND LEADS LIVING BEINGS TO THE BODHIMANDA/ It leads all creatures to the field of enlightenment.

ONCE I WAS ATTACHED TO DEVIANT VIEWS/ Once, I had an attachment. I held to deviant knowledge and views. AND WAS A TEACHER OF THE BRAHMINS/ an outside Way teacher. THE WORLD HONORED ONE KNEW MY HEART/ The Buddha knew what was in my heart, he knew my nature; he understood my previous causes and latter effects; he knew me quite thoroughly. PULLED OUT THE DEVIANT, TAUGHT ME NIRVANA/ He plucked out my deviant views and replaced them with the Dharma of Nirvana, non-production and non-extinction, enabling me to certify to the fruit of sagehood.

I RID MYSELF OF DEVIANT VIEWS/ CERTIFIED TO THE DHARMA OF EMPTINESS/ the dharma of True Emptiness, the wonderful fruit of Nirvana.

THEN I SAID TO MYSELF/ THAT I'D ARRIVED AT EXTINCTION/ I thought that certifying to the first, second, third, or fourth fruits of Arhatship was arriving at the level of extinction. I was wrong.

Sutra: T.11a14

BUT NOW AT LAST I REALIZE
IT IS NOT REAL EXTINCTION,
FOR WHEN I BECOME A BUDDHA,
COMPLETE WITH THIRTY-TWO MARKS,
REVERED BY GODS, HUMANS, AND YAKSHA HORDES,
DRAGONS, SPIRITS, AND OTHERS,
ONLY THEN WILL I BE ABLE TO SAY,
"THIS IS ETERNAL EXTINCTION, WITHOUT RESIDUE."
THE BUDDHA, IN THE GREAT ASSEMBLY,
HAS SAID I SHALL BECOME A BUDDHA.
HEARING SUCH A DHARMA SOUND,
ALL MY DOUBTS HAVE BEEN DISPELLED.

Outline:

I3. Conclusion.
J1. Conclusion itself.
K1. Conclusion proper.

Commentary:

BUT NOW AT LAST I REALIZE/ Shariputra says, "Before, I thought I had gained extinction. Who would have guessed that it was nothing but Transformation City![1] It was not the treasure trove! So now I have awakened. IT IS NOT REAL EXTINCTION/ FOR WHEN I BECOME A BUDDHA/ The position I previously attained was merely certification to the principle of one-sided emptiness.[2] It was not the true, real extinction. It was not the true attainment of Nirvana. In the future, when I become a Buddha COMPLETE WITH THE THIRTY-TWO MARKS/ of a great man, REVERED BY GODS, HUMANS, AND YAKSHA HORDES/ honored by the gods in the heavens, the human beings, and all the ghosts, the entire eight-fold division, DRAGONS, SPIRITS, AND OTHERS/ ONLY THEN WILL I BE ABLE TO SAY/

---

[1]The Transformation City and the treasure trove are discussed in "Chapter Seven, Transformation City."

[2]偏空理-*p'ien k'ung li.*

At that time I will be able to say, "THIS IS ETERNAL EXTINCTION, WITHOUT RESIDUE/ I have truly attained extinction and entered Nirvana without residue.

THE BUDDHA, IN THE GREAT ASSEMBLY/ Presently, the Buddha, from amidst the great assembly HAS SAID I SHALL BECOME A BUDDHA/ He has conferred a prediction upon me saying that I shall, in fact, become a Buddha. HEARING SUCH A DHARMA SOUND/ ALL MY DOUBTS HAVE BEEN DISPELLED/ All my doubts have disappeared.

Sutra: T.11a20

WHEN I FIRST HEARD THE BUDDHA SPEAK,
MY HEART WAS FILLED WITH GREAT FEAR.
IS THIS NOT MARA DISGUISED AS THE BUDDHA,
COME TO DISTURB AND CONFUSE MY HEART?

Outline:

K2. Narrating the doubts.

Commentary:

WHEN I FIRST HEARD THE BUDDHA SPEAK/ the Dharma, MY HEART WAS FILLED WITH GREAT FEAR/ I thought, IS THIS NOT MARA DISGUISED AS THE BUDDHA/ Has the demon come and turned himself into a "Buddha?" How else could he be speaking such strange things? COME TO DISTURB AND CONFUSE MY HEART/ to ruin my cultivation of samadhi?" Shariputra admits that when he first heard the Buddha speak this wonderful Dharma, he had some doubts.

Sutra: T.11a22

THE BUDDHA, BY MEANS OF VARIOUS CONDITIONS,
ANALOGIES, AND INGENIOUS SPEECH,
MAKES ONE'S HEART CALM AS THE SEA.
HEARING HIM THE NET OF MY DOUBTS WAS RENT.
THE BUDDHA SAYS THAT IN THE PAST
THE LIMITLESS BUDDHAS, NOW EXTINCT,

DWELT CALMLY IN EXPEDIENTS,
AND ALSO SPOKE THIS DHARMA--EACH OF THEM.
THE BUDDHAS OF THE PRESENT AND THE FUTURE,
THEIR NUMBERS WITHOUT LIMIT,
ALSO USED EXPEDIENTS,
TO PROCLAIM THE DHARMA SUCH AS THIS,
JUST AS NOW THE WORLD HONORED ONE
FROM BIRTH UNTIL HIS LEAVING HOME,
HIS ATTAINING THE WAY AND TURNING THE
DHARMA WHEEL,
ALSO SPOKE BY MEANS OF EXPEDIENTS.
THE WORLD HONORED ONE SPEAKS THE REAL PATH.
THE EVIL ONE DOES NO SUCH THING;
HENCE I KNOW FOR CERTAIN
THIS IS NOT THE DEMON POSING AS A BUDDHA.
BECAUSE I HAD FALLEN INTO A NET OF DOUBTS,
I SAID IT WAS THE DOINGS OF A DEMON.
HEARING THE BUDDHA'S COMPLIANT VOICE,
PROFOUND, FAR-REACHING, SUBTLE AND FINE,
PROCLAIMING WIDE THE CLEAR, PURE DHARMA,
GREAT IS THE JOY WITHIN MY HEART.
MY DOUBTS ARE FOREVER ENDED,
AS IN REAL WISDOM I STAND FIRM.

Outline:

K3. Narrating his presently being led to understanding.

Commentary:

THE BUDDHA, BY MEANS OF VARIOUS CONDITIONS/ Shariputra says, "When I first heard the Buddha speak the Dharma, I thought a demon had come disguised as the Buddha to disturb my cultivation of samadhi. But the Buddha used all kinds of conditions, ANALOGIES, AND INGENIOUS SPEECH/ speaking the Dharma to me with his unobstructed eloquence. He MAKES ONE'S HEART AS CALM

AS THE SEA/ The Buddha's heart was as calm as the sea and caused my heart to become as calm as the sea. HEARING HIM THE NET OF MY DOUBTS WAS RENT/ Hearing the Buddha's analogies and clever speech, my doubts vanished.

THE BUDDHA SAYS THAT IN THE PAST/ THE LIMITLESS BUDDHAS, NOW EXTINCT/ DWELT CALMLY IN EXPEDIENTS/ They all were securely established in the application of expedient Dharma-doors in order to teach the Dharma to living beings. AND ALSO SPOKE THIS DHARMA--EACH OF THEM/ They all spoke *The Wonderful Dharma Lotus Flower Sutra*.

THE BUDDHAS OF THE PRESENT AND THE FUTURE/ THEIR NUMBERS WITHOUT LIMIT/ ALSO USED EXPEDIENTS/ TO PROCLAIM THE DHARMA SUCH AS THIS/ the wonderful Dharma which is "thus."

JUST AS NOW THE WORLD HONORED ONE/ FROM BIRTH UNTIL HIS LEAVING HOME/ HIS ATTAINING THE WAY AND TURNING THE DHARMA WHEEL/ ALSO SPOKE BY MEANS OF EXPEDIENTS/ The Buddha manifested Eight Signs of Accomplishing the Way:

1. The Buddha descended from the Tushita heaven. The Buddha descended from the Tushita heaven to be born in India, in Kapilavastu, in the palace of King Shuddodana.

2. He entered the womb.

3. He dwelt in the womb. When the Buddha entered the womb, day and night he spoke the Dharma for the gods, dragons, ghosts and spirits.

4. He left the womb. He was born in the world. When the Buddha Shakyamuni was born, he pointed one forefinger to the sky and one to the ground and said,

"In the heavens, and below,
I alone am honored."

5. He left home.

6. He accomplished the Way. While sitting beneath the Bodhi tree one night he saw a bright star and awakened to the Path.

7. He turned the Dharma wheel. He spoke Dharma for all living beings.

8. He entered Nirvana.

In the T'ien T'ai Teachings they omit the third, "dwelling in the womb," and substitute "he defeated Mara" as the fifth, "he accomplished the Way," as sixth, and so forth. Actually, it amounts to the same thing because in the Great Vehicle, the defeating of Mara is included within the "accomplishing of the Way."

So the Buddha manifested these eight signs which are referred to in the lines of text above.

THE WORLD HONORED ONE SPEAKS THE REAL PATH/ The Buddha speaks *The Wonderful Dharma Lotus Flower Sutra*. THE EVILONE DOES NO SUCH THING/ This is the true, real wisdom, the doctrine of the Real Mark. The demon doesn't talk about such things. HENCE I KNOW FOR CERTAIN/ THIS IS NOT THE DEMON POSING AS A BUDDHA/ Why did I think it was the demon acting as the Buddha? It was because I had fallen into the net of doubts. So I didn't believe even the Buddha! I doubted him. BECAUSE I HAD FALLEN INTO A NET OF DOUBTS/ I SAID IT WAS THE DOINGS OF A DEMON/ I said, "The Buddha speaking the Dharma is actually a demon king speaking wildly!" HEARING THE BUDDHA'S COMPLIANT VOICE/ the wonderful sound which is compassionate, kind, joyous and generous, PROFOUND, FAR-REACHING, SUBTLE AND FINE/ PROCLAIMING WIDE THE CLEAR, PURE DHARMA/ GREAT IS THE JOY WITHIN MY HEART/ I am very happy. MY DOUBTS ARE FOREVER ENDED/ AS IN REAL WISDOM I STAND FIRM/ I now abide securely in Real Wisdom.

Sutra: T. 11b7

I AM CERTAIN TO BECOME A BUDDHA,
REVERED BY GODS AND HUMANS.
I SHALL TURN THE UNSURPASSED WHEEL OF DHARMA,
TO TEACH AND TRANSFORM THE BODHISATTVAS.

Outline:

J2. Final statement.

Commentary:

I AM CERTAIN TO BECOME A BUDDHA/ In the future it is for sure that I will become a Buddha. REVERED BY GODS AND HUMANS/ dragons and spirits and so on. I SHALL TURN THE UNSURPASSED WHEEL OF DHARMA/ In the future I, too, shall turn the supreme Dharma wheel TO TEACH AND TRANSFORM BODHISATTVAS/ all the great Bodhisattvas.

Gods (cover detail)

Shakyamuni Buddha (cover detail)

Shariputra receives a prediction

PART TWO: SHARIPUTRA'S PREDICTION

Sutra: T.11b9

AT THAT TIME THE BUDDHA TOLD SHARIPUTRA, "I, NOW, AMIDST THE GREAT ASSEMBLY OF GODS, HUMANS, SHRAMANAS, BRAHMINS, AND OTHERS, DECLARE THAT IN THE DISTANT PAST, IN THE PRESENCE OF TWENTY THOUSAND MILLIONS OF BUDDHAS, FOR THE SAKE OF THE UNSURPASSED PATH, I HAVE CONSTANTLY TAUGHT AND TRANSFORMED YOU. AND YOU, THROUGHOUT THE LONG NIGHT, HAVE FOLLOWED ME AND RECEIVED MY INSTRUCTION. I HAVE USED EXPEDIENT DEVICES TO GUIDE YOU TO BE BORN WITHIN MY DHARMA."

Outline:

F3. The Thus Come One tells of Shariputra's realization.
- G1. Shariputra was taught the Great Vehicle in the past.

Commentary:

AT THAT TIME THE BUDDHA TOLD SHARIPUTRA...Right then, the Buddha said, "I, NOW, AMIDST THE GREAT ASSEMBLY OF GODS, HUMANS, SHRAMANAS...Shramana is a Sanskrit word which means "diligent and resting." They diligently cultivate morality, samadhi, and wisdom, and put to rest greed, hatred, and stupidity.

BRAHMINS are those of outside ways who cultivate pure conduct.

AND OTHERS, DECLARE THAT IN THE DISTANT PAST, IN THE PRESENCE OF TWENTY THOUSAND MILLIONS OF BUDDHAS FOR THE SAKE OF THE UNSURPASSED PATH I HAVE CONSTANTLY TAUGHT AND TRANSFORMED YOU." The text says, "For the sake of seeking the unsurpassed path." There are seven aspects to the adjective "unsurpassed" as follows:

1. The unsurpassed body.
2. The unsurpassed receiving and upholding.
3. The unsurpassed completeness.
4. The unsurpassed wisdom.
5. The unsurpassed inconceivability.
6. The unsurpassed liberations.
7. The unsurpassed conduct.

The Buddha says, "I have constantly taught and transformed you, Shariputra. AND YOU, THROUGHOUT THE LONG NIGHT, HAVE FOLLOWED ME AND RECEIVED MY INSTRUCTION. Before you had understood, before you had become enlightened, it was as if you were following me in a dark, long night, receiving my teaching. I taught you the Buddhadharma.

"I HAVE USED EXPEDIENT DEVICES TO GUIDE YOU TO BE BORN WITHIN MY DHARMA. I have used all manner of expedient devices and Dharma-doors to lead you and so, Shariputra, you have been born within my Buddhadharma."

Sutra: T.11b12

"SHARIPUTRA, IN THE PAST I TAUGHT YOU TO RESOLVE YOURSELF ON THE BUDDHA PATH, BUT YOU HAVE COMPLETELY FORGOTTEN THIS, AND SO YOU SAY OF YOURSELF THAT YOU HAVE ALREADY ATTAINED EXTINCTION."

Outline:

G2. Halfway through he forgot it and grasped at the Small Vehicle.

Commentary:

"SHARIPUTRA," Shakyamuni Buddha called out again, "I have used various expedients to lead you to be born within my Dharma. IN THE PAST I TAUGHT YOU TO RESOLVE YOURSELF ON THE BUDDHA PATH. I instructed you to set your sights on the Great Vehicle, to vow to accomplish the Buddha Path. BUT YOU HAVE COMPLETELY FORGOTTEN THIS. You have now no recollection of the Dharma-door I taught you then."

This is like before, I taught you all *The Shurangama Sutra* but you have all forgotten it now.

"AND SO YOU SAY OF YOURSELF THAT YOU HAVE ALREADY ATTAINED EXTINCTION. You say that you have attained the Dharma-door of genuine extinction.

Sutra: T. 11b14

"NOW, AGAIN, WISHING YOU TO RECALL THE PATH YOU HAVE PRACTICED ACCORDING TO YOUR PAST VOWS, I, FOR THE SAKE OF THE SOUND HEARERS, SPEAK THIS GREAT VEHICLE SUTRA BY THE NAME OF *THE WONDERFUL DHARMA LOTUS FLOWER*, A DHARMA FOR INSTRUCTING BODHISATTVAS OF WHOM THE BUDDHAS ARE PROTECTIVE AND MINDFUL."

Outline:

G3. Once again he is taught the Great Vehicle.

Commentary:

"NOW, AGAIN, WISHING YOU TO RECALL THE PATH YOU HAVE PRACTICED ACCORDING TO YOUR PAST VOWS...I wish to cause you to remember, to think back and recall the vows you made in past lives. You have made vows to the effect that in every life you would support my Dharma. What is more, you vowed you would study the Buddhadharma under me and realize the Buddha Path. Do you remember? You vowed you would not be satisfied with studying the Small Vehicle Buddhadharma or with realizing the fruit of Arhatship by any means. You should think over the vows you made in the past, vows to cultivate the Buddha Path. I, FOR THE SAKE OF THE SOUND HEARERS, for those who are Shravakas, SPEAK THIS GREAT VEHICLE SUTRA BY THE NAME OF *THE WONDERFUL DHARMA LOTUS FLOWER*, A DHARMA FOR INSTRUCTING BODHISATTVAS OF WHOM THE BUDDHAS ARE PROTECTIVE AND MINDFUL." When you study this Sutra all the Buddhas throughout the ten directions will come to protect you and be mindful of you.

Sutra: T. 11b16

"SHARIPUTRA, IN A FUTURE AGE, AFTER LIMITLESS, BOUNDLESS, INCONCEIVABLE AEONS...

Outline:

F4. Shariputra is given a prediction.
G1. Prose.
H1. Time.

Commentary:

"SHARIPUTRA, IN A FUTURE AGE, AFTER LIMITLESS, BOUNDLESS, INCONCEIVABLE AEONS...I am now conferring a prediction upon you to the effect that, after a number of aeons which is infinite and boundless, which cannot be conceived of with the mind or expressed in words...

Sutra: T. 11b17

"...HAVING MADE OFFERINGS TO SOME THOUSANDS OF MYRIADS OF MILLIONS OF BUDDHAS, HAVING REVERENTLY UPHELD THE PROPER DHARMA, AND HAVING PERFECTED THE PATH PRACTICED BY THE BODHISATTVAS...

Outline:

H2. Causal practices.

Commentary:

"...HAVING MADE OFFERINGS TO SOME..."Some" here refers to a number that is uncountable. The exact figure is not known, but in general Shariputra made offerings to a great many Buddhas--a thousand, ten thousand million? Who knows how many? "HAVING REVERENTLY UPHELD THE PROPER DHARMA... You will have most reverently practiced the proper, orthodox Dharma, not the deviant dharma.

"...AND HAVING PERFECTED THE PATH PRACTICED BY THE BODHISATTVAS..." Having completed the practices essential to Bodhisattvas, the Six Perfections and the Ten Thousand Conducts...

Sutra: T. 11b19

"...YOU SHALL BECOME A BUDDHA BY THE NAME OF FLOWER-LIGHT THUS COME ONE, ONE WORTHY OF OFFERINGS, OF PROPER AND UNIVERSAL KNOWLEDGE, ONE WHOSE UNDERSTANDING AND CONDUCT ARE COMPLETE, A WELL-GONE ONE WHO UNDERSTANDS THE WORLD, AN UNSURPASSED LORD, A TAMING AND REGULATING HERO, A BUDDHA, A WORLD HONORED ONE."

Outline:

H3. Attainment of the fruition.

Commentary:

"...YOU SHALL BECOME A BUDDHA BY THE NAME OF FLOWER-LIGHT THUS COME ONE..." Here we are given the list of the Buddha's ten titles. The first is "Thus Come One." The Buddha, the Thus Come One,"takes the Vehicle of the way which is 'Thus' to 'Come' to the realization of proper enlightenment."[1]

---

1 以如是之乘来成正覺 -*i ju shih chih ch'eng, lai ch'ung cheng chiao (chüeh).*

The way which is "Thus" is the real, substantial Buddha Way, the path of the realization of Buddhahood. The path of the realization of Buddhahood is most certainly not an illusion; it is real and substantial. Therefore, an explanation of the term "Thus Come One" is that the Buddha takes the Vehicle of the way which is "Thus" to "Come" to the realization of proper enlightenment, that is, Buddhahood.

One of the best explanations of the term Thus Come One, however, is to be found in *The Vajra Sutra*. It says, "The Tathagata does not come from anywhere, nor does he go anywhere. Therefore he is called the Tathagata."[1] The Tathagata, or Thus Come One, neither comes nor goes.

"Thus" also represents stillness. "Come" represents movement. Movement does not obstruct stillness; stillness does not obstruct movement. Movement itself is stillness and stillness itself is movement. Movement and stillness are of one "thusness."

Why is there movement? Movement is manifest through stillness. Why is there stillness? Stillness appears out of movement. Stillness is produced from movement. Movement comes from stillness. That is why movement and stillness are of one "thusness." They are dual and yet non-dual. Although they are two, they are one. They are like water and ice. Water is ice and ice is water. The principle is the same. So, movement does not obstruct stillness and stillness does not obstruct movement. Stillness, at its extreme point becomes movement and movement at its extreme point turns into stillness.

We human beings move during the day and are still at night. However, sometimes during the time of stillness people move. Sometimes during the time of movement people are still. For instance, during the day people are supposed to be on the move, but some of them may take a nap. Sleeping is stillness and waking is movement. At night, one should sleep. But some people don't. That's movement.

Thus Come One, then, is the first of the Buddha's ten titles.

---

[1]Master Hua, *A General Explanation of the Vajra Prajna Paramita Sutra*, Buddhist Text Translation Society, San Francisco, 1974, p. 147.

The second title is ONE WORTHY OF OFFERINGS. One ought to make offerings to the Buddha. Living beings should make offerings to the Buddha, the Dharma, and the Sangha. On the part of the Buddha, the Buddha is worthy and should rightfully receive the offerings of gods and humans. It is said, "Where there is seeking there will be a response. There is no influence that does not come through." When you make offerings you do so because you are seeking something. You seek blessings and wisdom, and therefore you make offerings to the Triple Jewel.

The third of the Buddha's ten titles is ONE OF PROPER AND UNIVERSAL KNOWLEDGE. What is meant by "proper knowledge? It means that one knows that the mind produces the ten thousand dharmas. "Universal knowledge" means that one knows that the ten thousand dharmas are only the mind. All dharmas come from the mind:

> The Buddha spoke all dharmas,
> for the minds of living beings.
> If there were no minds,
> what use would dharmas be?

The fourth title is ONE WHOSE UNDERSTANDING AND CONDUCT ARE COMPLETE. "Understanding" refers to the light of wisdom. "Conduct" refers to his cultivation. Because the Buddha is replete with wisdom he is said to be complete in understanding and conduct.

Fifthly, the Buddha is the WELL GONE ONE WHO UNDERSTANDS THE WORLD. "Well" means good. "Gone" means that he has gone to a good place. He understands and is clear about everything in the world. There are no dharmas, either mundane or transcendental, which he does not understand.

His sixth title is that of UNSURPASSED LORD. Only

the Buddha can be called the Unsurpassed Lord. Other living beings cannot. No one is higher than the Buddha.

TAMING AND REGULATING HERO: To steer a car, you have to turn the steering wheel. In northern China, they have horse carts. The driver cracks the whip and they go forward. This is just "regulating." The Buddha is a great hero who tames and regulates those in the three realms: the desire realm, the form realm and the formless realm.

TEACHER OF GODS AND HUMANS: The Buddha is a leader for both the gods in the heavens and the people on the earth. THE BUDDHA has three meanings, "self-enlightened," "enlightening others," and "complete in enlightenment and practice." It is said,

> Having perfected the three
> kinds of enlightenment,
> And replete with the ten thousand virtues,
> He is therefore called "the Buddha."

WORLD HONORED ONE means that the Buddha is honored both in and beyond the world.

Sutra: T.11b20

"HIS COUNTRY SHALL BE CALLED 'APART FROM FILTH.' ITS GROUND WILL BE LEVEL, PURE, AND ADORNED, TRANQUIL AND PROSPEROUS, AND ABOUNDING WITH GODS. IT SHALL HAVE LAPIS LAZULI FOR SOIL AND EIGHT INTERSECTING ROADS BORDERED WITH GOLDEN CORDS AND BY WHICH SHALL STAND ROWS OF TREES MADE OF THE SEVEN JEWELS CONSTANTLY BLOOMING AND BEARING FRUIT."

Outline:

H4. Buddhaland.

Commentary:

"HIS COUNTRY SHALL BE CALLED 'APART FROM FILTH.' ITS GROUND SHALL BE LEVEL, PURE, AND ADORNED...Not only will it be level, it will also be pure. There will be no garbage in it whatsoever, no unclean things. TRANQUIL AND PROSPEROUS, AND ABOUNDING WITH GODS. The land will be peaceful and without any trouble at all. It will be, for the most part, a happy place. Not only will ordinary people live in this country, but many gods will dwell there, their numbers flourishing, like a blaze of flame.

"IT SHALL HAVE LAPIS LAZULI FOR SOIL AND EIGHT INTERSECTING ROADS BORDERED WITH GOLDEN CORDS...Where the roads intersect, golden ropes will mark off the boundaries. BY WHICH SHALL STAND ROWS OF TREES MADE OF THE SEVEN JEWELS WHICH CONSTANTLY BLOOM AND BEAR FRUIT."

Sutra: T.11b23

"THE THUS COME ONE FLOWER-LIGHT WILL ALSO TEACH AND TRANSFORM LIVING BEINGS BY MEANS OF THE THREE VEHICLES. SHARIPUTRA, WHEN THIS BUDDHA COMES INTO THE WORLD, ALTHOUGH IT WILL NOT BE AN EVIL AGE, BECAUSE OF HIS PAST VOWS, HE SHALL TEACH THE DHARMA OF THE THREE VEHICLES."

Outline:

H5. Speaking of the Dharma.

Commentary:

"THE THUS COME ONE FLOWER-LIGHT WILL ALSO TEACH AND TRANSFORM LIVING BEINGS BY MEANS OF THE THREE VEHICLES. The Buddha Flower-Light will also use the Three Vehicles: Sound Hearers, Conditioned-Enlightened Ones, and Bodhisattvas, to teach and transform living beings.

"SHARIPUTRA, WHEN THIS BUDDHA COMES INTO THE WORLD, ALTHOUGH IT WILL NOT BE AN EVIL AGE, an age of the five turbidities, BECAUSE OF HIS PAST VOWS HE SHALL TEACH THE DHARMA OF THE THREE VEHICLES. Because of his original vows, he will speak the Three Vehicles. Why is this? It's because the teacher he studied the Buddhadharma under in the past will have been Shakyamuni Buddha. Since his teacher spoke the Dharma of the Three Vehicles, the disciple also will make a vow to imitate his teacher. Although the age he will be born in will not be one of the five evil turbidities, he will nevertheless teach the expedient dharmas of the Three Vehicles."

Sutra: T.11b25

"THAT AEON WILL BE CALLED 'ADORNED WITH GREAT JEWELS.' WHY WILL IT BE CALLED 'ADORNED WITH GREAT JEWELS?' BECAUSE IN THAT LAND, BODHISATTVAS WILL BE CONSIDERED GREAT JEWELS."

Outline:

H6. Name of the aeon.

Commentary:

When the Thus Come One Flower Light becomes a Buddha, "THAT AEON WILL BE CALLED 'ADORNED WITH GREAT JEWELS.' WHY WILL IT BE CALLED 'ADORNED WITH GREAT JEWELS?' BECAUSE IN THAT LAND, BODHISATTVAS WILL BE CONSIDERED GREAT JEWELS." This is because in that country they will take Bodhisattvas to be great jewels. During that aeon a great many Bodhisattvas, Mahasattvas, will emerge. The Bodhisattvas will adorn the age.

Sutra: T.11b27

"THESE BODHISATTVAS WILL BE LIMITLESS, BOUNDLESS, INCONCEIVABLE IN NUMBER, BEYOND THE REACH OF CALCULATION OR ANALOGY. WITH

THE EXCEPTION OF THE POWER OF THE BUDDHA'S WISDOM, NO ONE SHALL BE ABLE TO KNOW THEIR NUMBER."

Outline:

H7. Size of the assembly.

Commentary:

"THESE BODHISATTVAS WILL BE LIMITLESS, BOUNDLESS, INCONCEIVABLE IN NUMBER..." The term Bodhisattva has been explained many times. But perhaps some of you have forgotten, so today I will take a little time to explain it.

Where do Bodhisattvas come from?

Bodhisattvas come from living beings. Bodhisattvas originally were living beings.

Then where do living beings come from?

Living beings come from the Buddha.

Where does the Buddha come from? He comes from living beings. Therefore, the Buddha comes from living beings; living beings come from the Buddha. Coming and going--going and coming; not coming and not going, not going and not coming...

How many Bodhisattvas will there be? You could never count them. You could never find their limits. Why is that? It's because their number is inconceivable. If it had a limit or a boundary it would be "conceivable."

"BEYOND THE REACH OF CALCULATION OR ANALOGY... Because the number is inconceivable, it cannot be reckoned. The number of Bodhisattvas can't be counted, can't be alluded to. Who knows how many there will be? Their numbers will be like the grains of sand in the Ganges River. The entire land will be covered with them. That's why the aeon will be called 'Adorned with Great Jewels.' Take a look at the Ganges River. Can you count the grains of sand in it? The number of Bodhisattvas is even greater than that!

"WITH THE EXCEPTION OF THE BUDDHA'S WISDOM, NO ONE SHALL BE ABLE TO KNOW THEIR NUMBER. Without the Buddha's wisdom, the Ten Wisdom Powers of the Buddha, no one could know how many Bodhisattvas there will be.

Sutra: T.11b29

"WHEN THEY WISH TO WALK, JEWELED FLOWERS WILL SPRING UP BENEATH THEIR FEET. THESE BODHISATTVAS WILL NOT BE THOSE WHO HAVE JUST BROUGHT FORTH THEIR THOUGHTS. THEY WILL HAVE PLANTED THE ROOTS OF VIRTUE FOR A LONG TIME, AND IN THE PRESENCE OF LIMITLESS HUNDREDS OF THOUSANDS OF MYRIADS OF BUDDHAS PURELY CULTIVATED BRAHMAN CONDUCT, CONSTANTLY RECEIVING THE BUDDHAS' PRAISE. CONSTANTLY CULTIVATING THE BUDDHA'S WISDOM AND COMPLETE WITH GREAT SPIRITUAL PENETRATIONS, THEY WILL BE WELL-VERSED IN ALL THE DOORS OF DHARMA, STRAIGHT-FORWARD, INGENUOUS, AND STRONG-WILLED. BODHISATTVAS SUCH AS THESE WILL FILL THAT COUNTRY."

Commentary:

"WHEN THEY WISH TO WALK...Perhaps they are standing there, or sitting down--that's not extraordinary. However, as soon as they move to walk JEWELED FLOWERS WILL SPRING UP BENEATH THEIR FEET. When they walk, lotuses will spring up to receive their feet. THESE BODHISATTVAS, boundless in number, WILL NOT BE THOSE WHO HAVE JUST BROUGHT FORTH THEIR THOUGHTS. They haven't just now brought forth their resolve. They have cultivated good roots for a long time and certified to unobstructed wisdom. These Bodhisattvas, you might say, are old Bodhisattvas, not young ones.

Last summer, during the Summer Session,[1] I told you:

> Fish eggs, and the Amala fruit,
> and the newly resolved Bodhisattva--

---

[1]Ninety-six-day *Shurangama Sutra* Study and Cultivation Session, Summer, 1968.

> Of these three there are many in the cause,
> But few of them bear fruit.

Newly resolved Bodhisattvas sometimes don't make it. Fish spawn in the Spring, and although they lay many eggs, all the eggs don't turn into fish. Some do, but many others are turned into mush by the current in the sea.

The Amala tree has lots of blossoms, but bears little fruit. Bodhisattvas find that bringing forth the first thought is easy:

> The heroic heart is easy to bring forth,
> But enduring determination is hard to keep.

The heroic heart may suddenly arise, "Ah! I have brought forth the Bodhisattva heart. I am going to give this and that valuable gift." Easy to say. But if you try to give that way every day, you will find it's not easy, not easy. It's easy to bring forth the first thought to become a Bodhisattva, but in cultivating the Bodhisattva Way you must practice for a long, long time. It's very difficult. Sometimes people may being forth the thought and then retreat. Haven't I said that, in cultivating the Way, people will suddenly advance, and then, just as suddenly, retreat.

"Today, I'm thinking about my old friends. They're all dead. And my young friends, too, are no longer in this world. My middle-aged friend died in an auto accident. The old, middle-aged, and young ones are all dead. Human life is truly meaningless. In the future everyone is going to die. What day am I going to die? Don't know..."

Yesterday we went to "take across" someone who had died. It is the Chinese Buddhist custom that when someone dies, those who have left home recite Sutras to take them across. One person over eighty asked us to go recite Sutras, so the entire company--three novices and a Bhikshu--mobilized and went. Why do I bring this up? It's because in the future everyone is going to die. The question is: After we die, where are we going? Where did we come from in the first place? That, too, is a question. Therefore, you must find out where you came from before you were born and where you will be going after you die. When you are clear about that, then you won't have lived your human life in vain. You won't have come here for nothing. So the Bodhisattvas who have just brought forth the mind, seeing that everyone is bound to die, will get nervous, "I'd better hurry up and cultivate the Way, recite the Buddha's name, meditate, keep precepts, listen to Sutra lectures. I've simply got to cultivate. There's a lecture every night at 125 Waverly Place, Fourth Floor. We ought to take it in."

So they go to one lecture, find it utterly tasteless, and never return. That's called "The Bodhisattva bringing forth the first thought--for a day." The first day they are quite enthusiastic. The second day they have cooled off considerably. By the third day their hearts are frozen solid. They have entered the ice-box when it comes to the Buddhadharma.

It's easy to bring forth that initial thought, but difficult to sustain it for any length of time. So these old Bodhisattvas, who knows how many little Bodhisattvas were in the group that they began in? Anyway, when they walk, lotuses spring up to catch their feet. When Shakyamuni Buddha walks, there are lotuses beneath his feet, and he walks four inches above the ground. He doesn't need to have his feet touch the ground in order to make footprints!

"Now, that I don't believe," you say. "How could someone make footprints whose feet don't even touch the ground?"

I don't care if you believe it or not. What difference does it make to me whether or not you believe it? I'm lecturing the Sutras in accord with the truth. If you don't believe it--so much the better! That's my fondest wish, in fact. If you believed, I wouldn't have to lecture on the Sutras. As long as you don't believe, I can keep on lecturing, just to get you to disbelieve! See? The inconceivable is right there.

These Bodhisattvas will not be those who have just recently brought forth their hearts. THEY WILL HAVE PLANTED THE ROOTS OF VIRTUE FOR A LONG TIME. For a long time they will have planted the roots of Way-virtue, merit and blessings. What are the roots of virtue? They are obtained by planting blessings. If you do a lot of good deeds, you are planting the roots of virtue. If you do a lot of evil deeds, you are planting the roots of offenses. These Bodhisattvas did no evil and practiced every kind of good deed. For a long time they had been planting the roots of their virtue, not just for a day or two, a month or two, a year or two, but in every life throughout limitless, countless aeons. If they found out there was a good deed to be done, they did it, regardless. They benefitted all living beings.

"AND IN THE PRESENCE OF LIMITLESS HUNDREDS OF THOUSANDS OF MYRIADS OF BUDDHAS PURELY CULTIVATED BRAHMAN CONDUCT. "Purely" means clean, sparkling clean, not defiled by a single speck of dust:

> Not defiled by a single speck of dust,
> The myriad thoughts are all empty.

If one wishes to be truly pure, one must not handle money. If you have money, that's impure. Having no money is a form of purity. Why? Money is the filthiest thing there is. In spite of the fact that it's filthy, everyone takes it for a treasure. When people count money they spit on their hands to count the bills. How filthy would you say that was? The germs are crawling all over the money, but that doesn't stop anyone from putting it right in their pockets, germs and all. The more the better! People like to be unclean. They take dirty things as gems. The pure cultivation of Brahman conduct means that you don't handle money.

"I can't manage that," you say.

Of course you can't. If you could, you'd be a Bodhisattva. But you can't, and so you aren't! That's putting it simply.

"CONSTANTLY RECEIVING THE BUDDHA'S PRAISE means that the Buddhas praised them all the time, saying, "You're really good old Bodhisattvas, great Bodhisattvas." Why do they praise them? Because they have been cultivating their roots of virtue for a long time. They are naturally deserving of the Buddhas' praises.

"CONSTANTLY CULTIVATING THE BUDDHA'S WISDOM: What is the Buddha's wisdom? It is real, genuine wisdom. COMPLETE WITH GREAT SPIRITUAL PENETRATIONS, not small ones. They don't just have the power of knowing others' thoughts or past lives, or the heavenly eye or the heavenly ear. It's not that simple. They have great spiritual powers. With great spiritual penetrations one does not have to use an act of deliberate mentation and observation to thoroughly comprehend everything. Those with small spiritual penetrations, such as the Arhats, have to "deliberately think and observe."[1] This means that, if they want to know about something they first have to quiet their minds and deliberately think, "I want to know this..." They have a wisdom which comes from mental activity. Those with great spiritual powers, on the other hand, don't have to do that. They don't have to settle their minds and sit down to meditate for five minutes or so before they can know something. They don't have to meditate because at all times and in all places there is nothing they do not know and nothing they do not see. That's great spiritual penetrations. If you study the Buddhadharma you should know the difference between great and small spiritual penetrations.

"THEY WILL BE WELL-VERSED IN ALL THE DOORS OF DHARMA: The great Bodhisattvas know the entrance into the Dharmas, that is, how to get into them, so to speak. They will be able to penetrate the Real Mark of all Dharmas.

"STRAIGHTFORWARD means that their behavior is straightforward and not sneaky. INGENUOUS means that they are not false. They are truthful in all they do. AND STRONG-WILLED. When it comes to the Buddhadharma, their determination is extremely firm. They can't be side-tracked, and they would never retreat. BODHISATTVAS SUCH AS THESE WILL FILL THAT COUNTRY: Great Bodhisattvas like these will completely fill the land of the Thus Come One Flower Light during the aeon called 'Adorned with Great Jewels.'"

Sutra: T.11c4

"SHARIPUTRA, THE LIFESPAN OF THE BUDDHA FLOWER-LIGHT WILL BE TWELVE SMALL AEONS, NOT

---

1 作意觀察 -*tso i kuan ch'a*

COUNTING THE TIME DURING WHICH, AS A PRINCE, HE WILL NOT YET HAVE BECOME A BUDDHA. THE LIFESPAN OF THE PEOPLE IN THAT COUNTRY WILL BE EIGHT SMALL AEONS."

Outline:

H8. The lifespan.

Commentary:

Shakyamuni Buddha called out, "SHARIPUTRA, THE LIFESPAN OF THE BUDDHA FLOWER-LIGHT WILL BE TWELVE SMALL AEONS.

What is meant by a "small aeon?"

Every one hundred years the average human lifespan decreases by one year, and the average height decreases by one inch. We are now in a period of a "decreasing aeon." When the lifespan has decreased to ten years--it is now on the average of sixty or seventy years--it will begin to increase again. One period of increase and one period of decrease is considered to be an aeon. One thousand of those aeons is a small aeon. Twelve small aeons--how long is that? You'll need some time to figure it out.

"NOT COUNTING THE TIME DURING WHICH, AS A PRINCE, HE WILL NOT YET HAVE BECOME A BUDDHA. The lifespan of twelve small aeons does not count the time during which he is a prince and hasn't yet become a Buddha. THE LIFESPAN OF THE PEOPLE IN THAT COUNTRY WILL BE EIGHT SMALL AEONS."

Sutra: T.11c6

"AFTER TWELVE SMALL AEONS, THE THUS COME ONE FLOWER-LIGHT WILL CONFER UPON THE BODHISATTVA SOLID FULLNESS A PREDICTION OF ANUTTARASAMYAKSAMBODHI, AND ANNOUNCE TO THE BHIKSHUS, 'THE BODHISATTVA SOLID FULLNESS SHALL NEXT BECOME A BUDDHA BY THE NAME OF FLOWERY FEET PEACEFULLY WALKING, TATHAGATA, ARHAT, SAMYAKSAMBUDDHA. HIS BUDDHA COUNTRY

WILL BE OF LIKE CHARACTER."

Outline:

H9. The successor

Commentary:

"AFTER TWELVE SMALL AEONS, THE THUS COME ONE FLOWER-LIGHT WILL CONFER UPON THE BODHISATTVA SOLID FULLNESS A PREDICTION OF ANUTTARASAMYAKSAMBODHI." He will give the Bodhisattva Solid Fullness a prediction. "Solid" means firm; "fullness" means complete. What is solid? His vow power. What is complete? His vow power. What is his vow? To become a Buddha! Since his vow to become a Buddha is complete, the Thus Come One Flower-Light will give him a prediction of Buddhahood. "AND ANNOUNCE TO THE BHIKSHUS, 'THE BODHISATTVA SOLID FULLNESS SHALL NEXT BECOME A BUDDHA BY THE NAME OF FLOWERY FEET PEACEFULLY WALKING." The word "Bhikshu" here includes the four-fold assembly. His Buddha name will be Flowery Feet Peacefully Walking because when he walks there will be flowers springing up to catch his feet. He will walk very peacefully. "TATHAGATA" is the Thus Come One. "ARHAT" means One Worthy of Offerings. "SAMYAKSAMBUDDHA" means One of Right and Universal Knowledge. "HIS BUDDHA COUNTRY WILL BE OF LIKE CHARACTER."

Sutra: T.11c10

"SHARIPUTRA, WHEN THE BUDDHA FLOWER-LIGHT HAS PASSED INTO EXTINCTION, THE PROPER DHARMA SHALL DWELL IN THE WORLD FOR THIRTY-TWO SMALL AEONS. THE RESEMBLANCE DHARMA SHALL DWELL IN THE WORLD ALSO FOR THIRTY-TWO SMALL AEONS."

Outline:

H10. Duration of the Dharma's dwelling.

Commentary:

"SHARIPUTRA, WHEN THE BUDDHA FLOWER-LIGHT HAS

PASSED INTO EXTINCTION, THE PROPER DHARMA SHALL DWELL IN THE WORLD FOR THIRTY-TWO SMALL AEONS. There is the Orthodox Dharma Period, the Dharma Resemblance Period, and the Dharma-ending Period. THE DHARMA RESEMBLANCE PERIOD SHALL ALSO DWELL FOR THIRTY-TWO SMALL AEONS. During the Orthodox Dharma Period people are strong in Dhyana Samadhi. During the Dharma Resemblance Period people are strong in building temples and monasteries and Buddist images. During the Dharma-ending Period, people are strong in fighting.

Dharma-ending means that there is no more Dharma. The Dharma has come to its final stages, like the tips of the branches of a tree. The Orthodox Dharma Period could be likened to the root of the tree, the Dharma Resemblance Period to the branches, and the Dharma-ending Period to the twigs, the tips of the branches. In the Dharma Resemblance Period, people will still create Buddha images, but in the Dharma-ending Period they won't even do that. What will they do? They will be strong in fighting. "You fight me. I fight you." Everybody will be thinking only of fighting with one another, and so the good Dharma will turn into "no-Dharma." Without the good Dharmas,the Buddhadharma will become extinct. Presently, there are words on the printed Sutra texts. When the Dharma-ending Period descends, the words will disappear from the paper. Why? Scientific progress in the field of weaponry has created pollution in the air to the point that there is not a single place at present where the air is clean. It is all full of poison and so when people breathe it, if they don't get cancer, they come down with some other incurable disease. Because of this impure air, gradually the words of the Sutra will be poisoned right off the paper. The first Sutra to disappear will be *The Shurangama Sutra*. So, in the West, the first order of business is to investigate *The Shurangama Sutra* and promote it. Why do we recite the Shurangama Mantra twice every day, once in the morning and once at night? If there is no one in the world who can recite the Shurangama Mantra, the demons and strange creatures can get into the world. As long as there is one person in the world who recites the Shurangama Mantra, they don't dare come into the world. Also, the Forty-two Hands work the same way. If one person has mastered the Thousand Arm Dharani Dharma, not a single demon in the great trichiliocosm will have the gall to appear in the world. So now our recitation of the Shurangama Mantra supports and maintains the Orthodox Dharma Period. We are now turning the Dharma-ending Period into the Orthodox Dharma Period!

Sutra: T.11c12

AT THAT TIME, THE WORLD HONORED ONE, WISHING TO RESTATE THIS MEANING, SPOKE VERSES SAYING,

SHARIPUTRA, IN A FUTURE AGE,
THERE SHALL BE A BUDDHA, HONORED AND ALL-WISE,
BY THE NAME OF FLOWER-LIGHT,
WHO WILL SAVE LIMITLESS MULTITUDES.

Outline:

G2. Verse.
H1. Verse introduced.
I1. Transcendance to attain the fruition.

Commentary:

AT THAT TIME, when Shakyamuni Buddha had conferred the prediction upon Shariputra, THE WORLD HONORED ONE, WISHING TO RESTATE THIS MEANING, the Buddha wanted to use verses to speak the meaning once more, in greater detail, and so he SPOKE VERSES SAYING,

SHARIPUTRA, IN A FUTURE AGE/ in the future THERE SHALL BE A BUDDHA, HONORED AND ALL-WISE/ a Buddha who saves all living beings and is honored for his wisdom BY THE NAME OF FLOWER-LIGHT/His Buddha name will be Flower-Light Thus Come One. WHO WILL SAVE LIMITLESS MULTITUDES/ limitless, boundless living beings.

Sutra: T.11c15

HAVING MADE OFFERINGS TO COUNTLESS BUDDHAS,
AND PERFECTED THE BODHISATTVA CONDUCT,
THE TEN POWERS AND OTHER MERITORIOUS QUALITIES,
HE SHALL CERTIFY TO THE UNSURPASSED PATH.

Outline:

I2. Verse of causal practices.

Commentary:

HAVING MADE OFFERINGS TO COUNTLESS BUDDHAS/ Why will he become a Buddha? Because he will have made offerings to countless numbers of Buddhas AND PERFECTED THE BODHISATTVA CONDUCT/ practiced the Six Perfections and the Ten Thousand Conducts, the path that Bodhisattvas are supposed to practice, that of benefitting oneself and benefitting others, enlightening oneself and enlightening others--the Bodhisattva Way. THE TEN POWERS AND OTHER MERITORIOUS QUALITIES/ The Ten Powers, the Eight Liberations, and the Dhyana samadhis. The Ten Powers have been discussed.[1] As to the seventh of the ten, that of knowing where all paths lead, this means that the Buddha knows that living beings who cultivate the five precepts and the ten good deeds can be born in the heavens. If one cultivates the Four Holy Truths, one can certify to the fruit of Arhatship. If one cultivates the Twelve Conditioned Causes one can certify to the fruit of Pratyeka Buddhahood. If one practices the Six Perfections and the Ten Thousand Conducts one can certify to the fruit of Bodhisattvahood.

Because he has perfected the meritorious qualities of the Ten Powers as well as other meritorious qualities, including the Eighteen Unshared Dharmas and the Four Truths, the Twelve Conditioned Causes, the Six Perfections and the Ten Thousand Conducts--all the Dharma-doors HE SHALL CERTIFY TO THE UNSURPASSED PATH/ to the position of the supreme path.

Sutra: T.11c17

> WHEN LIMITLESS AEONS SHALL HAVE PASSSED,
> THERE SHALL BE AN AEON NAMED "ADORNED WITH
> GREAT JEWELS,"

---

[1]see *The Dharma Flower Sutra, Vol. III,* BTTS, 1979, pages 437-9.

Outline:

I3. Verse of time and name of aeon.

Commentary:

WHEN LIMITLESS AEONS SHALL HAVE PASSED/ THERE SHALL BE AN AEON NAMED "ADORNED WITH GREAT JEWELS"/ After unlimited aeons have gone by, and Shariputra has become a Buddha, there will be an aeon named Adorned with Great Jewels.

Sutra: T.11c18

AND A WORLD BY THE NAME OF "APART FROM FILTH,"
BEING PURE AND WITHOUT FLAW,
WITH LAPIS LAZULI AS ITS GROUND,
AND ITS ROADS BORDERED WITH GOLDEN CORDS,
WITH MULTICOLORED TREES MADE OF SEVEN JEWELS,
WHICH CONSTANTLY BLOOM AND BEAR FRUIT.

Outline:

I4. Verse about the country.

Commentary:

AND A WORLD BY THE NAME OF "APART FROM FILTH"/ Why will it be called "Apart From Filth?" Because there will be no unclean things there. It will be extremely clean. BEING PURE AND WITHOUT FLAW/ It will not have the slightest flaw, no "blemishes on the jade," so to speak.

WITH LAPIS LAZULI AS ITS GROUND/ This blue gem shall be its ground. AND ITS ROADS BORDERED WITH GOLDEN CORDS/ WITH MULTICOLORED TREES MADE OF SEVEN JEWELS/ The combination of colors--blue, white, red, yellow, green--will cause those who see the trees to bring forth the Bodhi heart. Why are they so beautiful? So that when people see them, their hearts want to seek the Way. "This place is so fine," they will think, "I had better hurry up and cultivate so I can go there." WHICH CONSTANTLY BLOOM AND BEAR FRUIT/ The trees will always be in bloom and will constantly be bearing fruit.

Sutra: T.11c20

THE BODHISATTVAS IN THAT LAND,
WILL BE ALWAYS FIRM IN MINDFULNESS,
WITH SPIRITUAL PENETRATIONS AND PARAMITAS,
ALL THOROUGHLY PERFECTED.
IN THE PRESENCE OF COUNTLESS BUDDHAS,
THEY WILL HAVE WELL-LEARNED THE BODHISATTVA PATH.

Outline:

I5. Verse concerning the assembly.

Commentary:

THE BODHISATTVAS IN THAT LAND/ in the world Apart From Filth, during the aeon called Adorned with Great Jewels, WILL BE ALWAYS FIRM IN MINDFULNESS/ Their resolve and their thoughts will be extremely firm. They will have all attained to the Three-fold Irreversibility: 1) Irreversible in position, 1) Irreversible in thought, and 3) Irreversible in conduct. WITH SPIRITUAL PENETRATIONS AND PARAMITAS/ ALL THOROUGHLY PERFECTED/ They will have obtained great spiritual powers and the paramitas, having gone to the other shore. They will have perfected them all.

IN THE PRESENCE OF COUNTLESS BUDDHAS/ THEY WILL HAVE WELL-LEARNED THE BODHISATTVA PATH/ They will have studied the practice of the Bodhisattva Path, the Dharma-door of the cultivation of the Six Perfections and the Ten Thousand Conducts.

Sutra: T.11c24

GREAT LORDS SUCH AS THESE
SHALL HAVE BEEN TRANSFORMED BY THE
BUDDHA FLOWER-LIGHT.

Outline:

I6. Verse about the teaching of the Dharma.

Commentary:

GREAT LORDS SUCH AS THESE/ So many limitless, boundless great Bodhisattvas SHALL HAVE BEEN TRANSFORMED BY THE BUDDHA FLOWER-LIGHT/ taught and transformed by the Buddha Flower Light.

Sutra: T.11c25

THAT BUDDHA, WHEN STILL A PRINCE,
SHALL RENOUNCE HIS LAND AND WORLDLY GLORY,
AND, IN HIS FINAL BODY,
LEAVE HOME TO REALIZE THE BUDDHA PATH.
THE BUDDHA FLOWER-LIGHT SHALL DWELL IN THE WORLD
FOR A LIFESPAN OF TWELVE SMALL AEONS.
THE PEOPLE OF HIS LAND
SHALL LIVE FOR EIGHT SMALL AEONS.

Outline:

I7. Verse about the lifespans.

Commentary:

THAT BUDDHA, WHEN STILL A PRINCE/ SHALL RENOUNCE HIS LAND AND WORLDLY GLORY/ He basically should have become the king, but he won't. He won't want his kingdom. He will renounce it and let go of all the wealth and honor he was due to receive. AND, IN HIS FINAL BODY/ In his very last life he shall LEAVE HOME TO REALIZE THE BUDDHA PATH/ He shall go forth from the home-life, become a Bhikshu, and cultivate to accomplish the Buddha Way.

THE BUDDHA FLOWER-LIGHT SHALL DWELL IN THE WORLD/ FOR A LIFESPAN OF TWELVE SMALL AEONS/ THE PEOPLE OF HIS LAND/ SHALL LIVE FOR EIGHT SMALL AEONS/ eight minor kalpas.

Sutra: T.11c29

WHEN THAT BUDDHA HAS BECOME EXTINCT,
THE PROPER DHARMA SHALL REMAIN IN THE WORLD
FOR THIRTY-TWO SMALL AEONS,
WIDELY SAVING LIVING BEINGS.
WHEN THE PROPER DHARMA'S ALL EXTINCT,
THE RESEMBLANCE DHARMA SHALL REMAIN FOR THIRTY-TWO.
THE SHARIRA SHALL BE DISTRIBUTED WIDELY,
FOR THE OFFERINGS OF GODS AND HUMANS.

Outline:

I8. The Dharma's dwelling.

Commentary:

WHEN THAT BUDDHA HAS BECOME EXTINCT/ When the Thus Come One Flower-Light has entered Nirvana, THE PROPER DHARMA SHALL REMAIN IN THE WORLD/ The Orthodox Dharma will remain in the world FOR THIRTY-TWO SMALL AEONS/ WIDELY SAVING LIVING BEINGS/ During the thirty-two aeons of the Orthodox Dharma Age, vast numbers of living beings will be taken across the sea of suffering.

WHEN THE PROPER DHARMA'S ALL EXTINCT/ When the Orthodox Dharma has passed out of existence, THE RESEMBLANCE DHARMA SHALL REMAIN FOR THIRTY-TWO/ also for thirty-two small aeons. THE SHARIRA SHALL BE DISTRIBUTED WIDELY/ The sharira of the Buddha Flower-Light shall be distributed widely throughout the world and many stupas shall be erected. FOR THE OFFERINGS OF GODS AND HUMANS/ The gods in the heavens and the humans below shall make offerings to the shariras, to the jeweled stupas containing them.

Sutra: T.12a4

THE DEEDS OF THE BUDDHA FLOWER-LIGHT,
SHALL BE SUCH AS THESE.
THAT SAGELY HONORED ONE, TWICE COMPLETE,
SHALL BE SUPREME AND BEYOND COMPARE.

AND HE IS JUST YOU, YOURSELF!
SO IT'S FITTING THAT YOU DO REJOICE.

Outline:

H2. Concluding praise.

Commentary:

THE DEEDS OF THE BUDDHA FLOWER-LIGHT/ The actions of the Buddha Flower-Light, SHALL BE SUCH AS THESE/ in general shall be as just enumerated. THAT SAGELY HONORED ONE, TWICE COMPLETE/ The One Complete in blessings and wisdom, SHALL BE SUPREME AND BEYOND COMPARE/ He will be the most excellent; no one will be able to compare with him.

AND HE IS JUST YOU YOURSELF!/ And just who is this Flower-Light Buddha? He is just you, Shariputra. In the future you shall become the Buddha Flower-Light. SO IT'S FITTING THAT YOU DO REJOICE/ You should be happy and rejoice, for in the future you shall become a Buddha.

the assembly (cover detail)

the burning house

PART THREE: THE PARABLE

Sutra: T.12a7

AT THAT TIME, THE FOUR-FOLD ASSEMBLY OF BHIKSHUS, BHIKSHUNIS, UPASAKAS, UPASIKAS, AS WELL AS THE GREAT MULTITUDE OF YAKSHAS, GANDHARVAS, ASURAS, GARUDAS, KINNARAS, MAHORAGAS, AND SO FORTH, SEEING SHARIPUTRA, IN THE PRESENCE OF THE BUDDHA, RECEIVE A PREDICTION FOR ANUTTARASAMSAKSAMBODHI, GREATLY REJOICED IN THEIR HEARTS AND LEAPT FOR UNBOUNDED JOY.

Outline:

F5. Rejoicing of the great assembly.
G1. Prose.
H1. Editor of Sutra tells of the assembly's rejoicing.

Commentary:

AT THAT TIME, after Shakyamuni Buddha had bestowed the prediction upon Shariputra, THE FOUR-FOLD ASSEMBLY

OF BHIKSHUS, BHIKSHUNIS, UPASAKAS, AND UPASIKAS: Bhikshus are men who have left home; Bhikshunis are women who have left home. Upasakas are men who are at home and Upasikas are women who are at home. Not only was the four-fold assembly of disciples present, but the gods and dragons and the eight-fold division was there, too. AS WELL AS THE GREAT MULTITUDE OF YAKSHAS, "speedy ghosts" who run very fast. GANDHARVAS are musical spirits in the court of Shakra. ASURAS are those who have heavenly blessings but not heavenly authority. They don't have the virtuous practice of the gods. Asuras are sometimes found in the Three Good Paths and other times they are counted in the Four Evil Paths. The Three Good Paths are those of gods, humans, and asuras. The Four Evil Paths are the asuras, hell-beings, hungry ghosts, and animals. Why are asuras put into the Four Evil Paths? Because their temperment is very fiesty. They are always trying to pick fights with people. Because of their strength in fighting, they are counted among the Four Evil Paths. There are asuras, too, among humans, in the hells, in the heavens, and among the animals, and the hungry ghosts. Asuras are just those who like to fight. No matter what kind of living being it is, if it likes to fight, it's an asura. GARUDAS are the great golden-winged P'eng birds. These birds have a wingspan of three hundred yojanas. With a single flap of their wings they can dry up the entire ocean, exposing all the dragons to view. They gobble up the dragons just like we eat noodles! They open their mouths and pop in a dragon, open their mouths and pop in a dragon. Their bodies are huge, so their lips are big, too, and they can swallow dragons just like we eat noodles. KINNARAS are also musical spirits in Shakra's court. MAHORAGAS are the big snakes. When the Buddha spoke the Dharma, the gods, dragons, and the rest of the eight-fold division all went to listen. This is just a general list. There were also a lot of other kinds of beings there.

SEEING SHARIPUTRA, IN THE PRESENCE OF THE BUDDHA, RECEIVE A PREDICTION FOR ANUTTARASAMYAKSAMBODHI: The great assembly saw Shariputra receive a prediction of his future Buddhahood as the Thus Come One Flower-Light. GREATLY REJOICED IN THEIR HEARTS. See? The Great Wise Shariputra in the future can become a Buddha! They were ecstatic! AND LEPT FOR THEIR UNBOUNDED JOY. They jumped around just like when people are happy to the extreme they may jump for joy, not dancing, but just expressing their happiness.

Sutra: T.12a10

EACH REMOVED HIS UPPER GARMENT AND PRESENTED IT AS AN OFFERING TO THE BUDDHA. SHAKRO DEVANAM INDRAH AND THE BRAHMA HEAVEN KING, TOGETHER WITH COUNTLESS GODS, ALSO MADE OFFERINGS TO THE BUDDHA OF HEAVENLY WONDERFUL GARMENTS, HEAVENLY MANDARAVA FLOWERS AND MAHAMANDARAVA FLOWERS, AND SO FORTH.

Outline:

H2. Explaining the offerings.

Commentary:

EACH OF THEM REMOVED HIS UPPER GARMENT: Each of them removed his most expensive upper garment. AND PRESENTED IT AS AN OFFERING TO THE BUDDHA. Now, as to making offerings to the Buddha, in the Indian custom, Bhikshus had a precept that they could have only three robes in their possession. One was the Samghati robe, also called the host robe, which is twenty-five strips and one hundred and eight patches. There is also the seven-piece robe and the five-piece robe. These are the only three robes they were allowed. Now, if they removed their robe and offered it to the Buddha, wouldn't they be left without a robe and be thereby breaking a precept? Wherever left-home people go, their three robes have to go with them. But if they removed their most upper garment, their most expensive garment of course being the host robe, wouldn't they be missing a robe?

You shouldn't have an attachment at this point and look at it as so stuffy. At that time the Bhikshus might have had the offerings of some other people, extras of which they gave the newest ones to the Buddha. Or perhaps some Bhikshus had already died and had entrusted their clothing to others who took this happy occasion to offer them to the Buddha. There are a lot of ways you could explain this. Lay people of course can give away their valuable clothing as they like. "Upper" garments can refer to the clothes they wore on the upper part of their bodies or it can refer to the finest, most expensive garments.

SHAKRO DEVANAM INDRAH, the Lord of the Heaven of

the Thirty-three, also known as Shakra, THE BRAHMA HEAVEN KING, the King of the Great Brahma Heaven, TOGETHER WITH COUNTLESS GODS, ALSO MADE OFFERINGS TO THE BUDDHA OF HEAVENLY WONDERFUL GARMENTS, the wonderful clothing of the gods, HEAVENLY MANDARAVA FLOWERS, white flowers, AND MAHAMANDARAVA FLOWERS, big white flowers, AND SO FORTH includes the Manjushaka flowers and the Mahamanjushaka flowers, that is, the red flowers and the big red flowers.

Sutra: T.12a13

THE HEAVENLY GARMENTS THEY TOSSED ALOFT REMAINED IN EMPTY SPACE AND WHIRLED AROUND. THEN ALL AT ONCE IN EMPTY SPACE A HUNDRED THOUSAND MYRIADS OF KINDS OF HEAVENLY MUSIC BEGAN TO PLAY, AND THERE FELL A RAIN OF HEAVENLY FLOWERS.

Commentary:

THE HEAVENLY GARMENTS THEY TOSSED ALOFT REMAINED IN EMPTY SPACE AND WHIRLED AROUND. They revolved in empty space as if they were flying, and twirled around and around. THEN ALL AT ONCE IN EMPTY SPACE A HUNDRED THOUSAND MYRIADS OF KINDS OF HEAVENLY MUSIC BEGAN TO PLAY, all at the same time. AND THERE FELL A RAIN OF HEAVENLY FLOWERS.

Sutra: T.12a15

AS THEY UTTERED THESE WORDS, "LONG AGO IN VARANASHI, THE BUDDHA FIRST TURNED THE WHEEL OF THE DHARMA. NOW, HE TURNS AGAIN THAT UNSURPASSED, MAGNIFICENT DHARMA WHEEL."

Outline:

H3. Leading to understanding proper.

Commentary:

AS THEY UTTERED THESE WORDS: "LONG AGO, IN VARANASHI, in the Deer Park, THE BUDDHA FIRST TURNED THE WHEEL OF THE DHARMA. He turned the Dharma Wheel of the Four Truths, called The Three Turnings of the Dharma Wheel of the Four Holy Truths. NOW, HE TURNS AGAIN THE UNSURPASSED MAGNIFICENT DHARMA WHEEL. He is speaking *The Wonderful Dharma Lotus Flower Sutra*.

Sutra: T.12a17

AT THAT TIME ALL THE GODS, WISHING TO RESTATE THIS MEANING, SPOKE VERSES SAYING,

LONG AGO IN VARANASHI,
YOU TURNED THE DHARMA WHEEL OF FOUR TRUTHS,
DISCRIMINATINGLY SPEAKING OF THE DHARMAS,
THE PRODUCTION AND EXTINCTION OF FIVE HEAPS.
NOW AGAIN YOU TURN THAT WONDROUS,
UNSURPASSED, GREAT WHEEL OF DHARMA.
THIS DHARMA'S DEEP AND RECONDITE,
AND FEW ARE THOSE WHO CAN BELIEVE IT.

Outline:

G2. Verse
H1. Verse of opening the provisional to reveal the one reality.

Commentary:

AT THAT TIME, after the gods, dragons, and the eightfold division heard that the Buddha was about to turn the Dharma Wheel again, ALL THE GODS, WISHING TO RESTATE THIS MEANING, SPOKE VERSES SAYING,

LONG AGO IN VARANASHI/ The World Honored One, previously, in the Deer Park, YOU TURNED THE DHARMA WHEEL OF FOUR TRUTHS/ You expounded the Three Turnings of the Dharma Wheel of Four Truths. DISCRIMINATINGLY SPEAKING OF THE DHARMAS/ suffering, origination, extinction, the Way, the Twelve Conditioned Causes, THE PRODUCTION AND EXTINCTION OF FIVE HEAPS/ form, feeling, perception, impulse, and consciousness. The truth of suffering is produced from the truth of origination. When there is production, there is extinction. If there is no production, there is no extinction. Because of the truth of origination, the truth of suffering arises. Not long after it is produced, it is extinguished. The extinction of both production and extinction is the truth of extinction.

What is extinguished? Suffering and origination. The extinction of suffering and origination is the truth of the path. Therefore, suffering, origination, extinction and the path have their roots in the five skandhas.

NOW AGAIN YOU TURN THAT WONDROUS/ SUPREME, GREAT WHEEL OF DHARMA/ Long ago you spoke the dharmas of the Four Truths and the Twelve Conditioned Causes and now you speak the most wonderful Dharma. What is that? It's *The Wonderful Dharma Lotus Flower Sutra*. This Sutra is the King of Dharmas. It is supreme. There is nothing more lofty than it. It is the genuine wisdom. In this Sutra the provisional wisdom is done away with and the true, real wisdom is taught.

THIS DHARMA'S DEEP AND RECONDITE/ AND FEW ARE THOSE WHO CAN BELIEVE IT/ This Sutra is extremely deep and most wonderful. Because it is so wonderful, most people's wisdom can't fathom it. Unable to fathom it, they disbelieve it. For example, over a thousand years ago in China there were "flying cars." When the Yellow Emperor was battling with *Ch'ih-yu*[1], the leader of a barbarian tribe, there were already flying cars. The Yellow Emperor invented the compass because during the battle, *Ch'ih-yu* was able to set off a poisonous fog which screened their vision. So the Yellow Emperor invented the compass so he could know the four directions. But, a thousand years ago, if you had told someone, "In the future there will be planes which will fly in space," to say nothing of rockets, no one would have believed you. "Impossible," they would have said. Why wouldn't they have believed you? Because it's too wonderful. "How could people possibly fly around in space? Absurd."

Before Columbus discovered America, if you had gone around saying, "I know where there is another continent. It's rich with gold and silver," most people wouldn't have believed you. Ultimately, did it exist or not? It did. But for the most part, people

---

[1] 蚩尤

didn't believe it. It was there all the time, but no one believed in it. After it was "discovered," it wasn't the case that it suddenly sprang into existence It was there all the time.

The Wonderful Dharma Lotus Flower Sutra says that everyone can become a Buddha--all living beings can become Buddhas. Nobody believes it. "How can I become a Buddha? It's ridiculous to think that all living beings can become Buddhas and I don't believe it." Ultimately, can people become Buddhas? If not, then how did the Buddha realize the fruit of Buddhahood? Shakyamuni Buddha was just a person. We, too, are people, but we haven't cultivated. We haven't practiced as bitterly as Shakyamuni Buddha in our cultivation, and so we have not yet become Buddhas. If we imitate Shakyamuni Buddha in his bitter cultivation we would very quickly become Buddhas. Why haven't we become Buddhas? Because we're lazy! Because we do not diligently cultivate the good Way.

Why has Shakyamuni Buddha become a Buddha? Because he diligently cultivated the good Way. There's no other esoteric secret involved. It's like traveling. If you want to go somewhere, you have to start walking, or else get in your car, take a bus, a train, or a plane. In any case, you've got to start moving. If you just say, "I'm going to New York," and don't go, you'll never get there. You've got to set yourself in motion. Shakyamuni Buddha knew that becoming a Buddha was a possibility, and so he began cultivating the Path to Buddhahood. Finally, he realized it. We are now still living beings and we don't think it's bad at all. "I am a human being. I am quite intelligent." Who knows how large our mark of self looms--higher than Mount Sumeru! The mark may loom high, but the things we do aren't high at all. They are very base and lowly. How are they base and lowly? We have not rid ourselves of greed, for one thing, and that is base and lowly. Our hatred and stupidity we find impossible to put down, too. We take ourselves too lightly. That is why the text says, "Few are those who can believe it."

Sutra: T.12a22

WE, FROM OF OLD,
HAVE OFTEN HEARD THE WORLD HONORED ONE SPEAK,
BUT NEVER HAVE WE HEARD SUCH DHARMA,
SO DEEP, SO WONDROUS, AND SUPREME.
THE WORLD HONORED ONE HAS SPOKEN THE DHARMA,
AND WE REJOICE ACCORDINGLY,
AS THE GREAT WISE SHARIPUTRA
NOW RECEIVES THE HONORED ONE'S PREDICTION.
WE, TOO, ARE LIKE THIS,
AND WILL SURELY BECOME BUDDHAS,
THROUGHOUT ALL THE WORLDS,
MOST HONORED AND SUPREME.
THE BUDDHA'S PATH IS INCONCEIVABLE,
TAUGHT EXPEDIENTLY ACCORDING TO WHAT IS FITTING.
MAY ALL OF OUR BLESSED KARMA,
IN THIS LIFE AND IN LIVES GONE BY,
AND THE MERIT AND VIRTUE GAINED FROM
SEEING THE BUDDHAS,
BE DEDICATED TO THE BUDDHA PATH.

Outline:

H2. Rejoicing and dedicating the merit as they gain understanding.

Commentary:

WE, FROM OF OLD/ The gods say, "All of us from limitless aeons in the past up until the present. HAVE OFTEN HEARD THE WORLD HONORED ONE SPEAK/ "Often" means not just once, but many times, a countless number of times. BUT NEVER HAVE WE HEARD SUCH DHARMA/ Although we have heard the Buddha speak the Dharma, we have never heard a Dharma as wonderful as this. SO DEEP, SO WONDROUS, AND SUPREME/ It's profound, miraculous, lofty, and supreme.

THE WORLD HONORED ONE HAS SPOKEN DHARMA/ the wonderful Dharma, AND WE REJOICE ACCORDINGLY/ All the gods and the rest of those assembled listen to this Dharma joyfully. Especially, AS THE GREAT, WISE SHARIPUTRA/ The wisest among the Sound Hearers, NOW RECEIVES THE HONORED ONE'S PREDICTION/ He receives a prediction of his future Buddhahood, the most valuable, most glorious of predictions. WE, TOO, ARE LIKE THIS/ All the gods also have this hope, AND WILL SURELY BECOME BUDDHAS/ In the future we will most surely become Buddhas. This is because in the Dharma Flower Assembly, there is not one being who will not become a Buddha. . THROUGHOUT ALL WORLDS/ When we become Buddhas, in all the worlds we shall be MOST HONORED AND SUPREME/ We shall also be the most venerable. No one shall be above us. No one shall be more lofty. THE BUDDHA'S PATH IS INCONCEIVABLE/ TAUGHT EXPEDIENTLY ACCORDING TO WHAT IS FITTING/ It is through expedient devices that the Buddha accords with the potentials of living beings and speaks the Dharma appropriate to them.

MAY ALL OF OUR BLESSED KARMA/ IN THIS LIFE AND IN LIVES GONE BY/ all of the blessings, virtue, and good karma of the gods, AND THE MERIT AND VIRTUE GAINED FROM SEEING THE BUDDHA/ BE DEDICATED TO THE BUDDHA PATH/ We, together, take this merit and virtue and dedicate it to our future attainment of the Buddha Path.

the assembly (cover detail)

The great white ox cart.

Drawn by Sara (age 11) and Pearl (age 8) of Instilling Virtue School.

Sutra: T.12b2

AT THAT TIME, SHARIPUTRA SPOKE TO THE BUDDHA SAYING, "WORLD HONORED ONE, I NOW HAVE NO FURTHER DOUBTS OR REGRETS, HAVING RECEIVED FROM THE BUDDHA A PREDICTION FOR ANUTTARASAMYAK-SAMBODHI. BUT THE TWELVE HUNDRED WHOSE HEARTS HAVE ATTAINED SELF-MASTERY, AND WHO FORMERLY DWELT IN THE STAGE OF STUDY, WERE CONSTANTLY TAUGHT BY THE BUDDHA WHO SAID, 'MY DHARMA CAN ENABLE ONE TO SEPARATE FROM BIRTH, OLD AGE, SICKNESS, AND DEATH AND ATTAIN ULTIMATE NIRVANA.' BOTH THOSE WHO STUDY AND THOSE BEYOND STUDY ALIKE HAVE SEPARATED FROM THE

VIEW OF A SELF, THE VIEWS OF EXISTENCE AND NON-EXISTENCE, AND SO FORTH, AND CLAIM THAT THEY HAVE ATTAINED NIRVANA.
YET NOW, HEARING FROM THE WORLD HONORED ONE THAT WHICH THEY HAVE NEVER HEARD BEFORE, THEY HAVE ALL FALLEN INTO DOUBT AND DELUSION.
GOOD INDEED, WORLD HONORED ONE. I BEG THAT YOU WOULD, FOR THE SAKE OF THE FOUR-FOLD ASSEMBLY, SPEAK OF THESE CAUSES AND CONDITIONS, TO FREE THEM OF THEIR DOUBTS AND REGRETS."

Outline:

E2. Circuit of speaking the parable.
F1. Opening the three to reveal the one.
G1. The request.

Commentary:

AT THAT TIME, when all the gods had finished speaking their verses and dedicating all their merit and virtue towards their future attainment of the Buddha Path, SHARIPUTRA SPOKE TO THE BUDDHA, SAYING, "WORLD HONORED ONE, I NOW HAVE NO FURTHER DOUBTS OR REGRETS."Hearing the Dharma the Buddha has spoken, I have no doubts." This is because the great and wise Shariputra understood the wonderful Dharma the Buddha spoke. He had no doubts becuase he had already caught on to it. He couldn't ever doubt it again.

"HAVING RECEIVED FROM THE BUDDHA A PREDICTION FOR ANUTTARASAMYAKSAMBODHI, a prediction for the unsurpassed proper, equal, right enlightenment, saying that his Buddha name would be the Thus Come One Flower-Light"

"BUT THE TWELVE HUNDRED WHOSE HEARTS HAVE GAINED SELF-MASTERY, all of the 1250 disciples who have gained self-mastery, all the great Bhikshus, WHO FORMERLY DWELT IN THE STAGE OF STUDY: The stage of study refers to stages prior to the attainment of Fourth Stage Arhatship. WERE CONSTANTLY TAUGHT BY THE BUDDHA, WHO SAID: The Buddha continually taught them saying, 'MY DHARMA CAN ENABLE ONE TO SEPARATE FROM BIRTH, OLD AGE, SICKNESS, AND DEATH AND ATTAIN TO ULTIMATE NIRVANA.' From within my Buddhadharma, you can release yourself from the sufferings of birth, old age, sickness, and death.

Birth, old age, sickness, and death: When people are born, it is extremely painful. But, because you were so small and didn't understand what was going on, you quickly forgot the experience.However, when we get old, we shall all suffer the bitterness of old age. In what way is old age a form of suffering?

As you grow old, your eyes grow dim and your hearing fails, your teeth fall out, and so your food is tasteless. Your eyes, ears, and teeth all fail to help you. Pretty soon your legs won't help you, and soon neither will your hands. Your hands may want to pick something up, but when the time comes, they shake uncontrollably, and it becomes impossible to pick anything up. Americans like to eat with knives and forks, but when you're old, you can't even pick them up! They seem to weigh several thousand pounds. Would you say that was suffering or not? You can't even manage even the simplest, most basic things. After a while your body quits on you, and all you can do is lie in bed all day long. Finally you get sick on top of that, and suffer the bitterness of sickness. Recently, former President Eisenhower died. He was a very old man. Despite the fact that he was the President, he still had to die. A few days ago the newspapers reported that he had been hospitalized with a grave illness. That's the suffering of sickness. Then, he underwent the suffering of death. He had occupied the most glorious position there is, but when the time came for him to die, the spirit of death was not polite at all, and forced him to undergo great pain. Why? Because he had never studied the Buddhadharma. If one can understand the Buddhadharma and put everything down, one will not have to undergo the sufferings of birth, old age, sickness and death. One can put an end to them all.

Birth, old age, sickness, and death are very democratic. Everyone is born, grows old, gets sick, and dies. However, if you understand the Buddhadharma, truly wake up and put everything down, you can obtain control over your own birth and death. Otherwise, you cannot. Once you have gained self-mastery, for you there is no birth, old age, sickness or death. That's the happiness of the attainment of ultimate Nirvana. Why did Shakyamuni Buddha toil so at his cultivation? It was just because he looked upon the process of birth, aging, sickness, and death as entirely meaningless. Everyone kept being born and dying, being born and dying:

Birth, aging, sickness, death: suffering;
Death, birth, aging, sickness: suffering;
Sickness, death, birth, aging: suffering;
Aging, sickness, death, birth: suffering;

Over and over again, this suffering never stops.

"It's just too stupid to stay here and keep turning around like this," thought Shakyamuni Buddha. "I am determined to separate from the sufferings of birth, old age, sickness, and death." So he left home to cultivate. Why? Just because he wished to remove himself from the sufferings of birth, old age, sickness, and death.

In realizing Buddhahood, the Buddha separated himself from these sufferings, but he couldn't part with the other living beings who had not. "All these living beings haven't left the sufferings behind. I shall take the wonderful Dharma which I have attained and spread the message to all these living beings." He told them, "My Dharma can enable one to separate from birth, old age, sickness, and death and attain ultimate Nirvana."

"BOTH THOSE WHO STUDY AND THOSE BEYOND STUDY ALIKE HAVE SEPARATED FROM THE VIEW OF A SELF, AND ALSO FROM THE VIEWS OF EXISTENCE AND NON-EXISTENCE AND SO FORTH, AND CLAIM THAT THEY HAVE ATTAINED NIRVANA." This is Shariputra speaking. Those who study and those beyond study thought that they had left the view of self, and the views of existence and non-existence, that is the view of permanence and the view of annihilationism.

"YET NOW, HEARING FROM THE WORLD HONORED ONE THAT WHICH THEY HAVE NEVER HEARD BEFORE, THEY HAVE ALL FALLEN INTO DOUBT AND DELUSION." Now, in the presence of the World Honored One, they all hear the wonderful Dharma which they have never heard before, and they have fallen into the pit of doubts and delusion. They do not understand.

"GOOD INDEED, WORLD HONORED ONE. I BEG THAT YOU WOULD, FOR THE SAKE OF THE FOUR-FOLD ASSEMBLY, SPEAK OF THESE CAUSES AND CONDITIONS, TO FREE THEM OF THEIR DOUBTS AND REGRETS." The Bhikshus, Bhikshunis, Upasakas, and Upasikas all wish to put aside their doubts. Basically, Shariputra had no doubts. But he saw that the four assemblies had not yet understood, and so, on their behalf, he requested the Dharma.

Former President Eisenhower has left the world. Also, Yü T'ien-hsiu, one of the Lecture Hall's Dharma Protectors, and a Dharma Protector called T'ang have left the world. Eisenhower was a two-term President who benefitted America in many ways. Since we are living in America we should transfer merit to him to take him across so that he may soon hear the Buddhadharma and realize Buddhahood. He did not hear the Buddhadharma in his last life, but perhaps he can in his next life. We should use our true hearts in dedicating merit to him and it will certainly be efficacious.

Also, next Saturday is Kuan Yin's anniversary.[1] In the Chinese custom, everyone likes to bow to the Buddha on that day. So next Sunday we will bow the Great Compassion Repentance in the morning at eight o'clock and also in the afternoon. The Dharma lecture will be here in the Lecture Hall and *The Earth Store Bodhisattva Sutra* will be lectured as usual. If you want to bow twice, you can continue bowing after the lecture. On this day, bowing repentances and reciting Kuan Yin's name yields several thousand millions of times greater merit than on ordinary days. Everyone should know this. In the Lecture Hall, each night, we will recite the Buddha's name five minutes for President Eisenhower and for the Lecture Hall's Dharma Protectors. Tomorrow we will set up memorial tablets for them and put them up in the merit and virtue hall to cross them over. We shall do this for a month, inviting them to the lectures. They didn't hear the Sutras while they were alive, but now that they are dead they can come to the lectures and in the future, when they understand, they can also leave the sufferings of birth, old age, sickness, and death. Tuesday is Shakyamuni Buddha's Nirvana anniversary and everyone should recite "Namo Original Teacher Shakyamuni Buddha" a little more on that day. We shall now recite for President Eisenhower.

---

[1]This lecture was delivered on March 30, 1969.

Sutra: T.12b8

AT THAT TIME THE BUDDHA TOLD SHARIPUTRA, "HAVE I NOT SAID BEFORE THAT ALL THE BUDDHAS, WORLD HONORED ONES, SPEAK THE DHARMA BY MEANS OF VARIOUS CAUSES AND CONDITIONS, PARABLES, AND PHRASES, AND EXPEDIENT DEVICES, ALL FOR THE SAKE OF ANUTTARASAMYAKSAMBODHI? ALL OF THESE TEACHINGS ARE FOR THE SAKE OF TRANSFORMING THE BODHISATTVAS. HOWEVER, SHARIPUTRA, I SHALL NOW AGAIN MAKE USE OF A PARABLE IN ORDER TO FURTHER CLARIFY THE PRINCIPLE, FOR ALL THOSE WHO ARE WISE GAIN UNDERSTANDING THROUGH PARABLES."

Outline:

H1. The arisal.

Commentary:

When Shakyamuni Buddha heard Shariputra request the Dharma on behalf of the four assemblies, in order to clear up their doubts, AT THAT TIME THE BUDDHA TOLD SHARIPUTRA, "HAVE I NOT SAID BEFORE...Didn't I already say this? Haven't we been through this one before?" The question implies that, of course, the Buddha had told him before. "I did not *not* tell you. I did tell you, didn't I? Isn't that right?" It's a rhetorical question and you shouldn't take it to mean that he actually did not say it before. That's not what it means. It means, "Didn't I tell you this already?" Tell him what?

"THAT ALL THE BUDDHAS, WORLD HONORED ONES, SPEAK THE DHARMA BY MEANS OF VARIOUS CAUSES AND CONDITIONS: All the Buddhas throughout the ten directions use various kinds of causes and conditions, PARABLES, AND PHRASES, clever speech, AND EXPEDIENT DEVICES. But although all manner of dharmas are spoken, they are ALL FOR THE SAKE OF ANUTTARASAMYAKSAMBODHI? The dharmas are all spoken for the sake of nothing else but the unsurpassed, proper, equal and right enlightenment. ALL OF THESE TEACHINGS ARE FOR THE SAKE OF TRANSFORMING BODHISATTVAS." This passage is a slight reprimand. It implies, "I already told you this, and you still don't understand! Ah, and you ask again?" But the word "HOWEVER" takes the sting out of it and reassures Shariputra, "You are a good child, you are very intelligent."

"SHARIPUTRA, I SHALL NOW AGAIN MAKE USE OF A PARABLE IN ORDER TO FURTHER CLARIFY THE PRINCIPLE. I will use another analogy to make the doctrine a little clearer for you. FOR ALL THOSE WHO ARE WISE GAIN UNDERSTANDING THROUGH PARABLES. Through the use of analogies they can understand the doctrine."

The following section of text is very difficult to explain, so you should pay particular attention to it."

Sutra: T.12b13

"SHARIPUTRA, SUPPOSE THAT IN A COUNTRY, A CITY, OR A VILLAGE, THERE IS A GREAT ELDER, AGED AND WORN, OF LIMITLESS WEALTH, POSSESSING MANY FIELDS, HOUSES, AND SERVANTS."

Outline:

H2. Parable proper.
I1. Prose.
J1. Setting up parable.
K1. Generable parable.
L1. Parable of the elder.

Commentary:

"SHARIPUTRA, now I am going to use a parable to teach you the wonderful Dharma. SUPPOSE, hypothetically speaking, THAT IN A COUNTRY: 'Country' here is an analogy for the Real Retribution Adorned Land,[1] which is where the Bodhisattvas live. A CITY is an analogy for the Land of Expedients with Residue,[2] which is where those of the Two Vehicles dwell. A VILLAGE is

---

1 實報莊嚴土 -*shih pao chuang yen tu.*

2 方便有餘土 -*fang pien yu yü tu.*

an analogy for the Land in which the Common and Sagely Dwell Together,[1] which is where you and I now live. The Buddha dwells in the Land of Permanent Still Pure Light.[2]

The word "country" also refers to the large, inclusive aspect, as its boundaries are very large. A country is then divided up into smaller states. The country represents that which reaches the farthest and that which is the largest. A city is ruled by minor officials. San Francisco and New York are cities. Cities are neither far-reaching nor nearby; they are middle-sized. Villages are very small. Their boundaries do not extend for any great distance. They are small towns or hamlets.

"THERE IS A GREAT ELDER: The great elder is an analogy for the Buddha. The Buddha is the great elder. In terms of worldly dharmas, the elder has ten kinds of virtuous practices:

The Ten Virtues of an Elder

1. His name is honored. The elder has an honorable name. In Chinese, when you ask a person what their name is, you say, "What is your honorable name?" But this is just a polite formality. It is not the same as having an honorable name.

What is meant by having an honorable name?

In terms of worldly people, being born in the household of an Emperor, or a noble lord is honorable. In India, the Kshatriyas are an honorable clan. One born in the family of a king can become a king in the future. One born in the family of a noble lord will become a noble lord.

2. He is of lofty position. The elder has a high position. His rank is especially high. What is meant by this? A Prime Minister or perhaps a great general has a high rank.

---

1 凡聖同居土 *-fan sheng t'ung chü tu.*

2 常寂光淨土 *-ch'ang chi kuang ching tu.*

3. He has great wealth. He is very rich. Most people have storehouses full of rice or other grains, but his storehouses are completely filled with gold!

4. He has awesome courage. He is brave and courageous. It is said, "His majesty makes one tremble." It is also said, "His awesomeness is to be feared." Everyone who sees such a person, although he has never struck, scolded, or killed anyone, is still afraid of him. That's because he is awesome. Courage means bravery. He is dignified and impressive, solemn, like the great generals in military array who look very deadly. One knows not how many people they control.

5. His wisdom is profound. He has wisdom, and this wisdom is the highest, transcending all other wisdom. Such wisdom is extremely deep. All things are to him as clear as if in the palm of his hand. Nothing gets past his deep wisdom. Within his mind is contained all existence; he knows everything. All of his clever expedient devices are better than those of ordinary people. He is positively outstanding, smarter than even the most intelligent people.

6. He is advanced in years. He is very old. Although he is very old, the older he gets, the stronger he becomes. The older he gets, the healthier he becomes. He is a model for people, a leader for them.

7. His practice is pure. His conduct is pure, extremely lofty and clean. He is like a piece of white jade without a single flaw. This shows that he is immaculately pure.

In *The Book of Songs, (Shih-ching)*, it says,

"A flaw in a mace of white jade
may be ground away;
But for a flaw in speech,
nothing can be done."

If there is a black spot on a mace of white jade, you can slowly polish it away. If what you say has a flaw in it, there is no way to erase it.

So, the seventh virtue of an elder is that his conduct is pure. Ordinary people can't even come close to measuring up to it.

8. His propriety is perfect. The elder is polite to everyone. He would never lack manners. He is courteous towards all. Whether you are rich or poor, noble or lowly, he is polite to you. He entertains people according to the proper rules. For example, if a friend comes he may invite him to have a cup of coffee. If his friend likes soda pop, he will treat him to a bottle. In general, he entertains guests appropriately.

9. He is praised by his superiors. It is not unusual to receive praise from ones inferiors. It is rare to be praised by those above one. However, the elder is, in fact, praised by those above him.

10. He is a refuge for his inferiors. Those beneath him all return respectfully to him. He is honored by all within the four seas, and all people are like brothers and sisters to him. All people come to him for support.

For example, the King is supported by his subjects, and the President is supported by the citizens.

an elder

In this analogy, the elder represents the Buddha. Let us now discuss the Ten Virtues of an Elder as they apply to the Buddha:

1. The Buddha is born from the real limit, the true suchness of the three periods of time, and therefore his name is honored. True Suchness is also called the nature of the Thus Come One's Storehouse. Because he is born from the principle substance of the real limit, the Buddha's name is honored.

2. The Buddha's cultivation of merit and virtue is perfect, his Way karma has been realized, and he has certified to the attainment of the Ten Titles of the Buddha. Having certified to the highest position, that of Buddhahood, he has a lofty position.

3. The Buddha has the wealth of the Dharma and the ten thousand virtues. The Buddha's Dharma is the greatest form of wealth there is, and his myriad virtues are perfect and interpenetrating. His Dharma wealth and myriad virtues are completely perfect, and so he is said to have great wealth.

4. The Buddha has Ten Wisdom Powers, and heroic courage with which to subdue demons and regulate those of external paths. He conquers the heavenly demons and regulates those of outside ways. In order to do this, he uses the Ten Powers. Since he conquers heavenly demons and subdues those of outside ways, he is said to have great awesome courage.

5. Profound wisdom. As to the Buddha:

> The one mind and the three wisdoms--
> There are none he hasn't penetrated.

What is meant by "one mind, three wisdoms?" When the Buddha cultivates the Contemplation of Emptiness, he obtains All Wisdom. By cultivating the Contemplation of the Truth of Falseness, he obtains the Wisdom of the Way. By cultivating the Contemplation of the Middle

Way, he obtains the Wisdom of All-Modes. With one mind he obtains three kinds of wisdom. There are none he hasn't penetrated. This represents the profound wisdom of the Buddha.

6. Advanced in years. Shakyamuni Buddha did not leave home just in this one life. Limitless aeons ago he had already accomplished Buddhahood, realized Right Enlightenment. Therefore, in *The Brahma Net Sutra* it says, "I have come to this Saha world 8,000 times." Thus, he is advanced in years.

7. Pure in practice. The three karmas of the Buddha all accord with the conduct of wisdom. All of his body karma accords with the conduct of wisdom; all of his speech karma accords with the conduct of wisdom; all of his mind karma accords with the conduct of wisdom. He never make mistakes or errors. Because his three karmas accord with the conduct of wisdom, his practice is pure.

8. His propriety is perfect. The Buddha has perfected the awesome deportment. His heart is as big as the great sea. The Buddha's awesome deportment is never off in the slightest degree. He has three thousand awesome deportments and eighty-thousand minor practices.

9. Praised by his superiors. The greatly enlightened ones of the ten directions, that is, the Buddhas of the ten directions, all praise Shakyamuni Buddha. The Buddhas are basically of one mind and there is nothing seen as above or below, high or low. But the ten direction Buddhas became Buddhas long ago, and so they are, so to speak, older in years.

10. A refuge for his inferiors. The Seven Expedients all return to him. What are the Seven Expedients? There are many different ways to explain them. However, according to the *T'ien-t'ai* Teaching they are:

Seven Expedients

A. The vehicle of people.
B. The vehicle of gods.

C. The Vehicle of Sound Hearers.
D. The Vehicle of Conditioned Enlightened Ones.
E. The Vehicle of the Storehouse Teaching Bodhisattva.
F. The Vehicle of the Pervasive Teaching Bodhisattva.
G. The Vehicle of the Separate Teaching Bodhisattva.

Living beings of these Seven Expedients, also called the Seven Vehicles, all rely upon the Buddha. Thus, he is a place of refuge for his inferiors. This concludes the discussion of the Ten Virtues of the Elder as they apply to the Buddha.

***

Four Methods of Explaining Sutras

In lecturing Sutras, there are four methods one can use:

1. Causes and conditions.
2. The essential teaching. That is, to explain according to the essential points of the teaching, telling which particular teaching each point belongs to, to the Storehouse, Pervasive, Separate or Perfect Teachings.
3. The roots and traces.
4. The contemplation of the mind.

These are four different ways to explain each passage of text. However, if we applied them all to every passage it would take too much time. But now, I will explain the Ten Virtues of the Elder according to the method of contemplation of the mind. The previous explanation was done according to the causes and conditions method.

The Ten Virtues of the Elder according to the method of Contemplation of the Mind

The Ten Virtues of the Elder do not go beyond one thought of the mind. According to the method of contemplation of the mind we shall explain them one by one:

1. His name is honored. Where does the wisdom of contemplation of the mind come from? It comes from the Real Mark. The wisdom of contemplation of the mind is born in the Real Mark. Born into the family of the Buddhas, through the Real Mark, his name is honored.

2. His is of lofty position. He does not give rise to the three kinds of delusion: a) view delusion, b) thought delusion, or c) delusions as many as dust and sand. You can also say that they are a) coarse delusion, b) subtle delusion, and c) delusions of ignorance. Not giving rise to the three delusions means not having these three confusions, no view delusion, no thought delusion, and no delusions as many as dust and sand.

What is meant by "view delusion?" It means that when you see something you are confused by it. View delusion refers to producing greed and love when faced with a state. When something happens, you give in to greed and attachment. Why do you give rise to greed and love? Because you are confused.

Thought delusion means to be confused about the principle and give rise to discrimination. Unclear about the principle, you start giving rise to various kinds of discrimination. These are the easiest kinds of delusions of have.

Delusions as many as dust and sand means that in your mind there are countless subtle doubts, as many as the grains of sand in the Ganges River.

View delusions are sometimes called coarse delusions. Thought delusions are sometimes called subtle delusions. Delusions like dust and sand are sometimes called delusions of ignorance.

3. He has great wealth. How does this relate to contemplation of the mind? In contemplation of the mind, his great wealth is explained in terms of the Three Truths: a) The truths of emptiness, b) the truth of falseness, and c) the truth of the middle way. These Three Truths contain all merit and virtue, and are replete with the wealth of Dharma, the precious storehouse. Therefore, he has great wealth.

4. He has awesome courage. With awesome courage he uses wisdom to conquer love and views. While contemplating the mind he has a kind of wisdom which can subdue love and views.

Love is something that everyone has. Views are something which everyone clings to. Without views, there is no clinging. Without clinging there is no love. Without love there is no affliction. Why do we have affliction? It's because of love. There is love because of the attachment of love. In the wisdom of contemplation of the mind, the Buddha conquers the affliction of love and views. Therefore, he has awesome courage.

5. His wisdom is profound. Previously, the awesome, courageous wisdom had not yet reached the level of being profound. It was only capable of conquering love and views. Now, at the level of profound wisdom, he has united with the Middle Way. The Middle Way illuminates the Real Mark of all Dharmas. He knows what is provisional Dharma and what is real Dharma, and knows this very clearly. The two wisdoms, provisional and real, are just the two Dharmas, provisional and real. He understands the clever provisional expedients and the real Dharmas without obstacle.

6. He is advanced in years. At this time, his ability to cultivate this kind of contemplation enables him to transcend the Seven Expedients listed above. Having transcended them, he is advanced in years.

7. His practice is pure. Cultivating the contemplation of the mind, you observe your own mind and nature. The contemplation of one's own mind and nature is called "superior concentration." It is the highest form of samadhi power. This kind of samadhi power enables one to be without error in the three karmas. In the karma of body, mouth, and mind, one is without error. Therefore, his practice is pure.

8. His propriety is perfect. The mind, when encountering causes and conditions or a particular state, does not lose the awesome deportment. One is always in accord with the Dharma's regulations. His propriety and manners are perfect.

9. His superiors praise him. If one is able to cultivate this kind of contemplation, then with deep faith one can understand the marks of dharmas. This causes

all the Buddhas to rejoice. Since they are happy, they praise the cultivator.

10. He is a refuge for his inferiors. If one has cultivated, the gods, dragons, and those of the eightfold division as well as the four assemblies of disciples revere one. Above, didn't the Sutra text say, "Though worshipped by the gods and dragons/ They do not find it cause for joy?" The gods and dragons come to pay their respects, but they do not disturb one's mind and nature which remain, "thus, thus, unmoving." This is an indication of one's samadhi power. Because one has samadhi power, those beneath one find one a place of refuge and and gods, dragons, and the eightfold division all revere and trust one.

This concludes the discussion of the Elder as an analogy for the Buddha.

"AGED:" It is said that as one grows older, one acquires virtue. Virtue can be spoken of in terms of inner and outer virtue. Inner virtue refers to wisdom. If one has wisdom, one will have virtue. Outer virtue is wealth. With resources, you can cultivate outer virtue. The Elder is very old, and he knows the past and present. He knows what happened in the past and he understands what is going on now. This penetration of the past and present is also an analogy for the Buddha's wisdom virtue.

"AND WORN:" This means that his strength is deteriorating, although his basic disposition and his determination remain robust. He is very experienced. "Worn" represents the Buddha's severing virtue. Severing virtue is the virtue gained through severing attachments and afflictions. The Buddha is not like us. We find it hard to cut off afflictions and bad habits. However, it is said,

> Not severing what should be severed,
> One must bear the consequences.

If you should have stopped doing something and you haven't, you will have to take the unpleasant repercussions. The Buddha is not that way. He cuts off what he should cut off because he has the severing virtue. Why does he have it? Because he has the wisdom virtue. Because he has the wisdom virtue, he sees everything very clearly. He wouldn't be confused. He would not see a state unclearly. This represents the Buddha's severing virtue.

"OF LIMITLESS WEALTH:" This is an analogy for the Buddha's unlimited blessings and virtues. Because the Buddha is adorned with the myriad virtues, it is said that he is of limitless wealth.

"POSSESSING MANY FIELDS:" Fields are where crops are planted; they sustain life. We plant the fields, reap the harvest, and in this way maintain our livelihood. That's the function of fields. The fields here referred to can nourish the wisdom-life of our Dharmabodies and the life of our wisdom.

How do we cause our Dharmabody's wisdom-life to grow? We investigate Dhyana and perfect our skill in samadhi. That is how we cause it to grow. While cultivating the skill of Dhyana samadhi, you must simultaneously cultivate Prajna wisdom. Therefore, the analogy is that of Dhyana samadhi assisted by the strength of Prajna wisdom which increases the wisdom-life of the Dharmabody. Such is the meaning of the word "field."

"HOUSES:" What use are houses? They are places to put our bodies; our bodies live in houses. What does this represent? It represents the "realm of reality" which dwells within wisdom. People live in houses. The Real Mark dwells in genuine wisdom. Thus, the houses are an analogy for the true wisdom of the realm of reality.

In speaking of the blessings and virtue of the Buddha, he has extensively cultivated the Six Perfections and the Ten Thousand Conducts, without failing to cultivate even the smallest, finest conduct. In terms of his wisdom, there is no realm it does not illuminate. There's not one state it doesn't shine upon.

"AND SERVANTS:" Servants are those employed to work for one. The Buddha doesn't actually have servants. They are an analogy for the Buddha's expedient knowledge and vision which is perfect and complete. With expedient knowledge and vision, he can do anything at all. This means that, among those who turn in the six paths of rebirth, he is able to harmonize the light.

Lights do not struggle with each other. Lights easily mix. In the six paths, coming and going, although the Buddha manifests as undergoing birth and death, still, he is not attached to birth and death. Why does he harmonize the light among the six paths? Because he wishes to accomodate all the many beings with the potential for being taught. He uses expedient methods in teaching the Dharma. He doesn't teach it straightaway, but finds ways "around" living beings. He employs clever expedient devices to teach and transform them. The servants referred to in the text, then, represent this use of expedient knowledge and vision, expedient knowledge and vision being, as it were, the servants of real wisdom.

Sutra: T.12b15

"HIS HOUSE IS SPACIOUS AND LARGE...

Outline:

L2. Parable of the house.

Commentary:

"HIS HOUSE IS SPACIOUS AND LARGE... The Elder's house is vast and not small. Ultimately, how big is it? I'll tell you: It is as large as the desire realm, the form realm, and the formless realm. It is as large as the three realms in which living beings run back and forth, being born and then dying over and over. They are born and then they die; they die and are then reborn, and never succeeed in freeing themselves from the turning wheel in the three realms. They run around inside of it, but they don't know how to get out.

Shakyamuni Buddha came into this world to manifest a response/transformation body to point out to all living beings that this house is not a peaceful one.

Sutra: T.12b15

"...HAVING ONLY ONE DOOR...

Outline:

L3. Parable of only one door.

Commentary:

This house may indeed be spacious and large, but there is ONLY ONE DOOR. The house is an analogy for the three realms. In the three realms, there is no peace. It is like a burning house. Later on in the chapter, the house catches fire. The one door represents the Buddha Path of the One Vehicle. It is only through the One Vehicle of the Buddha Path that one can escape the three realms, that one can separate from this place of unrest. Later it speaks of the children inside the great burning house who are not afraid, but continue to play happily at their games. They don't know the seriousness of the fire raging in the house. This represents all of us in the three realms who think it a very delightful place. You are unaware that you are about to be burned to death by the fire. Thus, there is only one door out of the three realms.

Sutra: T.12b15

"...BUT WITH A GREAT MANY PEOPLE--ONE HUNDRED, TWO HUNDRED, EVEN FIVE HUNDRED OF THEM--DWELLING WITHIN IT."

Outline:

L4. The parable of the five hundred people.

Commentary:

"BUT WITH A GREAT MANY PEOPLE, and beings from the five paths as well, ONE HUNDRED, TWO HUNDRED, EVEN FIVE HUNDRED OF THEM, DWELLING WITHIN IT." The one hundred people represents the path of the gods. The two hundred people represents the path of human beings. Three, four, and even five hundred represent the animals, ghosts, and the beings in hell.

"But," you may ask, "what about the Six Path Wheel? What happened to the asuras?"

Not a bad question. We do speak of the Six Path Wheel, but the present passage of text merely refers to the five paths. This is because asuras may be found in all the five paths and so they are omitted. This doesn't mean that they are left out altogether. It means that they are subsumed under the other five paths, and are therefore a secondary classification, not a path proper.

"But with a great many people" represents the beings in the five paths.

Asura is a Sanskrit word which means "ugly." How are they ugly? Most people's noses are below their eyes, but the asuras' noses are above their eyes! Would you say that was good looking? Also, their eyes, nose, ears, and mouth are all bunched together in the middle of their faces. Would you call that attractive? That's just the male asuras, however. The female asuras are very beautiful. Do you remember the story I told you about the asura king's beautiful daughter?[1]

Asura also means "no wine." They have the blessings of the gods, but not the power of the gods and so they are not allowed to drink wine. If they were, their tempers would be even more fierce. Since they have no wine, although they are hostile, it's not as bad as it might be. Asuras love to fight and make war. The asuras in the heavens fight with the heavenly troops. The asuras among human beings fight in the national armies. Animal asuras are, for example, the wild horse. Horses are usually pretty docile, and eat together in harmony. The wild horse, however, does nothing but bully the other horses and hurt them. That's an asura horse for you. Didn't one of my disciples say that he had an asura dog? I said, "You aren't exactly included outside of the asura realm yourself. You're an asura person." When he translated, he only translated the asura dog part. He didn't translate the part about the asura person. Hah!

There are also asura ghosts who specialize in hurting people. In general, their tempers are very big. They are like fire-crackers at New Year's. If you would rather be a Bodhisattva, don't explode all the time.

---

[1] See *The Dharma Flower Sutra, Vol. II.*, BTTS, 1977, p. 173.

In the five paths, the path of the gods alone is divided into many, many categories. Among humans, there are the rich and the poor, the citizens and the officials. There are also armies and police forces. Some people are very poor and some are wealthy. Some are born very good looking and others are ugly, like the asuras. Some have no eyes, some no noses. Some can't speak, some are deaf, and some blind. There are many kinds of people. Some people are as intelligent as spirits. Some people say, "He's as intelligent as a ghost," but actually ghosts have intelligence that belongs to the *yin*, or dark side. Intelligent people are like spirits. It is said, "Intelligent and properly wise, they are called spirits." It is also said, "*Ts'ao-ts'ao* was as crafty as a ghost. Emperor *Yao* was as wise as a spirit." Some people are intelligent and others are outstandingly stupid.

For example, I have two disciples here who are very intelligent. They have very good memories. I remember when they memorized the Shurangama Mantra and were the first to learn it. The Shurangama Mantra usually takes at least six months to learn, but they only needed one month or so. It's not easy to memorize it. Now that some Westerners suddenly can recite it is inconceivable!

What is more, my disciples now lecture on the Sutras and they do so much better than I do. Why? Because I speak in Chinese and they speak in English. So, unless you don't have time, you really should come and listen to them speak the Dharma. Don't miss it. I would come myself, but sometimes I'm too busy. I don't really need to come because they learned it from me, anyway! So don't think, "The Master isn't here so let's leave, too." You have to investigate the Buddhadharma. I'm not trying to act like a big shot, but I have been studying for several decades and you are just beginning. So you cannot be lazy.

So there are many kinds of people. There are also many kinds of animals and hungry ghosts. You're all no doubt very familiar with hungry ghosts. Although you probably haven't been hungry ghosts, those who study the Buddhadharma should know what they are all about. Hungry ghosts have nothing to eat. They keep looking for food, but never find any. Why are they hungry ghosts? Because when they were people they were greedy for food. As people they ate too much, so as ghosts, they are "hungry."

There were five hundred people in the big house, that is in the desire realm, the form realm, and the formless realm. So it is said, "There's no peace in the triple world. It is like a burning house." Soon, in *The Dharma Flower Sutra,* the house is going to catch on fire. It won't be like a burning house, it will *be* a burning house. We haven't escaped from the burning house yet, either. We are in the burning house. Think it over. Is it dangerous or not? I don't need to say too much about it.

I'll tell you something more. Why are people intelligent? Why are they stupid? Intelligent people have recited many Sutras and studied the Buddhadharma. They have also printed Sutras. Why are people stupid? Because they haven't recited Sutras or studied the Buddhadharma, and they haven't printed Sutras. Life after life, they grow stupider. People who print Sutras grow more and more intelligent, life after life. So I just said I had two disciples who had very good memories. Probably in former lives they read many Sutras. And it's for sure that they have great affinities with *The Shurangama Sutra* and *The Dharma Flower Sutra*. So no one should be jealous of them because of their intelligence. The more jealous you are, the stupider you become. If you are jealous of smart people you will be stupid yourself. Why? Smart people got that way by planting blessings. Stupid people didn't cultivate blessings or print Sutras. We don't want to print just one Sutra, but many different ones. Now, in the Buddhist Lecture Hall, we are printing *The Thousand Hand, Thousand Eye Heart Dharani Sutra*. The Great Compassion Mantra contained within this Sutra is an inconceivable state, and whatever you seek from it shall be fulfilled. No one should pass up this chance to help print the Sutra. Do whatever you can, give whatever you can. You don't have to overdo it. Do what you can. Things should be done naturally and happily. If you want to be intelligent, print more. If you want to be stupid and know nothing at all, then you needn't take part. That's the news for now.

Sutra: T.12b16

"ITS HALLS AND CHAMBERS ARE DECAYING AND OLD; ITS WALLS ARE CRUMBLING. THE PILLARS ARE ROTTING AT THEIR BASES; THE BEAMS AND RIDGE-POLES ARE TOPPLING DANGEROUSLY."

Outline:

L5. The fire breaks out.
M1. Describing the house which is burning.

Commentary:

"ITS HALLS AND CHAMBERS ARE DECAYING AND OLD;" Halls represent the desire realm. Chambers represent the form and formless realms. The halls also represent the lower part of the human body. The chambers represent the upper part of the body and the head.

The halls represent the desire heavens in the triple realm. Chambers represent the heavens in the form and formless realms. That's the three realms.

Decaying represents the corruption, evil, and impermanence within the three realms. In the three realms, the revolution of living beings is unceasing. Sometimes things are good, but this never lasts. Things decay. Old means that the three realms were not created only recently, but were there before.

"ITS WALLS ARE CRUMBLING." In our houses we have walls, but what are the walls in the three realms? The walls represent the four elements, earth, air, fire, and water. They are the walls on the four sides. Also, the four walls are said to be wine, wealth, form, and anger. They are like four locks, which lock people up.

So a verse says,

Wine,wealth, form and anger
are four walls.
Many living beings are held within them.
If you can leap out of the walls,
You can be an ageless king
with eternal life.

Our bodies are like the three realms. The skin and flesh are like the walls. Crumbling means that there is no peace in the three realms. Our bodies quickly go bad.

"THE PILLARS ARE ROTTING AT THEIR BASES." Our human lives are like the pillars. You could also say that our two legs are the pillars. The pillars are rotting. This means that they are dangerously near to breaking down. There is no peace in the three realms; it is like a burning house. Soon the situation will be very dangerous. Our lives are soon over.

"THE BEAMS AND RIDGEPOLES ARE TOPPLING DANGEROUSLY." Our mind consciousness is like the ridepole. Toppling refers to the ceaseless changes in the mind. This is a very dangerous moment. The moment of death has come. That's the general meaning of this passage.

Upon reading this passage of text, we should realize that we are not going to live forever. No matter what great talents, what wealth, what riches, you have, when the time comes to die, your two hands will be empty. You won't be able to take any of it with you. In this world people fight for fame and scramble for benefits. That is a very stupid thing to do. You should return to the root and go back to the source, recognize your original face. Your original face--what is it like? It is like nothing at all. If it were "like" something, it would have a mark. If it had a mark, it would be subject to production and extinction. Our basic self-nature is not defiled or pure, not produced and not extinguished. It is not increased and not decreased. Our original face has no problems whatsoever. Our original face, as it says in *The Shurangama Sutra,* is the "eternally dwelling true mind, the bright substance of the pure nature."

If you return to your original face, understand it, then you can turn all of your afflictions into Bodhi. If you don't understand your original face, then you turn Bodhi right into affliction. So it is said,

> In this world, there's nothing going on.
> But stupid people stir up trouble.

Basically, there's nothing happening, but people have to find something to keep themselves busy. If you tell them they are acting stupidly, they say, "You're the stupid one!" Why do they say you are stupid? Because you don't do the things they do. You don't act like they do and so they say you are stupid. Basically, nothing is going on, but they create a lot of disturbance to keep themselves busy. If that isn't stupid, what is? If you have the skill to understand the self nature, then:

> The eyes view external forms,
> but inside there is nothing;
> The ears hear mundane sounds,
> but the mind does not know.

One person sees forms as forms, shapes as shapes. If you understand the original face, then, seeing forms, there is no form, seeing shapes, there is no shape. One person looks at forms and shapes and sees them as forms and shapes, but for someone who has understood his self nature, there are no forms or shapes. Forms and shapes--do they really exist? One person sees them and says that they exist. Another person sees them and says they don't. Ultimately, do they exist or not? If you see them as existing, they exist. If you see them as non-existent, then they do not exist. That's why it is said:

> Everything is made from the mind alone.

This means that it depends on what you do, how you think about it. The same matter isn't viewed in the same way. The ears hear all the sounds of the world, but the mind is not turned by them, is not moved by the states of the five desires.

You say, "You explain this principle, but I don't believe it."

I already knew that you wouldn't believe it. It's not just now that I found out. I knew long ago you didn't believe it. Why? Because you haven't yet reached that level. You don't have that skill and so you don't believe. If you had that skill you would be able to do something like this: See and yet not see, hear and yet not hear. Seeing, hearing, smelling, tasting, feeling, and knowing--these six states of consciousness would all listen to your orders. They would be obedient to your commands and under your control. If you told them to see, they would see. If you did not order them to see, they would not see. If you told them to hear, they would hear. If you did not tell them to hear, they would not hear. The same applies to smelling, tasting, feeling, and knowing. So, in studying the Buddhadharma, you can study for any number of years, but when you encounter a situation your mind must not move. If you can have an unmoving mind, then you have samadhi power. If you see a state and are turned by it, then you have no samadhi power. If you have no samadhi power, you can study the Buddhadharma until you are old and die, but it will have been of no use whatsoever.

Therefore, we are now lecturing *The Dharma Flower Sutra*, which tells us that the world is a very bad place. It is as dangerous as a burning house. It is very easy to get burned to death in this fire.

Then how can we avoid burning to death? It is just as I said, do not be turned by states.

> The eyes view external forms,
> but inside there is nothing.
> The ears hear mundane sounds,
> but the mind does not know.

Understand your original face. Originally,who are you? Originally, you're the Buddha! Since originally you are the Buddha, you should return to the root and go back to the source, go down the road to Buddhahood. The Buddha has perfected the adornments of the myriad virtues. As we walk down the road to Buddhahood, we should do all kinds of good deeds to help us to succeed. That's the most important thing. We should do all the good deeds we have the power to do. What are good deeds? Helping others and benefitting others. Bodhisattvas benefit themselves and benefit others, enlighten themselves and enlighten others. Do these things.

You say, "I've heard that a lot."

Really? How many times?

"Several dozen times."

Well, how many times have you done it? Right, you've heard it a lot: "Benefit others and benefit yourself," but how many times have you done it? How many "others" have you benefitted? How many "others" have you caused to become enlightened? One..two...probably not. If you haven't even benefitted or enlightened one or two people, what use is you having just heard of it? No use at all. The Way must be walked. Do it truly! Do it sincerely! Plant your feet firmly on the ground and do the work straightforwardly. What is meant by "doing it truly?" The same deed can be done by two people differently. Some may do it with the thought to benefit themselves and some may do it with the thought to benefit others. Doing it to benefit others is doing it truly.

Some people may understand a principle and leave it at that, not worrying about whether or not anyone else understands it. If understanding it yourself, you can then in turn teach it to others and cause them to understand, that is to enlighten oneself and enlighten others. In general, there are different ways of doing everything in this world. One person may be selfish and seek his own benefit, and someone else may do nothing but benefit other people. Those who are selfish and seek their own benefit go to the hells. Why? They are simply too selfish. Those who benefit others also go to the hells. What for? To rescue living beings. Their goal is to undergo suffering themselves in order to teach those in the hells how to leave suffering and attain bliss. Earth Store Bodhisattva, for example, is in the hells all day long being a friend to all the hungry ghosts. But his intention is to take the ghosts across from suffering to bliss. There are a lot of confused people in the world, and as much understanding as I possess I will pass on to them so that they may also understand. That's called "enlightening oneself and enlightening others." To sum it up, there are different ways of doing everything.

One should benefit oneself and benefit others. If you want to know what someone is like, watch and see if what they do is for their own benefit or for the benefit of others. That's what you should take note of.

I just said that wine, wealth, form, and anger were the four walls. The Bodhisattva also has four walls--wine, wealth, form, and anger--which he has not jumped over. The Bodhisattva takes saving living beings as his wine. The more living beings he saves, the more he "drinks" and the "drunker" he becomes.

The Bodhisattva takes the twelve divisions of the Tripitaka as form, and so he wants to study them. The Bodhisattva also loves the wonderful Dharma as his wealth. Thus, he is tremendously wealthy. The Bodhisattva also has a "temper." He takes the Six Perfections and the Ten Thousand Conducts as his energy source and practices them every day. Without the Six Perfections and the Ten Thousand Conducts, he would have no energy; he would die. Bodhisattvas have everything we people have; the names are the same, the things themselves are different. The more the Bodhisattva drinks the wine of saving living beings, the more he enjoys himself. He loses himself altogether! How can he lose himself? He has no self. *The Vajra Sutra* says, "If a Bodhisattva has a mark of self, a mark of others, a mark of living beings, or a mark of a life, he is not a Bodhisattva."[1] Tell me, if he wasn't drunk, how could he not even have a self? It's because he has imbibed too much of the wine of saving living beings and has thereby lost himself. Not only has he lost himself, he has no mark of living beings, people, or a life. He has nothing at all.

"Hey, come on, you mean he has *nothing at all?*" you ask.

That's right! I hope you all master this, too, and drink the wine of saving living beings.

Basically, there is nothing to say about the Buddhadharma. So I just say things that people don't like to hear.

---

[1]Ven. Master Hua, *Vajra Sutra,* p.34.

Sutra: T.12b17

"ALL AT ONCE, THROUGHOUT THE HOUSE, A FIRE BREAKS OUT, SETTING THE HOUSE ABLAZE."

Outline:

M2. Describing the fire.

Commentary:

"ALL AT ONCE, THROUGHOUT THE HOUSE..." Throughout means all around, on all sides, everywhere. This refers to the eight sufferings. The eight sufferings pervade the four elements and the four types of birth. The eight sufferings have been discussed many times before. They are

1. The suffering of birth.
2. The suffering of aging.
3. The suffering of sickness.
4. The suffering of death.
5. The suffering of being separated from loved ones.
6. The suffering of being together with those one hates.
7. The suffering of not getting what one seeks.
8. The suffering of the raging blaze of the five skandhas.

The four types of birth are:

1. Birth by womb.
2. Birth by egg.
3. Birth by moisture.
4. Birth by transformation.

Each type of birth has its own suffering. However, creatures born from wombs know only the sufferings of womb-birth and know nothing of the pain involved in egg, moisture, or transformation birth. When you become one of those kinds of beings you will know the suffering that type undergoes. Now, we have not entered the other classes of birth, so why talk about their sufferings? Because the greatly wise Buddha has already pointed the Way for us clearly, we know the eight sufferings pervade the four births.

Throughout means the sufferings pervade the four births and the four elements.

All at once refers to the four types of birth and the four elements and the eight sufferings as all impermanent. Because they are impermanent, it says, "all at once." You could also say that the eight sufferings exist "all at once," or that one kind of suffering comes to exist all of a sudden. They are all impermanent.

"A FIRE BREAKS OUT..." Quite suddenly, a fire arose. Fire refers to suffering. The suffering basically does not exist, but because of ignorance various forms of suffering arise. Ignorance is the worst thing. Our tempers are just the fire-energy of our ignorance. Once the fire of ignorance arises, one doesn't understand anything at all. One has no judgement,no reason, and understands nothing at all. That is just stupidity. Because of stupidity, these sufferings come into being, and the fire of ignorance arises. You might also say that the fire of the five skandhas, form, feelings, perceptions, impulses, and consciousness, arise. The five skandhas are like a fire.

"SETTING THE HOUSE ABLAZE." This refers to the five skandhas which burn our bodies. The house represents the body. The five skandhas dwell within the house of the body and they set five kinds of fires which burn the house down. The fire is our tempers. It is said:

> The body of a tiger, and ignorance's blaze,
> Are the roots of errors from former live's days.

The fire of ignorance is as fierce as a tiger and it comes from former lives. In former lives one created too many offenses and so one now has no merit and virtue. Therefore in this life one has a big temper. This big temper is terrible! But you might also say it was the very best. How can you say it is both the very best and the very worst? No matter what it is, within the good, there is bad and within the bad, there is good. Things get good bit by bit, and things go bad, bit by bit, too. In what way is anger the very worst thing? After you get angry you feel uncomfortable all over, even very pained. Wouldn't you say that was bad? It is very bad for the body.

In what way is anger the very best thing? Once you get angry and realize it is painful, you won't let it happen anymore. Thus, you get rid of your anger. No more tiger; no more fire of ignorance. They are gone because you have awakened. You know that anger is not good. It's like slapping yourself. If you get angry, you suffer. Realizing it is painful, you quit doing such stupid things as getting angry. Isn't that the very best? You have escaped from what is not good. If you can fight your way out of the enemy's trap, you are a hero. Although the fire of your ignorance is fierce, if you can escape from it, you are a Buddhist hero. Students of the Buddha-dharma must break through ignorance. How? As I just said: Wake up. If you don't wake up, if you get angry and don't even realize it's a stupid thing to do, you get angry again and again, three times, four, five, up to countless times--ah! Inorance, ignorance, and--pop!--you die of rage!

Buddhists must cultivate patience.

What is patience?

When the most unbearable thing happens to you, you view it as if nothing were happening. You put it down. You cool off your brain and steady yourself. When something happens, don't immediately get angry. Cool off, and approach it in a reasonable manner. Then you won't set off the fire of ignorance. There's no end to talking about this, but in general, the fire of ignorance can burn our bodies and ruin them. It can burn your house to ashes.

Sutra: T.12b18

"THE ELDER'S SONS, TEN, TWENTY, EVEN THIRTY OF THEM ARE INSIDE THE HOUSE."

Outline:

L6. Parable of the thirty sons.

Commentary:

THE ELDER as previously stated, is the Buddha, the Thus Come One. His SONS refers to his "true sons," and initiate sons." TEN refers to the Bodhisattvas. TWENTY refers to the Sound Hearers, and THIRTY refers to the Conditioned-Enlightened Ones. Others say that the ten are the Sound Hearers, the twenty are the Conditioned-Enlightened Ones, and the thirty are the Bodhisattvas. Either way is all right. This is just an analogy, after all. The Dharma is flexible, not fixed, especially analogies, because they aren't real to begin with. Even though they aren't true in fact, they are true in principle.

The disciples of the Three Vehicles are within the triple realm, so the text says, ARE INSIDE THE HOUSE. They had heard the Buddhadharma in the past. In former lives, for limitless aeons, they had listened to the Buddhadharma, and so they had a very close, natural relationship, like that of blood relatives, like father and son. Because their affinities were so strong, they became the Buddha's "sons," Dharma Princes. The Dharma Princes of the Great Vehicle were the Bodhisattvas. The Dharma Princes of the Middle Vehicle were the Conditioned-Enlightened Ones. The Dharma Princes of the Small Vehicle were the Sound Hearers. The number in each category is not fixed, however, for some of the Small Vehicle may have gone over to the Middle Vehicle and some of the Middle Vehicle may have gone over to the Great Vehicle. They were all within the burning house. The thirty sons represent the Buddha's retinue. Other than the thirty sons, there were beings in the five paths, the "five hundred people," who were not as close to the Buddha. So, the sons represent those of the Three Vehicles.

Sutra: T.12b19

"THE ELDER, SEEING THE FIRE ARISE FROM THE FOUR SIDES, IS GREATLY ALARMED AND MAKES THE FOLLOWING REFLECTION: 'ALTHOUGH I HAVE BEEN ABLE TO ESCAPE SAFELY THROUGH THIS BURNING DOORWAY, ALL MY CHILDREN REMAIN INSIDE THE BURNING HOUSE, HAPPILY ATTACHED TO THEIR AMUSEMENTS, UNAWARE, UNKNOWING, NOT ALARMED AND NOT AFRAID. THE FIRE PRESSES UPON THEM AND THE PAIN

WILL SEAR THEM, BUT AT HEART THEY DO NOT MIND IT, NOR HAVE THEY ANY THOUGHT TO ESCAPE."

Outline:

K2. Specific parable.
L1. Parable of the Elder seeing the fire.

Commentary:

The ELDER is the Thus Come One. SEEING represents the Buddha vision with his Buddha Eye, and this is not ordinary seeing. SEEING THE FIRE ARISE represents the Buddha with the vision of his Buddha Eye, viewing the living beings in the six paths.

ON ALL FOUR SIDES: The beings in the six paths undergo the sufferings of the five skandhas. This suffering arises from the four directions. The four directions represent the Four Applications of Mindfulness: Mindfulness with regard to the body, feelings, thought, and dharmas. This was explained earlier in the passage about "Thus have I heard."[1] You should know that the body is a very unclean thing, a useless thing. Do not act as a slave for the body, a servant for the body. As the poet *T'ao Yüan-ming* said, "My mind has been my body's slave." In his elegant essay, *The Return*, he writes,

> I am going home!
> My fields and gardens are choked with weeds.
> Why should I not return?
> My mind has been my body's slave,
> But why should I remain melancholy?
> Having awakened to the past,
> I need not reproach myself.
> I know that in the future I can make up for it.
> I know that I am not far from the path
> of confusion,
> But I'm now awake to the present as
> "right" and the past as "wrong."

He says, "I am going home/ I want to go back. I should return to my home." But we shall change the meaning here a bit and say, "I want to return to my Buddha-home."

"My fields and gardens are choked with weeds/

---

[1] see *DFS, Vol. II*, p.72.

We can change it and say, "The field of my mind is choked with weeds." The mind is like a field, and it has been badly neglected. Why? Because we have not studied the Buddhadharma, and the "grass" has grown up in our minds. The more "grass" there is, the stupider we become. The weeds are choking the garden of our minds and if we don't hurry and study the Buddhadharma, our minds will be wild and uncultivated.

"Why should I not return?/ I should hurry right up and go back. My mind has been my body's slave/ My mind has been working for my body. But why should I remain melancholy?/ Why should I be so unhappy and so depressed? Having awakened to the past, I need not reproach myself"/ Awakened means to understand. "Ah! I know that everything I did before was incorrect."

T'ao Yüan-ming called himself on his own faults. We all make mistakes. The only thing to be afraid of is that you aren't aware of them. If you know about your own faults, then you are on your way to being a good person. Knowing that he was wrong in the past, there is no use wasting time in self-reproach.

"But I know that in the future I can make up for it/ In the future I can do better.

"I know that I am not far from the path of confusion/ I am like a lost sheep on a crooked path. The path of confusion, the stupid things I did, are still close at hand, but

"I am now awake to the present as "right" and the past as 'wrong'/ I know that what I did before was wrong. I plan to do better in the future."

This essay is extremely good. I like it very much. Later, if you want to learn it, I will explain it to you.

The Elder saw the big fire arise from all four directions. The four directions refers to the Four Applications of mindfulness, the first of which is to contemplate the body as impure. It is not a clean thing. Knowing this, you will not act as a slave for the body, as *T'ao Yüan-ming* so aptly wrote, "My mind has been my body's slave." His meaning was much like that of the Sutra.

Ten Types of Wisdom of those of the Three Vehicles:

Why does the text say "thirty" sons? Why doesn't it say "eight" or "nine?" If you add them up, 10 + 20 + 30 = 60. Sixty represents the Six Perfections of those of the Great Vehicle.

Why does the text say "ten?" This is because the Bodhisattvas, Sound Hearers, and Conditioned-Enlightened Ones, these Three Vehicles, all have ten kinds of wisdom.

1. Worldly wisdom. Although it is said to be worldly wisdom, it includes transcendental wisdom, because the sages of the Three Vehicles have used worldly wisdom to enlighten to all worldly dharmas. After that, they seek world-transcending Dharmas. Therefore, although it is said to be worldly wisdom, it is also transcendental wisdom. To put it another way, worldly wisdom itself is just transcendental wisdom. If you don't have worldly wisdom, how could you possess transcendental wisdom? World-transcending wisdom is born from worldly wisdom.

2. The wisdom of other's minds. Sound Hearers, the Conditioned-Enlightened Ones, and the Bodhisattvas all have this wisdom. It is the spiritual penetration of knowing the thoughts in other people's minds. This spiritual penetration is produced from samadhi. The Arhats, that is, the Sound Hearers, find it necessary to "intentionally observe" by means of the "wisdom of other's minds." This means that they have to use their mind to observe. If they do not, they won't know what it is someone else is thinking, and what it is they are about to do.

The wisdom of other's minds which the Conditioned-Enlightened Ones possess also involves this "intentional observation." However, they do not need to be sitting in Dhyana cultivating samadhi to carry it out. They just "intentionally observe," and, whatever you had it in mind to say or do, they know. Thus, the Conditioned-Enlightened Ones are one level higher in this respect than the Sound Hearers.

At the Bodhisattva level, the wisdom of other's thoughts does not require them to "intentionally observe." They can know anytime. Thus, they are one level higher than the Conditioned-Enlightened Ones. There are a lot finer discriminations which can be made, if one were to explain it in detail.

3. The wisdom of suffering. What does suffering have to do with wisdom? If you understand suffering, you will want to end suffering. If you want to end suffering, you can be rid of suffering. If you have no wisdom, how can you understand suffering? If you have no wisdom, you will suffer and not even realize you are suffering! If you have the wisdom to understand suffering, you can end suffering.

4. The wisdom of origination. This is the second of the Four Truths. Origination refers to the accumulation of afflictions. What does it have to do with wisdom? If you can know that origination involves affliction, if that isn't wisdom, what is it? If you lack the wisdom of origination, you won't even know it is affliction. When affliction besets you, you'll think of it as bread and butter and eat your fill! Why? Because you lack wisdom. With wisdom, when it comes you'll be aware: "Ah hah! That's affliction." That awareness is just wisdom.

5. The wisdom of extinction. What is extinguished? Affliction. With the wisdom of origination, you still need the wisdom of extinction which eradicates affliction. When affliction is extinguished, Bodhi is produced and thus you obtain the Four Virtues of Nirvana:

1. Permanence,
2. bliss,
3. true self,
4. purity.

6. The wisdom of the Way. In cultivating the Way, you also need wisdom. If you have no wisdom, you won't be able to cultivate. You'll waste your time all day long, and time will run out on you. In cultivating the Way, you need the wisdom of the Way.

7. The wisdom of Dharma. Dharma is the Buddhadharma. If you want to cultivate the Buddhadharma, you must have the Selective Dharma Eye. The Selective Dharma Eye is just wisdom, our wisdom eye. With the wisdom eye you won't do stupid things. Without it, you will.

What are stupid things? In studying the Buddhadharma, it is of primary importance that you not commit the Ten Evil Acts. Secondly, you must diligently cultivate the Ten Good Deeds.

The Ten Evil Acts

Three are committed with the body:
1. Killing,
2. stealing, and
3. sexual misconduct.

Three are committed with the mind:
4. Greed,
5. hatred, and
6. stupidity.

Four are committed with the mouth:
7. Abusive speech.
8. double-tongued speech,
9. frivolous speech, and
10. false speech.

The majority of our offense karma is created with our mouths. How can the mouth create offenses? By talking. If you say good things, there is no offense involved. Strangely enough, the mouth delights in speaking evil, in gossip, and in slander. That's the easiest place for the mouth to go wrong and create offenses. One gossips because one lacks the Selective Dharma Eye, one lacks wisdom. No matter what Bodhimanda it is, don't speak of its shortcomings. Their faults and problems are their own. We don't want to go there and put in our two cents. This is because:

> Others' wrongs, other's obsessions,
> Are their bad karma and their transgressions.

It is also said,

> Good and evil are two diverging roads.
> You can cultivate the good,
> or commit offenses.

If you cultivate the Way, you cultivate it. If you create bad karma, you create it. That's just the way things are. There's nothing strange about it. Those who cultivate the Way should support the Bodhimanda. Then you will be creating merit and virtue. You should not try to break up the Bodhimanda. If you break up the Bodhimanda you create offenses. If you support it you establish merit. If you have the Selective Dharma Eye you will not ruin the Bodhimanda. If you do not have it, you will get involved in various stupid actions.

8. The wisdom of comparison. Like the wisdom of the Dharma in which one uses the Selective Dharma Eye, this wisdom is one of comparing and choosing the superior Dharma-doors to cultivate.

9. The wisdom of the ultimate. Among the Three Vehicles this is wisdom at its extreme point, exhausting all principles, in which nothing is not known and seen.

10. The wisdom of non-production. This is the wisdom of the Patience with the Non-production of Dharmas. If you obtain this Patience then, in the Three Realms you do not see a single dharma produced and you do not see a single dharma extinguished. This experience cannot be fully expressed in words, nor can it be forgotten. You bear it in your mind; you know it yourself. It is like a person who drinks water and knows for himself whether it is cold or warm.

These are the Ten Types of Wisdom, and each of the Three Vehicles has these ten. Thus, the text says "ten, twenty, or even thirty." The people of the Three Vehicles are all in the burning house. The Elder, that is, the Buddha, using the Buddha eye, sees the living beings in the six paths being burned by the fire of the five skandhas, and, seeing the fire arise from the four sides...

The four sides, as I mentioned earlier, represent the Four Applications of Mindfulness.

The Four Applications of Mindfulness

1. Contemplate the body as impure.

2. Contemplate feelings as suffering.

3. Contemplate thought as impermanent.

4. Contemplate dharmas as without a self.

Our bodies are unclean things. In what way? Take a look. Perspiration flows from the entire body, and once you perspire, you smell. Tears and matter flow from the eyes. Wax oozes from the ears and mucus flows from the nose. Saliva and phlegm flow from the mouth. These seven orifices are always leaking unclean substances. Then, add the eliminatory orifices and you have nine holes which constantly ooze with impurities. Everyone is familiar with these impurities.

In our flesh and blood there are many kinds of bacteria as well which are impure. Someone may not believe this at all, but in the future, advances in science will no doubt prove that the flesh and blood are unclean. It's all very complex. Especially when people eat a lot of strange things which get into their systems and do strange things. The matter in the digestive system is also unclean. So why should you be so caught up in working for your body? First of all, contemplate the body as impure.

Secondly, contemplate feelings as suffering. Pleasurable sensations are enjoyable at first, but one soon grows tired of them, and they become disagreeable. It's a very obvious principle that there is nothing much to pleasure in itself.

Thirdly, contemplate thought as impermanent. thought after thought changes and moves on. Thoughts are like the waves on the sea. When one thought passes, another takes its place. Produced and extinguished, produced and extinguished, thoughts do not stop. Therefore, contemplate thoughts as impermanent. Past, present, and future, none of the three phases of thought can be got at. So contemplate thought as impermanent.

We are never aware of where our thoughts have gone off to. Mencius said, "If people's chickens and dogs run off, people go after them. But if their thoughts run off, they don't know to go after them." If someone's dog runs away, they may even go so far as to put an ad in the paper saying, "I have lost my dog! It's such and such a color and weighs so many pounds, and is of such and such a breed." If their chickens run off, they look for them everywhere. But when their minds go running off, they don't go after them. Where did their thoughts run off to? How can thoughts run off? When you have false thinking, that is just your mind running off. You may false think all day long. You think about getting rich, think about being an official, think about seeking fame and profit--these are all false thoughts. If you are destined to become an official, you will quite naturally do so.If you are destined to be famous or wealthy, it will happen according to your fate. You don't need to have false thinking about it and seek after it. Nevertheless, people insist on seeking after fame and profit, wealth and position, and don't understand that they should do good deeds. If you want your future to be bright you should merely do good deeds and not ask what the future will bring. If you do good things, things will naturally go well for you.

Fourthly, contemplate all dharmas as without self. Not only is there no self, there are no dharmas either! Make empty both people and dharmas. Empty the emptiness as well.

The Four Applications of Mindfulness are very important. But if I spoke of them in detail, what with *The Dharma Flower Sutra* being so long, when would I ever finish? So I have just commented on them briefly.

Seeing the fire break out on all four sides, the Elder IS GREATLY ALARMED. What does this mean? Doesn't the Elder represent the Buddha? How can the Buddha be afraid? The Buddha is fearless. How can he be frightened? His great alarm is a manifestation of his great kindness and great compassion. The Buddha is afraid that living beings will retreat from their resolve for Bodhi and so he is alarmed. If they retreat from their resolve for Bodhi, they will enjoy no bliss. With kindness, the Buddha bestows joy upon living beings. With compassion, he relieves them of their sufferings. The Buddha's fright represents his kindness and compassion for the living beings undergoing all the manifold miseries they must suffer if they retreat from the thought for Bodhi.

AND MAKES THE FOLLOWING REFLECTION: 'ALTHOUGH I HAVE BEEN ABLE TO ESCAPE SAFELY THROUGH THIS BURNING DOORWAY...' "I" is the Elder referring to himself. The door represents the doctrines of emptiness and existence. The four sides of the door represent exitence. The center of the door which one goes through represents emptiness. Although we speak of emptiness and existence, originally there is no emptiness or existence, because the Buddha, in the "burning house" relies upon the final principle of the Middle Way to cultivate and accomplish the fruition of Buddhahood. He has escaped the burning house through the burning doorway.

The Buddha has safely escaped because he is not harrassed by either the Five Skandhas or the Eight Sufferings. Nor is he shaken by the Four Inverted Views. The Four Inverted Views are four types of upside-down understanding and views. Common people and those of external religions take the Four Virtues of Nirvana and wrongly apply them to conditioned existence. Thus, their views are upside-down. The Buddha is not shaken by these four, and so he has escaped safely. He is secure and tranquil, having escaped the Three Realms.

The Four Inverted Views

1. Taking what is impermanent as permanent.

2. Taking what is not bliss as bliss.

3. Taking what is not true self as true self.

4. Taking what is not pure as pure.

Although the Buddha has escaped, ALL MY CHILDREN REMAIN INSIDE THE BURNING HOUSE. We living beings are still inside the burning house and we cause the Buddha to worry. HAPPILY ATTACHED TO THEIR AMUSEMENTS. In the burning house, the children, the disciples of the Three Vehicles and the five hundred people and all beings in the Three Realms are busy playing. Amusements refers to their attachment to views and to love. They have been shaken by states of love and views. In the Great Compassion Repentance it says, "Love and views are the root, the body and mouth are the conditions for the creation of all offenses within all of existence." Love and views are at the heart of the problem. The body and mind are the agents. Within the twenty-five planes of existence in the Three Realms, one is caught and does not wake up.

Amusements means that one accomplishes nothing. Attached to the five defilements: forms, sounds, smells, tastes, and tangible objects, to the the five desires: wealth, sex, fame, food, and sleep, in the end you do not obtain the slightest advantage. Your birth into this world has been in vain. You live and die in vain and your whole life amounts to nothing. Born muddled, you die muddled. Although you are born and die in a muddle, you have no thought to escape.

If you ask, "How were you born?"

"I don't know," you answer.

"How do you plan on dying?"

"I don't know," you answer.

You have no thought to escape birth and death. This is just like children playing. They play together and jump about all day. As they play, they are UNAWARE. Although they are within the burning house, they don't realize it's on fire. They don't say, "It's on fire. Let's get out!"

UNKNOWING means that they don't understand that fire is a "hot dharma." In the hot dharma of fire, their bodies may be seriously harmed, but they don't know this and so they are...

NOT ALARMED. Children who have never seen a tiger may be told about tigers, but they won't recognize one when they see one. If they accidentally run into one, they'll say, "Where did that big kitty come from?"

UNAFRAID, they don't know that the fire can rob them of their very lives. They don't understand how fierce the fire is.

What is more, living beings are unaware of suffering, unknowing when it comes to origination, and not alarmed at what injures the Way or frightened at the prospect of losing extinction. We haven't awakened to suffering, don't know about origination, and are not alarmed when our karma of the Way becomes obstructed, and are not frightened at the thought of losing the happiness of Nirvana. Not having heard the dharma of the Four Truths means that they lack "hearing" wisdom and "considering" wisdom.

Three Types of Wisdom

1. Hearing wisdom. This refers to listening to the Dharma. After hearing the Dharma, one needs,

2. The wisdom of consideration. With this wisdom, one thinks about what one has heard.

3. The wisdom of cultivation refers to putting what one has heard into actual practice.

If one lacks hearing and considering wisdom, one is unaware. If one does not then cultivate while in the burning house, one is unknowing. Without vision and understanding, one is not alarmed. If one lacks the understanding that comes from consideration, one is not frightened.

THE FIRE PRESSES IN ON THEM, AND THE PAIN WILL SEAR THEM. Living beings in the five paths of re-birth and those of the Three Vehicles are within the burning house and yet they are not afraid. The fire will soon burn them to death. The fire pressing in on them refers to the three sufferings which oppress the body:

The Three Kinds of Suffering

1. The suffering of suffering. This refers to the suffering of poverty. If poverty is suffering, what about prosperity?

2. The suffering of decay. When one's blessings run out, things go bad. This is the suffering of decay.

3. The suffering of process. This refers to the suffering involved in the life process itself, from birth to middle age, from middle age to old age, and finally death.

These three kinds of suffering, also called three kinds of feelings, are like a fire pressing in on one.

The pain will sear the living beings, those of the Three Vehicles, and the Buddha. The living beings and those of the Three Vehicles are like the Buddha's sons. The Buddha's sons will be burned in the fire. Won't this cause the Buddha to suffer? The pain will sear them and the Buddha himself will personally undergo great suffering, just as if his body were being stripped of its flesh.

BUT AT HEART THEY DO NOT MIND IT, NOR HAVE THEY ANY THOUGHT TO ESCAPE. The fire burns right beside them, but they are not disturbed by it in the least. Heart refers to the sixth/mind consciousness. The first five consciousnesses are linked to the sixth and the sixth has no thought to escape. Would you say this was delusion or not? If it were not delusion, how could they be seared by the fire and not even think about running away? Deluded by what? The three poisons: greed, hatred, and stupidity. Greed, hatred, and stupidity have deluded them to the point that they add suffering atop their suffering and grow more and more deluded.

Now, I will explain this passage in terms of the Five Evil Turbidities:

HAPPILY ATTACHED TO THEIR AMUSEMENTS: This refers to the turbidity of views and the turbidity of afflictions, in other words, love and views. Once you have views, you turn your back on enlightenment and unite with the dust. You have afflictions because you have love. Where there is love, there are afflictions. Take a look: There are some very intelligent people who are so caught up in love that they do nothing all day but laugh and then cry, laugh and then cry. When they have finished crying, for some reason unknown to them, they start to laugh. When they have laughed for a while they start crying again. Why? It's because there is affliction inside of love and it creates a lot of problems.

UNAWARE, UNKNOWING, NOT ALARMED, AND NOT AFRAID refers to the turbidity of living beings. THE FIRE PRESSES UPON THEM, AND THE PAIN WILL SEAR THEM refers to the turbidity of the lifespan. BUT AT HEART THEY DO NOT MIND IT, NOR HAVE THEY ANY THOUGHT TO ESCAPE refers to the turbidity of the aeon. We living beings, caught up in the five turbidities, have forgotten about returning home. Giving rise to views of people and self, right and wrong, all day long we run about hither and yon in the five turbidities, rising and sinking without cease. Sometimes they bob to the surface, other times they sink to the bottom, just like fish in the water having such a good time! But who knows when the fisherman's net will come and rob them of their very lives?

We living beings in the five turbidities are trapped in a net which is even fiercer. What is the net? It's our karma, our offense karma. When your offense karma hooks you, you'll be just like fish caught in a net. When people are caught by their own offense karma in King Yama's net, they are dragged into the hells to undergo suffering. Is this frightening or not? You shouldn't think this is such a peaceful place. Don't assume that the world is such fine place. It only seems fine to you because you haven't awakened from your dreams. Once you wake up you will know that this is not such a safe place to be.

Tonight there was a small earthquake. Originally, everyone has been saying for a long time that San Francisco was due for an earthquake. Why hasn't that big earthquake happened yet? I'll tell you: It's because of the power derived from our recitation of the Shurangama mantra. This power has scared away the demon kings who do not dare come near to disturb us. After this, whenever you recite Sutras or mantras, you should contemplate and concentrate on causing San Francisco to be very calm and peaceful, without any trouble.

We are here studying the Buddhadharma, and when new people come, we should treat them warmly. You should welcome them as you would your own brothers and sisters. The Dharma-protecting laypeople of long-standing should give up their seats to the new people and let them sit at the tables because the old-timers can get by sitting just anywhere. And don't look down on new people saying, "That person is crawling with demons! He doesn't understand the rules or how to bow or how to recite mantras..." While we don't go out into the streets and drag people in for lectures, when they do come we must certainly invite them to the lecture and give them a place to sit. We should be especially polite to new people and not slight them because they don't understand the Buddhadharma. When all of you first came, did I look down on you? Was I aloof towards you? I welcomed you all. But now, you must welcome the new people. Before, I didn't have so many Western disciples. Now that you have taken refuge with me you should support your Master and take a share of his load. Don't let new people feel very disappointed and make them want to leave. This isn't such a large group, after all. We must lead many people to study the Buddhadharma and then there will be hope for the future. Take note of this. The Master's disciples should support the Bodhimanda. Supporting the Bodhimanda is just supporting the Master. Being good to everyone is just supporting the Bodhimanda. So treat all the new people well. Look after them and don't look down on people. You were once just like them, you know. Now that you are a bit different you should think of a way to cause them to be different, too. That's the attitude that students of the Buddhadharma should have.

Sutra: T.12b23

"SHARIPUTRA, THE ELDER THEN REFLECTS, 'I HAVE A STRONG BODY AND ARMS. I MIGHT GATHER THEM IN A CLOTH POUCH OR ON A TABLE AND TAKE THEM FROM THE HOUSE.' HE FURTHER REFLECTS, 'THIS HOUSE HAS ONLY ONE DOOR AND IT IS NARROW AND SMALL. MY SONS ARE YOUNG AND IMMATURE AND AS YET KNOW NOTHING. ATTACHED TO THEIR PLACE OF PLAY, THEY MAY FALL AND BE BURNT IN THE FIRE.'"

Outline:

L2. Parable of casting aside table to use carts.

M1. Parable of casting aside the table.
N1. Method of exhortation not suitable.

Commentary:

Shakyamuni Buddha calls out again to SHARIPUTRA, saying THE ELDER THEN REFLECTS... This is a reference to the time when, for twenty-one days, the Buddha thought about what dharma he should speak that would be best suited to wake living being up from their dreams.

I HAVE A STRONG BODY AND ARMS. The Buddha is speaking about himself. The body represents the Buddha's spiritual penetrations which are ineffably wonderful. The arms represent the Buddha's wisdom which raises up all living beings.

The Buddha's spiritual penetrations conquer the karmic force which bears down heavily upon all living beings, carrying the load of their karmic forces. The Buddha uses his wisdom to teach living beings gradually and to lead them to understanding. This wisdom is manifest from samadhi. The samadhi is the Buddha's virtue of severing as discussed previously. When the Buddha says he is going to sever something, he does it. He's not like us. We talk about getting rid of our faults, but don't get rid of them. Then we have to undergo the consequences.With the virtue of severing, the Buddha can discriminate the Real Mark of all dharmas.

The Buddha also has the virtue of wisdom. With this wisdom, he speaks the Dharma. In speaking the Dharma, the Buddha uses both the virtue of severing and the virtue of wisdom. Thus, he accomplishes the Dharmabody.

To enter the two qualities of the virtue of severing and the virtue of wisdom, you must do so by means of the two doors of exhortation and admonishment. Exhortation means to encourage people to do something. To admonish is to warn people not to do something. These two doors can be related to the Four Types of Complete Giving, which are:

1. Complete giving for the sake of the person.

2. Complete giving in order to cure.

3. Complete giving which is mundane.

4. Complete giving of the primary principle.

The door of exhortation is the first, the complete giving for the sake of the person. The door of admonishment is the second, the complete giving in order to cure.

Basically, there is nothing to say about the Buddhadharma. That which is spoken is only superficial. Previously, I said,

> In the non-dual Dharma-door
> one doesn't open one's mouth.
> In the ground of the primary principle
> there are basically no words.

What is the ground of the primary principle? There is also nothing one can say about it.

If the Dharma cannot be spoken, then why do we speak the Dharma? Why did Shakyamuni Buddha speak the Dharma?

His speaking of the Dharma was based upon the Four Types of Complete Giving. "Complete" here means universally pervading. One universally gives with the four types of giving.

The exhortation door belongs to the complete giving for the sake of the person. The admonishment door belongs to the complete giving to effect a cure. "For the sake of the person" means to speak the Dharma for living beings. "To effect a cure" means to speak the Dharma to counteract the bad habits and faults of living beings. These two types of complete giving are spoken for the sake of the complete giving of the primary principle. The complete giving which is mundane is also spoken for the sake of the primary principle. They are set forth as preliminary expedient dharmas.

Therefore, when the Buddha first spoke the Dharma, he spoke the exhortation door to cause all living beings to offer up all good deeds. They must do all kinds of good things.

And what is the use of doing good deeds? What advantages does it have? A lot of them! In general, it enables you to accomplish the Ten Powers of the Thus Come One.

By means of the exhortation door one also accomplishes the Four Fearlessnesses of the Buddha:

1. The fearlessness of all-wisdom.

2. The fearlessness of speaking Dharma. When the Buddha speaks the Dharma it is like the roar of the lion which terrifies all the wild beasts. The heavenly demons and those of external religions all come and take refuge.

3. The fearlessness of speaking about dharmas which obstruct the Way. The Buddha teaches which dharmas obstruct the Way and which do not, discriminating the Real Mark of all dharmas, causing living beings to wake up.

4. The fearlessness of speaking of the dharmas which lead to the end of the path of suffering.

If we rely upon the exhortation door spoken by the Buddha and offer up all good deeds we, too, can obtain these Four Fearlessnesses and also obtain the wisdom of all modes. However, living beings have bad tempers and if you teach them to do good things, they won't necessarily do them. If you teach them to do evil things, they do them right away.

Since living beings are unable to accept the exhortation door, the Buddha teaches them the admonishment door. He says, "Hey! Don't you dare do that!!" giving them a loud and stern warning just like parents teaching their children not to do improper things. "DO NO EVIL!!" You are not permitted to do any evil deeds! Since it didn't work before when I taught you to do good things, I am now forbidding you to do anything evil." Strange. Living beings have a habit of doing the evil things you don't permit them to do. If you teach them to do good things, they won't do them. Living beings have habits which are too deeply ingrained for even the Buddha to do anything about. They deliberately insist on doing an evil deed just to try it out, just to see what trouble it brings. They try it out and try it out until eventually they fall. If you tell people to do no evil, they insist on doing it. If you teach them to do good, they refuse. The Buddha thinks, "They are so disobedient, then I will not teach living beings!" and he wants to quit teaching them. "Hah!"

What is the advantage of doing no evil? You can

certify to the great Nirvana, to its four virtues of permanence, bliss, true self, and purity. But living beings insist upon doing evil and are unable to accept the admonishment door. The Buddha tried the exhortation door, but they didn't listen. Then he tried to warn them with the admonishment door but they still didn't listen. Since there were no teachable living beings, the Buddha decided to take a rest and not teach and transform living beings. But then again, if he did not teach living beings, the Buddha would have nothing to do and he would feel compelled by his idleness to find himself a job. So he thought he would try speaking the Great Vehicle Dharma, teaching by means of spiritual powers and wisdom.

Adorned with the power
of samadhi and wisdom,
With these one saves living beings.

Previously, when praising the Elder, it was said that he was advanced in years. This represents the virtue of wisdom and the virtue of severing. These two virtues are also represented by the phrase "a strong body and arms."

I MIGHT GATHER THEM IN A CLOTH POUCH. In India cloth sacks were used to carry flowers in. The cloth pouch represents the Buddha's knowledge and vision. The cloth pouch,although one thing, can contain many things. It represents that the Buddha's knowledge and vision, although a simple thing in itself, can contain the knowledge and vision of all living beings within it. Knowledge refers to the wisdom of all modes. Vision refers to the Buddha eye. The wisdom of all modes means that there is nothing the Buddha does not know. The Buddha eye means that there is nothing the Buddha does not see. Using his knowledge and vision, the Buddha can rescue all living beings from the revolving wheel of the six paths of rebirth.

OR ON A TABLE: The Chinese text gives two characters, the first of which is 几 -*chi*, and is a small table. The second is 案 -*an*, a large table. Here in the lecture hall we have put several small tables together to make a large table. The small table represents the Four Fearlessnesses which are used to teach and transform living beings so that they may escape from the suffering in the Three Realms and avoid the difficulties in the six paths. The small table represents the Four Fearlessnesses, but this dharma is comparatively small, not broad and expansive. The large table represents the Ten Wisdom Powers of the Buddha.

In hearing the Dharma, you shouldn't be afraid of hearing it spoken once, twice, three, four, or even five times. Why? Hearing it once, it has "walked through" your eighth consciousness and planted a vajra seed. Don't think that once you hear a dharma you need not hear it again. The Dharma is like our food and drink. If you eat today does that mean you won't have to eat tomorrow? No. You have to eat everyday. After you eat, you wait a while and then you get hungry again and eat again. Hearing the Buddhadharma works the same way. You hear it once and then you hear it again. Don't fear hearing it too many times. If you do, it means there's some question about the wholesomeness of your roots. What question? The question of retreating from the heart of Bodhi. It doesn't matter who is lecturing on the Dharma, as long as there is a lecture, we should take time from our busy schedules to go listen to the Dharma. You should think, "I listen to the Dharma, and whether the lecture is good or not, I still am going to listen. If, out of a hundred sentences, the speaker says only one thing that strikes a responsive chord in me, a sentence which helps me get rid of my faults, then I will not have listened in vain."

You should not think, "His lecturing is meaningless. I'm not going to listen." When you listen to the Dharma, first of all you plant your own vajra seeds, and secondly you are supporting the Dharma Assembly and the Bodhimandala. You should look upon the Bodhimandala as you look upon your own household. You should feel the same responsibility for it. "I listen to the lectures everyday. I hear the Dharma everyday. Everyday I take care of my household affairs and I also protect the Bodhimandala."

The Buddha uses the Ten Wisdom Powers to teach and transform living beings in the Six Paths of rebirth so that they may leave suffering and attain bliss. Previously the Four Fearlessnesses represented by the small table was a relatively simple dharma. The Ten Powers save beings both horizontally and vertically, and are more expansive and inclusive.

For twenty-one days after his enlightenment, the Buddha thought and pondered, "What dharma should I use to teach and transform living beings? Should I use the great or the small dharma?" He thought about it for twenty-one days and the dharmas he decided to use are grouped under the exhortation door. The exhortation door is a dharma which "gathers in." It gathers in living beings in the same way a magnet attracts iron filings. Thus it belongs to the first of the four types of complete giving, complete giving for the sake of the person.

The admonishment door warns us to do no evil and is a kind of suppressing Dharma. Since you didn't listen to the exhortations, I'll scold you a good one! I'll use a strict method to teach you. The exhortation door was a compassionate door. The admonishment door was a severe door. Thus the Buddha used both the gathering and the suppressing dharma to teach and transform living beings. The Four Fearlessnesses, the Ten Powers, and the knowledge and vision of the Buddha were used to lead all living beings from the burning house.

HE FURTHER REFLECTS, "THIS HOUSE IS NARROW AND SMALL AND HAS ONLY ONE DOOR." What is the one door? It is the One Buddha Vehicle, the door of the White Ox Cart, the Great Vehicle. It is a very small door. Although it is the Great Vehicle, there are so many people to come through it that it will certainly be too small.

The One Vehicle is represented by the one door. You could also say the one door represents the doctrine of the One Vehicle, the Purity of the One Way. What is the door? It represents the proper teaching, the orthodox Buddhadharma. Further, a door is something which people can go through. In the same way, the proper teaching teaches and transforms living beings.

What is meant by "narrow and small?" Externalist religions cannot go through this door because they are attached to the concepts of permanence or annihilationism. The living beings in the Seven Expedients are also unable to get through this door. Only the Bodhisattvas of the Great Vehicle's Perfect Teaching are able to go through this door. The Seven Expedients are made up of those with the disposition of the Small Vehicle and so they are not able to get through the door. That is an explanation according to the Small Vehicle. Explained in terms of the doctrine itself, this door is the largest door, for only the Buddha and the Bodhisattvas of the Perfect Teaching can go in and out of this door. Small Vehicle people don't understand the perfectly interpenetrating doctrine of the Great Vehicle. Although it is said to be a small and narrow door, it's not really. It's the biggest. The Small Vehicle people neither understand nor comprehend it, and so for them it is narrow and small.

The wonderful doctrine of the One Buddha Vehicle is said to be the doctrine of uniformity because it is not mixed with any other doctrines. Since the doctrine is one, the path is especially pure. This pure path is the only path, and so it is said that there is one door. Why is the door said to be small? Because the oneness of the doctrine and the oneness of the Way are fine and subtle, inconceivable. Inconceivable means that it is difficult to understand. This is to speak of it in terms of the theory.

To explain it in terms of the teaching, it is the Perfect Teaching, the teaching in which the provisional and real are non-dual. Ordinary people don't know how to get through the door, they don't understand the provisional. They also don't know how to get in the door, they don't understand the real. The provisional and the real, these two teaching doctrines, are not understood by common people. Although those of the Two Vehicles understand how to get out, they never understand how to get in. Thus, they also don't understand this doctrine. Although the Bodhisattvas know exactly how to get out, they also don't know how to get in. This refers to the Bodhisattvas of the Special Teaching and below, the Bodhisattvas of the Seven Expedients. The Seven Expedients don't understand this teaching doctrine and so the teaching of the One Buddha Vehicle is "narrow and small." Since they are unable to travel it, for them the great becomes small and narrow. This Dharma-door belongs only to the One Buddha Vehicle. So the door is narrow and small and there is only the One Buddha Vehicle.

The one door is the Great Vehicle's white ox cart door which represents the One Buddha Vehicle. We have explained the One Buddha Vehicle according to the teaching and according to the theory. Now, we will explain it according to the conduct.

Conduct refers to the cultivation of the Perfect Teaching. It is a direct conduct, not a crooked or round-about conduct, because nothing can obstruct it or block it up. Therefore, the conduct is one. In cultivating the Bodhisattva Way, you go directly to the position of Buddhahood, to the Bodhimanda, where you realize the Buddha fruit. It is a "door" because you go straight through it. However, walking through the door is a kind of wonderful conduct which is not easy to cultivate. The Great Vehicle Buddhadharma is hard to cultivate. No expedient Dharma-doors are used, and so the door is said to be narrow and small. In reality, this Dharma-door is by no means narrow or small. It is the broadest and greatest of doors.

MY SONS ARE YOUNG AND IMMATURE, the ten, twenty, or thirty sons mentioned previously, that is, those of the Three Vehicles: Sound Hearers, Conditioned-Enlightened Ones, and Bodhisattvas.

What is meant by "young and immature?" Everyone knows that children are immature. They have no sense and so they are not afraid or alarmed. Although during the time of the twenty thousand Buddhas, those of the Three Vehicles have both studied the unsurpassed Way· and cultivated the Bodhisattva dharmas, and although they have been both taught how to cultivate the Way and transformed by those twenty thousand Buddhas, still their good roots are small and weak, and without strength. Since their Great Vehicle roots are weak, they are young and immature. In the Buddhadharma, those of the Three Vehicles are looked upon as little children.

AND AS YET KNOW NOTHING: Because their good roots are so scanty, when those of the Three Vehicles hear the Great Vehicle Buddhadharma, they slander it as did those arrogant five thousand people who walked out at the beginning of the speaking of the Sutra. When they heard the Buddhadharma, they did not believe it. They ran off because the "knew nothing." They had no common sense.

ATTACHED TO THEIR PLACE OF PLAY: They are caught up in their place of play. Not only are they unable to accept the Great Vehicle Buddhadharma, they also wish to retreat from their resolve for Bodhi. Having retreated, where do they end up? Attached to love and views! Having retreated from the Bodhi heart, they are harrassed by the eight kinds of suffering and become attached to the Dependent and the Proper Retribution Worlds. The Dependent Retribution World refers to the mountains, the rivers and the earth and all the vegetation and buildings. The Proper Retribution World is our bodies. The Proper Retribution World is also called the sentient world and the Dependent Retribution World is also called the material world. Having retreated from the Bodhi heart, they undergo the eight sufferings and become attached to these two worlds. That is what happens to ordinary people.

There are Three Realms: the realm of desire, the realm of form, and the formless realm. Beings in the realm of desire are attached to the five desires: wealth, sex, fame, food, and sleep. The five desires may also be said to be form, sound, smells, tastes, and tangible objects, that is, the objects of the five senses.

Beings in the realm of form also have their attachments. They are attached to the flavor of Dhyana. Beings in the four heavens of Dhyana are attached to the delight of Dhyana and the bliss of the Dharma. All day long they are extremely happy, happy to the point that you couldn't even describe their happiness. That is why the first Dhyana is called the blissful ground of leaving production, the second is called the blissful ground of the production of samadhi, the third is called the wondrous ground of leaving bliss, and the fourth is called the pure ground of getting rid of thought. The flavor of Dhyana is the taste of meditation. All of a sudden these beings become attached to their happiness, like children who eat one piece of candy and then want another and another. Those in the form heavens are attached to the flavor of Dhyana.

Beings in the formless realm have their attachments, too. They are attached to their samadhi. You shouldn't think that hearing "precepts, samadhi, and wisdom" talked about all day is all there is to it. If you get attached to your samadhi and are born in a formless heaven, you will not be able to get out of the Three Realms.

But let's not speak of the beings in the desire, form, and formless realms--which of us has no attachments? If we had no attachments, we could escape the Three Realms. A person might basically be very intelligent, but ends up doing all kinds of crazy things because he is attached, caught up in his place of play. Today he runs south and tomorrow he runs north; the next day he runs east, and then he runs west. People cannot put down their stupid behavior. They are all attached to their places of play. Why? It's a lot of fun here! They are like people in a movie theatre who forget all about their homes. Or they run off to gamble and forget to go home, forget everything. You might say they have entered the gambling samadhi, or the movie-samadhi, or the dancing samadhi, the drinking, smoking, or dope samadhi. Crazy mixed-up antics! They are attached to their places of play. And what happens then? The next sentence lays it right on the line:

THEY MAY FALL AND BE BURNT IN THE FIRE: Luckily the text says "may." It doesn't say for sure that they will fall, and so there is still some hope. This means that if you are able to reform yourself and become unattached, if you know to turn back from the confused path, you may not fall. If you don't wake up, you will fall. It's not for sure. This is like when a person has been arrested and has not yet been convicted or sentenced. It could go either way.

Why might they fall? Because they are young and immature, that is, stupid. Children have no sense. They are very stupid. Likewise, attachment to the five desires which causes one to fall is also very stupid. They fall because they are young and immature, too young to understand things. They fall because they know nothing, they simply don't know any better. They take what is suffering as bliss and turn their backs on enlightenment in order to unite with the dust. They go against the doctrine of enlightenment and think the most painful things are pleasurable. People like this fall into the three evil paths. Once they fall, they will be burnt in the fire. What is the fire? The eight sufferings, the five skandhas and the five turbidities. Once burned, it will be even harder for them to wake up.

Sutra: T.12b27

> "'I MUST TELL THEM OF THIS FRIGHTFUL MATTER, THAT THE HOUSE HAS CAUGHT FIRE, AND THEY MUST HURRY AND COME OUT SO AS NOT TO BE BURNED.' SO THINKING, HE SPEAKS TO HIS SONS, SAYING,'COME OUT, ALL OF YOU, QUICKLY!' ALTHOUGH THE FATHER, IN HIS PITY, INDUCES THEM WITH GOOD WORDS, STILL ALL THE SONS ARE HAPPILY ATTACHED TO THEIR AMUSEMENTS AND PLAY AND REFUSE TO BELIEVE HIM. THEY ARE NOT FRIGHTENED OR AFRAID AND HAVE NOT THE SLIGHTEST INTENTION OF LEAVING. WHAT IS MORE, THEY DON'T KNOW WHAT IS MEANT BY 'FIRE,' WHAT IS MEANT BY 'HOUSE' OR WHAT IS MEANT BY 'BEING LOST.' THEY MERELY RUN FROM EAST TO WEST IN PLAY, STARING AT THEIR FATHER."

Outline:

N2. Method of admonishment not suitable.

Commentary:

"I MUST SPEAK TO THEM OF THIS FRIGHTFUL MATTER. I should tell the people of the Three Vehicles and those in the five paths of rebirth, THAT THE HOUSE HAS CAUGHT FIRE. It's a terrifying situation. AND THEY MUST HURRY AND COME OUT SO AS NOT TO BE BURNED. If they don't leave they will be burned by the fire.

SO THINKING, HE SPEAKS TO HIS SONS, SAYING, "COME OUT, ALL OF YOU, QUICKLY! Hurry up and get out. If you don't come out right away you will be burned by the five skandhas and the five turbidities. You don't want to be burned to death, do you? Hurry and escape so that you may leave suffering and attain bliss."

ALTHOUGH THE FATHER, IN HIS PITY, INDUCES THEM WITH GOOD WORDS, STILL ALL THE SONS ARE HAPPILY ATTACHED TO THEIR AMUSEMENTS AND PLAY AND REFUSE TO BELIEVE HIM. They don't believe what the Elder says, and so THEY ARE NOT FRIGHTENED OR AFRAID of losing their very lives. AND HAVE NOT THE SLIGHTEST INTENTION OF LEAVING. The children have no thought whatever to leave the burning house.

WHAT IS MORE, because they are so young, THEY DON'T KNOW WHAT IS MEANT BY "FIRE;" this represents the living beings in the five paths who don't know that the eight sufferings and the five skandhas can burn our Dharma bodies and burn off our good roots. THEY DON'T KNOW WHAT IS MEANT BY "HOUSE;" they also don't know that the five skandhas and the six sense organs, the twelve places, and the eighteen realms are the apparatus which creates suffering; they are the origin of suffering.

OR WHAT IS MEANT BY "BEING LOST." "Lost" means to turn your back on the light and go towards the darkness, to travel back and forth between birth and death and further rebirth. They don't know the cause of the injury to their Dharma bodies.

THEY MERELY RUN FROM EAST TO WEST IN PLAY, STARING AT THEIR FATHER.They run to the east for a while, and then they run to the west.They have no sense of direction, no principle, and no idea of where they are going. They are just running around confusedly. This running is just turning one's back on the light and going towards the darkness. By running headlong into the darkness, they are born and die, over and over again. Suddenly, they are in the heavens; suddenly,they are in the hells. There is nothing fixed about it. No one is in control. They just run to the east and west.

"Staring at their father" means that, even though their father warns them, since they don't know what a fire is, what a house is, or what it means to be hurt, they just go right on revolving in birth and death and are not the slightest bit afraid. They just stare at their father, playfully as if nothing were happening. This represents their not venerating the Great Vehicle Buddhadharma and not listening to the Great Vehicle teaching. So it says, "they just stare at their father" and laugh, because they don't cultivate according to the Great Vehicle Buddhadharma.

This passage is the Admonishment Door, a warning to the children, but they don't listen. The Buddha considers quitting teaching and transforming living beings. Although it occurs to him to stop teaching, he is very compassionate and he can't bear to forsake living beings. So he decides to think up some other method.

Sutra: T.12c4

> "THEN THE ELDER HAS THIS THOUGHT, 'THE HOUSE IS ALREADY ABLAZE WITH A GREAT FIRE. IF MY SONS AND I DO NOT GET OUT IN TIME WE CERTAINLY SHALL BE BURNED. I SHALL NOW DEVISE AN EXPEDIENT DEVICE SO THAT MY SONS CAN AVOID THIS DISASTER.'"

Outline:

M2. Parable of using the carts.
N1. Suitability of the three carts.

Commentary:

Having decided not to use the table, the Elder now decides to use carts to entice the children to leave the burning house.

THEN, when the Elder told the children to leave the burning house and they just ignored him, THE ELDER HAS THIS THOUGHT, "THE HOUSE IS ALREADY ABLAZE WITH A GREAT FIRE. It is ablaze with the fire of the eight sufferings and five skandhas. IF MY SONS AND I DO NOT GET OUT IN TIME WE CERTAINLY SHALL BE BURNED." The Buddha and the disciples of the Three Vehicles and the beings on the five paths will be burned in the fire.

Previously, the Elder said, "Although I have been able to escape safely through this burning doorway..." and now he says that he, too, is about to be burned. Isn't this a contradiction?

Previously, he was speaking about his Dharma body, saying that it could escape safely. Here, in referring to being burned with the children in the fire he is talking about his Response body. So, in reading Sutras, you have to be able to tell what is going on.

"I SHALL NOW DEVISE AN EXPEDIENT DEVICE SO THAT MY SONS CAN AVOID THIS DISASTER." The Buddha thought, "I should set up some clever expedient method to lead living beings to escape being burned in the fire of the skandhas, sufferings, places, and realms. They will then be able to escape this disaster, this harm, and not get burned in the fire.

Sutra: T.12c6

"THE FATHER, KNOWING BOTH THE PREDISPOSITIONS OF HIS SONS AND THE PREFERENCES EACH HAS FOR VARIOUS PRECIOUS TOYS AND UNUSUAL PLAYTHINGS TO WHICH THEY HAPPILY RESPONDED..."

Outline:

N2. Knowing the children's former delights.

Commentary:

THE FATHER, the Buddha, KNOWING BOTH THE PREDISPOSITIONS OF HIS SONS AND THE PREFERENCES EACH HAS..."It is said, "No one knows a child as well as his father." A father will surely know how his children are predisposed, that is, he will know what they like. It is also said, "No one knows living beings as well as the Buddha." The Buddha knows all the desires of living beings. He knows what they like and what their dispositions are. The Buddha knows the natures and preferences of all living beings. "Predispositions" refers to the Small Vehicle Buddhadharma which they cultivated in the past. Everyone has his own preference. Some people cultivate giving, some cultivate the Four Truths, others cultivate the Twelve Conditioned Causes. The Dharmas each person cultivates are the preferences they have. So the Buddha knows living beings' hearts, what they prefer. What do they prefer?

VARIOUS PRECIOUS TOYS AND UNUSUAL PLAYTHINGS: This represents the Four Truths, the Twelve Conditioned Causes and so forth. All beings have their preferences when it comes to the Dharma-doors of the Three Vehicles. TO WHICH THEY HAPPILY RESPONDED: I will take a guess, according to the situation, and figure out what dharmas they will like.

Sutra: T.12c8

"...SPEAKS TO THEM SAYING, 'THE THINGS YOU WILL LOVE TO PLAY WITH ARE RARE AND HARD TO GET. IF YOU DO NOT TAKE THEM YOU WILL CERTAINLY REGRET IT LATER. THINGS SUCH AS THESE: A VARIETY OF SHEEP CARTS, DEER CARTS, AND OX CARTS, ARE NOW OUTSIDE THE DOOR FOR YOU TO PLAY WITH. ALL OF YOU SHOULD QUICKLY COME OUT OF THIS BURNING HOUSE AND I SHALL GIVE YOU WHATEVER YOU WANT.'"

Outline:

N3. Praising the three carts as rare.

Commentary:

SPEAKS TO THEM SAYING, "THE THINGS YOU WILL LOVE TO PLAY WITH ARE RARE AND HARD TO GET. The toys you have now aren't that fine. You shouldn't be attached to them. In the burning house, there is nothing to be fond of; it is, in fact, very dangerous. All of you should not play with those toys because I have some other fine things. I have some really *super* toys. You've never seen toys as much fun as these. They are brand new. See? They are very rare. They are imported! IF YOU DO NOT TAKE THEM YOU WILL CERTAINLY REGRET IT LATER. You'll be sorry. Now, come right out and I'll give them to you. THINGS SUCH AS THESE: A VARIETY OF SHEEP CARTS, DEER CARTS, especially beautiful. You've never seen anything like them. So pretty! If you want a sheep cart, I'll give you a sheep cart. If you want a deer cart, I'll give you a deer cart. OX CARTS are even less of a problem. Just hurry and get out. They ARE NOW OUTSIDE THE DOOR FOR YOU TO PLAY WITH. I have put them right here, outside the door. So come on out! The sheep cart represents the Sound Hearer Vehicle. The deer cart represents the Conditioned-Enlightened Vehicle. The ox cart represents the Bodhisattva Vehicle. The three carts are the Three Vehicles.

A sheep drawn cart can only pull small things, and so it represents the Small Vehicle. The deer has more strength than the sheep and can pull more things. An ox cart is more powerful than a deer drawn cart. It can pull people and things--a lot of them. So the carts represent the Small, Middle, and Great Vehicles. They are all right outside the door, and they are lots of fun to play with. You can get in them and go wherever you want.

ALL OF YOU SHOULD QUICKLY COME OUT OF THIS BURNING HOUSE. Come on, you kids, hurry and get out. Quick! Pronto! AND I SHALL GIVE YOU WHATEVER YOU WANT. Don't hang around in the burning house. Hurry right out!"

children playing in the burning house

Sutra: T.12c11

"THEN THE CHILDREN, HEARING THEIR FATHER SPEAK OF THESE PRECIOUS PLAYTHINGS WHICH SUITED THEIR WISHES EXACTLY, EAGERLY PUSH AND SHOVE ONE ANOTHER ASIDE IN A MAD SCRAMBLE, ALL FIGHTING TO GET OUT OF THE BURNING HOUSE."

Outline:

N4. Granting the kids wishes.

Commentary:

THEN THE CHILDREN, those of the Three Vehicles, HEARING THEIR FATHER SPEAK OF THESE PRECIOUS PLAYTHINGS, the Dharma-doors of the Three Vehicles, WHICH EXACTLY SUITED THEIR WISHES...They were so new and wonderful they aroused the children's curiosity. They were exactly what they wanted, what they had hoped for. They had hoped for the Dharma of the Three Vehicles and so the Buddha spoke it to them as a clever expedient. He could not speak about the One Buddha Vehicle because they were so busy playing that they had forgotten everything. They had forgotten all their dharmas and were caught up in the three realms.

It was not until the very end that the Buddha spoke of the One Buddha Vehicle, the real, genuine Dharma. *The Dharma Flower Sutra* sets forth this real, wonderful Dharma. There is nothing in it which is provisional. So the Great Master *Chih-che* spoke of this Sutra as purely perfect and solitarily wonderful. It is the Dharma-door of the Perfect Teaching.

In studying the Sutras we must certainly be respectful. We cannot call the Patriarchs by their names. For example, the Sixth Patriarch can't be called "Hui-neng." He should be called the Great Master the Sixth Patriarch. For a common person to call out a Great Master's name is a most disrespectful thing. The First Patriarch Bodhidharma, for example, must be called by his title with the addition of the phrase "Great Master." The Great Master Chih-che can't just be called "Chih-che." If students of the Buddhadharma don't pay proper respect to the ancients and the patriarchs, they will be unable to understand the Buddhadharma. You must be very respectful and add the term "Great Master" or "Venerable" to their names. You can't just call out "Hui-neng" to show that you are higher than he is! You can call children by their names, but not your elders. This is something that students of the Dharma must take note of. Don't study the Buddhadharma on one hand and create offenses on the other. In studying the Dharma you should eradicate offense karma. If you study it on one hand and fail to respect it, you will only increase your offense karma. It will increase to the point that people who were clear-headed will become confused and not follow the rules.

To speak of this passage in terms of the Three Kinds of Wisdom, the phrase "which suited their wishes exactly" refers to the Wisdom of Hearing. It shows that "the potential beings and the teaching are well-suited to one another." Each of the children had a favorite toy. This represents the Buddha setting up clever expedient Dharma-doors in which all beings take delight. Since this passage indicates the Wisdom of Hearing, it points to the cultivation of the Four Applications of Mindfulness.

The word "eagerly" here means that their hearts became very bold. It represents the Wisdom of Thought. This kind of thought is done by means of Contemplative Prajna. It is not the false thought of ordinary people. This kind of thought comes from the investigation of Dhyana. If you are eager, vigorous, and go forward in your cultivation, you must have the sword of wisdom. This sword of wisdom can distinguish right from wrong and prevent one from taking the wrong path.

What is the wrong path? It means to know clearly that something is wrong, but deliberately do it. One may know that something is wrong, but insist on doing it anyway. This is because one lacks the wisdom sword and is stupid. Not only is such a person stupid, he is the stupidest of people.

Before we have understood the Buddhadharma, if we take the wrong road, it's because we don't understand true principle. Having entered the door of the Dharma, and even taken refuge with the Triple Jewel, one must offer up one's conduct in accord with the teaching. If one does not, in the future one is sure to fall into the hells. There's not the slightest doubt about it. Why? Because one clearly knew that it was wrong and did it anyway. If one has genuine wisdom, one won't do wrong things. "Push and shove" means that when the children, those of the Seven Expedients, heard there were new toys, they looked into the Four Holy Truths and having done so they were able to subdue and sever view delusion.

ONE ANOTHER ASIDE: This refers to their contemplation of the Four Holy Truths: suffering, origination, extinction, and the Way. In so doing, they are able to sever the view delusions. Thus, the phrase "push and shove one another aside" refers to their investigation of the Four Truths which leads to the subjugation of view delusion.

This passage also refers to the four additional practices: "One another aside" refers to the first two, heat and summits. "In a mad scramble" refers to the third, patience. "All" refers to the fourth, highest mundane Dharma. These four additional practices were discussed in *The Shurangama Sutra*.

A MAD SCRAMBLE refers to the position of seeing the way, that is, the first fruit of Arhatship. At this position view delusions have been severed. View delusion is defined as giving rise to greed and love when facing an external state. Now these delusions have been severed and one "sees as if not seeing," "loves and yet does not love." There is no view delusion. However, having reached first stage Arhatship one has only ended share section birth and death. One has not ended change birth and death. One has not yet reached the place where the "two deaths eternally cease."

What is share section birth and death? It refers to each person having his own share and his own section. Your share refers to your body, from the soles of your feet to the top of your head. Your section refers to your alloted lifespan from your day of birth to your dying day, including your actions from birth until death which are controlled by your karma. Sages of the first fruit have ended this share section birth and death.

FIGHTING TO GET OUT: This refers to the Way of thought, that is, cutting off the last of the thought delusions in order to certify to the stage beyond study, fourth stage Arhatship. When one has certified to fourth stage Arhatship one can escape the Three Realms. If one has not certified to the fourth stage of Arhatship, one cannot escape the Three Realms. At fourth stage Arhatship, view delusions and thought delusions have both been cut off. At that time:

One passes beyond the three realms,
Is not within the five elements.
One is not confined by one's temper or
Pressured by desire for things.

"Temper" refers to our nasty dispositions inherited from our parents. We may try to get free of our bad tempers, but it's not easy. We are tied up by our dispositions and can't get free of them.

You may think, "I am very free. I just do what I please." It's just your "doing as you please" that makes you unfree! You are being controlled by your disposition. You like the movies, and so all day long you watch movies. Ultimately what use is it?

"Well, it's fun."

When the fun is over, then what? What benefit is it?

"Well, at least I'm happy for a short time."

So you're happy for a short time, but who knows how much time you will spend suffering? At the very least, after a movie your eyes are tired and you lack energy. That's an obvious form of suffering. Or perhaps you enjoy various forms of pleasure thinking they are blissful when actually they are the roots of suffering. You take suffering as bliss, and you have been tied up by your habits. You would like to transcend the three realms, but you can't get out. You want to study the Buddhadharma? Your temperament grabs you and prevents you from doing so. "Studying the Buddhadharma is of no great use. It would be better to take a nap or have something to eat. At least that will help out the body."

"Not pressured by desire for things." You are not pushed or covered over with desire for material things. What gets covered over? Your wisdom.

"No!" you say, "I feel like I get smarter and smarter everyday."

If you like to smoke, drink, or take drugs, these are all desires for material things which cover over your self-nature's bright light and Prajna wisdom, so that you do things that are upside-down, things involved with deviant knowledge and views. Because we are confined by our tempers and pressured by a desire for things, we are caught in the three realms and never make it out. Would you like to get out? Then use your Prajna wisdom sword to cut off all your temper and lust for things, and then you can certainly transcend the three realms.

Like the children, we should fight to get out of the burning house. Don't dally thinking it's fun. It may be "fun" but it's also the most dangerous place you could possibly be. Students of the Buddhadharma must grab ahold of proper knowledge and views in order to get out of the three realms.

A few days ago I heard one of my disciples gossip. He said he knew that before he was climbing on conditions to get people to make offerings and now he knows that this is wrong. This proves that he hasn't wasted his time in cultivation. He has obtained a bit of the benefits of Dhyana samadhi, and he should take care to guard his state and not relax. His state is the same as the First Dhyana, but he must continue to work hard. There are very few Westerners who cultivate the Way. People who are confused about the Way are many. Before you left home, you were also very confused. Now everyday you meditate and work hard and investigate the Buddhadharma; this means that you have made progress.

After this, you should address left-home people as "Dharma Master." You can't just call out their names. A few days ago I told you that you can't casually call out the names of the past patriarchs. You also shouldn't call out the names of the present patriarchs. You now are future American patriarchs. All you need to do is do a good job. In the future when you become enlightened and have a bit of spiritual powers, you will have success. So now, all my disciples must call each of the left-home people by the title "Dharma Master." We shall set up rules now so that it will become a custom in the future. The Dharma-name is basically a name that only one's Master or other high monks can use. Ordinary people don't call people by their Dharma-name. They may use their other names. Lay people should not look at the faults of those who have left home. If they have faults, they will gradually improve and you shouldn't blame them for them.

Today we received notice of the upcoming precept-transmission in Taiwan. This time the transmission will be very good because they will provide the three robes and the bowl and sitting cloth as gifts to create affinities. In the past, on the mainland, they did not always do this. They sent a lot of forms, but we don't know how many people will be going to take the precepts. If you would like to go, you should apply early.

I am very happy that some of my disciples are going to leave home. I'm so happy in fact that I can't even sleep at night! I just think, "Oh, they really work hard." But though the left-home people work hard and eat one meal a day, you lay people should work hard, too. You should work even harder than the left-home people and not just go to sleep all day, fail to listen to the lectures, and when the time comes, refuse to recite the Sutras. If you act like that in the future you will become a snake. If as a lay person in the temple you don't recite Sutras or cultivate the Dharma it's very, very dangerous. You shouldn't think you can get off so cheaply. If things get dangerous, I will be even more on edge and lose more sleep at night. When I'm too happy I can't sleep. When I'm worried, I can't sleep, either. If my lay disciples don't cultivate and turn into snakes, I'll lose sleep over it. So everyone of you should work hard. Don't wait until someone is watching over you to start working. You should be diligent.

Lay people should be addressed as "Layman so and so..." If you call them by that title they will think, "I ought to do a good job." When you say "Dharma Master" they think, "He's calling me 'Dharma Master,'" and even if they wanted to relax a little, they won't. "I am a Dharma Master and I should study a little more Buddhadharma," or "I am a lay person and I ought to support the Buddhadharma." So everyone will live up to their names and walk down the road to Buddhahood. "Oh ho! So that's what becoming a Buddha is all about!" you'll think when you get there. So from today on the lay people must respect one another and be compassionate towards all. The best thing would be to look at other's strong points and ignore their weaknesses. Those with strong points should be encouraged to make them even stronger. Those with weaknesses should gradually turn them into strong points. This is my hope for each of you. I have the same equal compassionate regard for all of you and certainly am not closer to any one of you than to any other. Whoever cultivates, and genuinely works and practices the Buddhadharma is my real "jewel" of a disciple. If you don't work hard, then I can only sigh, "This person...I have no way to save him," and I won't be able to sleep. That's the way it is.

Sutra: T.12c13

"AT THAT TIME, THE ELDER, SEEING THAT ALL HIS SONS HAVE GOTTEN OUT SAFELY AND ARE SEATED ON THE GROUND AT THE CROSSROADS, IS WITHOUT FURTHER OBSTRUCTION; HIS MIND IS AT PEACE AND HE IS FILLED WITH JOY."

Outline:

L3. Parable of giving all a great cart.
M1. The father rejoices on seeing the children escape the danger.

Commentary:

AT THAT TIME, THE ELDER, the Buddha, SEEING THAT ALL HIS SONS HAVE GOTTEN OUT SAFELY AND ARE SEATED ON THE GROUND AT THE CROSSROADS...The Buddha saw the living beings had gotten out of the burning house and were sitting on the ground at the crossroads. The crossroads represents the method of contemplation of the Four Truths: The method of contemplation of suffering, the method of contemplation of origination, the method of contemplation of extinction, and the method of contemplation of the Way. This contemplation leads to the wisdom of suffering, the wisdom of origination, the wisdom of extinction, and the wisdom of the Way. "On the ground" means that, in cultivating the Four Truths to certify to the fruit, one severs entirely the delusions of views and thought in the three realms. "Seated" means they have certified to the fruit and do not seek further progress. Certifying to the first fruit, one does not seek the second; certifying to the second fruit one does not seek the third and so on. One just sits there and stops.

People in the three realms are as if tied up by the revolving wheel of the six paths. Now, seated at the crossroads they have transcended the revolving wheel. What is meant by HIS MIND IS AT PEACE? The Buddha's heart was at peace because he had seen all living beings safely get out of the burning house and certify to the fruit of Arhatship. HE WAS FILLED WITH JOY, because the disciples had avoided the disaster. What disaster? That of being burned by the eight sufferings, five skandhas, six senses, twelve places, and the eighteen realms--the various kinds of suffering, and so the Buddha was filled with joy.

A father may have sons or daughters who have to undergo some danger or trouble.When he hears that his sons and daughters have escaped danger, he is very happy. This is like now, everyone here is very vigorous in studying the Buddhadharma and comes to listen to the Dharma. During the day they work and it's very tiring. When time comes for the Sutra lecture, no matter how far away they are, they come to listen. This causes your teacher's heart to be very happy. He thinks,"These students of the Dharma are so sincere." If none of you came to hear the Buddhadharma as I was lecturing here, it would be like when Dharma Master Yin-kuang lectured in Nanking--only one person was in the audience, night after night. Finally, he spoke with him and said, "So you find my Sutra lectures interesting, do you?"

The man replied, "I don't have any idea what you are talking about. I don't understand any of it."

"Then what are you doing here?" said Master Yin-kuang.

"I'm waiting for you to finish so I can put the chairs away," he said.

Master Yin-kuang's heart was pained. "I thought I had a real friend here when all the time there wasn't a single one!" Master Yin-kuang had a lot of Way virtue. He went into seclusion on Mount P-u-t'ou for eighteen years and saw no guests in all that time. What was he doing those eighteen years? Reading the Tripitaka. Later, he wrote many articles. They are extremely good because he developed his wisdom by reading the Tripitaka. He was the Thirteenth Patriarch of the Pure Land School. He had a lot of virtuous practice, yet no one listened to him lecture on the Sutras. Why not? Because he didn't do a lot of advertising or pressure people into coming. He never put ads in the paper.

Now, when I am lecturing in Chinese and so many Westerners come to listen, my lectures are translated into English. Whose merit is this? The translator's. If no one translated, no one would know what I was saying. So I am very happy.

A Story: Don't Let Your House Burn Down!

Speaking of children fighting to get out of the burning house, that reminds me of a story. There was once an old married couple who cultivated the Pure Land Dharma-door. They recited "Namo Amitabha Buddha" everyday. Someone told them, "When you recite, you should get the Buddha-recitation samadhi. After you obtain that samadhi, when the wind blows it won't blow on you, and the rain won't fall on you. At that time you will certainly gain great advantage."

One day, the old couple's daughter-in-law had to go to work. She couldn't find a baby-sitter for her three and four year-old children, so she gave them to the old couple to look after. The children were very mischievious and started playing with matches, lighting little fires. The old man told the old lady, "Go tell the kids not to light fires. They could burn the house down!"

The woman said, "You just keep minding trivial matters. How can you expect to attain the Buddha-recitation samadhi that way? The Buddha-recitation samadhi means you can't pay attention to any external matters at all. What are you doing watching over the kids?"

The old man thought, "All right. I'll just forget it," and continued his recitation. "If I keep reciting the Buddha's name, it will generate enough merit to keep the house from catching on fire."

So the two of them kept reciting until, finally, the house did catch on fire! The old couple didn't even know because they weren't paying attention. When a neighbor came over to put out the fire, he saw the house was half-burned already and the other half was going fast, but the old couple was just sitting there reciting the Buddha's name. "How can you ignore the children, let the house burn down, and not even get out yourselves?" he cried.

The old man glanced at his wife and said, "See? I told you the kids were playing with fire, and you said not to pay any attention to it but to concentrate on getting the Buddha-recitation samadhi. The house has burned down; have you got the samadhi?"

The old woman said, "Well, why wasn't the recitation effective? We recited and the house burned down anyway. Probably there's nothing efficacious about recitation at all."

Actually, she was just superstitious. Kids don't know what is going on. They have to be watched over.

You can't just let them play with fire. Thus, a perfectly good home turned into a burning house. Although they didn't get out themselves, luckily a good knowing advisor was able to rescue them at the last minute.

Now, we are talking about getting out of the burning house; we shouldn't act as stupidly and superstitiously as that old couple. Don't think that just because you recite the Buddha's name there will be no fires. Recitation brings its own merit and virtue, but if you don't watch over the children, the danger of fire is still ever-present.

Someone asks, "The Sutra says that if one who recites the name of Kuan-yin Bodhisattva happens to enter into a great fire, they fire will not burn them. Why, when they were reciting Amitabha Buddha did the house catch on fire?"

The Sutra is referring to one who accidentally "happens" to enter a great fire. If someone is standing there while the house accidentally catches fire, that situation differs from the former. The first is a fire which couldn't be prevented. The latter is one which the old man already knew about, but ignored. They knew the kids might start a fire, but paid them no mind. Thus, the house caught fire.

Students of the Buddhadharma shouldn't be like that muddled old couple. Don't think that you can rely on reciting the Buddha's name and nothing will happen. That's just being stupid. Reciting the Buddha's name is reciting the Buddha's name, but if something happens, you have to be prepared. It is said, "If you are prepared, there are no emergencies."

Sutra: T.12c15

"THEN THE CHILDREN ALL SPEAK TO THEIR FATHER SAYING, 'FATHER, THE FINE PLAYTHINGS YOU PROMISED US A WHILE AGO, THE SHEEP CARTS, THE DEER CARTS, AND THE OX CARTS, PLEASE GIVE THEM TO US NOW.'"

Outline:

M2. The children demand the carts.

Commentary:

This is the section of text in which the children all demand their carts. The three carts are an analogy for the positions of the Three Vehicles. Because they wish to obtain the Three Vehicles, they must transcend the three realms. Once one has transcended the three realms, the Three Vehicle fruits are ultimately unobtainable. The Three Vehicles are all the provisional teaching, ultimately unobtainable and non-existent. During the Vaipulya Teaching Period those of the Three Vehicles were scolded by the Buddha. During the Vaipulya Period the three teachings were all reprimanded: the Storehouse Teaching, the Pervasive Teaching, and the Separate Teaching. He told them, "You are withered sprouts and sterile seeds! You are all just self-ending Arhats who only watch over themselves. You are corrupt elements. You have no guts at all. When I teach you,you pay no attention and you don't even follow the rules. You don't practice any of the Dharma methods I teach you. You are so lazy!" Thus, he scolded those of the Storehouse and Pervasive Teachings.

Then he spoke in praise of the Special Teaching. He said, "You of the Special Teaching are not bad. You have a bit of spunk." He rewarded those of the Perfect Teaching, those beings with potential which is perfectly penetrating without obstruction. "They really cultivate well. Their skill has about matured."

During the Vaipulya Period the Buddha scolded the partial and the small and praised the great and rewarded the Perfect.

During the Prajna Period of the Buddha's teaching a process of selection went on, to see which had the Great Vehicle dispositions and which had the Small Vehicle dispositions. All the disciples went through many selection processes. So the Buddha, in several decades, taught and transformed Sages who had certified to the fruit, obtaining Arhatship and cultivating the Bodhisattva Vehicle. This was the result of several decades of work.

The Dharma Flower Sutra itself says, "The expedients are not real." This means that the three types of provisional dharmas taught previously were nothing but expedients. They are not real, actual Dharma. You should not misunderstand. Before, you were not ready to receive the true Dharma, and so I did not teach it to you. Now, in The Dharma Flower Assembly the truth is coming out, the genuine Dharma is being spoken. Shariputra very respectfully requested the Buddha three times to speak the Sutra, until the Buddha finally agreed to speak it. The three requests are what is represented in the analogy by "asking for the three carts," the deer cart, the sheep cart, and the ox cart. They want the Three Vehicles from the Buddha.

Shariputra and the entire assembly were extremely sincere and earnest in their request that the Buddha speak the true Dharma. The three requests refers to the Sound Hearers, the Conditioned-Enlightened Ones, and the Bodhisattvas asking for the carts. The children want their toys.

Previously, the three types of provisional dharma were taught; now the one real Dharma is being taught. That is the Great Vehicle, which is for living beings with the Great Vehicle potential. They have brought forth the resolve to cultivate the Great Vehicle, to go from the small towards the great. However, we must realize that during the Vaipulya period those of the Three Vehicles received a lot of scoldings from the Buddha. He taught and transformed them for a long time. Sometimes the Buddha reasoned with them and other times he upbraided them. However, they didn't know what to do.There were living beings then who wanted to seek the Great Vehicle Dharma, but they didn't know how to go about asking for it. It was not until the Prajna Assembly, when Prajna was being taught, that "the teaching was passed on and the wealth was bequeathed." The teaching passed from the small vehicle to the Great Vehicle, just as a father will hand down his wealth to his children.

In the Prajna period, when the teaching was passed on, the living beings did not know ultimately whether or not they could obtain the wonderful Great Vehicle Dharma. It was at this point that they got the idea to seek the Great Vehicle. Although the idea arose, they didn't understand until the Dharma Flower Assembly when Shariputra earnestly requested three times, speaking up and asking for the carts. Thus, this passage of text is the kids speaking up and demanding the carts. They said, "FATHER, THE FINE PLAYTHINGS YOU PROMISED US A WHILE AGO, THE SHEEP CARTS, DEER CARTS, AND THE OX CARTS, PLEASE GIVE THEM TO US NOW. Daddy, you promised to give us those neat toys. We want them right now!"

Sutra: T.12c18

"O SHARIPUTRA, AT THAT TIME THE ELDER GIVES TO ALL OF HIS SONS EQUALLY A GREAT CART."

Outline:

M3. Giving all the children a great cart.
N1. Statement of giving the carts.

Commentary:

Shakyamuni Buddha calls out again, "O SHARIPUTRA, AT THAT TIME THE ELDER GIVES TO ALL OF HIS SONS...The sons represent all living beings. Because all living beings are equal, it says, "all the sons." Equal means that they are equal with the Buddha. Living beings and the Buddha are equal. Living beings and the mind are also equal. This is an analogy showing that all living beings have the Buddha nature and all can become Buddhas.

Since the Buddha nature is the same in all of them, they are all the Buddha's children. The Buddha's heart is not particularly fond of any one living being. They are all treated alike. He is extremely compassionate towards all living beings, and so he GIVES TO ALL OF HIS SONS EQUALLY A GREAT CART. The equal giving of the great cart represents the Buddhadharma as equal, without distinctions. There, it is said, "All dharmas are the Buddhadharma." The analogy is to the Great Vehicle Mahayana Teaching, the genuine Buddhadharma. It is different from the three provisional dharmas which preceded it. However, the preceding provisional dharmas are also subtle, wonderful, and inconceivable. Although they are provisional dharmas, they were set forth for the sake of the real. They are essentially the same. hus, he gives them all the Great Vehicle Dharma. All the sons get a big cart. Though he gives them the Great Vehicle Buddhadharma, each of them in the distant past had their habits and their particular emphasis in study and practice. For example, some had cultivated the Four Truths. Some studied the Twelve Conditioned Causes. Others practiced the Six Perfections. The Truths, Conditions, and Perfections, the Four Unlimited Thoughts of the Buddha--these were all practiced. There were also the form dharmas and the mind dharmas. There were opposing the according dharmas, dharmas of dependent and proper retribution, phenomenal and noumenal dharmas. There were those who cultivated cause and those who cultivated effect, those who cultivated their own dharmas and those who cultivated dharmas of others. There were those who cultivated the dharmas of understanding and those who cultivated dharmas of delusion, that is, dharmas of liberation and dharmas of confusion. There were those who cultivated many or great dharmas and those who cultivated small or few dharmas. There were those who cultivated dharmas of blessings and those who cultivated dharmas of wisdom. How did they cultivate blessings? In all situations, they took the short end of the deal and didn't try to get off cheap. They benefitted others and not themselves. They helped others and didn't ask others to help them. If you help others for long enough, you will naturally obtain blessings. Suppose you see a person who has no blessings at all. If he has twenty cents in his hand he is likely to buy something that makes him sick or something that will cause him some other kind of trouble. Why doesn't he have any blessings? He has never cultivated blessings. Cultivating blessings isn't just helping people out. It means also not obstructing people and not causing them to be unhappy with you. If you obstruct others you are throwing away your blessings.

You may argue, "But isn't that practicing giving?"

Right. It's giving. But if you give away your blessings like that, no one actually receives your gift, and no one gets any benefit out of the transaction.

For example, you give away your blessings by slamming the door when entering the hall where others are meditating, studying, or doing other types of work. If you cause those meditating to jump, keeping them from entering samadhi, then you've just given away your blessings. Or if the sound scatters the students' concentration as they translate Sutras, then you have just given away your blessings, thrown them away. In general, anything which gets in other people's way and makes them unhappy is all "giving away" your blessings.

As another example: You have all taken refuge with the Triple Jewel, and bowed to me, such a stupid person, as your teacher. Why do I say that I am stupid? Because I often give rise to afflictions and that is a manifestation of stupidity. How do I give rise to afflictions? Perhaps one of you disobeys. When you took refuge with me you said that you would offer up your conduct in accord with the teaching. But after you took refuge you just turn your back on the teaching and refuse to practice it. You reject my teachings and don't obey them. Why did you take a teacher? If you want to study the Buddhadharma, you must do so in a straightforward manner, not just haphazardly. In China, when Dharma Master Hsüan-tsang went to India to get the Sutras, he was tormented by demons and suffered considerably to obtain the Dharma. Now, it's very simple to listen to the Sutras and study the Dharma. If you don't study properly now, you are really lacking virtuous practice. In previous lives you planted no good roots, and so now you can't study the Dharma properly. Because you don't study properly, you make your stupid teacher very upset. Last year I remember there were two disciples to whom I said, "You do a good job. Study the Buddhadharma and don't give me a lot of trouble. If you continue to give me trouble, and fail to study properly, then not only are you failing to support your teacher's Dharma, but you are destroying it."

The causes and effects involved with destroying the Dharma bear consequences which are so dangerous they can't even be spoken of. If you make trouble in a Bodhimanda, make trouble for your teacher, or make trouble for the Triple Jewel, you are "giving away" your blessings, and soon you will have none. If you have no blessings, then you will most certainly not succeed in your cultivation of the Way.

As to cultivating wisdom, one must respect the Sutras. You can't just read them and expect to develop wisdom. You must treat them with great respect. The T'ien-t'ai Master Chih-che, for example, after hearing only the title of *The Shurangama Sutra*, bowed to-towards India, where the Sutra was, everyday for eighteen years, but he never saw the Sutra. In China, Great Master Chih-che was enlightened while reading *The Dharma Flower Sutra*. There were also many other Dharma Masters who bowed to *The Dharma Flower Sutra*, *The Shurangama Sutra*, and to *The Avatamsaka Sutra*, to every word in them. They bowed once for every word in the Sutra, using an ancient coin, the kind with a hole in it, to mark their place. They bowed to them in that way for their entire lifetime. You can open your wisdom either by bowing to Sutras or by reading them. I will tell you something that is extremely important, and don't let it go in one ear and out the other: You must practice what you know. You can't just read the Sutra and think, "I understand the principle," and let it go at that. You must actually do what the Sutras instruct you to do. The Sutras tell you to get rid of all your faults and you must do that. If you don't get rid of your faults, you might as well not study the Buddhadharma. The Buddhadharma is just that inconvenient. If you think you can study it and hold on to your imperfections, it can't be done. This is one point to which everyone should pay special attention. I'm not joking with you. If you don't get rid of your faults and deliberately violate the Dharma's regulations, then you'd be better off not studying the Dharma at all. If you do, you'll certainly wind up in the hells.

Another thing, in cultivating the Way, everyone has to watch over themselves and do everything they can to get rid of their habits and faults. I look upon all of you equally. I'm not insisting that you improve instantly, but I hope that you will gradually improve and get rid of your faults. I am deeply concerned for all of you and I watch after you. I worry about your faults more than I do my own, in fact, because I hope that all of you can be better than me. I hope that you will blaze the trail for Buddhism in the West, and be pioneers, as it were. Don't look upon yourselves lightly.

If you were to speak about dharmas in detail, there are limitless and boundless dharmas, and so it is said,

All dharmas are the Buddhadharma.

All you need to do is understand and it's the Buddhadharma. When you don't understand, it is still the Buddhadharma. The only difference is that you don't understand it.

So you have now understood a bit of the meaning of the Buddhadharma. You should go forward and actually practice it. Don't be sloppy about it. The Sound Hearers, the children, all of them had their dharmas which they had practiced in former days, but they were all provisional teachings. They were not the real teaching. Now the real begins. That is why, today, I have told you all some real Dharma. No one should be afraid of making a mistake. Just be afraid you won't correct it. If you don't correct your mistakes, not only do I have no way to help you, but even Shakyamuni Buddha himself couldn't save you!

The dharmas they studied before were all different, and so the text says, EACH. Although they were different then, now they are all EQUAL. You all get the Mahayana Teaching.

In the Great Vehicle Dharma:

One includes all.
It is universally perfect,
universally accessible.

The Great Vehicle Dharma includes all dharmas. It is complete with all dharmas. All living beings can obtain it. That's why it is called the Great Cart! It is just the Great Vehicle, real wisdom. So the Buddha says, "Shariputra! At that time the Elder gave each of his sons equally a great cart." Every living being gets a cart. There is no partiality and no one is excluded. Everyone gets one. That's why *The Dharma Flower Sutra* is said to open the provisional to reveal the real. This is the wonderful doctrine of the Great Vehicle.

Sutra: T. 12c18.

"THE CART IS HIGH AND WIDE, ADORNED WITH A MULTITUDE OF INTERTWINING JEWELS, SURROUNDED BY RAILINGS, AND HUNG WITH BELLS ON ITS FOUR SIDES. FURTHER, IT IS COVERED WITH CANOPIES, ADORNED WITH VARIOUS RARE AND PRECIOUS JEWELS, STRUNG WITH JEWELED CORDS AND HUNG WITH FLOWERED TASSELS. THE CART IS HEAPED WITH BEAUTIFUL MATS AND SET ABOUT WITH ROSY CUSHIONS. IT IS YOKED TO AN OX, PLUMP AND WHITE AND OF FINE APPEARANCE, OF GREAT MUSCULAR STRENGTH, WHO WALKS WITH EVEN TREAD, AS FLEET AS THE WIND, HAVING ALSO MANY SERVANTS WHO FOLLOW AND GUARD IT."

Outline:

N2. Explaining the equality of the carts.

O1. Explaining the substance of the carts.

Commentary:

THE CART IS HIGH AND WIDE: Ultimately, how high and how wide is it? High and wide describes the appearance of the cart, but the cart itself is an analogy, so no one can tell exactly how high or wide it is. The cart is an analogy for the Great Vehicle Dharma.

Someone once said to me, "That person cultivates the Great Vehicle and that person cultivates the small vehicle."

I replied, "How big is the Great Vehicle? How small is the small vehicle? How big does it have to be before it qualifies as 'Great?' How small does it have to be before it is considered 'small?' Where do you draw the line?"

The Great Vehicle is so high you cannot see its top, and so broad you cannot see its borders. This, again, is an analogy. High and wide represent the knowledge and vision of the Thus Come One. The knowledge of the Thus Come One is all-wisdom, and the vision of the Thus Come One is the Buddha-eye. With his vision, there is nothing the Buddha fails to see; with his knowledge, there is nothing he doesn't know. Horizontally, its boundaries encompass the entire Dharma Realm. And how far do the boundaries of the Dharma Realm extend? There is nothing beyond them. No one can discover the borders of the Dharma Realm. No one can determine the boundaries of the Dharma Realm. Why not? Because the Dharma Realm includes the Three Thousand Great Thousand World systems within it.

Can we measure the Three Thousand Great Thousand Worlds in terms of numbers?

We cannot.

Therefore, horizontally the Thus Come One's knowledge and vision encompasses the borders of the Dharma Realm.

Vertically, it plumbs the depths of the Three Truths. The Three Truths are: the empty, the false, and the middle. These Three Truths include all the Buddhadharmas. Therefore, the knowledge and vision of the Thus Come One is complete with all the Buddhadharmas.

Thus, the cart is high and wide.

ADORNED WITH A MULTITUDE OF INTERTWINING JEWELS: The jewels are hooked together and strung as adornments. There are many different kinds of them strung together to adorn the cart and make it beautiful.

This, too, is an analogy. It represents the ten thousand practices adorning our Dharma body. "Adorned and intertwining" means that we must cultivate in order to perfect the ten thousand practices. If you don't cultivate, you can't perfect them. So the cart is adorned with a multitude of intertwining jewels, and this means that we must very reliably practice the methods of the ten thousand conducts.

SURROUNDED BY RAILINGS: According to the words of the text, we would say that the cart was surrounded by railings on all four sides. HUNG WITH BELLS ON ITS FOUR SIDES: These bells make beautiful sounds. These phrases are also analogies, as is the entire chapter. You can't explain them according to the literal meaning.

The Parable Chapter is the hardest chapter in the entire Sutra to explain and the hardest to understand. However, if you deeply enter the principles of the Sutra, then this chapter is the most valuable and the most important to explain. If you can understand the Parable Chapter of *The Lotus Sutra*, you will be able to understand the other chapters very easily.

You could also say that this was the easiest chapter to explain. How's that? If you understand it, it's easy! If you don't understand it, then it's very difficult. In fact, everything works this way.

The railings represent Dharani. Dharani is a Sanskrit word which means "uniting and holding." The phrase above "adorned with a multitude of intertwining jewels" referred to cultivation on the causal ground of the ten thousand conducts and the resulting fruit of the ten thousand virtues. "Surrounded by railings" represents the Dharani.

What are the uses of the Dharani? They are limitless and boundless. "Uniting" means that it unites all dharmas; it collects all dharmas together. "Upholding" means that is upholds limitless meanings. Dharani also means that you "unite and uphold" the three karmic vehicles, body, mouth, and mind, and commit no violations. You uphold all the Buddhadharmas. Why do we say that they surround the cart? This means that the Dharani can uphold the ten thousand good deeds. It also supresses the mass of evils. It supresses the mass of evils so that, without any outward manifestation, they are all eradicated. It supports all good deeds, so they can be done. This is what is meant by saying:

> Do no evil;
> Practice all good deeds.

The bells make a sound when they are struck or when they move. This represents the Four Types of Unobstructed Eloquence:

1. Unlimited eloquence in speech.

2. Unlimited eloquence in dharma.

3. Unlimited eloquence in meaning.

4. Unlimited eloquence in delight in speech.

As to the first, unlimited eloquence in speech, the poem I lectured earlier, "The Return" is a good example of a work by one who possessed this eloquence. Although a recluse, *T'ao Yüan-ming* still wrote this poem. He couldn't hide away. In fact, even today people still read his work. The things he said were phrased very well, and his words were moving. People who did not believe in the Buddhadharma were influenced to believe through his writing.

The second, unlimited eloquence in dharma, means that, although it may be the same dharma, one can express it in terms of the ten thousand dharmas. Then, one can bring it back to the one dharma.

It is said,

> The single root divides into
> ten thousand branches;
> The ten thousand branches
> return to the single root.

This means that one principle expands into limitless doctrines and those limitless doctrines again return to the one doctrine. Thus,

> One is all and all is one.

"All" come into being through the accumulation of many "ones." And where does the "one" come from? It appears out of the many. Therefore, one is many and many are one. There are no fixed dharmas. Whether you speak horizontally or vertically--no matter how you speak--it's still dharma.

The third is unobstructed eloquence in meaning. Meaning refers to the principles and what they mean. There are a great many of them. Yet the great number of meanings are just "no meanings." So there is unobstructed eloquence in dharma.

The fourth is unobstructed eloquence in delight in speech. The speaker of Dharma does not speak for those who are not interested. For those who are interested, he speaks the Dharma like flowing water. The doctrines he explains are limitless and endless, and he enjoys speaking the Dharma.

FURTHER, IT IS COVERED WITH CANOPIES: Beautiful silks and satins covered the cart. This is an analogy for the Four Unlimited Minds of the Buddha, kindness compassion, joy, and giving.

Kindness means to make living beings happy. Compassion means to relieve them of their sufferings. Joy means to rejoice in teaching and transforming living beings. Giving means that he gives to all poor living beings. The Buddha has great virtuous conduct because he has unlimited kindness, compassion, joy, and giving.

Of all the virtuous practices, kindness and compassion are the highest. They are the greatest, and so the Buddha protects all beings. The Sutra says, "With compassion you can perfect the Ten Powers and Four Fearlessnesses." This is the Thus Come One's compassion. The Buddha's kindness, compassion, joy, and giving are boundless. The canopies represent these Four Unlimited Minds. He cultivates the practices of the Four Unlimited Minds and therefore accomplishes his pure Brahma conduct.

ADORNED WITH VARIOUS RARE AND PRECIOUS JEWELS. This represents the cultivation of the ten thousand conducts in order to adorn the Four Unlimited Minds. The beauty of the cart means that in the Great Vehicle Dharma one must perfect the Six Perfections and the ten thousand conducts, that is, all the Dharma-doors to adorn the Great Vehicle Dharma.

STRUNG WITH JEWELED CORDS: This represents the Four Vast Vows:

1. I vow to save the infinite number of beings.

2. I vow to sever the endless afflictions.

3. I vow to study the limitless Dharma-doors.

4. I vow to realize the Supreme Buddha Way.

But the Four Vast Vows are not something simply to be

recited. You must actually put them into practice. You, personally, must do all you can to fulfill these Four Vows. If you just recite them, that's useless. You must return the light and reverse the illumination and ask yourself: "I have vowed to save the infinite number of beings. Have I saved any? If I have, well, that's the Bodhisattva Way. If I haven't, I better start saving them." However, when you save living beings, you must not become attached to the mark of saving living beings. Don't say, "I saved that one, and that one..." Separate from all marks, for that is the essence of the Dharma.

I vow to sever the endless afflictions. Ask yourself everyday, "Have I severed them or not? If not, I better." Unless you sever your afflictions, you will never be free of them.

How does one sever afflictions? It's not hard at all. It's not a matter of taking a knife and slicing them off. You should know that affliction is Bodhi. Affliction itself is Bodhi, just like ice is water and water is ice. All you need to do is melt the ice of your afflictions into the wisdom water of Bodhi and you will have severed those afflictions. Do not search for afflictions apart from Bodhi. Do not look for Bodhi apart from afflictions. They are one thing. If you know how to use it, it's Bodhi. If you don't know how to use it, it's affliction. Why do we say that living beings are the Buddha and the Buddha is living beings? When you have saved all living beings, you are a Buddha. If you haven't saved all living beings, you are still a living being. There is no difference between living beings and the Buddha. All you need to do is wake up and then you are a Buddha. When you are confused, you are a living being. Don't search outside of yourself for living beings to save. That's just seeking outwardly. When you have saved all the living beings in your own self nature, then you have saved all living beings.

The Sixth Patriarch's Sutra says, "I vow to save the infinite number of beings in the self nature." Why doesn't it refer to the infinite number of living beings in someone else's nature? It says "self nature" because all living beings are one. There is no "you" or "me" or "them." All are included within the self nature.

"I vow to sever the afflictions in the self nature." Note that it says "self" nature. You can't say, "Hey, you've studied the Buddhadharma for so long, how come you haven't severed your afflictions?"

If you had severed your own afflictions, you would not see the afflictions of others. When you have severed afflictions, then even when living beings have afflictions, you do not see them as afflictions. You just think, "Well, that's the way living beings are. If they weren't like that, they wouldn't be living beings. They can't change their basic make-up. Living beings are just living beings."

What about the Buddha? He's just the Buddha! The Buddha is not different from living beings.

> Enlightened, you are a Buddha.
> Confused, you are a living being.

There is no difference between enlightenment and confusion, either. If you are not confused, you are enlightened. If you are not enlightened, you are confused. There's no real difference. It's just like ice and water.

"I vow to study the limitless Dharma-doors." "Have I studied them? Ah...All I did today was sleep. I didn't do anything." You didn't do anything? You've got to study!

"I vow to realize the supreme Buddha Path." Have you realized it? No? Would you like to realize it?

"Well, let me think it over..." If you think it over, you'll have to wait another three great kalpas. If you don't think it over, you don't have to wait. You can become a Buddha tomorrow, because you don't have to think it over! If you are determined to become a Buddha, you will. Those who are determined are successful. The Buddha is just waiting for you to realize Buddhahood. If you don't want to, the Buddha won't force you to. You must want to cultivate the Dharma and accomplish the Buddha Path. If you haven't realized Buddhahood, you've got to cultivate. If you don't cultivate, you can't arrive at the position of Buddhahood.

HUNG WITH FLOWERED TASSELS: These represent the Four Methods of Conversion:

1. Giving,

2. kind words,

3. beneficial conduct,

4. cooperation.

It is said,

> If you want to lead them
> to the Buddha's wisdom,
> First bait the hook
> with something they like!

If you want them to develop the wisdom of a Buddha, you must first determine what it is they like. Then you give it to them to induce them into the Buddha's wisdom. For example, people like money. If you give them some money, that's practicing the giving of wealth. Then they will think, "I was broke and he gave me some money," and they will be very happy. At that time, if you speak some Dharma to them, they will accept it. You put the Dharma in second place, although normally it is first. You did this because they weren't happy and you wanted to make them happy first. You give them a little money and then, when they are delighted with it, you speak the Dharma. "Ah, that has principle. It really makes a lot of sense," they think. That is the giving of the Dharma. Then you give them fearlessness. You say, "Don't worry about it. Everything is going to work out. No need to be afraid..."

Kind words: This refers to compassionate concern, like that of parents for their children. They fear their child will catch cold, or get too warm, or be hungry or thirsty. Children like people to be kind to them and so the parents say, "I like you a lot; I am very fond of you." This kindness is also present in the Buddhadharma. When you speak, you don't talk about "love," but just say things they like to hear, things that make them happy. When you speak kindly to them, living beings are attracted to you.

Beneficial conduct is also a way of attracting living beings. It means doing things that benefit living beings. You do all kinds of good deeds to benefit living beings.

Cooperation: If you want to teach and transform a living being, you must be the same as he, be his friend. If he is a businessman, then you are a businessman. If he is a student, then you become a student. In general, you do the same kind of work that he does. Eventually, you will be able to convert him to Buddhism, to take him from confusion to enlightenment. When Bodhisattvas teach and transform living beings, they are willing to do anything at all. They are more concerned for living beings than parents are for their children. Bodhisattvas practice the Bodhisattva Path, cultivating the Four Methods of Conversion. In this way they attain four kinds of spiritual penetrations. The Four Methods of Conversion are also called the Four Spiritual Powers. They cause all living beings to be happy. Living beings may clearly be in error, but the Bodhisattvas want to save them, to take them across. They forgive them, they overlook their faults, hoping that in the future the living beings will be able to reform, hoping that they won't remain sunk in confusion forever. Wait a bit! So they don't see the faults of living beings. No matter what kind of mistake a living beings makes, the Bodhisattva is compassionate and doesn't blame him. Those are the Four Methods of Conversion. It's not that they just do those things, but they carry out their work with a miraculous functioning of spiritual powers. Living beings are taught and transformed without even being aware of it. Sometimes living beings make mistakes, and without their knowing quite how, their mistakes are corrected, and they are "like new." They don't know that the Bodhisattva, without any outward manifestation, influenced them with his virtue so that the mind of that being was able to change and reform. But some living beings can't be so influenced. The Bodhisattve still doesn't give up hope that in the future he will change. So the Four Dharmas of Conversion are ineffably wonderful.

We are all living beings. When we think about the compassionate protection afforded us by the Bodhisattvas, we should hurry and thank them, and tearfully repent of our past stupidity. "The Bodhisattvas are so good to me, and I still don't even realize it." Thus, in the Sutra text, the phrase, "hung with flowered tassels" is an analogy for the Four Methods of Conversion.

THE CART IS HEAPED WITH BEAUTIFUL MATS: There are beautiful mats spread out in the cart, layer upon layer. This is an analogy for the cultivation of skill in the Dhyanas. Everyday you steep yourself in the cultivation of contemplative Prajna. Eventually, you will have an accomplishment. "Heaped up" means that they are piled up and soft. This represents sitting in Dhyana and attaining the state of "light peace." This makes you feel especially happy. You feel extremely blissful. In this state you sit again and again and the feeling keeps returning, without interruption. When you walk you feel that it is like the wind, not that you are walking fast, but, before you have even taken a step, you arrive at where you are going. It's like a light breeze, and you don't even feel that you are walking.

> The gentle breeze passes by,
> But there are no waves on the water.

You are sitting there, but you don't feel like you are sitting. Standing, you don't know you are standing. Reclining, you don't know you are reclining. But this state must be cultivated in order to be obtained. It's a state in which there are no others and no self. You must work hard in order to understand its wonderful advantages. If you don't work hard, you won't be able to know them. I have explained a bit of it, but to taste the true flavor, you will have to discover it for yourself.

SET ABOUT WITH ROSY CUSHIONS: This is an analogy for the dharma of non-discrimination. There are inner cushions and outer cushions on the cart. The inner cushions are used inside the cart. The outer cushions are used when the cart is stopped. They are used to prop up the front of the cart so that it won't sit right on the ground. This represents the time in cultivation when one applies effort. At this time movement does not obstruct stillness, and stillness does not obstruct movement. Movement is just stillness and stillness is just movement. Movement and stillness are one substance. When the cart is moving, it moves; when it stops, it is still. But whether it is still or moving it's the same cart. When we cultivate the Way, in movement and in stillness we are still people. That's what the outer cushions represent.

The inner cushions are used to support the body when it sits or lies down to rest. The resting of the body and mind represents the single-conduct samadhi. In the single-conduct samadhi, one can give rise to genuine Prajna wisdom. That's the inner cushions.

YOKED TO AN OX, PLUMP AND WHITE: The ox is tied to the cart. This represents people when they have no outflows. Haven't I spoken before about the non-outflow Prajna wisdom? "Yoked to an ox" just means "no outflows." But this is no easy matter. Every habit and fault we have is called an outflow and all our thoughts of desire are outflows. Why don't we become Buddhas? It's because we have outflows. Why haven't we become enlightened? It's because we have outflows. Why is our habitual energy so heavy? It's because we have outflows. Why do we have desires? It's because we have outflows. If one has no outflows, then one is liberated. When one has obtained the non-outflow wisdom, if one cultivates the Four Truths, one succeeds in that cultivation. If you hold on to your non-outflow wisdom, you don't do things which reflect deviant knowledge and deviant views. If you cultivate the Twelve Causal Conditions, you realize them and become enlightened. If you cultivate the Six Perfections, you arrive at the other shore. In general, if you can look after your own household, that is what is meant by non-outflows.

What are "no-outflows?" In China there is a saying:

> Everyday, guard against fire;
> Every month, guard against thieves.

You have to watch over your own house. Guard against the fire of ignorance. When ignorance arises, one fears neither heaven nor earth nor spirits nor ghosts. "If a monster comes, I'll take him on!" Why does one act like that? Because the fire of ignorance has been lit. So we must guard against such fires of ignorance every day.

Every month one must guard against the thieves within one, not those on the outside. It is said, "It's hard to defend yourself from the thieves in your own house." If a thief comes from the outside, he won't know where you have put your treasures. If you've got a thief inside your house, however, he will know right where to go to steal your valuables. You must guard yourself from your eyes, ears, nose, tongue, body and mind--the six thieves. These six can turn your mind upside-down, and you get all afflicted. Isn't this pitiful? The eye, ear, nose, tongue, body and mind steal the Dharma treasures from your self nature. You let your house get out of control and you have outflows. Once the outflows start, they keep on flowing, and you end up just like everyone else. If you can maintain the non-outflow state you will certainly realize Buddhahood. Outflows, however, are very quick to start.

If you have no outflows, then you are yoked to a white ox cart. If you have outflows, then you haven't been yoked up to it. When I lectured on *The Heart Sutra*, one of the verses had a line which said:

The great white ox cart's
rapidly turning sound;
The yellow-faced child
jumping and thumping.

Your mind may jump and thump and race, but since it is yoked to the white ox cart, it doesn't get very far.

White is the base of all colors, the absence of any stain or defilment. It represents the basic substance of the Dharma which is pure and undefiled. It hasn't the least spot of dust on it, so it is white. It is interactive with the non-outflow wisdom. If there are defilements, there is no attainment. The great white ox cart represents the Four Applications of Mindfulness having been cultivated to the point of perfect accomplishment, to enlightenment.

The white ox also represents the Four Right Efforts:

1. Those good roots which have not come forth are caused to come forth.

2. Those good roots which have come forth are caused to grow.

3. Evil which has not come forth is caused not to come forth.

4. Evil which has already come forth is eradicated.

PLUMP AND WHITE: The two aspects of the good in the Four Right Efforts are represented by "plump." "White" represents the eradication of evil in the Four Right efforts.

The Four Bases of Psychic Power are:

1. Zeal,

2. Vigor,

3. Mindfulness, and

4. Consideration.

Zeal refers to the accomplishment of whatever you wish, that is, when it concerns the cultivation of the Buddhadharma. For example, if you wish to succeed in your cultivation, you will. Vigor: For example, one disciple wishes to bow to *The Dharma Flower Sutra* everyday. If he continues to keep his vow by bowing, he will perfect the psychic power of vigor. Thus, he will blaze a trail in Western Buddhism by doing things no one has ever done before.

With the psychic power of mindfulness things go just as your heart wishes them to go. Consideration means that you just think about them and you get your aim. But the Four Bases of Psychic Power must be based on the non-outflow wisdom. If you have outflows, you won't be able to succeed. You have to have no outflows, and this means no sexual desire. Sexual desire is the root of all outflows. If you have no sexual desire, that is the non-outflow wisdom. If you have sexual desire, you have not obtained the non-outflow wisdom.

AND OF FINE APPEARANCE: This represents the bringing forth of the Great Vehicle mind. All dharmas are complete in the mind and the mind indicates the total all-inclusive functioning of the Great Vehicle. The one word "mind" includes all dharmas.

OF GREAT MUSCULAR STRENGTH: The great white ox is powerful. Its muscles are large and strong. The muscles represent the Five Roots and the strength represents the Five Powers. The Five Roots are five kinds of good roots. Why are they called roots?

When the roots are deep,
the trunk is solid;
When the roots are solid,
the branches are luxuriant.

If the roots are deep the branches are lush. When the roots are solid, the branches and leaves are very beautiful. The Five Roots are:

1. Faith,

2. vigor,

3. mindfulness,

4. concentration, and

5. wisdom.

As to faith, the Buddhadharma is as vast as the sea and only by faith can one enter it. Therefore, faith is the root for studying Buddhism. You must have the root of faith. If you have faith, you can send down deep roots. Although I lecture on the Buddhadharma for you everyday, you still must believe it and send down your own roots.

Vigor: You can't just believe, you have to be vigorous and make progress. If you are not vigorous, and just believe without practicing, it's useless. You must go forward and practice.

Mindfulness: You must have presence of mind and never forget to practice. If you have the root of mindfulness, then you must not be moved.

Samadhi: You may think, "The Buddhadharma's not bad. I'll go save a few living beings and get them to believe in Buddhism." But as soon as you get near some living being, he says, "Christianity is the very best religion. Catholicism is the very best. Come and study with us." Since you have no samadhi, you become one of their converts! They transform you. You don't transform them. This happens because you have no samadhi. If you had samadhi, you would save those you wished to save and wouldn't be "saved" by them.

Wisdom: Out of the root of samadhi comes wisdom. When the root of wisdom is sent down then you are even less easily moved.

The Five Powers are just the Five Roots which have grown. The roots grow into the powers. Thus the Five Powers are the Powers of faith, vigor, mindfulness, samadhi and wisdom.

With the Five Powers, by means of the non-outflow wisdom, you can accomplish all kinds of good roots, and all kinds of Bodhi seeds and grow to fulfillment.

WHO WALKS WITH EVEN TREAD: Because the ox has great muscular strength his walk is steady. He never takes a wrong step. This represents the equality of samadhi and wisdom. If one has wisdom one also has samadhi, and if one has samadhi one also has wisdom. Samadhi and wisdom are evenly balanced. As one's samadhi increases so does one's wisdom, and as one's wisdom increases, so does one's samadhi. They are balanced. If you have samadhi and no wisdom you will be a stupid cultivator. If you have wisdom but no samadhi, you will become a frenzied cultivator. You must let wisdom aid samadhi and samadhi aid wisdom. They should support each other.

The even tread also represents the Seven Limbs of Enlightenment, also called the Seven Bodhi Shares, or seven Dharma-doors for enlightening to the Way. They are among the Thirty-seven Wings of Enlightenment which the Buddha taught those of the Two Vehicles.

However, the Great Vehicle includes them as well. The Thirty-seven Wings of Enlightenment are composed of:

1. The Four Applications of Mindfulness.

2. The Four Right Efforts.

3. The Four Bases of Psychic Power.

4. The Five Roots.

5. The Five Powers.

6. The Seven Limbs of Enlightenment.

7. The Eight Sagely Way Shares (the Eightfold Path)

The first of the Seven Limbs of Enlightenment is that of:

1. Selecting a dharma. In selecting a dharma, one chooses between the right and wrong dharmas, the proper and improper dharmas, true and false dharmas, real and illusory dharmas. How do you select them? You use the non-outflow wisdom and the Selective Dharma Eye to pick the dharma. We must pick out true, proper, real, and good dharmas to cultivate. Improper, false, and deviant dharmas should be avoided.

2. Vigor. Having selected a dharma, one must vigorously cultivate it. You must be vigorous in your cultivation of genuine dharmas, not in cultivation of false dharmas. If you are vigorous in cultivating false dharmas, that is just false vigor. You must have the Enlightenment Share of Vigor which just means that you need to understand what road it is you need to walk down in your cultivation.

3. Happiness. There is both proper and improper happiness. If you cultivate correctly, you will gain proper happiness. Some people obtain a kind of insane happiness. When this happens, you follow your insane desires and do insane things; you feel very happy, but you are actually just upside-down. You should take joy in both Dhyana and Dharma, take the joy of Dhyana as your food and be filled with the delight of Dharma. You should be happy to have obtained the Buddhadharma. You should think, "Before, I didn't understand the Buddhadharma at all. Now I understand all these principles and they

are so lofty and profound! I am truly happy!"

Those are the first three of the Seven Limbs of Enlightenment. There are four more:

4. Casting out. You must determine what is true and what is false. Keep the true, but get rid of the false. What is false? Afflictions. Cut off afflictions.

5. Renunciation. You must renounce those things which you should not hold on to. For example, when sitting in Dhyana, you can't get attached to the advantages gained thereby. Some people sit in Dhyana and get a bit of a state and promptly become attached to it. They can't put it down and constantly hanker after that happy state. When you have cast it aside, you need...

6. Samadhi. Samadhi refers to Dhyana samadhi. In cultivation when one is not attached to anything, then one gains accomplishment in the skill of Dhyana samadhi. Once you have this accomplishment, you have got the Enlightenment Share of Samadhi.

In other, non-Buddhist, religions, they "hold to a quiet darkness." This means that they supress the thoughts of the mind-consciousness so that they do not arise. This is a type of samadhi cultivated by external religions and you should avoid it. You must cultivate proper samadhi. And what is proper samadhi? If means not being attached to anything. If you have proper knowledge and proper views, you will then have proper samadhi.

The first three of the Limbs of Enlightenment are to be used when you feel depressed or drowsy. The second three are to be used when you are nervous or upset. The ability to use the first six to counteract these mental states is called the Enlightenment Limb of...

7. Mindfulness. Cultivators should know about the Seven Limbs of Enlightenment. Those who have brought forth the Bodhi heart should cultivate according to them. By means of these seven, one regulates the body and mind so that they are free of all danger. That is what is meant by "who walks with even tread." It is a manifestation of his spiritual skill.

AS FLEET AS THE WIND: The great white ox is pulling the cart as fast as the wind. There are many different kinds of winds. Hurricanes blow people and things right away. Everyone likes light breezes, however. This wind is not a light wind or a hurricane. On the other hand, you could say that is is both a light wind and a hurricane. Why? It's a light wind because it makes you feel refreshed and comfortable. It's a hurricane because it blows away the deviant knowledge and views of demons and externalists. The light breeze is also an analogy for the Eight Sagely Way Shares (the Eightfold Path). One should cultivate according to these eight:

1. Right views. If you have deviant knowledge and deviant views, you can't accept the Buddhadharma. You must have right knowledge and right views. Using the non-outflow wisdom, you break through all deviant knowledge and views to cultivate right knowledge and views. Right views means, "If it's not in accord with propriety, don't look at it."

2. Right thought. This means, "If it is not in accord with propriety, don't listen to it." Why would you think about it? Because you listened to it.

3. Right speech means "If it is not in accord with propriety, don't talk about it." Don't gossip.

Even if you know very clearly that someone is at fault, forgive them. People are just people, after all. If people didn't make mistakes, they would all have become Buddhas long ago. People have heavy habits and no one can avoid doing a few things wrong. So don't talk about people's faults. That's right speech. Don't get together with your friends and sit in judgement on other people. People in this world come together because of affinities. We have met here to study the Buddhadharma together so we should look at people's good points, not at their mistakes.

"But if they are wrong and refuse to change, then what will we do?"

Don't worry about whether or not they will change. Just have faith that they will. If you confront them head on with, "You're wrong!" they will resist. "Who are you to tell me what to do?" they will fire back. "I'll just boss you around instead, because I can see a few places where you are off--" and then the fight is on! Each one says the other is wrong when actually they are both in the wrong. They both get upset and then retreat from the Bodhi mind. "To heck with it. I'm not going to cultivate the Way. I'm leaving. I'm not going to leave home. I'm going back to lay-life!!"

How much offense karma have you created here? So speak properly and don't just talk about other's faults.

4. Right action. This means that you do proper things. "If it is not in accord with propriety, don't do it." Don't do deviant things like going into the gambling business and developing spiritual powers in the number's racket. That's deviant action.

What is right action? Sitting in Dhyana meditation without any false thinking. Studying the Buddhadharma. that is the most proper form of action.

"But," you ask, "if I study the Buddhadharma, where will I get food to eat?"

You shouldn't worry about that. If you study well, you will naturally have food to eat.

5. Right livelihood. During your life, you should do things properly, out in the open. As to deviant forms of earning a living, there are five types:

A. Manifesting a strange style. This means to act eccentrically. For example, a man wearing flowers in his hair walking around on the streets would attract attention. Or perhaps one wears some outlandish costume to attract a lot of attention to oneself.

B. Speaking of one's own merit and virtue. "I built a temple here. I built a bridge over there. I gave to this and that cause..." No one knows how great their merit and virtue is.

C. Telling fortunes. Perhaps you consult the *I-ching* for someone and say, "Oh no! You're really in for it. Tomorrow you are going to die! If you don't give me several hundred or several thousand dollars, you are going to lose your life." The person hears this and thinks, "What use will my money be to me if I am dead? Might as well give it to him and live a little longer." Thus he has been cheated out of his life savings. Or you say, "In the future you are going to be the President, but right now you have to do some merit and virtue. Give me five thousand dollars and do something good for me and I will guarantee your future success." The fellow thinks, "Gee, that is really cheap to be President," and he gives him the five thousand and waits to become President. By the time he realizes he will be waiting forever, the person he gave the money to has disappeared. He's gone somewhere else, or perhaps he's died. He could predict the other person's death, but he was unable to predict his own. This is just cheating people.

D. Speaking loudly and acting in an overbearing manner. The person speaks in booming tones so that those who hear him think he is very unusual. They respect him and make offerings to him.

E. Speaking of one's own offerings. "Oh, so and so gave me five hundred thousand dollars, and so and so gave me a million. They really believe in me." But you just talk that way to get someone else to make offerings to you. "They made offerings, you should too." This is climbing on conditions, trying to get offerings. All of you should listen carefully. When did I ever say, "So and so made offerings to me..." When I do, you will know that I am guilty of using a method of deviant livelihood and you shouldn't make offerings to me.

6. Right vigor. Some people are vigorous in proper ways and others in deviant ways. What is proper vigor? What is deviant vigor? Deviant dharmas harm other people. Those who cultivate deviant dharmas work very hard in the six periods of the day and night, cultivating all kinds of ascetic practices. These ascetic practices, however, are unbeneficial. They may imitate the behavior of cows or of dogs, and practice being like chickens. They imitate cows and eat grass and say they are being vigorous because cows eat grass all day long. This happens because they saw that a cow was born in the heavens. They didn't realize it was because of the merit and virtue which the cow had done in previous lives. They thought the cow was born in heaven because it ate grass! So they take a cow for their teacher. The cow has no understanding of dharma whatsoever, and if you study with a cow, that is called improper vigor. As to studying with a dog... Hah! They say that dogs watch over the door for people and that brings merit. Dogs eat excrement and that is a form of ascetic practice. So they imitate dogs. They also imitate chickens. Chickens go looking for food, pecking on the ground, and so they do this, too. They pretend that their hands are chicken legs, and they peck at the ground. They think this is an ascetic practice, that they can do something no one else can do. Actually, this is just an unbeneficial type of ascetic practice. Although it is unbeneficial, they

won't admit it as such. They think it's cultivation. They are not properly vigorous and they have no genuine wisdom. That is why they observe the morality of cows, dogs, and chickens.

Right vigor means to cultivate according to the Buddha's Four Applications of Mindfulness, Four Right Efforts, Four Bases of Psychic Power, Five Roots, Five Powers, the Seven Limbs of Enlightenment, the Eightfold Path, the Four Holy Truths, and the Twelve Causal Conditions. Cultivating according to the Six Perfections is also right vigor. Right vigor means to cultivate according to the Buddhadharma. One does not cultivate dharmas which the Buddha did not teach. This is called offering up your conduct in accord with the Buddha's instructions. Right vigor means vigor with the body and vigor with the mind. Mental vigor means recollecting the Triple Jewel, not neglecting it for a second. Vigor with the body means putting the teachings into actual practice. For example, bowing to the Buddha, reading the Sutras, bowing to Sutras, and bowing repentence ceremonies and reciting the Buddha's name are all manifestations of bodily vigor, actual upholding of the Buddhadharma.

7. Right mindfulness. This means mindfulness of the Buddha, the Dharma, and the Sangha. Deviant mindfulness means mindfulness of deviant views, prejudiced views, love and emotion. Deviant mindfulness means always thinking about yourself first. Right mindfulness means that whenever we have time we should recollect the Buddha, reciting, "Namo Amitabha Buddha," or "Namo Medicine Master Buddha," or "Namo Shakyamuni Buddha." We should recite the Great Compassion Master, the Great Vehicle Sutras--all these dharmas. There are several laywomen here to go to work all day and then skip dinner to come here at night and recite Sutras. That's right mindfulness.

Mindfulness of the Sangha. What Sangha? The worthy sages of the Sangha of the ten directions. Who are they? The great Bodhisattvas, Arhats, and Bhikshus. Now, in the world, all who have left the homelife are members of the Sangha. If you are mindful of the Sangha, you will make offerings to them. If you are mindful of the Dharma, you make offerings to the Dharma. If you are mindful of the Buddha, you make offerings to the Buddha. If you don't want to forget the Triple Jewel, you must make offerings to the Triple Jewel. By respectfully making offerings to the Triple Jewel, you plant blessings. If you want to have fields of blessings, you must plant them by making offerings to the Triple Jewel. There is a saying that goes:

> Although one can't plant blessings
> with the common Sangha,
> If you want blessings, you must
> seek them from the common Sangha.
> Although a clay dragon can't bring rain,
> If you want rain, you must seek it
> from a clay dragon.

The "common Sangha" refers to ordinary left-home people, those who have not certified to the fruit. Although they can't bring you blessings, when you seek blessings, you must seek them from the common Sangha. If you seek blessings from them with a sincere heart, then the sagely Sangha of the ten directions will naturally send you blessings. If you don't seek blessings from the common Sangha and go looking for the sagely Sangha, you can look to the ends of the horizon, to the end of the ocean, and you won't find one. If you seek blessings, you must start by seeking them from the common Sangha.

The "clay dragon" can't make rain. However, if you want rain, you have to seek for rain at the temple of a clay dragon. Westerners probably aren't familiar with this method, but in China when people want rain, they seek it by going to a dragon king temple. In the temple there is a clay dragon. If you seek rain there, you will gain a response. It will rain. Now, in the scientific age, they say that people don't have control over the rain. They say rain comes from condensation in the atomosphere. That is correct, but the condensation has no life of its own. It's like a computer. Unless someone operates the computer, it can't compute. The same principle applies. The rain comes from condensation, but still, imperceptibly, in a way people cannot see, the spirits and dragons are controlling it. But this is not something we common folk with our science can understand through research. Really, the rain is caused by the dragons!

"I've never seen any dragons," you say. "How can they make it rain?"

Well, if you haven't seen any dragons, we will just have to wait until you do and then I'll explain to you how it works. Now, you haven't seen any so I won't tell you about them. However, I remember when I was in Manchuria a very strange thing happened. I had a disciple there named Kuo-hsün. He worked hard at his cultivation and was even more sincere than I am! He was my favorite disciple. One day, he built himself a small hut. Beside it there was the Dragon King Temple. When he had finished building the hut, he asked me to perform the opening ceremonies. On opening day, ten dragons came over from the temple nextdoor and asked to take refuge with the Triple Jewel. Would you say this was strange or not? I had four disciples with me at the time and two of them had the Buddha Eye and the Heavenly Eye. When they meditated, they could observe all kinds of things. After the ten dragons asked to take refuge, I said to them, "It's been several months since there's been any rain. You're dragons. Why don't you make it rain. Why are you so lazy?"

They wanted to take refuge and so when I scolded them they didn't get angry. They said, "The Jade Emperor, Shakra, gives us orders to make it rain. If he tells us to make it rain then we can do it."

I said to the dragons, "Tell him that in the world here there is a left-home person by the name of so-and-so who is now asking for rain within a radius of forty miles from where he is. If it rains tomorrow, I will let you take refuge the day after tomorrow. If it doesn't rain tomorrow you can't take refuge, you can't be my disciples, and you can't take refuge with the Triple Jewel."

They went right up into the heavens with my message which turned out to be very efficacious. The next day, in fact, it rained and, what is most strange, it rained right within a forty-mile radius of where I was. There was no rain outside of forty miles. The day after, I let them take refuge. That's my experience with dragons and rain. But this is something that, although I personally experienced it, those who don't believe it far outnumber those who do. Ultimately, why is this? I don't know either! I don't pay any attention to whether or not people believe it. I just bring it up for your information. In the future, when you come to believe in it, you will know that what I told you today was really true.

There was another similar experience I had while in Hong Kong. One year Hong Kong had no rain during the spring and summer. All the temples, Buddhahalls, and places of cultivation were praying for rain. They sought for four or five months and didn't get any. I originally didn't pay attention to such matters, because I have never liked to get involved in things like that. Besides, there were so many people seeking for rain, surely their power would be greater than mine. So I ignored the whole thing. But after five or six months I couldn't ignore it any longer, because I was living at Hsi Le-yüan where the water was almost dried up. I said to one of my disciples,"You have three days in which to recite 'Namo Amitabha Buddha,' and seek for rain. If it doesn't rain in three days, you need not come back and see me ever again."She very obediently recited and after two days it rained. Then what do you think happened? All the Buddha Halls in Hong Kong advertised that the rain was a result of their having prayed for it. They all took out ads. Not a single person knew that the rain had come as a result of the recitation of my disciple. She never advertised it. Why did I give her three days to get rain? Because I knew I had ten dragon disciples, and if they were not lazy any one of them could make it rain. I told them to make it rain and sure enough in rained inside of two days. Things like this have happened often. One time we were making offerings to the heavens and the rain clouds gathered. Everyone said, "Call off the ceremony. It's going to rain." It takes four hours to do the ceremony and right after we were done and had just moved everything inside, it started pouring down rain! Whether you believe or not, if you have experienced these things, you know. In Hong Kong my disciples really believe in me. They know that when I say something it is efficacious.

Tomorrow is the first day of the fifth month and the fourth month (April) has already passed. I said there wouldn't be an earthquake in the fourth month and sure enough, my words were efficacious. There are a lot of causes and conditions involved in this, but there's not time to go into them now.

Once you have right mindfulness, you need...

8. Right concentration. Right concentration is the opposite of deviant concentration. What is deviant concentration? It's attached. You can't put it down. For example, some people like to drink and although you tell them not to, they continue to drink with great concentration because they have this deviant concentration. Or they like to take drugs. The more they take the stupider they get. When you tell them not to, they say, "I can get enlightened taking this stuff. When I take this, things really start happening. I go through changes. I see and hear differently. The world becomes adorned with the seven jewels. Isn't that a state?" It's deviant concentration, that's what it is! For example, one person came here to listen to the lecture,

but not a word could get in because he had his deviant concentration going and he was very attached. "I'm right! I can't listen to you!" That's deviant knowledge, deviant views, and deviant concentration.

Then what is right concentration? Right concentration is the cultivation of the Four Dhyanas, the Eight Samadhis. Don't have a self at all. Cultivate these Dharmas, but forget your "self." If you have forgotten your "self" how could you still keep on drinking, taking drugs, and indulging yourself? Everyone looks for advantages for themselves, but people who cultivate the Ch'an School forget about advantages. That's right concentration.

HAVING ALSO MANY SERVANTS WHO FOLLOW AND GUARD IT: The servants represent expedient Dharma-doors, the paramita of expedients. By means of expedient Dharmas, one arrives at the other shore. What are expedients? What are servants? Expedient Dharmas are those which are indirect and which accord with people's wishes. How do they do this? Say people do a certain kind of work, and you go help them out. That's being expedient. The heavenly demons and outside religions and those of the Two Vehicles cannot get away from expedients but follow the wisdom of expedients in their cultivation of the Way.

The servants can also be said to represent the spiritual powers gained on the result-ground by the Bodhisattvas. The result-ground Bodhisattvas have already certified to the fruit and attained to the position of the ten grounds. That is what is meant by "result" ground. These Bodhisattvas all have spiritual powers and their spiritual powers accord with the wishes in their minds. They can do whatever they think to do. This spiritual power is as their minds wish it to be and so the text says, "Having many servants who follow and guard it." This means that the Great Vehicle Dharma requires many expedients to bring it to accomplishment. With these spiritual powers, one can do anything at all. It's like having a lot of servants.

Looked at from the point of view of "contemplation of the mind," in this passage of text we observe each thought in the mind: Vertically speaking, the thoughts which come from our mind have no former or latter aspect and no beginning or end. Horizontally speaking, our mind has no boundary. The thoughts present in our mind reveal the truth of emptiness, the truth of the false, and the truth of the middle way. Because they contain all three truths, the cart is said to be broad and high.

The thoughts present in our minds also contain the Ten Dharma Realms. None of the Ten Dharma Realms go beyond the thoughts present in the mind. The cart is said to be broad, as are the Ten Realms. The virtuous qualities within our self-nature are more numerous that the grains of sand in the Ganges River. So the cart is "adorned with a multitude of intertwining jewels." The many virtuous qualities of the nature are the "multitude." The basic substance of those virtuous qualities is jewel-like, and so they are like a multitude of intertwining jewels.

As to the mind: Outside of the mind, there are no dharmas. Outside of the dharmas, there is no mind:

> The Buddha spoke all dharmas,
> for the minds of living beings;
> If there were no minds,
> what use would dharmas be?

The mind is just the dharma and the dharmas are just the mind. What are "outside Ways?" They are those who seek for the dharma outside the mind. Since there are no dharmas outside the mind, the mind includes both worldly and transcendental dharmas. That is what is represented in the text by "surrounded by railings."

"Hung with bells on its four sides" represents that the mind can universally influence all things. It proclaims the sounds of the teaching. None of them go beyond one thought of the mind.

"Further, it is covered with canopies." This represents the thoughts present in the mind. The mind is the most wonderful thing among all the dharmas. It includes all dharmas within it. There are no dharmas which are not inside the mind. The mind "covers" all dharmas, and so is represented by the canopies.

As to the mind, there are mind-king dharmas, and subsidiary mind dharmas. The eighth consciousness, also called the mind-king, sometimes performs an observation. When it does this, the subsidiary mind dharmas all respond to it and follow its orders. This is what is meant by "adorned with various rare and precious jewels." This is lecturing according to the contemplation of the mind.

As to subsidiary mind dharmas, when the wholesome subsidiary mind dharmas react favorably with the remaining subsidiary mind dharmas in an uninterrupted fashion, this is represented by the phrase "strung with jeweled cords."

From out of the wholesome subsidiary mind dharmas, limitless wisdom arises and limitless blessings and virtues are realized; this is represented by the phrase, "hung with flowered tassels."

Further, that thought present in the mind is complete with pliant and light dharmas; not only is it replete with pliant and light dharmas, it is complete with all dharmas. It is complete with all dharmas--multilayered and without end. Layer after layer, you could never speak of them all. It's just that thought present in the mind which has such a versatile functioning. This is represented by the phrase, "heaped with beautiful mats."

Take another look at the mind. It itself is movement; it is also stillness. It can move and it can be still. Movement does not obstruct stillness and stillness does not obstruct movement. Movement and stillness are one suchness, non-dual. The singularity of the suchness and their non-duality is represented by the phrase "set about with rosy cushions."

"Yoked to an ox..." If you observe it at a deeper level, the doctrine of the mind is manifest through the wonderful observing wisdom, and this is represented by the phrase "yoked to a white ox."

"Plump and white..." The merit and virtue of the nature is subtle and inconceivable; this is represented by the word "plump." If in the mind there is no affliction, then it is "white." It's color is pure. Why? Because in your mind there is no admixture of ignorance or affliction.

The mind is complete with perfect penetration and comfort; this is represented by the phrase "of fine appearance."

"Of great muscular strength..." This wisdom of perfect contemplation can produce all good roots. The perfect contemplation can eradicate love and views within the Three Realms. Because love and views are upside-down, it takes great strength to eradicate them.

The perfect contemplation is the non-duality of samadhi and wisdom. Wisdom is samadhi and samadhi is just wisdom. Wisdom and samadhi perfectly interpenetrate; this is represented by the phrase "who walks with even tread."

The perfect contemplation easily arrives at the other shore; this is represented by the phrase "as fleet as the wind." This perfect contemplation leads all the subsidiary mind dharmas, controls them all; this is represented by the phrase "having also many servants who follow and guard it."

Sutra: T.12c24

"AND WHY IS THIS? THAT GREAT ELDER HAS LIMITLESS WEALTH AND ALL MANNER OF STOREHOUSES FULL TO OVERFLOWING."

Outline:

O2. Explaning the source of the carts.

Commentary:

Having explained that the cart was so high and broad, with little bells hanging from the four sides and covered with canopies and rare treasures, the question is raised, AND WHY IS THIS? THAT GREAT ELDER, the Buddha, HAS LIMITLESS WEALTH AND ALL MANNER OF STOREHOUSES FULL TO OVERFLOWING. The wealth refers to Dharma treasures, Dharma-doors taught by the Buddha.

The storehouses refer to all kinds of jewel-treasuries filled with precious things. These treasuries are all the Dharmas. This is an analogy for all the Dharmas. In general, you could say there are Six Perfections and Ten Thousand Conducts. The Six Perfections are giving, morality, patience, vigor, Dhyana samadhi, and wisdom. These six are not just to be recited in order to perfect them. We can't just learn to rattle off the names and think we understand them. You have to practice them. You have to give. You can give wealth, Dharma, or fearlessness--but you have to *do* it. "Morality" means to do no evil and to practice all good. Patience...well, that's the hardest. Giving is pretty easy. Morality is not too hard. But patience is the hardest of all. Why? In order to be patient you have to empty yourself of your concept of "self." Otherwise, you can't be patient. Patience means taking the hard things easy. If people are not good to you, you must act as if they were being good to you.

"But that's just being stupid!" you may object.

Students of the Buddhadharma should not act too smart. If you are too smart, you've gone overboard. If you have no mark of self, no attachment to self, no view of self, then you can be patient. If you think, "Before I was born, who was I? Now that I have been born, who am I? Where did this 'me' come from? It's just an empty name. When I blink my eyes and the dream ends, then who will I be? When I die, where will I go? Who will I be then?" then you can bear what is hard to bear. If you always look on the "self" as empty, then you can easily bear up. Although people are bad to you, you won't feel that it is any problem. If you study the Buddhadharma, you can't just listen to it. In order to understand it, you must actually practice it. If you just eat candy all day long, and it's really sweet, thinking you are being patient with your eating of candy, you are fooling yourself. It takes something you don't like, some vexing situation, then you act as if nothing were the matter. It's no problem. It doesn't phase you because you really understand and you have control over it. That's what patience is all about. But it's not easy to be that way. If you can do it, you have grasped the essential message of *The Wonderful Dharma Lotus Flower Sutra*. Don't look upon your "self" as so important. That "self" in the future is going to die. Why scramble to get the best for it? Why compete for fame and profit? You should look on the mark of self as empty. There is no self.

"What if someone slugs me?" you ask. "What do I do then?"

Think of it this way: "In the past I must have hit that person, and so he is hitting me now. If I didn't hit him in this life, I must have hit him or scolded him in a previous life. Last year during the Summer Session, I said that if in this life you scold people, in your next life you will be beaten. If you beat people in this life, in a future life you may be murdered. If in this life you pester people, in a future life, they will pester you. Former cause and latter effect are very severe.

You say, "I don't believe it."

You don't? Do you have troubles? If you do, that's where they came from. You can't be patient. You can't put everything down. Whether you believe it or not, that's the way it is!

"But why is it so severe?" you ask.

If you put money in a bank, over a period of time it will collect interest. If you scold people and give them a lot of trouble, they are going to collect a little interest, too. If, in a former life, you scolded people, they may beat you in this life. If you beat them, they may kill you. If you kill someone, they may end up killing your entire household. The retribution is very severe. That is why cultivators should always refrain from giving others trouble. Watch over yourself. Don't be aggressive and make trouble for no reason.

If someone beats or scolds you, you may try to act as if there were no self, but then you feel: "Well... here I am, I mean...I'm in my body right here. I have feelings, you know. How can I have no self? How can I put it down?"

There's a wonderful Dharma here and I'll tell you what it is: If someone hits you, you can just think, "Oh, gees, I ran into the wall. I wasn't looking where I was walking..." or "Something fell on me." If a brick fell on you you wouldn't want to hit the brick. If you did that, you hand as well as your foot would hurt. If you fight it, it's going to hurt more. If you don't, if you pretend nothing happened, that you ran into the door or whatever, then it's all over. It's hard to listen to someone scold you, but you can just pretend you don't understand them. "Oh, he's speaking Japanese or Spanish or something. I have no idea what he's talking about." Or else you can think, "He's praising me! His scolding is just a song. He's making music!" Think of ways to cope with it, and then you will have no anger or affliction. If you get afflicted that means you have a karmic obstacle. People without karmic obstacles do not have afflictions. Those with afflictions have karmic obstacles. Since you have karmic obstacles, you should find ways to eradicate them. In this world there's nothing that is unbearable if you really know how to practice patience. I have often told you about Maitreya Bodhisattva's verse, which, no doubt, all of you have rejected, thinking it too silly; but since you don't want it, I'll just give it to you again:

The Old Fool wears ragged robes,
And fills himself with tasteless food,
And mends his clothes to keep out the cold,
Just letting things take their course.

Should someone scold the Old Fool,
The Old Fool just says, "Fine."
Should someone hit the Old Fool,
He just lays down to sleep.

Spit right in his face,
He just lets it dry,
Saving his energy
And giving you no affliction.

This kind of paramita
Is the jewel in the wonderful.

Having heard this news,
Why worry about not realizing the Way?

If you can't perfect patience, it's because you can't put down your "self." Your "self" is bigger than Mount Sumeru, and there's no place to put it because it won't fit anywhere! Wherever you put it, that place is filled up. You must put your "self" down. Then you can understand the Buddhadharma. Those who understand the Buddhadharma cultivate patience. We who study the Buddhadharma must take care to cultivate it. Otherwise when something happens you won't be on top of it, and the fire of ignorance will blaze thirty thousand feet in the air, burning off all your merit and virtue.

Firewood gathered in a thousand days,
Burns up in a single spark's blaze.

One match can burn it all up. Cultivating patience is very important.

Not to speak of other people, you might think I have no problems in this line, but actually a lot of people berate me. But if you want to scold me or hit me, go right ahead. There was a person who came and bullied me until there was nothing I could do but bow to him! And he was one of my disciples! Now that's a first in the history of Buddhism, but I won't mention his name or else you will all start bowing to him and that wouldn't be too good.

Sutra: T.12c25

"SO HE REFLECTS THUS: 'MY POSSESSIONS ARE BOUNDLESS. I SHOULD NOT GIVE MY CHILDREN SMALL OR INFERIOR CARTS. ALL OF THESE YOUNGSTERS ARE MY CHILDREN WHOM I LOVE WITHOUT PARTIALITY. HAVING SUCH GREAT CARTS MADE OF THE SEVEN JEWELS, INFINITE IN NUMBER, I SHOULD GIVE THEM TO EACH ONE EQUALLY. WHY? IF I GAVE THEM TO AN ENTIRE

COUNTRY, THEY WOULD NOT RUN SHORT; HOW MUCH THE LESS IF I GAVE THEM TO MY CHILDREN!"

Outline:

N3. Explaining the equality of the mind.

Commentary:

SO HE REFLECTS THUS, the Elder thinks like this, "MY POSSESSIONS ARE BOUNDLESS. Nothing is higher or more valuable than my Dharmas. I SHOULD NOT GIVE MY CHILDREN SMALL OR INFERIOR CARTS. I should not use Small Vehicle Dharmas to cross over all living beings, all the thirty children, the Sound Hearers, Conditionally Enlightened Ones and the Bodhisattvas. NOW ALL OF THESE YOUNGSTERS: The children represent those of the Three Vehicles who have not been cultivating the Way for very long. They are just beginners, like children without much experience. Even though they don't have a lot of common sense, still THEY ARE MY CHILDREN WHOM I LOVE WITHOUT PARTIALITY. I love all my children. The Buddha has no partiality towards any living being one way or the other. His compassion is impartial. HAVING SUCH GREAT CARTS MADE OF THE SEVEN JEWELS, INFINITE IN NUMBER: The Seven Limbs of Enlightenment, the Eightfold Path, the Five Roots, Five Powers, Four Bases of Psychic Power, Four Right Efforts, Four Applications of Mindfulness, the Thirty-seven Wings of Enlightenment adorn the Great Vehicle Buddhadharma. I SHOULD GIVE THEM TO EACH ONE EQUALLY: Every kid should get a cart. There should be no discrimination. WHY? IF I GAVE THEM TO AN ENTIRE COUNTRY THEY WOULD NOT RUN SHORT. The country represents the Land of Eternal Still Light and Purity. "Run short" means that the Buddhadharma never runs out. HOW MUCH THE LESS IF I GAVE THEM TO MY CHILDREN! If I gave them to everyone in the country, there would still be carts leftover. How much the less would they run short if I gave them to my children with whom I have such a great affinity. So now, I certainly will give each one a Great White Ox Cart.

Everyone should take a look at himself. See whether or not you have afflictions. If you have no afflictions, then you have obtained the Buddhadharma. If you still have afflictions, you have to go forward and cultivate reliably. If you keep getting angry all the time, that means you have to look more deeply into the Buddhadharma. At whatever time you cease to have afflictions, that will be the time you have obtained the good points of the Buddhadharma. This is very important.

Sutra: T.13a1

"MEANWHILE, ALL OF THE CHILDREN ARE RIDING AROUND ON THE GREAT CARTS, HAVING GOT WHAT THEY NEVER EXPECTED TO HAVE, BEYOND THEIR ORIGINAL HOPES."

Outline:

M4. Parable of the children attaining the carts and rejoicing.

Commentary:

MEANWHILE, that is, when the Elder gave away the great carts. If he had limitless wealth, but they were not his children, he would not have given the great carts away. If they were his children, but he didn't have any wealth, he also wouldn't have given them away. But now, the Elder has the wealth, limitless treasuries, and they are overflowing. The children are true disciples of the Buddha and so the Buddha gives them all a great cart. This is because the children originally had no hopes of getting a great cart. They were hoping for deer carts or sheep carts and that alone would have satisfied them. They would have played in them happily. But now the Elder, because he is so wealthy, gives each of them a great cart. This is using the Great Vehicle Dharma to save living beings. All of the children had not had such great hopes. Now they have all obtained the great carts, the beautiful and expensive white ox carts, so ALL OF THE CHILDREN ARE RIDING AROUND ON THE GREAT CARTS, HAVING GOT WHAT THEY NEVER EXPECTED TO HAVE, BEYOND THEIR ORIGINAL HOPES. They had never before seen anything so fine. They had never had such fine toys. This is beyond their wildest dreams. They had just wanted small carts to begin with. Now they have the great carts. This represents those of the Two Vehicles who originally cultivated Small Vehicle Dharmas and have ended share-section birth and death. But now they don't need to work on anything more, no extra trouble for them, and they obtain the Great Vehicle Buddhadharma. On the basis of their original cultivation and practice, they accomplish the karma of the Great Vehicle. Quite naturally they also bring change birth and death to an end, and this takes them beyond their original hopes. It's not what they were originally after, but now they've got it, and it surpasses their former aspirations.

Sutra: T.13a2.

"SHARIPUTRA, WHAT DO YOU THINK? WHEN THAT ELDER GIVES EQUALLY TO ALL OF HIS CHILDREN THE GREAT JEWELED CARRIAGES, IS HE GUILTY OF FALSEHOOD OR NOT?"

Outline:

L4. Parable of no falsehood involved.
M1. The question.

Commentary:

Was the Elder lying? SHARIPUTRA, WHAT DO YOU THINK? WHEN THAT ELDER GIVES EQUALLY TO ALL OF HIS CHILDREN THE GREAT JEWELED CARRIAGES, IS HE GUILTY OF FALSEHOOD OR NOT? Did he lie to them? Did he do wrong?

Sutra: T.13a3.

SHARIPUTRA REPLIED, "NO, WORLD HONORED ONE. THE ELDER IS NOT GUILTY OF FALSEHOOD, FOR HE HAS ONLY ENABLED HIS CHILDREN TO AVOID THE CALAMITY OF FIRE, AND HAS THEREBY SAVED THEIR LIVES. WHY IS THIS? IN SAVING THEIR LIVES HE HAS ALREADY GIVEN THEM A FINE PLAYTHING. HOW MUCH THE

MORE SO HIS SETTING UP OF EXPEDIENTS TO SAVE THEM FROM THE BURNING HOUSE."

Outline:

M2. The answer.

Commentary:

The Buddha asked Shariputra what he thought about the situation. The Elder gave them the great cart. Was he lying? Now, in this passage of text he is answering the Buddha's question by saying that the Elder was not lying. Someone may ask, "Why didn't the Buddha explain this himself? Why did he ask Shariputra? He could have just made the question rhetorical and answered it himself."

He asked Shariputra because the Elder is an analogy for the Buddha. If he had explained that he himself had not lied, most people would not have believed him. He had the greatly wise Shariputra answer the question so that everyone could understand that the Buddha does not lie.

Shariputra answered saying, "No, he does not lie. The Buddha doesn't lie." SHARIPUTRA REPLIED, "NO, WORLD HONORED ONE, THE ELDER IS NOT GUILTY OF FALSEHOOD, FOR HE HAS ONLY ENABLED HIS CHILDREN TO AVOID THE CALAMITY OF FIRE, AND HAS THEREBY SAVED THEIR LIVES. They didn't burn to death. This alone is enough to prove that he was not speaking falsely. WHY IS THIS? IN SAVING THEIR LIVES THEY HAVE ALREADY GOT A FINE PLAYTHING. You could say that getting out with their lives was getting out with fine playthings. This is because the most important thing to people, after all, is their life. Since they got out with their lives, you could say they got the toys they wanted and so the Buddha did not lie. HOW MUCH THE MORE SO HIS SETTING UP OF EXPEDIENTS TO SAVE THEM FROM THE BURNING HOUSE." The Buddha set up many expedients to save living beings from the burning house of the Three Realms.

Sutra: T.13a6

"WORLD HONORED ONE, IF THAT ELDER HAD NOT GIVEN THEM EVEN SO MUCH AS A SINGLE SMALL CART, HE STILL WOULD NOT HAVE BEEN SPEAKING FALSELY. WHY? BECAUSE THE ELDER PREVIOUSLY HAD THIS THOUGHT, 'I SHALL USE EXPEDIENTS TO LEAD MY CHILDREN OUT.' FOR THIS REASON HE IS NOT GUILTY OF FALSEHOOD. HE IS EVEN LESS GUILTY SINCE, KNOWING HIS OWN WEALTH TO BE LIMITLESS AND WISHING TO BENEFIT ALL HIS CHILDREN, HE GIVES TO THEM EQUALLY A GREAT CART."

Commentary:

Even if THAT ELDER HAD NOT GIVEN THEM EVEN SO MUCH AS A SINGLE SMALL CART, a little sheep cart, HE STILL WOULD NOT HAVE BEEN SPEAKING FALSELY. WHY? BECAUSE THE ELDER PREVIOUSLY HAD THIS THOUGHT, 'I SHALL USE EXPEDIENTS TO LEAD MY CHILDREN OUT.' I will use a clever expedient device to cause all the children to leave the burning house. FOR THIS REASON HE IS NOT GUILTY OF FALSEHOOD. Why not? He had formed the intention of using expedient devices, and they are only provisional, used to save the children. By saving them alone he was not guilty of lying.

HE IS EVEN LESS GUILTY SINCE, KNOWING HIS OWN WEALTH TO BE LIMITLESS AND WISHING TO BENEFIT ALL HIS CHILDREN, HE GIVES TO THEM EQUALLY A GREAT CART." He wanted to benefit all the children. This passage of text points out that the Buddha, in order to save living beings, doesn't use the Small Vehicle Dharma. Thus he has already lived up to his word, to say nothing of his now giving all beings the Great Vehicle Dharma. Since he saves all beings with the Great Vehicle Buddhadharma, he can't be considered a liar.

Sutra: T.13a10

THE BUDDHA TOLD SHARIPUTRA, "GOOD INDEED, GOOD INDEED! IT IS JUST AS YOU SAY."

Outline:

M3. Praise.

Commentary:

The Buddha heard Shariputra's answer and then he told him, "You are exactly right, Shariputra. IT IS JUST AS YOU SAY."

Sutra: T.13a11

"SHARIPUTRA, THE THUS COME ONE IS ALSO LIKE THIS IN THAT HE IS A FATHER TO ALL IN THE WORLD. HE HAS FOREVER ENDED ALL FEAR, WEAKNESS, WORRY, IGNORANCE AND OBSCURITY. HE HAS COMPLETELY REALIZED THE LIMITLESS KNOWLEDGE AND VISION, POWERS, AND FEARLESSNESSES. HE HAS GREAT SPIRITUAL MIGHT AND THE POWER OF WISDOM. HE HAS PERFECTED THE PARAMITAS OF EXPEDIENTS AND WISDOM. HE IS GREATLY KIND AND COMPASSIONATE. NEVER TIRING, HE EVER SEEKS THE GOOD, BENEFITTING ALL. AND THUS HE IS BORN IN THE THREE REALMS WHICH ARE LIKE A BURNING HOUSE..."

Outline:

J2. Correlating the dharmas with the analogy.
K1. Correlation to the general parable.
L1. Elder as the Buddha.

Commentary:

SHARIPUTRA, THE THUS COME ONE IS ALSO LIKE THIS. The Buddha teaches and transforms living beings in the same way as the Elder saves his children. HE IS A FATHER TO ALL IN THE WORLD, a compassionate father. HE HAS FOREVER ENDED ALL FEAR, WEAKNESS, WORRY, IGNORANCE, AND OBSCURITY. They are gone forever. He has no worries or cares, no afflictions or false thinking. Not a trace remains. HE HAS COMPLETELY REALIZED THE LIMITLESS KNOWLEDGE AND VISION...Since ignorance and obscurity are gone forever, in their place we find limitless wisdom and the limitless knowledge and vision of the Buddha.

Each has his own method by means of which he accomplishes his karma of the Way. Take Shariputra, for example. He opened the knowledge and vision of the Buddha through the door of wisdom. Mahamaudgalyayana did so through the door of spiritual powers. Each one has his original practice and work. By taking one more step forward in that direction, they were able to open up to the Buddha's knowledge and vision.

POWERS, the Ten Powers, AND FEARLESSNESSES, the Four Fearlessnesses.

HE HAS GREAT SPIRITUAL MIGHT AND THE POWER OF WISDOM. With his great spiritual powers, the Buddha saves living beings, taking them from suffering to bliss. The Buddha's great wisdom is of four kinds:

1. The wonderful observing wisdom. Why does the Buddha know everything? Because he has the wonderful observing wisdom.

2. The equality wisdom. The Buddha is equal towards all living beings. He makes no discriminations among them.

3. The perfecting wisdom. He succeeds in whatever he does because he has the perfecting wisdom.

4. The great perfect mirror wisdom. The Buddha's wisdom is like a big mirror. When something comes along, it relects it; when it goes, the image is gone. It illumines all dharmas as empty marks; it is perfectly fused without obstruction.

HE HAS PERFECTED THE PARAMITAS OF EXPEDIENTS AND WISDOM. The Buddha uses whatever method is necessary in order to save any living being. There are no fixed dharmas. He also has the paramita of wisdom, which goes all the way to the other shore. HE IS GREATLY KIND AND COMPASSIONATE. Kindness bestows happiness. The Buddha grants their wishes and makes them happy. Compassion relieves living beings of their sufferings.

NEVER TIRING, HE EVER SEEKS THE GOOD, BENEFITTING ALL. He never grows weary, lax, or tired. He never gets sick of working or takes a break because he's tired. No matter how tough the job is, the Buddha doesn't rest. He's not lazy.

What kind of work does the Buddha do? He teaches and transforms living beings, leading them all to Buddhahood. So the Venerable Ananda made this vow:

> "If a single living being
> hasn't become a Buddha,
> I will not enter into Nirvana."

That's a great vow. Why doesn't the Buddha ever rest? Because he sees living beings in this world are too miserable. In pursuit of the false, they forget the truth and they have no thought to escape the burning house. The Buddha is very busy, thinking of ways to pluck his sons and daughters out of the sea of suffering. He uses the power of his great compassion and wisdom, his spiritual powers, and various provisional expedients to save living beings. If one single being hasn't been saved, he's uneasy. Saving living beings is his job. He has no time to rest, no time to look for happiness for himself. He doesn't need to benefit himself, because he has already become a Buddha. He just wants to benefit living beings.

AND THUS HE IS BORN IN THE THREE REALMS WHICH ARE LIKE A BURNING HOUSE. The desire, form, and formless realms are like a burning house. The house is already falling apart. It's rotten and very dangerous. Why does the Buddha enter the burning house? To save all the little children. The children are so caught up in their play they they are oblivious to everything. Therefore, the Buddha comes to the Three Realms to teach and transform living beings so that they can quickly wake up.

Sutra: T.13a15

"...IN ORDER TO SAVE LIVING BEINGS FROM THE FIRES OF BIRTH, OLD AGE, SICKNESS, DEATH, GRIEF, MISERY, STUPIDITY, DULLNESS, AND THE THREE POISONS. HE TEACHES AND TRANSFORMS THEM, LEADING THEM TO THE ATTAINMENT OF ANUTTARASAMYAKSAMBODHI."

Outline:

L2. Thirty sons.

Commentary:

Why did the Buddha come into the flaming house of the Three Realms? He came to liberate all living beings. This is because living beings in the burning house don't know enough to be afraid. They don't wake up to the fact that there is no peace in the Three Realms.

The Buddha came IN ORDER TO SAVE LIVING BEINGS FROM THE FIRES OF BIRTH...When we are born, it is great suffering. It is as painful as ripping the shell from a live tortoise. OLD AGE is even more painful. You are not free in any respect. Your four limbs, your internal organs, your eyes and ears all refuse to help you out. It's really rough. While you are young, you feel strong and healthy. But when you get old, you aren't in control. When you get old, if you then get sick, it's even worse. You have to lay in bed all day as the SICKNESS wears on and grows more painful. Then, there is DEATH which is as painful as flaying the skin from a live cow. There is all this GRIEF, MISERY, STUPIDITY, AND DULLNESS, AND THE THREE POISONS, greed, hatred, and stupidity. HE TEACHES AND TRANSFORMS THEM, LEADING THEM TO THE ATTAINMENT OF ANUTTARASAMYAKSAMBODHI. He leads living beings to enlightenment The Buddha came into the world to teach living beings. Because we living beings have no idea how compassionate the Buddha is, we don't think to escape the Three Realms. The Buddha exhausts himself waiting, waiting for us, and getting nervous on top of it all. We should strike up our spirits to hurry and get out of the Three Realms. Don't hang around in the burning house!

Sutra: T.13a15

"HE SEES ALL LIVING BEINGS ARE SCORCHED BY BIRTH, OLD AGE, SICKNESS, DEATH, GRIEF, AND MISERY. THEY UNDERGO VARIOUS SUFFERINGS BECAUSE OF THE FIVE DESIRES, WEALTH AND PROFIT. FURTHER, BECAUSE OF THEIR CLINGING AND GRASPING, THEY PRESENTLY UNDERGO A MASS OF SUFFERING AND IN THE FUTURE WILL UNDERGO SUFFERING IN THE HELLS, AMONG THE ANIMALS, OR HUNGRY GHOSTS. IF BORN IN THE HEAVENS OR AMONG HUMAN BEINGS, THEY WILL SUFFER POVERTY AND DISTRESS, THE SUFFERING OF BEING SEPARATED FROM WHAT ONE LOVES, THE SUFFERING OF BEING JOINED TOGETHER WITH WHAT ONE HATES, AND ALL THE VARIOUS SUFFERINGS SUCH AS THESE. HOWEVER, LIVING BEINGS SUNK IN THIS MORASS, JOYFULLY SPORT, UNAWARE, UNKNOWING, UNALARMED AND UNAFRAID. THEY DO NOT GROW SATIATED NOR DO THEY SEEK LIBERATION. IN THE BURNING HOUSE OF THE THREE REALMS THEY RUN ABOUT FROM EAST TO WEST. ALTHOUGH THEY ENCOUNTER TREMENDOUS SUFFERING, THEY ARE NOT CONCERNED.

"SHARIPUTRA, HAVING SEEN THIS, THE BUDDHA FURTHER THINKS, 'I AM THE FATHER OF LIVING BEINGS. I SHOULD RESCUE THEM FROM THIS SUFFERING AND DIFFICULTY, AND GIVE THEM THE LIMITLESS, BOUNDLESS JOY OF THE BUDDHA-WISDOM TO PLAY WITH.'"

Outline:

K2. Correlation of specific parts of the parable.

L1. Correlation of seeing the fire.

Commentary:

HE SEES ALL LIVING BEINGS SCORCHED BY BIRTH, OLD AGE, SICKNESS, DEATH, GRIEF, AND MISERY. These sufferings are like a great fire in which living beings burn. They are like hot water in which they boil. THEY UNDERGO VARIOUS SUFFERINGS BECAUSE OF THE FIVE DESIRES, wealth, sex, fame, food, and sleep. The five desires are also explained as forms, sounds, smells, tastes, and tangible objects. They turn people upside-down. Why do people do evil deeds? It's because they are turned by the five desires. Why do people do good deeds? It's because they look upon the five desires with indifference. They have seen them for what they are and have broken their attachment to them. "So that's what they are all about," they think. "No matter how much money I get, I can't take it with me. No matter how lovely the partner, when I die, it's all over. No matter how good the food, once it hits my stomach it changes. Once it has turned to excrement, no matter how fine it was to begin with, no one would want to eat it. If you put even the tiniest speck of excrement on a plate of exquisite food, no one would go near it. Once it goes through the machine, it's completely different. So food can't be all that important. Now, sleep...the more you sleep the more you want to sleep. All day long you are in a daze. If you have a good reputation, when it's time to die, it evaporates!" You should see through the five desires. Then you can do good deeds and foster merit and virtue. *The Shurangama Sutra* tells us that if you become a Buddha it is through the use of your six senses. If you commit offenses and fall into the hells, it is also because of your six senses. The five desires work in the same way. If you don't understand, you are attached to the five desires, you lust after them and can't put them down. People with understanding put them down and they use the strength they have to do good deeds. The five desires work that way. WEALTH AND PROFIT: Because of their greedy pursuit of the five desires, wealth and self-benefit, they use many tricks to get them and when they fail, they suffer in many ways.

FURTHER, BECAUSE OF THEIR CLINGING AND GRASPING, THEY PRESENTLY UNDERGO A MASS OF SUFFERING. Because they are greedy for the five desires in this life they suffer a lot. They suffer from the frustration of their ambitions. They create much offense karma and so IN THE FUTURE WILL UNDERGO SUFFERING IN THE HELLS, AMONG THE ANIMALS, OR HUNGRY GHOSTS. IF BORN IN THE HEAVENS OR AMONG HUMAN BEINGS, THEY WILL SUFFER POVERTY AND DISTRESS. They will be poor and utterly wretched. Poor people find it hard to give. Even if they want to do merit and virtue, they don't get a chance. They just keep getting poorer and poorer. Pretty soon they have no home, no land, nothing at all. Cultivators who practice giving keep increasing their wealth. Why? Because they give it away! The more they give, the more good roots they have and so the more wealth they aquire. Because of this, while we have the strength, we must nourish our good roots.If you wait until the last minute, you won't be able to even if you want to.

THE SUFFERING OF BEING SEPARATED FROM WHAT ONE LOVES, THE SUFFERING OF BEING JOINED TOGETHER WITH WHAT ONE HATES: Hatred means there is no affinity between people. If you have an affinity with someone, you won't mind it even if they scold you or beat you. You'll still feel good about them. If you have no affinity with a person, no matter how you praise them and respect them, there are still no good feelings between you. You may praise them, but they will say you are ridiculing them. You may be speaking well of them, but they will say you are being sarcastic. Lots of misunderstandings occur. No matter how good you are to them, they continue to despise you. There's not a darn thing you can do about it! That's the suffering of being joined with what you hate. If you hate them, you may even move somewhere else to get away from them, but as soon as you get there you run into someone exactly like them. They bring you much grief. This is because you did not create an affinity with them in former lives. You set up antipathy instead.

AND ALL THE VARIOUS SUFFERINGS SUCH AS THESE. HOWEVER, LIVING BEINGS SUNK IN THIS MORASS, JOYFULLY SPORT, UNAWARE, UNKNOWING, UNALARMED AND UNAFRAID. Sunk in this suffering, they don't realize they are suffering. They play happily thinking it is great fun. Like the thirty children in the burning house, they aren't afraid of dying, they aren't scared in the least.

THEY DO NOT GROW SATIATED NOR DO THEY SEEK LIBERATION. Because they don't know suffering leads to affliction, they don't grow satiated. Because they don't seek the Way to certify to extinction, they do not seek liberation. IN THE BURNING HOUSE OF THE THREE REALMS THEY RUN ABOUT FROM EAST TO WEST. ALTHOUGH THEY ENCOUNTER TREMENDOUS SUFFERING, THEY ARE NOT CONCERNED. Everything in this world is a form of suffering. They don't worry, however, because they take suffering as bliss.

SHARIPUTRA, HAVING SEEN THIS, THE BUDDHA FURTHER THINKS, "I AM THE FATHER OF LIVING BEINGS. I am the guide of the Three Realms, the compassionate father to all beings in the four classes of birth and I SHOULD RESCUE THEM FROM THIS SUFFERING AND DIFFICULTY, help them escape it. AND GIVE THEM THE LIMITLESS, BOUNDLESS JOY OF THE BUDDHA-WISDOM TO PLAY WITH. I should save them from their troubles--that's the Buddha's great compassionate heart. Giving them the joy of the Buddha's wisdom--that's the heart of great kindness. In this way all living beings can play safely and happily in the great kindness and compassion of the Great Vehicle Buddhadharma.

We were just talking about the suffering of poverty. You may wonder, "What about people who are wealthy?" That, too, is a form of suffering. It is the suffering of happiness.

"But how can happiness be suffering?"

When happiness reaches its extreme, it turns into its opposite. Although it is said that it is hard to give when one is poor, it is also true that it is hard to cultivate the Way when one is rich. Was Shakyamuni Buddha wealthy? He was extremely wealthy. But he was able to cultivate the Way.

When the Buddha was in the world, the following incident took place: At that time, they used to burn oil lamps as a kind of offering to the Buddha. The person in charge of the lamps put them out during the day and lit them at night. One day a very poor man came to the temple with a gift of about a gallon of oil as an offering to use in the lamps. The person in charge of the lamps found that no matter how hard he tried, he couldn't put out the lamp that the poor man had lit. All the Bhikshus came and tried to blow it out, like candles on a birthday cake, but they just couldn't do it. Even Mahamaudgalyayana, foremost in spiritual powers, couldn't blow it out. He used his spiritual powers to create a wind, but that didn't work either. Then he rounded up the biggest wind around, and even that didn't work. So he went and asked the Buddha, "How come the lamp is playing such tricks today? No one can blow it out."

The Buddha said, "You don't know, but that person who came today with the oil is a poor beggar. The oil he bought took his entire life savings. His lamp will never go out."

And it never did.

Because he gave everything he had, the light just never went out, no matter what spiritual powers were used. If you are poor but can still give, then that is genuine giving, genuine merit and virtue. The less you have, the more your gift counts.

"If you have a lot and give, then does that not count?"

It's still giving, but those who are wealthy find it hard to cultivate. Those who are poor, if they can give, that's real giving. When rich people give, it's not that special.

Sutra: T.31a29

"SHARIPUTRA, THE THUS COME ONE FURTHER THINKS, 'IF I MERELY USE SPIRITUAL POWER AND THE POWER OF WISDOM, AND CAST ASIDE EXPEDIENTS, PRAISING FOR ALL LIVING BEINGS THE POWER OF THE THUS COME ONE'S KNOWLEDGE AND VISION, POWERS, AND FEARLESSNESSES, LIVING BEINGS WILL NOT BE ABLE TO BE SAVED IN THIS WAY. WHY IS THIS? ALL OF THESE LIVING BEINGS HAVE NOT YET ESCAPED BIRTH, OLD AGE, SICKNESS, DEATH, GRIEF AND MISERY. THEY ARE BEING SCORCHED IN THE BURNING HOUSE OF THE THREE REALMS. HOW COULD THEY UNDERSTAND THE WISDOM OF THE BUDDHA?'"

Outline:

L2. Correlation of casting aside table to use carts.
M1. Correlation of casting aside table.
N1. Corr. proper of casting aside table.

Commentary:

The Buddha calls out again, "SHARIPUTRA, THE THUS COME ONE FURTHER THINKS, 'IF I MERELY USE SPIRITUAL POWER AND THE POWER OF WISDOM, all wisdom, wisdom of the Way, and the wisdom of all modes AND CAST ASIDE EXPEDIENTS, PRAISING FOR ALL LIVING BEINGS THE POWER OF THE THUS COME ONE'S KNOWLEDGE AND VISION, POWERS AND FEARLESSNESSES, the Buddha's Ten Powers and Four Fearlessnesses, LIVING BEINGS WILL NOT BE ABLE TO BE SAVED. Living beings can't, by means of these causes and conditions, gain salvation.

"'WHY IS THIS? ALL OF THESE LIVING BEINGS HAVE NOT YET ESCAPED BIRTH, OLD AGE, SICKNESS, DEATH, GRIEF, AND MISERY. THEY ARE BEING SCORCHED IN THE BURNING HOUSE OF THE THREE REALMS. They are like children who have not understood the principles of human life. Therefore, in the flames of the Three Realms, they are being burned.

"'HOW COULD THEY UNDERSTAND THE WISDOM OF THE BUDDHA?'" They never knew about the Buddhadharma, so if you tell them about the Buddha's wisdom, they couldn't understand it. For example, in the West, many people have never heard the world "Buddha." Because of their unfamiliarity, many people are afraid of Buddhism, like the student who came today. I asked him, "Why have you stayed away so long?"

He said, "I was afraid."

I asked him what he was afraid of and he couldn't tell me. I said, "This person is afraid of becoming a Buddha, afraid of getting enlightened, afraid of gaining understanding." Once you understand, you can't continue to do confused things. Some people clearly know something is wrong, but want to do it anyway. They are quite clear that it is wrong to break precepts, but they are determined to do so. They know that taking drugs is wrong, but they do it anyway. Before you have studied the Buddhadharma, if you made mistakes, it's not important now. But once you understand the Buddhadharma, if you continue to make mistakes this is called "Clearly knowing and deliberately violating the rules." If you do this, your offenses are tripled. Say originally you didn't know about the law, broke it, and got five years in jail. If you get out and then break it again, you'll get twenty years for the second offense. Those of you who have made mistakes had better hurry and change. Those who haven't made mistakes should be even more vigorous in their cultivation. Don't deliberately violate the rules. That's just a mistake on top of a mistake, confusion atop confusion, suffering in suffering. It's very dangerous, dangerous within the dangerous. You're bound to be drawing very close to the hells, the realm of animals, and the realm of the hungry ghosts.

When people make mistakes, on the first offense, if they really repent, then there's still hope. When they commit it the second, third, fourth, fifth, or sixth time, their offense karma increases to astronomical proportions. The more you do it, the lower you are bound to fall. If you can return from the road of confusion, hurry and get back on the right track, then

> Although the sea of suffering is boundless,
> A turn of the head is the other shore.

The sea of pain has no limit whatsoever, but once you change, you have made it across. People who have made mistakes must change. Those who haven't should work even harder to do better. Confucius said, "If you have committed offenses, don't be afraid to reform." If you have made mistakes, don't be afraid to change. If you are afraid to reform, then your offenses will always be with you. But if you can reform, those offenses disappear.

Sutra: T. 13b4

"SHARIPUTRA, JUST AS THAT ELDER, ALTHOUGH HE HAD A POWERFUL BODY AND ARMS, DID NOT USE THEM, BUT MERELY APPLIED EXPEDIENTS WITH DILIGENCE TO SAVE ALL THE CHILDREN FROM DISASTER IN THE BURNING HOUSE, AND AFTERWARDS GAVE TO EACH OF THEM A GREAT CART ADORNED WITH PRECIOUS JEWELS, IN THE SAME WAY, THE THUS COME ONE,

ALTHOUGH HE HAS POWERS AND FEARLESSNESSES,
DOES NOT USE THEM."

Outline:

N2. Corr. of not using strength.

Commentary:

The Thus Come One's wisdom is hard to understand and hard to comprehend. That is why the Buddha bestows the provisional for the sake of the real. He sets forth expedient dharma-doors for the sake of real wisdom.

"SHARIPUTRA," the Buddha calls out again. Shariputra is foremost among the Sound Hearer Disciples in wisdom. However, when you talk about the wisdom of the Bodhisattvas, he certainly doesn't rank first there. Manjushri is the first of the Bodhisattvas in wisdom.

"JUST AS THAT ELDER, previously mentioned, ALTHOUGH HE HAD A POWERFUL BODY AND ARMS...This refers to the Buddha's spiritual powers, inexhaustible in their wonderful function. DID NOT USE THEM...The Buddha had both spiritual powers and real wisdom. He could use his spiritual powers to teach living beings, but he doesn't. He could teach living beings with real wisdom, but he doesn't. What does he keep them back for? Is the Buddha too stingy to use them? Is he afraid he will use them up? No.

"BUT MERELY APPLIED EXPEDIENTS WITH DILIGENCE: He is very busy and does not rest. He bestows the provisional for the sake of the real. He teaches the Three Vehicles for the sake of the One Buddha Vehicle.

"TO SAVE ALL THE CHILDREN FROM DISASTER IN THE BURNING HOUSE: He uses clever, expedient dharma-doors to save living beings. He rescues all the thirty sons, that is, those of the Three Vehicles. He saves the five hundred people, that is, the beings in the five destinies. The thirty children are the true sons of the Buddha. The five hundred people represent living beings in general. The Buddha rescues them all from disaster in the burning house, from the Three Realms in which no peace can be found. The burning house is very dangerous and if you don't find a way to get out, you are going to burn to death.

Burned by what fire? By the fire of the three poisons, greed, hatred, and stupidity. In the Three Realms, one is burned by the three poisons. It is incredibly dangerous.

"AND AFTERWARDS GAVE TO EACH OF THEM A GREAT CART ADORNED WITH PRECIOUS JEWELS. The Buddha used the sheep carts, deer carts, and ox carts, saying they were outside the door. In this way, he "cheated" the children into running out of the house. Then he gave each of them a great white ox cart adorned with the Six Perfections and the Ten Thousand Conducts. The great white ox cart is just the Great Vehicle , the Buddha Vehicle, not the Bodhisattva Vehilce.

There is only one vehicle;
There are no other vehicles.

Then why didn't Shakyamuni Buddha employ the great white ox cart before? Why did he say there were three carts? It was because if he had talked about the great white ox carts, the children wouldn't have been able to formulate any conception of what there were like. Little children like little things. If he had talked about a great cart, they might have gotten scared and not dared to think of wanting them. Likewise, if you don't mention the three vehicles, but start right out talking about the Buddha Vehicle, people will be afraid. "How could that be? How could we become Buddhas?" they think. And then, not only do they fail to go forward, they retreat. That is why the Buddha used clever expedients to babysit the kids. A babysitter has to know how to speak the child's language. Otherwise he can't do a good job. The Buddha knows that living beings haven't such great wisdom and that is why he speaks of the Three Vehicles. He waited until the Dharma Flower Assembly to let it all out in the open, to proclaim the entire substance of the Buddhadharma to all living beings. When he told them they could become Buddhas, that was like the gift of the great jeweled cart.

"IN THE SAME WAY, THE THUS COME ONE, ALTHOUGH HE HAS POWERS AND FEARLESSNESSES, DOES NOT USE THEM. He doesn't use the real wisdom of the Ten Powers or the strength of the Four Fearlessnesses. Didn't I just say that the Buddha didn't use his spiritual powers, his real wisdom? If he had used them, living beings would not have understood what he was doing. He spoke the expedients instead. But here, in the Dharma Flower Assembly, he opens the provisional to reveal the real. The entire Buddhadharma is told to living beings so that they can all quickly realize the Buddha Path.

Sutra: T.12b8

"HE MERELY USES WISDOM AND EXPEDIENTS TO RESCUE LIVING BEINGS FROM THE BURNING HOUSE OF THE THREE REALMS, SPEAKING TO THEM OF THREE VEHICLES: THAT OF SOUND HEARER, PRATYEKA BUDDHA, AND BUDDHA VEHICLE."

Outline:

M2. Correlation of using the carts.
N1. Corr. of suitability of three carts and knowing the children's former thoughts.

Commentary:

The Buddha's expedient dharmas are controlled by wisdom. With wise expedients, one observes the conditions and dispenses the teaching, speaking the dharma appropriate to the person. Like prescribing a drug for a certain illness, one teaches a certain dharma appropriate to that person. Living beings have many illnesses--greed, hatred, and stupidity being the most violent. These three poisons smother the wisdom of our Dharma body.

Greed means you can never get enough. The more the better! There's no time of satiation. Would you say this was violent or not? Since one is never satisfied, one lusts day and night, at all times.

When your greed is frustrated, it turns into hatred. "It's not the way I want it!" you shout as you explode with anger. You can't even sleep at night thinking of ways to get even. Once hatred arises, you manifest an asura face and that's ugly! Your contorted features move to the middle of your face--a big family, all united! They get together to do business. What business? Beating people! Refusing to speak! Scowling with a black face so that everyone runs off with their tails between their legs! "Let's get out of here. This guy's a human bomb! He's an atom bomb looking for a place to explode." Not only do you hurt yourself, you hurt other people as well. Not only do you hurt other people, you hurt yourself in the process. How's that? Once that ignorance is set ablaze, every bit of self-discipline you had accumulated goes up in a blaze along with your wisdom. I mean, take a look, angry people are incredibly stupid. If they weren't stupid, they wouldn't get angry! Which truly wise person has ever had a nasty temper?

When you get angry, your facial features move to the center of your face, ready for battle. Hatred works like that--the asura-face. Angry people are all asuras. Now, am I indulging in name-calling here? No. Asuras just like to get angry. They have no other talent. All day long they express themselves by getting angry. Why do they get angry? Because they are greedy. Without greed, one would have no reason to get angry. Why do they get angry? Because they are stupid. Intelligent people don't get angry. Those who habitually get angry can be lumped together in the Dharma Realm of the asuras. Greed, hatred, and stupidity burn off your inherent wisdom, the merit and virtue of your Dharma body. It's the biggest fire there is.

The Buddha uses wisdom to speak expedient Dharma-doors and knows which Dharma to speak when he meets any given person. The Buddha speaks the Dharma with a single sound and living beings understand it according to their kind. The Buddha explains the doctrine of cultivation which leads to the realization of Buddhahood. It wakes people up. When spirits hear it, they also give rise to the Bodhi-mind and cultivate. When Bodhisattvas hear it, they also give rise to the Bodhi-mind. When the Arhats hear it, they do, too. The same applies to the Conditioned-enlightened Ones. Living beings in the nine Dharma Realms all produce the Bodhi-mind when they hear the Buddha preach the Dharma. The Buddha uses one sound to speak the Dharma; the different kinds of living beings all understand the wonderfulness of it. That's what is meant by expedient wisdom. Using wise expedients, one teaches and transforms living beings.

TO RESCUE LIVING BEINGS FROM THE BURNING HOUSE OF THE THREE REALMS: He rescues them just as if extending his hand to living beings sinking in the mud, to pull them to safety. Living beings are trapped in the burning house of the Three Realms and are just on the verge of dying in the fire. Along comes the Buddha, the Cosmic Fireman, with fire extinguisher in hand to save living beings. He's not afraid of hurting himself. He runs right into the Three Realms to help us. Seeing how compassionate the Buddha is towards us, if we have even the slightest trace of conscience we should be weeping bitter tears, "The Buddha is so good to us. If we don't cultivate now...God!..we can't even be considered human. We're gonna fall right into the hells, right in with the hungry ghosts, right into the animal realm." So how can we cry over some long lost friend or some relative who's in trouble? Here we are, ourselves, just about ready to burn to death in the burning house, and the Buddha forsakes his very life to save all living beings. If we don't cultivate now we are really letting the Buddha down. We are flying in the face of the Buddha's kindness, compassion, joy and giving. His kindness bestows joy and his compassion relieves us of our suffering. He's saving us from our suffering so we can be happy. We really should bring forth the Bodhi-mind. Don't be lazy like you were before. You should know a little shame and not continue to be as obstinate as you have been. Wake up! The Buddha is waiting for us!

"But Dharma Master," you say, "you just told us that the Buddha freely parts with his very life in order to save us. Since he has already become a Buddha, does he still have to die?"

The Buddha doesn't die, right, but living beings do. Although the Buddha has ended birth and death and won't die again, we have not. Also, our lives are just the Buddha's life. That is why if we don't hurry up and end birth and death by cultivating the Way, we will in a sense be dragging the Buddha around to die with us! So you should hurry and bring forth the Bodhi-mind. Be vigorous. The Buddha discriminated and spoke of Three Vehicles in order to teach and transform living beings.

SPEAKING TO THEM OF THREE VEHICLES: THAT OF SOUND HEARER, PRATYEKA BUDDHA, AND BUDDHA VEHICLE: The three carts are hitched and waiting for us. Whichever cart you want, you pick it out. You can't just listen to the Sutra. Go and take your share. The Buddha has given us Three Vehicles. We all have a share in it. If you want a great white ox cart, he will give it to you. If you would rather have a deer cart, he's got one in stock. If you want a sheep cart, the compact model, that's okay, too. If you don't want any of them--then the Buddha has no way to save you.

"AND HE SAYS TO THEM, 'ALL OF YOU SHOULD TAKE NO PLEASURE IN DWELLING IN THE BURNING HOUSE OF THE THREE REALMS. DO NOT LUST AFTER VULGAR AND EVIL FORMS, SOUNDS, SMELLS, TASTES AND TANGIBLE OBJECTS. IF YOU ATTACH TO THEM GREEDILY AND GIVE RISE TO LOVE FOR THEM YOU WILL BE BURNT. YOU SHOULD QUICKLY ESCAPE THE THREE REALMS AND OBTAIN THE THREE VEHICLES: THE SOUND HEARER, PRATYEKA BUDDHA, AND BUDDHA VEHICLES.'"

Outline:

N2. Correlation of praising the three carts as rare.

O1. Correlation with demonstrating turning.

Commentary:

AND HE SAYS TO HIM, Shakyamuni Buddha says...This phrase was added by the Venerable Ananda when he compiled the Sutras. "ALL OF YOU SHOULD TAKE NO PLEASURE IN DWELLING IN THE BURNING HOUSE OF THE THREE REALMS." He is talking to the thirty children and the five hundred people. He is also talking to you and me and all living beings of the present. Don't go thinking that we are being left out. We are included in the phrase "All of you."

He says, "Don't think it is such great fun living in the burning house. It's really miserable. In the realm of desire, the form realm, and the formless realm the suffering is extreme. It's not fun and games by any means." Here the Buddha is talking about the first of the Four Holy Truths, the truth of suffering. Don't delight in it. It is suffering. There are limitless kinds of suffering, but living beings take suffering as bliss. That which is obviously bliss they take as suffering. For example, sometimes in the world, if you are competent, you can take bad situations and make them turn out for the better. If you don't know how to do things, then in doing good things, you make a mess of them.

Suffering is suffering, but living beings take it as a form of bliss. Basically, something may be blissful, but they take it as a form of suffering. Living beings are characterized by this kind of inverted thinking. Living beings are inverted, and in their confusion they don't know to turn back. They walk down the road of confusion without ever looking back. That's the truth of suffering and so here all living beings are told not to hang around in the burning house.

"DO NOT LUST AFTER VULGAR AND EVIL FORMS, SOUNDS, SMELLS, TASTES AND TANGIBLE OBJECTS." Don't be greedy. Don't lust after the vulgar, the coarse, the vile, the rotten...What's rotten? The suffering! The affliction! It disturbs our mind and nature and erodes our wisdom, making us stupid. The five sense-objects are also called the five desires. "Forms" refers to visible matter, what is in front of us and has material form. Sounds, smells, tastes, and tangible objects also delude our minds. Some beings are deluded by forms. Others like physical contact. Others like to smell fragrances or taste things. People are defiled by these states. They are not clear and pure. The realms of the five sense-objects confuse living beings completely. But if you can have no thought with regard to these states then:

> If you see affairs and awaken,
>   you can transcend the world;
> If you see affairs and are confused,
>   you fall beneath the wheel.

If, in a situation, you can wake up, that's just transcending the world. But if the situation gets out of hand and gets control over you, then you will fall. I always say,

> The eyes see forms,
>   but inside there is nothing.
> The ears hear defiling sounds,
>   but the mind knows it not.
> Facing a situation, to have no thought
> Means that you are not turned by that state.

This means that you control the situation and not vice-versa. If you reach this level then the objects of form, sounds, smells, tastes, and tangible objects cannot move your mind. If you see them and give rise to greed and love, then you have been confused by that state.

"IF YOU ATTACH TO THEM GREEDILY AND GIVE RISE TO LOVE FOR THEM YOU WILL BE BURNT." If you give rise to love and attachment, you will be burnt. Most people think that love is very important. Really, it's the very thing which keeps you from ending birth and death and becoming a Buddha. The nature flows out and becomes emotion. Emotion flows out to become desire. This emotional love is the root of birth and death and the source of outflows. If you can be without thoughts of emotional love, you can attain the non-outflow state. As long as you have emotional love, you cannot attain the state of no-outflows.

You will be burned by the fire of love. Love is a total burn. This refers to the second of the Four Holy Truths, that of origination. If you have emotional love, you will give rise to affliction. If you have no emotional love, no thoughts of love and desire, then there is no affliction. Why do you have emotional love? It's because you see your body as too important. You want to indulge in physical pleasures and this is the greatest of all mistakes. Shakyamuni Buddha cultivated bitter practices in the Himalayas. Why? Why did he go to realize the Way beneath the Bodhi tree? It was just because he was able to sever once and for all the thoughts of love and emotion which all worldly folk possess. He got rid of them and was thereby able to certify to the fruit and sever all affliction. He said,

> This is suffering, its nature is oppression.
> This is origination, its nature is seduction.
> This is extinction, its nature is certification.
> This is the Way, its nature is cultivation.

This was the first turning of the wheel of the Four Holy Truths, the Demonstrative Turning in which he pointed the Four Truths out to living beings.

"YOU SHOULD QUICKLY ESCAPE THE THREE REALMS AND OBTAIN THE THREE VEHICLES: THE SOUND HEARER, PRATYEKA BUDDHA, AND BUDDHA VEHICLES." He said, "You, that is you, plural, all of you should quickly escape. Don't linger in the three realms. Get out right now. Move! The more you dilly-dally around the father you will fall. Escape the burning house and obtain the Three Vehicles."

The Sound Hearers cultivated the Dharma of the Four Holy Truths and awakened to the Way when they heard the sound of the Buddha preaching Dharma. Pratyeka Buddhas are also called Conditioned-enlightened Ones. In the spring they watch the white flowers bloom and in the fall they watch the yellow leaves fall. Seeing the natural process of growth and decay, they cultivate the Dharma of the twelve conditioned-causes and attain the fruit. When they are born during the time when a Buddha is in the world, they are called Conditioned-enlightened Ones. When they are born at a time when there is no Buddha in the world, they are called Solitarily-enlightened Ones. Pratyeka Buddhas, most of them, live deep in the mountain valleys and have little contact with the outside world. They cultivate on their own to certify to the fruit.

The Buddha Vehicle is the vehicle of perfect enlightenment. Enlightenment is of three kinds: self-enlightenment, the enlightenment of others, and the perfection of enlightenment and practice. The Buddha Vehicle surpasses the Sound Hearer, Pratyeka Buddha, and Bodhisattva Vehicles.

The Dharma Flower Sutra says,

> There is only the one Buddha Vehicle;
> There are no other vehicles.

Previously, the three vehicles were provisional dharma. Only the Buddha Vehicle is real Dharma. Now, in the Dharma Flower Assembly, the Buddha opens the provisional to manifest the real. He sets expedient Dharmas aside in order to manifest the genuine Buddha Vehicle.

Sutra: T.13b13

> "I NOW GIVE MY PLEDGE FOR THIS AND IT SHALL NEVER BE PROVED FALSE. YOU NEED ONLY DILIGENTLY AND VIGOROUSLY CULTIVATE." THE THUS COME ONE USING THESE EXPEDIENT MEANS LEADS ALL CREATURES."

Outline:

02. Certification turning

Commentary:

In the second turning of the Three Turnings of the Four Truths, the Buddha testifies to his own attainment of certification. He says,

1. This is suffering, I already know about it. I

don't need to know anything more.

2. This is origination. I have already cut it off. I don't need to cut it off anymore.

3. This is extinction. I have already certified to it. I don't need to certify to it anymore.

4. This is the Way. I have already cultivated it. I don't need to cultivate it anymore.

Shakyamuni Buddha says, "I NOW GIVE MY PLEDGE FOR THIS. I guarantee this matter." What matter? The matter of becoming a Buddha. That is, if you cultivate according to the Great Vehicle, I guarantee that you will become a Buddha. I give you my word. "AND IT SHALL NEVER BE PROVED FALSE. YOU NEED ONLY DILIGENTLY AND VIGOROUSLY CULTIVATE. All you living beings should use your energy to go forward with vigor, practicing the Great Vehicle Dharma. In the Great Vehicle, one opens the provisional to reveal the real. But you must diligently cultivate. If you aren't diligent and vigorous in your cultivation, although it is the Great Vehicle, it will not benefit you. It is like speaking about food and not eating it, or like counting someone else's money. There is a saying,

> If all day long you count up other's wealth,
> When you haven't got a
> half a cent yourself--
> If you fail to cultivate the Dharma,
> You're making the exact same mistake.

The Shurangama Sutra says, "It is like speaking about food will never make you full." If you go to a restaurant and merely read the menu without ordering anything to eat, saying, "This is really good. And that's even more delicious. And that's a supreme treat!" your stomach will still be empty. You can't get full by talking about food.

You can't get rich by counting up other people's money. A bank teller counts up several million dollars a day, but none of it belongs to him. When he gets off work, not a dollar is his. This verse is pointing to the fact that if you just have an intellectual understanding of the Buddhadharma, but do not cultivate according to its methods, you might as well be counting someone else's money. You are making the same mistake. You gain nothing for yourself. If you sit at home sighing over how good Italian bread is or French bread--especially with butter and cheese!--it does nothing for your stomach. You can't just talk and not do anything. If you want any results, you have to put in the effort. Otherwise, you attain nothing. You must be vigorous with your mind and your body. This means bowing to the Sutras, reciting the Buddha's name, reciting the Sutras, meditating or reciting mantras. In general, you have to keep occupied because if our minds don't have anything to do, they get unreliable and start doing a lot of false thinking. They are like monkeys. Monkeys are always goofing off, running east and west, up and down trees all day long. Our minds are the same way. We have to give them some work to do and then they will settle down. One must not only be vigorous with the body but with the mind as well. Keep your thoughts to one point. The Buddhadharma has to be actually practiced. It is useless to merely talk about it. So I often say,

> Spoken wonderful, spoken well,
> If you don't walk down it,
> It's not the Way.

You have to put in the work. Then you can attain benefit. This requires vigor.

"THE THUS COME ONE USING THESE EXPEDIENT MEANS LEADS LIVING BEINGS." The Thus Come One uses the expedient dharmas of the Three Vehicles to lead living beings. You might even say he "cheats" them. How is this? He doesn't cheat us in a false way, but in a true way. He cheats us right into ending birth and death! If he didn't cheat us, we wouldn't know how to end birth and death. How can we prove that the Buddha cheats living beings? The Buddha is the great elder. The children in the house are all being burned by the fire and the elder says, "Hurry and come out! I have a sheep cart, a deer cart, and an ox cart! They are right outside the door!" But in reality there are no sheep, deer, or ox carts. Children like to play with the carts and when they hear about them they run out of the house and escape the fire. The elder thinks, "Well, I have so much wealth, I might as well give them a cart." He gives them each a great white ox cart. In the beginning he was using an expedient device to lead the children out of the burning house. Later he gave them the great cart and he was no longer being expedient. He was opening the provisional to reveal the real. The Buddha set aside expedients to teach the genuine Dharma in the same way. "Lead" in the text carries the meaning of "to entice." This is like the time the Buddha saved the child with his empty fist. The child, unaware of the danger, went crawling towards a well and was about to fall in. The Buddha used an expedient method. He said, "Little child, come back. I have here in my hand a piece of candy. Come on, I'll give it to you!" Kids love candy and so the child scrambled back. Did the Buddha have a piece of candy in his hand? No. He saved the child with his empty fist. Although he didn't have candy in his hand, he eventually went and got a piece for the child and so he didn't cheat the child after all. That's what is meant by the phrase "to lead." He uses expedients, giving living beings what they like, in order to teach and transform them. Living beings play up to each other for selfish reasons, but the Buddha uses their fondnesses to teach and transform them. We are all living beings, don't forget.

"I don't want Shakyamuni Buddha to cheat me," you say.

Then keep on being a living beings for a while. Hah! If you feel you haven't been one long enough, then continue to be one. If you don't want to be a living being, if you feel, "Now I want to understand the Buddhadharma and become a Buddha," then you will have to let Shakyamuni Buddha "cheat" you. You can't avoid it.

Sutra: T.13b14

"HE FURTHER SAYS, 'YOU SHOULD ALL KNOW THAT THE DHARMAS OF THE THREE VEHICLES HAVE BEEN PRAISED BY THE SAGES. THEY WILL MAKE YOU FREE, UNBOUND, AND SELF-RELIANT. RIDING ON THESE THREE VEHICLES, BY MEANS OF NON-OUTFLOW ROOTS, POWERS, ENLIGHTENMENTS, WAYS, DHYANAS, CONCENTRATIONS, LIBERATIONS, SAMADHIS, AND SO ON, YOU SHALL AMUSE YOURSELVES AND ATTAIN LIMITLESS PEACE AND JOY.'"

Outline:

O3. Exhortation turning.

Commentary:

In this, the third of the Three Turnings of the Four Truths, the Buddha exhorts his disciples to do what he has done. He says,

1. This is suffering. You should understand it.
2. This is origination. You should cut it off.
3. This is extinction. You should certify to it.
4. This is the Way. You should cultivate it.

"HE FURTHER SAYS, 'YOU SHOULD ALL KNOW THAT THE DHARMAS OF THE THREE VEHICLES HAVE BEEN PRAISED BY THE SAGES.'" The Buddhas of the past have praised them. The Buddhas of the present praise them. The Buddhas of the future will praise them. All the Buddhas throughout the three periods of time and the ten directions have used the Dharma-doors of the Three Vehicles as expedients to entice living beings. So they are praised and lauded by all the Buddhas. They say, "These Dharmas are the most wonderful. They are rare and hard to encounter."

"'THEY WILL MAKE YOU FREE, UNBOUND, AND SELF-RELIANT.'" What is freedom? When you obtain natural wisdom, that is freedom. When you have not obtained natural wisdom you are not free. What is natural wisdom? You might say that it is the wisdom of knowing the minds of others. That brings freedom. Unbound means that one leaves upside-down dream thinking far behind and so one is unbound. This refers to the attainment of the highest wisdom by means of which one can put everything down. That's being unbound. Self-reliant means that one relies on nothing and in one's heart one seeks nothing. "Not relying" means that when this life is over, one doesn't undergo further existence, because when one has ended birth and death, one has no future becoming, no future birth. Not to be born again, not to undergo future existence is to be self-reliant, to depend upon nothing. One shouldn't rely on others. Here we speak of two aspects: There is that which relies and that which is relied upon. That which depends is the self nature. That which is depended upon is birth and death. When there is no more birth and death, the object of reliance is gone so there is no more reliance.

When one is self-reliant, one seeks nothing. This means that one has done what one has to do. One has established one's pure conduct. One has succeeded in one's cultivation. One then seeks nothing because one has attained all one's wishes. At the level of self-reliance, one certifies to the fruit, ends birth and death.

"'RIDING ON THESE THREE VEHICLES, BY MEANS OF NON-OUTFLOW ROOTS, POWERS, ENLIGHTENMENTS, WAYS, DHYANAS, CONCENTRATIONS, LIBERATIONS, SAMADHIS, AND SO ON...'" This refers to the five roots, the five powers, the seven limbs of enlightenment, the eight sagely Way shares, the four dhyanas and the eight concentrations, and the eight liberations, and so on...

To explain the five roots once again, the first is faith. In studying the Buddhadharma, you must have faith. Otherwise, you will gain no reponse. The second is mindfulness. You must always be mindful and never forget what you are doing. Vigor is the third. You have to make vigorous progress. Don't get lazy in the Dharma assembly. Don't follow your own inclinations to be lax. You must be vigorous. Also you need the root of concentration, the fourth, and lastly, the roots of wisdom. Those are the five roots. "Root" means that they bring forth the growth of our good roots. From the five roots, five powers grow, the powers of faith, vigor, mindfulness, concentration, and wisdom.

There are four dhyanas. There are three heavens in each of the first three dhyanas and nine heavens in the fourth dhyana. The gods in the heaven of the fourth dhyana cultivate dhyana samadhi, but people can also attain the states of the dhyanas.

Those who attain the state of the first dhyana have merely attained a state. Not only the gods who dwell in the dhyana heavens, but even people who cultivate the dhyanas can enter the concentration of the first dhyana when they sit in meditation. The first dhyana is called "the joyous ground of leaving production." They leave afflictions behind and give rise to happiness. This happiness transcends all human happiness. Why don't they give rise to affliction? Because they have attained this kind of happiness and take the joy of dhyana as their food. Those who attain the state of the first dhyana feel very satisfied and comfortable all day long. Their bodies have never felt better. The pleasures of sexual intercourse are nothing compared to this feeling. This happiness makes them feel that anything less is quite common place.

They ground of the joy of leaving production occurs when you sit in meditation but also continued when you are not sitting. Walking, standing, sitting, and reclining, you are enveloped in this happiness. The more you cultivate this state, the more it increases. Then, as you are sitting, two hours seems like a couple of seconds. Or you can sit for two days and feel like it has only been five minutes. The Venerable Master

Hsü-lao sat on Chung-nan Mountain for eighteen days in this kind of state. All you need to attain this state is to meditate sincerely. It's not that hard. It's not hard at all, especially for young people. If you don't meditate or cultivate then of course you can't attain it. But if you work hard and cultivate you will attain this state of the first dhyana. This isn't something just belonging to the gods. You, in your ordinary human body can attain this state provided you cultivate. There's nothing very special about it. It's very common, very ordinary. It's the first step in cultivation, just getting in the door. It doesn't mean that you are real high or anything For example, a few days ago I said that there was someone here in our lecture hall who had attained this state. But it's only the first step on the journey. If you wish to attain the real advantages, you have to work extremely hard, and pour on the effort and go forward to certify to the sagely fruit. Don't just stop where you are.

The second dhyana is called the ground of the joy of the production of concentration. In this time of happiness, you must not become greedy and attach to it thinking how fine it is. Once that happens you come to a standstill and this is of no use. Remember you are cultivating concentration! Don't let the state move your mind, but keep your mind always in concentration. They say,

> The dragons are always in samadhi.
> There's no time they are not in samadhi.

Walking, standing, sitting, and reclining, one should remain in concentration and not let the mind become caught up in external conditions. Don't let the mind run outside to climb on conditions. The mind should be like still water, deep and clear, translucent and still. Then, as you continue to meditate and cultivate, not only will your pulse stop, but your breath will stop as well. You can sit there for any length of time, but it will seem like a very short time. However, you still have thought. In the first dhyana you haven't very much concentration going; in the second dhyana you've gotten a bit of concentration and your breath stops, but you haven't stopped thinking yet. You may be sitting there for some time when you suddenly think, "How long have I been sitting?" With that false thought, you come right out of samadhi. Before you had that false thought, you sat for a long time without knowing how long it was--no mark of people, no mark of self, no mark of living beings and no mark of a lifespan. As soon as thought arises, "Hmm...there's something I meant to do. I've got to go to the bank a little later and see how much I've got in my account. Then I'm going to go buy some vegetables. Let's see, what shall I have for lunch today?" As soon as you have these false thoughts you come out of samadhi and your thought hasn't stopped.

The third dhyana is called the ground of the wonderful bliss of leaving joy. In the first dhyana one is happy. In the second dhyana concentration arises, but this concentration is not separate from happiness. The joy of dhyana remains in the state of the second dhyana. In the third dhyana one leaves happiness behind and obtains a wondrous, never-before-experienced, inconceivable,subtle bliss. One leaves behind the state in which one takes dhyana as one's food and is filled with the joy of dharma. This happiness is the happiness of the heavens. It is not something experienced by human beings. If you want to try it out, work hard at your dhyana meditation.

The fourth dhyana is called the pure ground of casting out thought. In the third dhyana thought stops. Although one does not give rise to false thinking, thought hasn't been entirely cast out until one reaches the fourth dhyana. In the fourth dhyana one puts thought somewhere else entirely. In this state the afflictions of the guest-dusts have been completely purified. But this does not mean that one has certified to the fruit of sagehood. It is merely the attainment in cultivation of a state of "light peace."

To the four dhyanas one adds the four formless samadhis to obtain the eight concentrations. The four formless samadhis are:

1. The samadhi of the station of boundless emptiness.
2. The samadhi of the station of boundless consciousness.
3. The samadhi of the station of nothing whatsoever.
4. The samadhi of the station of neither perception nor non-perception.

The heavens of these four stations are called the heavens of the formless realm. The samadhis are therefore called the formless samadhis. The gods dwelling in the formless realm have only consciousness; they have no material form. The four are also called the four stations of emptiness, because they are formless.

There are eight liberations:

1. The liberation in which inwardly there is the mark of form and outwardly form is contemplated.

2. The liberation in which inwardly there is no mark of form and outwardly form is contemplated.

3. The liberation in which the pure body of wisdom certifies to the complete dwelling.

Add to these the liberations of the four formless samadhis:

4. The liberation of the station of boundless emptiness.

5. The liberation of the station of boundless consciousness.

6. The liberation of the station of nothing whatsoever.

7. The liberation of the station of neither perception nor non-perception.

Then add:

8. The liberation of the samadhi of the extinction of the skandhas of feeling and thought. These are also called "eight castings off the back." This means that one "gets affliction off one's back" and attains liberation.

To explain them in more detail:

1. The liberation in which inwardly there is the mark of form and outwardly form is contemplated. This means that within you, you still have the thought of sexual desire. People are just people after all. When they just begin cultivating they can't avoid the problem of sexual desire. You may wish to cut off this desire, but you have previously planted the seeds within you of desire and so you still have these thoughts and feelings. So, inwardly there is the mark of form. One counteracts this desire by the contemplation of outward form. What form? One uses the contemplation of the nine signs and the contemplation of impurity to look at outward forms. Once you understand the impurity of all forms, you won't be attached to the marks of form, i.e., you won't form sexual attachments.

You will thereby attain this first liberation. If you are attached, you can't be liberated. This means that you have to put everything down in order to be free. As long as you can't put it down, you won't be free. How do you put it down? You must see right through it, see it for what it really is. Then you can put it aside. If you can't see through it, you won't be able to put it down. As long as you can't put it down, you won't be free. So you first cultivate this contemplation.

2. The liberation in which inwardly there is no mark of form and outwardly form is contemplated. Those who apply effort for a time will, without realizing quite how, get rid of thoughts of sexual desire. Is that enough? No. You must continue to contemplate external forms. As you look at the most beautiful woman, you realize that eventually she will get old and die.

There are nine contemplations of a rotting corpse:

A. Tumefaction. When that lovely woman/man dies, her/his body will first swell up.

B. Secondly, it will turn a mottled green color.

C. Then it will start to rot.

D. It will break open and discharge blood.

E. It will ooze flesh and pus.

F. It will be devoured by birds and beasts and insects.

G. Its remains will be in a dismembered condition.

H. Finally it will be nothing but a skeleton,

I. which will finally turn to ashes.

Thus the four elements it was originally composed of will each return to where they came from. The element earth will return to the earth. The water will go back to the water. The fire will return to fire and the wind will go back to the wind. It's all empty once again. You contemplate one person like this, a hundred, a thousand, a million...Once you understand this contemplation of impurity--be they male or female, depending on your preference, you won't lust after them. The absence of lust is liberation.

3. Having broken through these marks of form, you then reach the next level of liberation in which "The pure body of liberation certifies to the perfect dwelling." Since you have seen through it and put it down, you obtain the pure wisdom body. You then certify to the perfect dwelling. "Perfect dwelling" is just liberation, that is, dwelling in purity's original substance.

Next, you become liberated with regard to: 4. Emptiness, 5. consciousness, 6. nothing whatsoever, 7. neither perception nor non-perception, that is, the four stations of emptiness.

8.Finally, you attain the liberation of the samadhi of the skandhas of feelings and thought. At that time your consciousness is just about to be extinguished, but has not quite yet been extinguished. After eighty-thousand great aeons that consciousness will arise again. Therefore, although one obtains the stations of emptiness and so on, one has not yet ended birth and death. The attainment of the samadhi of the extinction of feelings and thought is not the end of birth and death, either. In the four dhyanas and the four stations of emptiness plus the samadhi of the extinction of the skandhas of feelings and thought we have the nine successive samadhis.

The text continues with SAMADHIS. There are three kinds of samadhis. What are they? The samadhi of emptiness. The samadhi of signlessness. The samadhi of wishlessness. AND SO ON means as above all the principles just talked about...

YOU SHALL AMUSE YOURSELVES AND ATTAIN LIMITLESS PEACE AND JOY. By cultivating this skill, you attain the joy of dhyana as your food and are filled with the bliss of dharma. So you are extremely happy. Sporting in dhyana samadhi, you obtain that limitless peace and happiness. This means if you attain the Nirvana of true empitness, you forever leave all troubles and disasters. With no troubles or disasters your happiness and peace are unlimited.

Sutra: T.13b18

"SHARIPUTRA, IF THERE ARE LIVING BEINGS WHO INWARDLY POSSESS THE WISDOM-NATURE, AND HEARING THE DHARMA FROM THE BUDDHA, THE WORLD HONORED ONE, BELIEVED AND ACCEPTED IT, DILIGENTLY MAKING PROGRESS, WISHING QUICKLY TO ESCAPE THE THREE REALMS AND SEEKING NIRVANA FOR THEMSELVES, THEY ARE CALLED THOSE OF THE SOUND HEARER VEHICLE. THEY ARE LIKE THE CHILDREN WHO SOUGHT THE SHEEP CART AND THEREBY ESCAPED FROM THE BURNING HOUSE.

"IF THERE ARE LIVING BEINGS WHO HEARING THE DHARMA FROM THE BUDDHA, THE WORLD HONORED ONE, BELIEVED AND ACCEPTED IT, DILIGENTLY MAKING PROGRESS, AND WHO SEEK FOR THEMSELVES SPONTANEOUS WISDOM, DELIGHTING IN SOLITUDE AND FOND OF STILLNESS, DEEPLY UNDERSTANDING THE CAUSAL CONDITIONS OF ALL DHARMAS, THEY ARE CALLED THOSE OF THE PRATYEKA BUDDHA VEHICLE. THEY ARE LIKE THE CHILDREN WHO SOUGHT THE DEER CART AND SO ESCAPED THE BURNING HOUSE.

"IF THERE ARE LIVING BEINGS WHO HEARING THE DHARMA FROM THE BUDDHA, THE WORLD HONORED ONE, BELIEVED AND ACCEPTED IT, EARNESTLY CULTIVATING WITH VIGOR, SEEKING ALL-WISDOM, THE BUDDHA WISDOM, SPONTANEOUS WISDOM, UNTUTORED WISDOM, THE KNOWLEDGE AND VISION OF THE THUS COME ONE, HIS POWERS AND FEARLESSNESSES, PITYING AND COMFORTING LIMITLESS LIVING BEINGS, BENEFITTING GODS AND HUMANS, SAVING ALL, THEY ARE CALLED THOSE OF THE GREAT VEHICLE. BECAUSE THE BODHISATTVAS SEEK THIS VEHICLE, THEY ARE CALLED MAHASATTVAS. THEY ARE LIKE THE CHILDREN WHO SOUGHT THE OX CART AND SO ESCAPED THE BURNING HOUSE."

Outline:

N3. Correlation of granting the children their wishes.

Commentary:

"SHARIPUTRA, now I will tell you IF THERE ARE LIVING BEINGS WHO INWARDLY POSSESS THE WISDOM NATURE: This means that in past lives they heard the Buddha speak the Dharma, and therefore they have the seeds of wisdom within them. Formerly, they followed the Buddha and studied the Dharma-doors of the Three Vehicles, so now they have the wisdom nature within them. AND HEARING THE DHARMA FROM THE BUDDHA, THE WORLD HONORED ONE: In former lives they listened to the Buddha teach the Dharma. This represents the first of the three types of wisdom, the wisdom of hearing. If you just hear it but don't believe or accept it, you can't attain benefit. Once you have heard it, you must deeply believe it without having any doubts. So the text says BELIEVED AND ACCEPTED IT. You must believe and uphold it. If you can believe and accept and uphold it, then you can be assured of DILIGENTLY MAKING PROGRESS. Diligent refers to the second kind of the three types of wisdom: the wisdom of consideration. You diligently consider the Dharma and are vigorous. This vigorous progress represents the third of the three types of wisdom, the wisdom of cultivation.

"WISHING QUICKLY TO ESCAPE THE THREE REALMS: If you can be diligent and make progress you can quickly escape the desire, form, and formless realms.

"AND SEEKING NIRVANA FOR THEMSELVES: They pay no attention to anyone else. They just want to succeed in their own cultivation and forget it. THEY ARE CALLED THOSE OF THE SOUND HEARER VEHICLE. Because they only wish to enlighten and benefit themselves, they are called Sound Hearers. THEY ARE LIKE THE CHILDREN WHO SOUGHT THE SHEEP CART AND THEREBY ESCAPED FROM THE BURNING HOUSE. Hearing that there were sheep carts outside the door, they ran from the burning house and were saved."

The Sound Hearers are compared to sheep because they just care about themselves. They are only interested in their own welfare. They end birth and death for themselves, and pay no attention to others. They don't worry about the rest of the flock, they just run right ahead. That's the Sound Hearer Vehicle.

"IF THERE ARE LIVING BEINGS WHO, HEARING THE DHARMA FROM THE BUDDHA, THE WORLD HONORED ONE, BELIEVED

AND ACCEPTED IT: Someone asked me if the Buddhas and Bodhisattvas could give us faith. Does our faith come from ourselves or do the Buddhas give it to us? There are many ways to look at this question. However, we will say that faith arises from youself. It definitely is not something given to you from the outside. It is not like those of non-Buddhist religions who say that God gives you faith. Faith arises only from within you. Others can't give it to you. If others could give you faith, that would be like someone else eating lunch for you and you getting full. It doesn't work that way. In the same way faith can't be gotten from the outside. If you have faith, you will get the food of Dharma and be filled with it. If you don't have faith, and others try to give you faith, well, it's not your own faith! You won't get "full." Principles must be explained clearly. For example, one might ask if others can cultivate on your behelf. No. It's said,

> Eat your own food, fill yourself;
> End your own birth and death.

Faith works the same way. You have to give rise to it yourself. No one can do it for you.

"DILIGENTLY MAKE PROGRESS, SEEKING SPONTANEOUS WISDOM: This means very spontaneously and naturally giving rise to wisdom. How do they give rise to it? DELIGHTING IN SOLITUDE AND FOND OF STILLNESS. They cultivate by themselves in solitude; they are fond of stillness and are very pure. They don't like a lot of noise and commotion. DEEPLY UNDERSTANDING THE CAUSAL CONDITIONS OF ALL DHARMAS. They have profound understanding of the causes and conditions behind the production and extinction of all dharmas. They cultivate the twelve causal-conditions and by means of complete understanding of them they gain attainment. THEY ARE CALLED THOSE OF THE PRATYEKA BUDDHA VEHICLE. THEY ARE LIKE THE CHILDREN WHO SOUGHT THE DEER CART AND THEREBY ESCAPED THE BURNING HOUSE."They are like the kids who thought the deer cart the elder offered was the most fun. Deer are independent. They don't need anyone to help them. Pratyeka Buddhas are independent, too. When a Buddha is in the world, they are called Condition-enlightened Ones. When there is no Buddha in the world they are called Solitary-enlightened Ones. They like to be alone. They like things quiet. They profoundly understand the causes and conditions underlying all dharmas. Pratyeka Buddhas cultivate and certify on their own. The Sound Hearers and Pratyeka Buddhas are known as the Two Vehicles.

"IF THERE ARE LIVING BEINGS WHO HEARING THE DHARMA FROM THE BUDDHA, THE WORLD HONORED ONE, who follow the Buddha and cultivate the Way, BELIEVED AND ACCEPTED IT, EARNESTLY CULTIVATING WITH VIGOR, SEEKING ALL-WISDOM. All-wisdom means they want the wisdom regarding all transcendental and worldly dharmas. THE BUDDHA WISDOM, this wisdom of the Buddha which those of the Two Vehicles do not possess. SPONTANEOUS WISDOM was explained previously as also sought by the Pratyeka Buddhas. UNTUTORED WISDOM. Most people take this as wisdom which is gained without a teacher, but that is wrong. Untutored wisdom is something only the Buddha has because the Buddha is the leader of gods and humans, and no one acts as his teacher. Therefore his wisdom is untutored. This is just the Buddha wisdom. All-wisdom, Buddha wisdom, spontaneous wisdom, and untutored wisdom are all terms used to describe the Buddha's wisdom. Although four types of wisdom are named, in reality they are all the great, perfectly enlightened wisdom of the Buddha.

"THE KNOWLEDGE AND VISION OF THE THUS COME ONE: Seeking the knowledge of the Thus Come One refers to the wisdom of all modes and the vision of the Thus Come One refers to the Buddha-eye. HIS POWERS AND FEARLESSNESSES refers to the Buddha's Ten Wisdom Powers and Four Fearlessnesses. PITYING AND COMFORTING LIMITLESS LIVING BEINGS: They have pity on all living beings and make them happy. They bring forth hearts of great compassion pitying and comforting all creatures. LIMITLESS LIVING BEINGS. BENEFITTING GODS AND HUMANS. They benefit gods in the heavens and humans below. SAVING ALL: They want to deliver all beings. THEY ARE CALLED THOSE OF THE GREAT VEHICLE, Great Vehicle Bodhisattvas. BECAUSE THEY SEEK THIS VEHICLE, THEY ARE CALLED MAHASATTVAS, Great Bodhisattvas. THEY ARE LIKE THE CHILDREN WHO SOUGHT THE OX CART AND THEREBY ESCAPED FROM THE BURNING HOUSE. They sought the great ox cart and so got out of the burning house.

Sutra: T.13b29

"SHARIPUTRA, JUST AS THAT ELDER, SEEING ALL HIS CHILDREN SAFELY ESCAPE THE BURNING HOUSE TO A PLACE OF FEARLESSNESS, AND CONSIDERING HIS OWN UNLIMITED WEALTH, GIVES TO ALL OF HIS CHILDREN A GREAT CART...

Outline:

L3. Correlation of the giving of a great cart.
M1. Correlation of avoiding disaster and giving of a great cart.

Commentary:

"SHARIPUTRA, JUST AS THAT ELDER, SEEING ALL HIS CHILDREN SAFELY ESCAPE THE BURNING HOUSE TO A PLACE OF FEARLESSNESS: This refers to the thirty sons talked about earlier as well as the five hundred people. AND CONSIDERING HIS OWN UNLIMITED WEALTH, GIVES TO ALL OF HIS CHILDREN A GREAT CART,

Sutra:

JUST SO THE THUS COME ONE, IN THE SAME WAY IS THE FATHER OF ALL LIVING BEINGS. WHEN HE SEES LIMITLESS MILLIONS OF LIVING BEINGS USING THE GATEWAY OF THE BUDDHA'S TEACHING TO GET OFF THE FEARSOME AND DANGEROUS PATH OF THE SUFFERING OF THE THREE REALMS AND ATTAIN THE BLISS OF NIRVANA, HE HAS THIS THOUGHT, 'I HAVE LIMITLESS, BOUNDLESS WISDOM, POWERS, FEARLESSNESSES AND SO ON--THE COMPLETE STOREHOUSE OF THE BUDDHADHARMAS. ALL OF

THESE LIVING BEINGS ARE MY CHILDREN. I SHOULD GIVE TO ALL OF THEM A GREAT CART, NOT ALLOWING THEM TO GAIN INDIVIDUAL EXTINCTION, BUT CROSSING THEM OVER TO EXTINCTION BY MEANS OF THE THUS COME ONE'S EXTINCTION. HAVING ESCAPED THE THREE REALMS, ALL THESE LIVING BEINGS ARE GIVEN AS PLAYTHINGS THE BUDDHA'S DHYANA CONCENTRATIONS, LIBERATIONS, AND SO FORTH, ALL OF ONE MARK AND ONE KIND, PRAISED BY THE SAGES AND PRODUCTIVE OF PURE, WONDROUS, AND FOREMOST BLISS.'"

Outline:

M2. Giving of Great Vehicle.

Commentary:

JUST SO THE THUS COME ONE IN THE SAME WAY IS THE FATHER OF ALL LIVING BEINGS. WHEN HE SEES LIMITLESS MILLIONS OF LIVING BEINGS USING THE GATEWAY OF THE BUDDHA'S TEACHING TO GET OFF THE FEARSOME AND DANGEROUS PATH OF THE SUFFERING OF THE THREE REALMS AND ATTAIN THE BLISS OF NIRVANA, HE HAS THIS THOUGHT: The Three Realms are the realm of desire, the realm of form, and the formless realm. After you get out of the world of desire, you have no more desire. Once you trancend the world of form, there is no more form. Once you get beyond the formless realm, then there is no thought either. Everything in the Three Realms is suffering. Here the text says that it is not only suffering, but it is also very dangerous. Why is it dangerous? It is like a place that is overrun with thieves. The thieves are the six senses: eye, ear, nose, tongue, body, and mind. These six thieves rob you of the precious treasure of your own original wisdom. But if you can turn them around, the six senses can act as Dharma protectors, too. I will give you a simple analogy: For example, say there were some thieves who got tired of being thieves and decided to join the police force. Because they used to be thieves, they know very well where to go to look for theives, and they make very good policemen. They know all the sneaky thief tricks and can arrive at the scene of a crime before the criminals even get there! So it is with the six senses if they are turned around. The eyes that once ran after beautiful forms no longer are fooled by them. The ears quit running after fine sounds; the nose doesn't seek fragrances; the tongue doesn't crave fine flavors; the body doesn't run after things to touch; and the mind isn't preoccupied with dharmas. In this way they stand guard over the treasure of your original wisdom, and they have become Dharma protectors. Now, in the Three Realms there are many thieves. They are sneaking up the alleys, coming up the main highways, crawling in the windows, and leaping over the back fence. Would you say this is dangerous or not? The Three Realms are indeed fearful and dangerous, in addition to being places of great suffering and misery. The Buddha sees all the living beings using the teachings of the Buddha to walk right out of this suffering, dangerous world. He thinks, 'I HAVE LIMITLESS BOUNDLESS WISDOM, POWERS, FEARLESSNESSES AND SO ON--THE COMPLETE STOREHOUSE OF THE BUDDHADHARMAS. ALL OF THESE LIVING BEINGS ARE MY CHILDREN. I SHOULD GIVE TO ALL OF THEM A GREAT CART, NOT ALLOWING THEM TO GAIN INDIVIDUAL EXTINCTION, BUT CROSSING THEM OVER TO EXTINCTION BY MEANS OF THE THUS COME ONE'S EXTINCTION.' In the Three Realms there is no real happiness; there is nothing but suffering, and it is very dangerous. It is like standing on the edge of a deep abyss or walking on thin ice. What is meant by standing on the edge of a deep abyss? It's like standing on a cliff which hangs a hundred thousand feet right over the ocean. It's very easy to fall over the edge and lose your life. It's also like walking across some very thin ice--easy to fall right through into the water and also lose your life. That's what being in the Three Realms is like. It's like being in a dangerous burning house. The Buddha leads us out of danger to the joy of Nirvana, to the happiness of Nirvana--unproduced, undestroyed, not defiled, not pure, permanence, bliss, true self, and purity. Quite an advantage! The Buddha thinks, "Now that I have become a Buddha, my wisdom is limitless and boundless. It's endless for the taking and inexhaustible in its use. I also have ten powers and four fearlessnesses." The phrase "and so one" refers to the Dharma treasury of the Buddhas, that is, the Four Truths, the Six Perfections, the Twelve Conditioned-causes, the Thirty-seven Wings of Enlightenement. Since the Buddha has the complete storehouse of the Dharma, he decides to give to all his children a great cart, the Great Vehicle.

"I shouldn't let them gain individual Nirvana," he thinks. "I should lead them all to attain the Thus Come One's Nirvana so they can be just like the Thus Come One. I shouldn't allow them to attain simply a doctrine of one-sided emptiness. I should make sure that they all attain the perfect, supreme doctrine of true emptiness.

"'HAVING ESCAPED THE THREE REALMS, ALL THESE LIVING BEINGS ARE GIVEN AS PLAYTHINGS THE BUDDHA'S DHYANA CONCENTRATIONS, LIBERATIONS, AND SO FORTH, ALL OF ONE MAKE AND ONE KIND, PRAISED BY THE SAGES AND PRODUCTIVE OF PURE, WONDROUS, AND FOREMOST BLISS.'" When all of these living beings get out of the Three Realms, they all get the Dhyana concentrations of the Buddhas and the liberations--the very finest toys. You haven't attained that happy state of Dhyana concentration yet, but once you do--ah!--then you will be like children playing with new toys. Lot's of fun! Lot's of fun!

What is "one mark?" It is the Real Mark. The Real Mark represents the first of the Three Virtues, the Virtue of the Dharma body. Above, much principle has been discussed--the Thirty-seven Wings, The Six Perfections, the Four Truths, the Twelve Conditioned-causes. Now, the Parable Chapter is about to be finished and the Three Virtues are used to cap it off. So the text says, "all of one mark." They are all the Realm Mark. The Real Mark is without a mark. However, there is nothing which is does not mark. All marks arise out of the Real Mark. This is to say that within true emptiness, wonderful existence arises. Wonderful existence--you can't see it. That is why it is called "wonderful." You can't hear it, smell it, taste or touch it, either. Your mind's thoughts can't know of it. It is the Real Mark, the Virtue of the Dharma body.

"One kind" refers to the wisdom of all modes, a kind of wisdom, and represents the second of the Three Virtues, the Virtue of Prajna.

"Praised by the sages and productive of pure, wondrous, and foremost bliss" refers to the third of the Three Virtues, the Virtue of Liberation. This Dharma is praised by the Buddhas throughout the ten directions. It gives rise to a clear, pure, subtle, fine happiness, which knows no suffering. The absence of suffering is just liberation, the Virtue of Liberation. Such is the inconceivable storehouse of the Three Virtues.

Sutra: T.13c10

"SHARIPUTRA, JUST AS THAT ELDER FIRST HAVING USED THE THREE CARTS TO ENTICE HIS CHILDREN AND THEN LATER HAVING GIVEN THEM A GREAT CART ADORNED WITH JEWELS AND SUPREMELY COMFORTABLE, IS NOT GUILTY OF FALSEHOOD...

Outline:

L4. Correlation of "no falseness.
M1. The parable.

Commentary:

The greatly wise Shariputra is told that he should know that the Buddha is just like the great elder. "SHARIPUTRA, JUST AS THAT ELDER FIRST HAVING USED THE THREE CARTS TO ENTICE HIS CHILDREN: At the very beginning, he used expedients saying that outside there were three kinds of carts: sheep carts, deer carts, and ox carts. Basically the children were playing in the house and were totally unaware of the situation. They were not frightened or afraid at all. When they heard there were such beautiful toy-carts, they were enticed out. He cheated the children saying there were carts outside the door. The children were just on the verge of being burned in the fire so, even though there were no carts outside the door, the Elder told them there were. Since the toys he promised were more fun than the ones the children were playing with, they ran outside the door to safety.

"AND THEN LATER HAVING GIVEN THEM A GREAT CART: The Elder got them safely out of the house and then, because his own wealth was without limit--he could give to the entire country and not diminish his wealth--everyone got a great cart. ADORNED WITH JEWELS AND SUPREMELY COMFORTABLE. The cart was very comfortable. IS NOT GUILTY OF FALSEHOOD. You cannot rightfully say that the Elder lied to the children. He is without error."

Sutra: T.13c13

"...JUST SO IS THE THUS COME ONE LIKEWISE NOT GUILTY OF FALSEHOOD IN FIRST SPEAKING OF THE THREE VEHICLES TO ENTICE LIVING BEINGS AND THEN AFTERWARDS DELIVERING THEM ONLY BY MEANS OF THE GREAT VEHICLE. WHAT IS THE REASON? THE THUS COME ONE HAS LIMITLESS WISDOM, POWERS AND FEARLESSNESSES, A STOREHOUSE OF DHARMAS, AND IS ABLE TO GIVE TO ALL LIVING BEINGS THE GREAT VEHICLE DHARMA. NOT ALL LIVING BEINGS, HOWEVER, ARE ABLE TO ACCEPT IT. SHARIPUTRA, BECAUSE OF THESE CAUSES AND CONDITIONS YOU SHOULD KNOW THAT THE BUDDHAS, USING THE POWER OF EXPEDIENT DEVICES, IN THE ONE BUDDHA VEHICLE, DISCRIMINATE AND SPEAK OF THREE."

Outline:

M2. The correlation.

Commentary:

The Elder used expedient methods to get the children safely out of the burning house and he said there were carts when there really were none. Later, he gave all of them a great cart and so he is not guilty of telling lies. "JUST SO IS THE THUS COME ONE LIKEWISE NOT GUILTY OF FALSEHOOD IN FIRST SPEAKING OF THE THREE VEHICLES TO ENTICE LIVING BEINGS. He is just like the Elder. He did not lie. He used clever expedients to help living beings. He first spoke the Sound Hearer Vehicle. Then he spoke the Conditioned-enlightened Vehicle. Then he spoke the Bodhisattva Vehicle--the Three Vehicles. He did this to entice and lead all living beings. The Sound Hearer Vehicle was taught the Storehouse Teaching. The Conditioned-enlightened Ones were taught the Pervasive Teacning. The Bodhisattvas were taught the Separate Teaching. Then, lastly, he taught the Great Vehicle, the wonderful principle of the Real Mark the perfect-sudden Dharma-door, the Great Vehicle's wonderful Dharma found in this Sutra.

"AND THEN AFTERWARDS DELIVERING THEM ONLY BY MEANS OF THE GREAT VEHICLE. WHAT IS THE REASON? Why does the Buddha do this? THE THUS COME ONE HAS LIMITLESS WISDOM: The Buddha basically has limitless and boundless wisdom. He has all-wisdom, wisdom in the Way, and the wisdom of all modes. With such boundless wisdom, he also has ten wisdom POWERS, as well as four FEARLESSNESSES--A STOREHOUSE OF DHARMAS. He has all the Dharma-doors. AND IS ABLE TO GIVE TO ALL LIVING BEINGS THE GREAT VEHICLE DHARMA. NOT ALL LIVING BEINGS, HOWEVER, ARE ABLE TO ACCEPT IT. If you tell them about the Great Vehicle Dharma-door right off, since they have never heard of such a thing, not all will be able to accept it." For example the Buddha first spoke *The Avatamsaka Sutra*, and those of the Small Vehicle...

Had eyes but did not see
Nishyanda Buddha;
Had ears but did not hear
the perfect-sudden teaching.

They looked but did not see, listened but did not hear. They were as if deaf, dumb, and blind. So not only were they unable to accept it, they couldn't even understand it!

A layperson once asked me, "If those of the Two Vehicles couldn't even understand *The Avatamsaka Sutra*, how can we, who are not even as high as those of the Two Vehicles, possibly understand it?"

This is a good question. But right after the Buddha realized Buddhahood, no one at all understood the Buddhadharma. There wasn't any Buddhadharma. So if you spoke any profound principles to them, they wouldn't be able to understand them. Now, we know about the Buddhadharma and it is possible for us to understand it, and to understand its various levels, the Great and Small Vehicles and the profound and less profound teachings. Although we haven't certified to the fruit, and can't compare ourselves with those of the Two Vehicles, still our dispositions towards the Great Vehicle have been firmly established, and we have a chance to hear the Great Vehicle Buddhadharma.

The text tells us that living beings are unable to accept the Great Vehicle Dharma and so "SHARIPUTRA, BECAUSE OF THESE CAUSES AND CONDITIONS YOU SHOULD KNOW THAT THE BUDDHAS, USING THE POWER OF EXPEDIENT DEVICES, IN THE ONE BUDDHA VEHICLE, DISCRIMINATE AND SPEAK OF

THREE." Originally, there aren't three vehicles. There is only the Buddha Vehicle. Living beings' dispositions are such that they can't accept it completely and so the Buddha teaches the three for the sake of the one. The ultimate aim is for all living beings to become Buddhas through the cultivation of the Buddha Vehicle.

Sutra: T.13c18

THE BUDDHA, WISHING TO RESTATE HIS MEANING, SPOKE VERSES, SAYING:

SUPPOSE THERE WAS AN ELDER...

Outline:

I2. Verse section.
J1. Verse setting up parable.
K1. Verse about general parable.
L1. Verse about Elder.

Commentary:

THE BUDDHA, having finished speaking the prose sections, and WISHING TO RESTATE HIS MEANING, SPOKE VERSES. Because he was filled with compassion and afraid that living beings still hadn't understood his principles, he was not afraid to take the trouble to repeat himself. He spoke verses, SAYING...Some verses are four characters long, other five or six or seven. The length of the lines vary, but they elaborate upon the principles set forth in the previous prose passages. Sometimes they may speak them in a capsule form. The point is that they repeat them so that people who missed them the first time can pick up on them.

SUPPOSE THERE WAS AN ELDER/ Suppose, for example, there was an elder. And elder has ten kinds of virtuous practices which were mentioned before and which you no doubt remember very clearly. If you don't remember clearly, check back to that passage.

Sutra: T.13c19

WHO HAD A LARGE HOUSE,
WHICH WAS VERY OLD,
AND SO WAS COLLAPSING.
THE HALLS WERE HIGH AND PRECARIOUS,
THE PILLARS ROTTING AT THEIR BASES,
THE BEAMS AND RIDGEPOLES ASLANT,
THE FOUNDATIONS AND STAIRWAYS CRUMBLING.
THE WALLS AND PARTITIONS WERE
CRACKED AND RUINED,
THE PLASTER FLAKING AND FALLING OFF.
THE THATCH WAS FALLING EVERY WHICH WAY,
AND THE RAFTERS AND EAVEPOLES WERE COMING LOOSE.
THE PARTITIONS ON ALL SIDES WERE
BENT AND MISSHAPEN;
IT WAS FILLED WITH ALL KINDS OF FILTH.

Outline:

L2. Verse about the house.

Commentary:

WHO HAD A LARGE HOUSE/ The large house is the Three Realms, the desire realm, the form realm, and the formless realm. WHICH WAS VERY OLD/ It is said,

> There's no peace in the three realms;
> It is like a burning house.

AND SO WAS COLLAPSING/ It was just about to fall apart. We can also use the old house as an analogy for the human body. There is a poem which goes:

> Our bodies are like a house.
> The eyes are the windows, the mouth a door.
> Our four limbs are like the pillars,
> And our hair is like the thatch on top.
> Always keep it in good repair.
> Don't wait until it falls apart and then panic.

"Our bodies are like a house/ The eyes are the windows, the mouth a door"/ The mouth is like a door and the two eyes are like windows. Windows let light in the room, and our eyes allow us to see things. "Our hair is like the thatch on top"/ They don't have such houses in America, but in China some of the houses have grass thatch on the top, and it looks like the hair growing on our heads. "Always keep it in good repair"/ Keep up with the repairs as necessary. "Don't wait until it falls apart and then panic"/ When you are young, your house in in "good repair." Once you are old, then the "house" is about ready to fall over. When you are old and about to die, you'll realize that you can't live in that "house" anymore. You'll have to move. You may think to repair your house then, but it will be too late. The machine will have been overworked. That's how people's bodies work, too. They have to be kept in good repair when one is young. "Good repair" means to cultivate the Way. You should sit in Dhyana meditation, bow to the Buddha and to the Sutras, or recite mantras. Today I taught you your first Chinese lesson, and it was a good foundation for all of you:

"I got up today at four o'clock." The early morning is the best time to get up. It is said,

> The plans for one's life are made
> when one is young and strong.
> The plans for the year are made in the Spring.
> The plans for the day are made in the morning.

During one's life one must be vigorous. The most important time of the year is the Springtime, when the ten thousand things are blooming. As for the day, the most important time is early in the morning. It's best to get up early and take a walk in the garden, breathe some fresh air. That will give you energy. So, you get up at four and then wash your face, brush your teeth. Then, since there's nothing much to do, you can sit in meditation...Ahhh...At this time there is nothing moving at all. It's the very best time, the most precious time, to work hard. While you are sitting it is easy to get a response with the Way. Then, after a while when your legs start to hurt, or even if you have gotten past the pain, you may wish to get up and do some exercise. How? Bow to the Buddha. Bow and rise, and your circulation improves throughout your entire body. It's even better than doing yoga! When you have finished bowing to the Buddha, and you feel wide awake, then you can recite Sutras to regulate your breath and then secretly recite mantras. When you recite the mantras, you don't need to recite them out loud. We recite mantras here out loud, but that is for the public ceremonies. In real cultivation you recite them in your mind. This is called vajra mantra recitation. After that, you can go to work. When you get off work at five oclock you come to the Buddhist Lecture Hall to study Chinese and hear the Sutra lectures. You even skip dinner! The last sentence of the Chinese lesson says, "Are you hungry?" We will have to have to wait until tomorrow to answer that question.

THE HALLS WERE HIGH AND PRECARIOUS/ The Elder is the Buddha. His great house is the Three Realms in which all living beings live. The Three Realms are so old, we say they had no beginning. The house was just about ready to fall apart. It was already useless. This is speaking externally. If you use your own body as an analogy, you see that the house of the body eventually falls apart, too.

The halls represent the desire realm and the form realm. These halls are said to be high and precarious because it is very easy to fall and lose this human body. Sometimes one falls from the heavens, they are so high. A high place is very dangerous because when you fall, you lose your life. This means that in the desire and form realms, one doesn't know if one will fall into the hells, become an animal or turn into a hungry ghost. One doesn't know what path one will fall into and so it is extremely dangerous.

THE PILLARS ROTTING AT THEIR BASES/ You could say our legs are like the pillars. Our feet are the bases. They are rotting! This is talking about the sufferings of birth, old age, sickness and death. From birth one grows to adulthood, grows old, gets sick and then dies.

THE BEAMS AND RIDGEPOLES ASLANT/ Beams and ridgepoles are like our backs. They are crumbling and useless.

THE FOUNDATIONS AND STAIRWAYS CRUMBLING/ Foundations refers to, in the analogy of the body, the place where we "sit down." It also represents our karmic obstacles.

THE WALLS AND PARTITIONS WERE CRACKED AND RUINED/ The walls represent the skin and flesh of our bodies. When we get old, our skin gets cracked and wrinkled.

THE PLASTER FLAKING AND FALLING OFF/ The plaster

here refers to our complexions. THE THATCH WAS FALLING EVERY WHICH WAY/ AND THE RAFTERS AND EAVEPOLES WERE COMING LOOSE/ THE PARTITIONS WERE BENT AND MISSHAPEN/ IT WAS FILLED WITH ALL KINDS OF FILTH/ It was twisted out of shape. The thatch falling off is like our hair falling out. The rafters and eavepoles means our four limbs all falling apart. "Filth" refers to the things in our digestive systems, the urine and excrement inside us. We are entirely filled with these unclean things.

Each one of us has a "house." It is our own body. The body has "walls." They are the four elements and the four applications of mindfulness. When the walls fall apart, that is like when the four elements disperse. Earth, water, fire, and air--they all return to their origin. They disperse and the body dies.

As to the problem of human life, everyone should see it clearly. Don't let the mind become the body's slave, busy serving it all day long, with no time of waking up.

> From of old few have lived to be seventy.
> When you take off years for youth and age,
> There's not much time in between.
> And what's more, half of that is spent asleep!

There have never been very many people who have lived to age seventy. Most people die in their fifties or sixties. Some die in their twenties, some even younger. Few folks live to be seventy, but let's pretend that someone did. The first ten years of his live is pretty meaningless, because he doesn't understand what's going on around him. The last ten years he can't do anything either. That takes ten years off each end, leaving fifty years. Half of that is spent in sleep. That leaves just twenty-five years. There is also time to be taken off for eating, changing your clothes and going to the toilet, drinking tea and chatting about this and that. How much time is left? You have to take off at the very least another five years for that, leaving twenty years. Is that really so long? So what great meaning does human life have?

Yesterday, in Chinese class, I asked you, "Are you hungry?' Today, in your lessons you learned, "I don't feel hungry."

I asked you, "Why don't you feel hungry?"

You answered, "Because I get to listen to the Buddhadharma, and understand the true principles of human life." What I have just talked about here are the true principles of human life. If you understand them, you can be geuinely happy. When you are genuinely happy, you forget about being hungry. Do you see how wonderful this is? It may just look like a Chinese lesson, but it has a great deal of principle, if you look into it deeply. Your study of the Buddhadharma has brought you true peace of mind and real happiness, so you forget all about eating. Don't forget your Chinese lessons. People who study Buddhism should pay special attention to them. You're learning Chinese and the principles of the Buddhadharma at the same time. That's really great!! That's why I told our guest today that I charge a thousand dollars an hour for my Chinese lessons. That's not too much. If you get to end birth and death, that's simply priceless.

Sutra: T.13c23

THERE WERE FIVE HUNDRED PEOPLE

DWELLING WITHIN IT.

Outline:

L3. Verse about the five hundred people.

Commentary:

THERE WERE FIVE HUNDRED PEOPLE/ DWELLING WITHIN IT/ There were five hundred people in this big house. Five hundred stands for the living beings in the five destinies--gods, humans, hell-beings, hungry ghosts, and animals. It is the same as the six destinies with the ommision of the destiny of the asuras because asuras can be found in all of the other five destinies. Five hundred people, then, were living in the burning house of the Three Realms.

Sutra: T.13c25

THERE WERE KITES, OWLS, HAWKS, AND VULTURES,

CROWS, MAGPIES, PIGEONS, AND DOVES,
BLACK SNAKES, VIPERS, AND SCORPIONS,
CENTIPEDES AND MILLIPEDES.
THERE WERE GECKOES AND MYRIAPODS,
WEASELS, BADGERS, AND MICE--
ALL SORTS OF EVIL CREATURES,
RUNNING BACK AND FORTH.
THERE WERE PLACES STINKING OF EXCREMENT
AND URINE,
OOZING WITH FILTH,
WITH DUNG BEETLES
CLUSTERED UPON THEM.
THERE WERE FOXES, WOLVES, AND YEH KAN,
WHO NIBBLED AT, TRAMPLED ON,
AND DEVOURED CORPSES,
SCATTERING THE BONES AND FLESH.
THEN PACKS OF DOGS
CAME RUNNING TO GRAB THEM,
HUNGRY, WEAK, AND TERRIFIED,
SEEKING FOOD EVERYWHERE,
FIGHTING AND SHOVING,
SNARLING, HOWLING, AND BARKING.
THE TERRORS IN THAT HOUSE,
AND THE SIGHTS WERE SUCH AS THESE.
LI MEI AND WANG LIANG
WERE EVERYWHERE.
YAKSHAS AND EVIL GHOSTS
WERE EATING HUMAN FLESH.
THERE WERE POISONOUS CREATURES OF ALL KINDS,
AND EVIL BIRDS AND BEASTS,
HATCHING THEIR YOUNG,
EACH PROTECTING ITS OWN.
YAKSHAS RACED TO THE SPOT

FIGHTING ONE ANOTHER TO EAT THEM.
HAVING EATEN THEIR FILL,
THEIR EVIL THOUGHTS GREW MORE INFLAMED.
THE SOUND OF THEIR QUARRELING,
WAS DREADFUL TO THE EXTREME.
KUMBHANDA GHOSTS
WERE SQUATTING ON HIGH GROUND,
SOMETIMES LEAVING THE GROUND
A FOOT OR TWO,
AS THEY WANDERED TO AND FRO
AMUSING THEMSELVES AS THEY WISHED,
GRABBING DOGS BY TWO LEGS,
AND STRIKING THEM SO THEY LOST THEIR BARK,
TWISTING THEIR LEGS AROUND THEIR NECKS,
FRIGHTENING THE DOGS FOR THEIR OWN PLEASURE.
FURTHER THERE WERE GHOSTS,
THEIR BODIES VERY TALL AND LARGE,
NAKED, BLACK, AND THIN,
ALWAYS DWELLING THEREIN,
EMITTING LOUD AND EVIL SOUNDS,
HOWLING IN SEARCH OF FOOD.
FURTHER THERE WERE GHOSTS
WITH THROATS LIKE NEEDLES.
AGAIN THERE WERE GHOSTS
WITH HEADS LIKE OXEN,
NOW EATING HUMAN FLESH,
AND THEN DEVOURING DOGS.
THEIR HAIR WAS DISHEVELLED
THEY WERE HARMFUL, CRUEL AND DANGEROUS,
OPPRESSED BY HUNGER AND THIRST,
THEY RAN ABOUT SHOUTING AND CRYING OUT.
THERE WERE YAKSHAS, HUNGRY GHOSTS,
AND ALL SORTS OF EVIL BIRDS AND BEASTS,

FRANTIC WITH HUNGER, FACING THE FOUR DIRECTIONS,
PEEKING OUT THE WINDOWS.
SUCH WERE THE TROUBLES
AND TERRORS BEYOND MEASURE THERE.

Outline:

L4. Verse about the fire starting.
M1. Events above ground likened to the desire realm.
N1. The beings burnt.

Commentary:

THERE WERE KITES, OWLS...In *The Book of Songs* it says,

> The owl, the owl--
> The unfilial bird...

The owl is said to be unfilial because as soon as it is born, it eats its mother. The owl is hatched out of a lump of dirt that the mother sits on. As soon as it is born, the first thing it does it eat its mother. The mother just sits there and waits to be eaten. She is being very compassionate indeed, giving her life to her child, but you could also call it a kind of retribution. In past lives, the mother bird was unfilial, and so in this life she is a bird who ends up being eaten by her child. The head of an owl looks like a cat. They eat mice. In China, these birds are considered very unlucky. Whoever sees an owl is in for some hard times, some inauspicious events. Nothing is going to go right for them. In China there is a saying,

> "When the owl shows up in your house,
> Hard times is a-comin'."

If an owl flies into your house, someone's going to die, or else there's going to be a fire, or perhaps thieves will come and rob you--a lot of unlucky things are coming your way. So no one wants to set eyes on this bird.

How did it get to be an owl? When it was a person it was not filial to its parents, and was extremely arrogant. "See me? I'm bigger than my mom and dad." At home they acted like the Emperor and outside they acted like the President. Since they thought they were so incredibly fine, they forgot to be filial to their parents, and they turned into owls.

HAWKS are huge birds. AND VULTURES: Vultures and hawks like to eat dead things, human or animal corpses. Why? When these birds were people they liked to look down on everyone and make big plans for themselves. They liked being high, always thinking they were number one. They always schemed about how well-off they were going to be, but they never did anything. They had a lot of fancy plans, all right, but they did things very clumsily. They forgot their plans before they put them into action. They had fine ambitions, but they accomplished nothing. At night they had a thousand schemes going through their brains, but during the day they just took a lot of naps. False thinking all night and sleeping all day, they didn't benefit the world at all. They were of no use to themselves or to anyone else, but their minds created a lot of offenses. Because of all their wild plans, they turned into high-flying birds. People who like to "fly high" can turn into these high-flying, far-ranging birds.

The birds mentioned here represent arrogance, one of the Five Dull Servants: greed, hate, stupidity, arrogance, and doubt. There are eight kinds of birds which represent eight kinds of arrogance. Birds, when they were people, liked to "fly high," and they were very arrogant and conceited and looked down on other people. They didn't think anyone else measured up to them, and they pushed people around. If they had money, they looked down on the poor. If they had some talent, they look down on those less gifted. If they had a tiny bit of wisdom, they felt superior. In general, they looked on others as very low and upon themselves as very high. Birds swoop down from on high and feel that they are above it all. Yesterday we talked about the kites and owls. Hawks are very large birds and fly very high. They eat small animals, even deer and rabbits. They can swoop down, pick up a deer by the legs and fly up into the sky with it. Vultures like to eat rotting flesh, unclean things, like dead mice or dead cats, animals long dead and crawling with worms, terribly smelly.

CROWS are the opposite of owls. Crows are very filial birds. Why are they said to be filial? By the time the little crows are hatched out of their eggs and have learned to fly, the mother crow can't fly anymore. So the little crows go out and get food and drink and bring it back to the old mother crow. Although they are filial, they are still very arrogant. They are conceited.

Crows are black. MAGPIES are about the same size as crows. Chinese people consider them lucky. If they hear a magpie chattering in the morning, they are happy and think, "Today something lucky is going to happen. Perhaps an important guest will come. Something nice is going to happen." Everyone likes this bird.

PIGEONS: Most birds eat bugs, but pigeons just eat grains. They don't eat bugs. DOVES think they are very beautiful. Those are eight kinds of birds which represent the...

Eight kinds of Arrogance

1. Kites represent arrogance over one's prosperity.

2. Owls represent arrogance over one's name. When they were people they thought that they had the most noble family name.

3. Hawks represent arrogance over one's wealth. When they were people they took pride in being wealthier than everyone else. You could say that people who are very snobbish because of their wealth are just acting like hawks.

4. Vultures represent arrogance over one's freedom. They feel totally free and unfettered. They can eat whenever they feel like it, because they just eat rotten stuff anyway; they like it and considered it a practice which gives them a lot of freedom. Actually it's just an unbeneficial bitter practice.

5. Crows represent arrogance over longevity. They feel that they can live for a very long time. Even if they don't they still think that they do because they are conceited about their longevity.

6. Magpies represent arrogance over intelligence. Many people have this type of arrogance. They feel that they are the smartest of all.

7. Pigeons represent arrogance over good works. They

say, "See? You are all carnivores and I am not!" and they are arrogant over their good deeds.

8. Doves represent arrogance over beauty. They are always flying around and showing off in front of people. "See how lovely I am?" they say. They don't start flying until you get real close to them because they are waiting for you to get close enough to see how lovely they are when they fly around.

So the eight types of birds stand for eight kinds of arrogance, arrogance being the fourth of the Five Dull Servants. Arrogant people feel that when they are at home they are the Emperor and when they step outside, they are the President. They are always better than the next person.

BLACK SNAKES, VIPERS, AND SCORPIONS/ CENTIPEDES AND MILLIPEDES/ These are poisonous creatures. Black snakes are extremely poisonous, the most venemous of all snakes. Vipers are also a kind of snake. They are about three inches wide and extremely poisonous. Scorpions also sting people. Centipedes have red heads. The ones without red heads are millipedes. They, too, are very poisonous. On the first day of the fifth lunar month of each year, in Manchuria we go the mountains to gather mugwort, a medicinal herb. Then we put a tiny bit in our ears. This prevents the millipedes from crawling in our ears. After a long, long time they can turn into strange, wierd people. They are afraid of the medicinal properties of the mugwort plant, however. If someone gets one of these bugs in their ear they will die because it will poison their brain. The poisonous bugs represent hatred, which is the second of the Five Dull Servants. Whoever is hateful can easily turn into one of these creatures. So take care not to be hateful or get angry.

THERE WERE GECKOES AND MYRIAPODS/ WEASELS, BADGERS, AND MICE--/ ALL SORTS OF EVIL CREATURES/ RUNNING BACK AND FORTH/ Geckoes live in the walls of houses. In Chinese their name means, literally, "protectors of the palace."[1] This is because the old

---

1 -*shou kung*.

Emperors had many concubines. They would take the blood of the gecko and smear it on each concubine's arm. If the concubines had not engaged in sexual relations, the blood would stay on their arms even if they tried to wash it off. If they had had sexual relations, then the blood would disappear. The women in the place got smeared with this blood and their arms were checked everyday to see if they had been true to the Emperor. This is what the legend says, but there's no way to know for sure now whether it actually worked this way. Myriapods are creatures with a lot of legs. They are black and about three inches long.

As I said, the fifth month of the lunar year is the month for gathering medicinal herbs. From the first of the fifth month to the fifth of the fifth month, any grass or plant or herb you pick is medicinal. The mugwort gathered on that day is said to be especially potent. That's a legend in China.

In Manchuria, there are two kinds of weasels. One is called "huang-hsien" and one is called "hu-hsien." The "huang-hsien" is about three feet long, but not very tall, about as tall as a cat. It has a big tail, half as long as its body. They can let off a stink to discourage dogs from chasing them. It's sort of like the mace cans the police use. They set off their "stink bombs" to protect themselves from attack. It stinks worse than anything. Some are yellow, some are black and white. After a thousand years they turn black. After ten thousand years they turn white. After a hundred years they have a certain amount of spiritual penetrations. They are very talented, sort of like foxes.

Badgers eat chickens and cats and ducks, little animals. Mice: These mice are very strange. They are called "sweet mouth mice," because they can bite you are drink your blood, but you feel no pain.

The geckoes and myriapods represent the third of the Five Dull Servants, stupidity. This is because they have no wisdom. They also represent one of the two kinds of ignorance, "solitary head ignorance." The weasels, badgers, and mice represent the other kind of ignorance, "responsive ignorance," because they help each other out.

All sorts of evil creatures, those creatures discussed above, representing the two kinds of ignorance, were running back and forth. They ran from north to south, from east to west as the house caught fire. This is talking about the mark of karma in the three realms. The mark of karma cuts in a criss-cross through our lives without any end. It arises very fast, "running" as it were, throughout our lives.

THERE WERE PLACES STINKING OF EXCREMENT AND URINE/ OOZING WITH FILTH/ WITH DUNG BEETLES CLUSTERED UPON THEM/ Excrement and urine are found inside our bodies. No matter how well washed we are on the outside, we are still just as dirty on the inside, just as smelly. You can drink perfume if you want, but you'll still smell inside. Why love such an unclean thing as if it were a treasure. That's just being too stupid,really. They represent the stupidity of being attached to states.States are all impermanent, without a self, suffering, and impure. In what is impure, we become attached to purity. We greedily attach to this impurity and don't realize it stinks as much as it does.

Dung beetles live in excrement. People think that excrement is unclean, but the dung beetles like it a lot, yes they do. They think, "This is really a fine place I've got here!" Hah! See how they are? Sometimes they offer a piece of excrement to the Buddha. They eat it, I mean, so they think it's good to offer to the Buddha. Now, does the Buddha get upset over this? No. Even though it is unclean, still they are offering it with respect so the Buddha doesn't blame them. After all, they don't have anything else. That's it as far as their valuable things to offer the Buddha go. Since they made sincere offerings to the Buddha, they can eventually drop their dung-beetle bodies and in their next lives become people. But they are usually poor people, lowly people, or deaf, dumb, or blind people because their karmic obstructions from past lives are too heavy. Anyway, the dung-beetles were all clustered on the excrement and urine in the dirty places in the house. You might try to improve their lot, saying to them, "Hey, dung-beetles, it's too dirty there. Come on, I'm going to relocate you somewhere else." So you put them in a bottle of perfume thinking you are being very good to them and what happens? They die in less than an hour. They don't have the blessings to withstand it. They can only live in the excrement and urine. Move them and they die. Last year there were some people from another cultivating group who came here and I explained this principle to them. I said, "Wherever you have affinites, that is where you will go. If you like to study what is false, you will go somewhere where it is false. If you want to study what is true, you will find a true place. If you move the bugs in the toilet to a bottle of perfume, they won't be able to live there, they will feel very uncomfortable."

Hearing this principle, we students of the Buddhadharma should think it over. Don't choose a place that stinks. At the least, burn a bit of incense before the Buddhas everyday. Study the real Buddhadharma. Don't study improper Buddhadharma. Don't run into the pile of shit to stay. If you stay there, it is of no great advantage to you.

THERE WERE FOXES, WOLVES, AND YEH KAN/ WHO NIBBLED AT, TRAMPLED ON/ AND DEVOURED CORPSES/ SCATTERING THE BONES AND FLESH/ This section of text represents the last two of the Five Dull Servants, greed and doubt. In China, everyone knows about fox spirits. They specialize in confusing people. How do they do this? They confuse people to the point that they don't know anything at all. In China they have an analogy comparing "bad" women to foxes. They say, "She's a foxy lady..." about improper women. Also, foxes have a lot of doubts. When they walk across the ice, no matter how thick it is, they still walk a step and then cock their heads and listen to see if the ice creaks. If it doesn't they keep walking, take anouther step, and then stop and listen again.

Wolves are sort of like dogs. They are terribly cruel. No matter what kind of small animal it is they kill it; it doesn't matter whether they are going to eat it or not. They can drag off a hundred year old pig and eat it! They are the most violent of animals. When I was in Nanking I was living in Kung-ch'ing Mountain. I went to Lung-t'an and on the way back the sky suddenly grew dark and a whole pack of wolves descended. They have their own language and when one wolf howls all the wolves gather together, and they eat whoever is on the road. They rip them apart and split up the meat. That night I met a lot of wolves. It was about eight or nine o'clock at night, and they were all around in the trees right next to the road. As I walked along they followed me, protecting me. *I* thought they were protecting me. Of course, they thought they were getting ready to eat me. I thought they were guarding me. We walked along together for five or six miles, but they didn't eat me. They were my good friends. In fact I gave them the Three Refuges. You see, I have wolves for disciples. After I accepted them in the Three Refuges, they didn't think about biting people anymore. There were over twenty of them.

Yeh kan belong to the fox family. They are not

actually foxes, but they are even smarter than foxes, foxes being pretty smart in their own right. They live way out in the wilds where no one at all lives. They live in very dangerous places, places where no human could reach. Even hawks can't get there. They live high up in caves or atop very tall trees. They don't come out during the day, but roam at night in packs of four or five. They howl with a very strange sound to make all the other animals afraid. They are very weird animals, the yeh kan.

The yeh kan ate the corpses slowly, bit by bit. When there were a lot of corpses, they tramped on them. Then ran all over them, wasting them. When there were a lot, they just wasted them, they trampled on them. They devoured the corpses, ripping into the blood and bones with their lips and teeth. Then they scattered the bones and flesh everywhere, leaving everything in a shambles.

THEN PACKS OF DOGS/ CAME RUNNING TO GRAB THEM/ HUNGRY, WEAK, AND TERRIFIED/ SEEKING FOOD EVERYWHERE/ Once the flesh and bones were scattered about, the dogs came to fight over the leftovers. Hungry represents not understanding the Buddhadharma. If you don't understand the Buddhadharma, you are hungry. When your Dharmabody is not perfected you are weak. So, people who haven't heard the Buddhadharma are hungry and weak. Terrified means they were very frightened, very upset, not serene at all, running hither and thither, seeking food everywhere. The dogs came running to the scene greedy for food. This represents greed which is also one of the Five Dull Servants. Because they can't get any food, they fight for it.

FIGHTING AND SHOVING/ SNARLING, HOWLING, AND BARKING/ THE TERRORS IN THAT HOUSE/ AND THE SIGHTS WERE SUCH AS THESE/ The dogs were fighting, showing their teeth. They were howling and barking. Things were absolutely terrifying in that house of the five skandhas. From the beginning of the verse to this point we have been talking about greed, hatred, stupidity, arrogance, and doubt, the Five Dull Servants. Below, we will be talking about the Five Quick Servants. The Five Dull Servants turn people totally upside-down. They may want to wake up a bit, but it's not easy. They are as if tied up by the Five Dull Servants in this house where it is very dangerous. We better quickly find a way to slay the Five Dull Servants. That won't be a case of breaking the precepts, either, so don't worry about that.

LI MEI AND WANG LIANG/ WERE EVERYWHERE/ YAKSHAS AND EVIL GHOSTS/ WERE EATING HUMAN FLESH/ "Everywhere" speaking in broad terms means the entire three realms. In more specific terms, it refers to our bodies. No matter whether you speak of it in terms of the three realms or the body there are these creatures everywhere.

Li is a kind of ghost that stays very far away from people. Where are they found? They dwell in the mountains. They are weird creatures in the mountains, also called mountain essences.

The weird creatures you find in your house are called *mei*, and they play tricks on people. There are many kinds of them. There are very obvious ones; they can play all kinds of uncanny tricks and do thing which ordinary people can't even perceive.

Wang liang ghosts are transformations of stone or wood. After a long period of time, rocks can come to life. Not very many of them do this. For a rock to come to life it must have been touched with human blood. In fact, anything that is touched with human blood, specifically blood from a fingertip, can come to life. It does so by means of the person's blood and vital energy. The *wang liang* are the largest type of ghosts. They are as big as mountains. Sometimes Chinese people run into these ghosts while they are out walking at night. They try to walk forward, but it is as if there is a mountain blocking them and they can't move forward. I remember one of my brothers met one of these ghosts at night. When this happens no matter what you do you can't walk to any other place. You are stuck right there until dawn when the cock crows and then you can go again.

Li and *mei* are very tiny ghosts, about three feet high. *Wang liang* are sometimes thirty, forty, or even three hundred feet high.

These lines represent the Five Quick Servants. Previously we spoke about the Five Dull Servants and now we are speaking about the Five Quick Servants. They are:

1. The view of a body.

2. Extreme views.

3. Views of unprincipled morality.

4. Deviant views.

5. Views of grasping at views

The Five Dull Servants are called "dull" because they come on slowly. Quickly means that they come on very fast and are very sharp. The Five Quick Servants also turn people upside-down. They make them attached. They cause them to do wrong things.

1. The view of a body. The view of a body means that one is always attached to one's body. From morning until night one works on its behalf, buying it a little candy or sprinkling it with a little perfume, giving it some nice clothes and a nice place to live. That's called being attached to the body. One thinks, "My body is just me!" Actually, that is wrong. How is it wrong? The body can only be said to belong to you. You can say, "It's mine." But you can't say, "It's me." Why not? The body is like a house. When you are living in a house you can't tell people "My house is me." You can just say, "It's mine." Ultimately, you are not your body. Don't mistake the real owner. If you are attached to the body as yourself, you are wrong. I always say, if you look from the tip of the head to the soles of your feet, your head is called your head, your eyes are called eyes, your ears are called ears, your hair is called hair, your nose is called a nose, the mouth is called the mouth, the skin is called the skin, the hands are called the hands, the feet are called the feet. Everything has its name. Which one of them is called "me?" You can look all over your entire body, and you won't find a "me." This is because the body is "mine;" it is not "me." It is not you. It belongs to you, that's all. If you calculate on its behalf all the time, when, as the poet *T'ao Yüan-ming* said in his poem "The Return," your mind is acting as your body's slave. Your mind is your true self, the real owner in charge. The body is just like a house. The owner lives in the body. Here we are talking about the eternally dwelling real mind, the bright substance of the pure nature. That is really you, really me. It is also called the Thus Come One's Storehouse. It is also called the Buddha nature. So don't mistakenly think that the body is you. It's yours; it is not you. The real you is not produced and not destroyed, not defiled and not pure, not increasing and not decreasing. That's the real you. But instead of recognizing that real you, you reconize the false self and think that superficial thing, the body, is really you. If it is really you, then when the body dies, will you disappear, too? If you disappear, that is really meaningless. That's just a view of annihilation, which brings us to the second of the Five Quick Servants.

2. The view of taking sides. There are two sides: eternalism and annihilationism. In fact, when people die it is like their house has broken down and they have to move to a new one. They move to a new body. Where do they move to? It depends on what kind of karma they have created. If you create good karma, you move to a nice place. If you create evil karma, you move to an evil place. Death, then, is definitely not annihilation. We should see through the view of a body and put it down. Don't be attached to the view of a body.

To be attached either to eternalism or to annihilationism are the two kinds of attachments of non-Buddhist religions. The view of annihilation states, "When one dies it is like the lamp goes out. It's all over. If you do good, there is no retribution incurred. There is no retribution, either, for doing evil. If you do good deeds, when you die it's all over. If you do evil, again, when you die it's all over. There is no rebirth. So, don't believe in cause and effect. You don't have to because there is no cause and effect." These people deny cause and effect. They don't say that if you do good deeds you can become a Buddha or if you do evil things you can become a ghost. They don't believe in ghosts, they don't believe in the Buddha, and, in fact, they don't even believe in people! They think of people like grass or trees that get born and then die, and that's it. When one dies, another is born, but there is no rebirth of any specific living thing. One dies and another takes its place, that's all. What dies is forever dead; what is born is born anew. Because they don't believe in the revolution of the law of cause and effect, they deny the existence of the six paths of rebirth.

On the other side of the coin are those who hold to the extreme view of eternalism. They say that once you become a person it doesn't matter whether you do good or evil because you will always be a person. If you are a ghost, you are always going to be a ghost. Buddhas are always Buddhas. There is no change. God is eternal and he will always be god. Horses and cows will always be horses and cows. They say one never changes. Why not? Because you have that seed. People have the seed of people, Animals have the seed of animals. Ghosts have the seed of ghosts. If you fall into the hells you will always be there because you have the hell-seed in you. Everything is fixed and absolute. In reality there is nothing that is fixed for sure. There are no fixed dharmas. But they say that everything is fixed. There are no transformations. It's all ironclad. God is the only god. No one else can be god. That's the view of eternalism. Eternalism and annihilationism are the two views held by non-Buddhist religions. No matter how good you are you'll never be god because the whole show is fixed. They say you must believe in god. If you believe in god, even if you do evil, you will go to heaven. See? If you don't believe in god, no matter how many good things you do, you are still going to fall into hells. God! There is no true principle involved here. It doesn't even make sense! That's the view of eternalism.

Annihilationism and eternalism are both extreme views. They are not in accord with the Middle Way. For example, if someone has extreme views about another person, that is, if he is prejudiced on their behalf, then that other person can do terrible things, but they will overlook it and say that that person is good. There's a person here, in fact, who thinks that way about himself. He makes up principles on the spot to suit his motives, but makes them sound very logical because his views are extreme. This is sophistry. He thinks that his opinions are correct. He thinks, to put it bluntly, that he is better than everyone else. In China we say that such a person is holding on to a turd and if you offered him a doughnut, he wouldn't trade you. He's got a big turd in his hand, but if you offered him a cookie or a nice piece of pastry, he wouldn't let go of that turd to accept your gift. No way! That's just being extreme. Hah! Extreme views, extreme indeed...Extreme views are very difficult to reform because they arise very quickly. They are also entirely unprincipled, and that is why they are called "extreme" views.

Now, people all have within them the cause of realizing Buddhahood. However, you have to go and do it. Even though you have causal conditions for realizing Buddhahood, if you don't do the work, you won't arrive at that position. If you do the work, you will naturally arrive at your goal. For example, before studying the Buddhadharma, people may do a lot of confused things. A lot of young people take drugs and turn into "stoned" people. That's one thing when you haven't studied the Buddhadharma, because you have no true understanding of what it means to be human. But after you have studied the Buddhadharma, you have to change. You can't continue to use drugs. If you do, you are deliberately violating the rules, just like the person I just talked about who is holding on to a turd and won't accept a doughnut. I have brought up this analogy hoping that everyone will quickly wake up. If you have never taken drugs, that's even better. If you are still taking them, then *put that turd down right now!!* Don't be a dung-beetle, because if you live in the excrement too long you will turn into one for sure. If you get out of there fast, you still have a chance to find out what it is like to be human and have a share in the human race. If fact, you can even set up the causes for becoming a Buddha.

3. Views of unprincipled morality. This refers to non-Buddhist religions who practice unprincipled morality. They grasp at morality saying that what is not a cause is a cause, and what is not an effect is an effect.

What is meant by "taking what is not a cause as a cause?" They cultivate unbeneficial ascetic practices. They say that in doing this they can attain Nirvana and the fruit of highest bliss. Their asceticism is a side-trip as far as cultivation goes. Because they do cultivate asceticism, some of them may open their Heavenly Eyes. Then, they may see cows or dogs, pigs or chickens who have been born in the heavens. Seeing this, they decide to imitate the cows, dogs, pigs, and chickens. They eat grass along with the cows instead of eating regular food because they think it will get them into heaven with the cows. They think that the reason the cow was born in heaven is because it eats grass! They think that eating grass is a very pure precept, purer than just not eating meat. They think it's the optimal vegetarian diet! This is called keeping "cow precepts."

Others imitate dogs. Dogs live outside in dog-houses, and they watch the door for people. They think that this gives the dogs merit and that their ascetic practices are real cultivation. They imitate the dogs and live in doghouses! They act like dogs, too. Dogs eat excrement and so do they. They eat what dogs eat. They also imitate chickens and pigs. These are the ascetic practices cultivated by non-Buddhist religions. Because of their asceticism, sometimes they are born in the heavens. Within the framework of their unprincipled precepts they do cultivate the ten good acts. They are attached, though. They are attached to "taking what is not a cause as a cause and what is not an effect as an effect." Basically, their thinking does not make sense.

Some non-Buddhist religions practice sleeping on

the ground like pigs. They roll in ashes until you can't recognize them at all. Others pound nails in a board and sleep on the nails. Sometimes the nails stick them and they bleed. They claim, "I am really an outstanding ascetic. You all couldn't do this because you are afraid of pain. I sleep right on the nails, and I'm not afraid they are going to poke me."

Others say, "You all sleep lying down. Well, watch this!" and they tie two ropes around their feet and sleep hanging upside-down. It's hard to sleep that way, all right, but they think it is real good cultivation because nobody else can do it. Others don't eat. They don't eat food, that is. Everybody else eats food, but not them. When they are hungry they eat dirt. They say that this is the true, natural, organic way of life. There's so much dirt on the earth; might as well live on it. They don't have to eat very much of it either. A little bit goes a long ways. These are all examples of unprincipled morality, unbeneficial bitter practices. What good are they? No good at all. Still, they like to practice them.

4. Deviant views. Deviant means improper. For example, cultivators of the Way should be filial to their parents, but people with deviant views say it isn't necessary."What good is it? Don't bother. They give birth to children and that is their job. You don't have to be filial to them," they say.

Killing is wrong, but they say, "The more you kill, the better." The first of the five precepts prohibits killing, but they instruct people to kill. Would you call that deviant or not? Stealing is also not right, but they use all kinds of methods to teach people how to steal. If someone doesn't know how to steal, they teach them how.

Sexual misconduct is wrong, too, but they teach people to engage in it. One shouldn't lie, either, but they teach people to lie. They say, "Don't listen to that stuff about not lying. Everybody lies. Some people just cheat and get away with it. Don't believe in that." That's a deviant view. Taking intoxicants is against the precepts, but they say it doesn't matter. Some people like to smoke and claim that in the five precepts, the precept against taking intoxicants doesn't include tobacco. "Smoking isn't breaking the precepts," they say, but that is a deviant view. Other people say, "You are a vegetarian and don't eat meat? But all the cows and sheep and pigs were made to be eaten. If you don't eat them what use are they?" They have their reasoning, but their views are deviant. In general, what is right they say is wrong. They think up ways to say things that will make you go along with their deviant understanding and deviant views.

5. Views of grasping at views. When they see things they want to take them and make them their own. No matter what kind of finagling they have to go through, they find ways to help themselves out. They are showing their selfishness.

These Five Quick Servants block your genuine wisdom like five servants surrounding you so you can't do anything freely. They control you so you have to listen to them. They lock you up.

Students of the Buddhadharma, now that you know about these Five Quick Servants, you should pick up your wisdom sword and slay them all. After you have done so you can transcend the three realms.

This has been a general discussion of the Five Quick Servants. If one were to explain them in detail one wouldn't finish to the end of an aeon.

Someone asks, "You say that cows and dogs, pigs and chickens were born in the heavens? How could that be? If they didn't cultivate how could they be born there? If it is that easy it's no wonder the non-Buddhists tried to imitate them. Everyone could do it and be born in the heavens."

That's a good question. The non-Buddhists had the penetration of the Heavenly Eye and they could see these animals had been born in the heavens. What they couldn't see was the reason why they were born in the heavens. The cows, for example, had been born there because they had worked in the fields of a monastery, pulling carts, plowing fields, and things like that. They established a lot of merit for themselves by working for the Buddhadharma and, with that merit and virtue they were born in the heavens. The dogs had saved people's lives. One dog really loved his master. One day his master fell asleep in a thicket. Actually, he passed out from having had too much to drink. Anyway, he was asleep in the grass and the grass caught fire. The dog starting barking madly, but since the man was so drunk, he didn't hear it. So the dog ran to the river and jumped in, got himself all wet, and filled his mouth up with water. Then he ran and rolled over and over in the fire and spit out the water and put out the fire. Since he gained merit and virtue from saving his master, he was reborn in the heavens. It was because of the merit he gained that he was born in the heavens. It wasn't because he watched the door or ate excrement. And it wasn't because the cow ate grass that it was born in the heavens. The pigs and the chickens were sent to a temple by people who decided to give them away instead of killing them for food. While they lived at the temple they heard people recite Sutras in the mornings and in the evenings they heard people recite the Buddha's name. They started reciting Sutras and the Buddha's name in their hearts along with the people. Because of the merit and virtue they gained by hearing the Sutras and the Buddha's name, they were born in the heavens. But those of non-Buddhist religions with their Heavenly Eyes only saw them up there in the heavens and didn't know the real reason why they were born there. They simply slavishly imitated their behavior, hoping to be born in the heavens, too. They never asked why they were born there. They just copied them and expected to get results. But we have to know the reasons behind things. How do beings get born in the heavens? What makes them fall into the hells? We should understand these things. It is not right just to cultivate in a haphazard manner. You need genuine wisdom. You should look into things deeply and gain a true understanding of them.

From the sentence "Yakshas and evil ghosts/ eating human flesh/" to the sentence "The sound of their quarreling/ Was dreadful to the extreme/" discusses the first of the Five Quick Servants, deviant views. *Li mei* and *wang liang* and yakshas have a shadow, but no material form. They do things in a very sneaky manner, not out in the open. So they are like people with deviant views who do things in a very shadowy, dark manner. They don't see the sky. They don't see the light.

YAKSHAS AND EVIL GHOSTS/ WERE EATING HUMAN FLESH/ Human flesh represents good retribution. If you do good deeds, you gain good retribution; if you do evil deeds, you gain evil retribution. Eating human flesh represents the denial of cause and effect. People who deny cause and effect say, "You need not be afraid of cause and effect." In this way, it is as if they were "eating" the good retribution. They eat it all up so there is no more. They say, "There's no cause and effect, so don't worry about it. There is no hell. There is no heaven. What is all this about creating offense karma? Do whatever you like! There are no offenses and there is no merit. The world is a free place. Do what you want to do. If you want to kill, kill. If you want to steal, go ahead. If you like the opposite sex, well, do as you please. Don't worry about it. If you can cheat people and get away with it, more power to you. If you have wine to drink, what's the problem? There's nothing in this world finer than drinking wine, anway. Why worry about all that stuff?" Hah! This is called "eating human flesh," taking all the good retribution and eating it right up. Would you say this was extreme or not? These verses represent deviant views.

THERE WERE POISONOUS CREATURES OF ALL KINDS/ AND EVIL BIRDS AND BEASTS/ HATCHING THEIR YOUNG/ EACH PROTECTING ITS OWN/ There were snakes, scorpions, etc. and wolves, and all kinds of evil animals. There were fierce birds like hawks who eat deer. The birds protected their young and didn't let anyone see them. The animals gave birth to their young and protected them, too. If someone saw them they might steal and eat them. So they hid them. This is also an analogy for cause and effect in the world. Where there is a cause, there is certainly bound to be an effect. You could say that the effect is hidden in the cause. As you plant the cause, although the effect does not manifest at that time, still it is hidden there and in the future will certainly manifest. Where there is a cause,there will be an effect, and this is what is meant by "hidden." That effect is certain to be manifested and will not be lost, and that is what is meant by "protected." The cause will not be lost. This is an analogy for cause and effect. If you plant a good cause you will reap good fruit; if you plant an evil cause you will reap an evil fruit. It's for sure. No matter how you try, you can't get out of cause and effect. It remains, as it were, "hidden and protected."

YAKSHAS RACED TO THE SPOT/ FIGHTING ONE ANOTHER TO EAT THEM/ Because there weren't too many things to eat, and there were a lot of yakshas, they had to fight to get something to eat. This represents the denial of cause and effect. They think that there is neither cause nor effect. So they fight with one another to eat them. HAVING EATEN THEIR FILL/ THEIR EVIL THOUGHTS GREW MORE INFLAMED/This line represents the accomplishment of their deviant views. Before their deviant views have become a reality, they simply have thoughts of deviant views. Now their deviant views have manifested in reality and so they eat and are filled. Once their deviant views have become realized, then they increase. Day by day. their deviant views increase. Day by day they grow larger. THE SOUND OF THEIR QUARRELING/ WAS DREADFUL TO THE EXTREME/ They fought and argued. There is a saying,

> "Debating, thoughts of victory and defeat
> Stand in contradiction to the Way;

Giving rise to the four-mark mind,
How can samadhi be attained?"

The four marks are the mark of self, of others, of living beings, and of a lifespan. Once there is the mark of self, then there is the mark of others. The mark of self plus the mark of others turns into the mark of living beings. Once there are living beings, then there is a lifespan. You can't attain samadhi that way. The sound of their quarelling represents the deviant debates carried on by those who deny cause and effect. Basically, there is no principle in what they say, but they make it sound like there is. The sound was dreadful to the extreme. Terrifying, just horrifying. This line represents people who, hearing these deviant debates, become confused. Once they are confused, they create evil karma. Creating evil karma, they fall into the three evil paths. It is really scary. Once you fall into the three evil paths it is hard to get out again. Perhaps some special causal condition will enable you to get out, but still it's very, very hard.

KUMBHANDA GHOSTS/ WERE SQUATTING ON HIGH GROUND/ SOMETIMES LEAVING THE GROUND/ A FOOT OR TWO/ AS THEY WANDERED TO AND FRO / AMUSING THEMSELVES AS THEY WISHED/ GRABBING DOGS BY TWO LEGS/ AND STRIKING THEM SO THEY LOST THEIR BARK/ TWISTING THEIR LEGS AROUND THEIR NECKS/ FRIGHTENING THE DOGS FOR THEIR OWN PLEASURE/ These verses represent the third of the Five Quick Servants, that is, views of unprincipled morality. Kumbhanda ghosts are ghosts that look like watermelons. They haven't any head and they haven't any feet. They are round. They are also called *yen mei*, and they stay far away from people, except at night when they go and sit on them. When you wake up, they run far away. When you go to sleep, they come to get you. They are like great big melons who sit right down on you and make you feel like you can hardly breathe. You can't talk; you can't move. You're paralyzed. They have a dharma they do to cause you to be unable to speak. You can stare out into space, but you can't say anything. Some people even get crushed to death by them. Kumbhandas represent the views of unprincipled morality.

The ghosts were squatting on high ground and this represents the six heavens in the realm of desire. These heavens are like "high places." In non-Buddhist religions, they keep the cow, dog, pig, and chicken precepts and, by keeping to their unprinciple morality they cultivate the ten good acts and thereby gain rebirth in the various desire heavens.

1. The heaven of the four kings.

2. The heaven of the thirty-three.

3. The suyama heaven.

4. The tushita heaven.

5. The nirmanarati heaven.

6. The paranirmitavashavartin heaven.

The ghosts sometimes leave the ground a foot or two. This represents those non-Buddhists, who, relying on unprincipled morality, cultivate the Way. One foot off the ground represents ascending to the form realm to be born in the Four Dhyanas. Two feet off the ground represents their ascending to the formless realm to be born in the four formless concentrations.

They wandered to and fro: "To" represents those being born in the form and formless realms. "Fro" represents those returning to be born in the desire realm again. Within the three realms we are sometimes born in the upper realms and sometimes we fall into the lower realms. People in this world are in an extremely dangerous position. We are like motes of dust suddenly high, suddenly low, suddenly above, suddenly below. In the burning house of the three realms, if you do deeds of merit and virtue, you will be born in the heavens. If you create offenses, you will fall into the hells or turn into an animal or a hungry ghost. So it is very dangerous. The motes of dust float with the wind. They go where the wind blows, from one place to another. People float with the wind of their karma. The karma you create, if good, will enable you to be born in the heavens. If you create evil karma, you will fall into the hells. That is what is meant by the sentence of text "As they wandered to and fro."

"Amusing themselves freely" means just doing whatever they feel like doing, that is, not following the rules. Freely means being lazy and doing what you like. They played and sported in the three realms thinking it a lot of fun, when actually it is very dangerous. This line represents people not understanding true principle and having no real happiness. All their happiness is nothing more than a kind of shallow amusement, like going to a play. Is the pleasure of watching a play ultimately real or not? Does it last? It's entirely false.

The ghosts grab the dogs by two legs and strike them so they loose their bark. This represents those non-Buddhist religions who cultivate ascetic practices. They falsely think that their bitter practices will eventually bring about the realization of their karma of the Way. In reality, their ascetic practices are all without benefit. They imitate the dogs, pigs, chickens, and cows. What is the use of such practices? Eating grass? Eating excrement? Rolling in ashes? No use. Grabbing them by the two legs represents those who cultivate unbeneficial ascetic practices and falsely think that they will gain the fruit of purity. Striking them so they loose their bark represents those non-Buddhists who, in cultivating their unbeneficial ascetic practices take what is not a cause to be a cause. They think, "Now I am cultivating ascetic practices and things are certainly going to be good for me in the future. I won't reap any bitter fruit." That is just taking what is not a cause to be a cause.

Twisting their legs around their necks represents non-Buddhists and their bitter practices, taking what is not an effect to be an effect. They won't gain the result of happiness, but they falsely think that their practices will result in happiness, in the fruit of Nirvana.

They frighten the dogs for their own pleasure. When the dogs are scared they cry out. The ghosts are really happy because the dogs are afraid of them. When the dogs are afraid of them, they are delighted. This represents those of non-Buddhist religions using their unbeneficial bitter practices to temporarily subdue their afflictions. This is like using a rock to smother grass. Their afflictions are like the grass and their bitter practices are like the big rock. The rock may cover the grass, but as soon as you remove the rock, the grass grows right back, even thicker than before because you have not pulled the grass out by its roots. Non-Buddhist ascetics may subdue their more obvious afflictions temporarily, but they do not wipe them out at the root. Sometimes they attain a bit of the flavor of Dhyana. What is the flavor or Dhyana? It is bliss, great happiness. This is the stage where one is just on the verge of attaining the first Dhyana, the stage of the bliss of leaving production.

FURTHER THERE WERE GHOSTS/ THEIR BODIES VERY TALL AND LARGE/ NAKED, BLACK, AND THIN/ ALWAYS DWELLING THEREIN/ EMITTING LOUD AND EVIL SOUNDS/ HOWLING IN SEARCH OF FOOD/ These lines represent the first of the Five Quick Servants, the view of a body. There were many different kinds of ghosts, fat ghosts and thin ghosts, black ghosts and white ghosts, and naked ghosts. Some were very tall, as big as those *wang liang* we talked about before. Some had no clothes and some were black, with no flesh on their bones at all. They were all within the burning house. "Tall" represents the assumption of a self which pervades, vertically, the three periods of time, past, present, and future. "Large" represents the assumption of a self which pervades, horizontally, the five skandhas. "Naked" means that they are very free and don't cultivate good dharmas; they have no shame. They don't feel that they are wrong because they have no shame. People without shame are as if naked. Only a shameless person would run around without any clothes on, someone who didn't realize how ugly he was. "Black" means that they adorn themselves with offense and evil. Because their entire being is pervaded with offense and evil they are said to be black. "Thin" means that they have no merit or virtue whatsoever to help them. One without merit or virtue is as if very thin. They are always within the burning house, in the three realms, and don't think to get out. They never get out. They are always there.

EMITTING LOUD AND EVIL SOUNDS/ This represents those of non-Buddhist religions who proclaim their doctrines of various types of marks of self. They never get away from the concept of a self. They cultivate various non-Buddhist ascetic practices and so they are emitting loud and evil sounds because their mark of self is too heavy.

HOWLING IN SEARCH OF FOOD/ Howling, they cry out for food. The black ghosts have nothing to eat. Those skinny, black, naked ghosts with a view of a body are starving! They scream out with loud, evil sounds for people to give them something to eat. This represents their false assumption that there is a self which can attain Nirvana. Having the mark of self, the attachment to self, they think to attain Nirvana. So they howl in search of food, the food, here, being Nirvana.

And what is Nirvana? It is not produced and not destroyed. It is marked with the Four Virtues of permanence, happiness, true self, and purity. With the mark of self, they try to attain Nirvana. This is just false thinking! As long as you have the mark of self you cannot attain Nirvana. If you wish to attain Nirvana, you must break through the attachment to self. Do not attach to self. If you attach to self and try to attain Nirvana, it will be impossible to do so.

FURTHER THERE WERE GHOSTS/WITH THROATS LIKE NEEDLES/ These lines represent the fifth of the Five Quick Servants, the view of grasping at views. These ghosts had throats as skinny as needles, but their stomachs, let me tell you, were as big as bass drums! Do you think, with a shape like this, that they could ever get full? No matter how much they ate they would never get full because their stomachs were too big and their throats too small. In fact, it takes a tremendous amount of time for them to even drink a mouthful of water. Would you say that was suffering or not? Ghosts like this represent the view of grasping at views. With such little needle-throats, their very lives are in danger. They are constantly running around looking for food. This represents those who have attained to the heaven of neither perception nor non-perception and assume that it is Nirvana. Basically, this heaven is impermanent, even though the lifespan of one born there is eighty-thousand great aeons. When that time is up, they still fall. Those in the heaven of neither perception nor non-perception think that they have attained Nirvana. They are like the ghosts with the needle-throats.

AGAIN THERE WERE GHOSTS/ From this line to "They ran about shouting and crying out/" refers to the second of the Five Quick Servants, that of extreme views. WITH HEADS LIKE OXEN/ The ghosts had heads like oxen, with two horns on top. Their faces also looked like oxen. You may wonder, "How can ghosts have faces like oxen?" Well, not only do some of them look like oxen, there are ghosts with all kinds of faces. There are ghosts who look like pigs, dogs, and chickens. There are ghosts which look like every kind of animal there is, in fact. There are tiger-head ghosts and lion-head ghosts. Now, these ghosts have horns on their heads, like oxen, and this represents extreme views. The horns grow on top of their heads in the same way extreme views rely upon the view of a body. Once there is a view of a body, then there can be extreme views. Extreme views and the view of a body give rise to two views of annihilation and eternalism. The two horns, then, represent the two views of annihilationism and eternalism. These two views are very harmful because they can sever one's transcendental good roots. For this reason the text says, NOW EATING HUMAN FLESH/ The eating of human flesh is like the severing of one's transcendental good roots. AND THEN DEVOURING DOGS/ Perhaps they were eating dogs. This represents severing one's mundane good roots.

Just what are transcendental good roots? They are created by diligently cultivating morality, samadhi, and wisdom and by destroying greed, hatred, and stupidity. They are also cultivated by practicing of the Four Truths, the Twelve Causes and Conditions, the Six Perfections, and the Ten Thousand Conducts. The merit and virtue gained from cultivating these make up the transcendental good roots. What are mundane good roots? Cultivating the five precepts and the ten good deeds. The extreme views of annihilationism and eternalism sever both transcendental and mundane good roots.

THEIR HAIR WAS DISHEVELLED/ Basically, one's hair should be kept neat, but these ghosts had hair going every which way. This represents those of non-Buddhist religions who sometimes put forth views of annihilationism and at other times put forth views of eternalism. Sometimes they say that everything is eternal."The saints in heaven,"they claim,"are now and ever will be saints in heaven. The human beings will always be people and the animals will always be animals. It's all fixed. It doesn't ever change. Gods are gods; ghosts are ghosts; people are always people. Grass and trees will always be grass and trees. There is no possibility for change."But then sometimes they have reservations about this doctrine, and they switch to a view of annihilationism. "People won't be people forever. When they die they disappear entirely. Horses, cows, sheep, chickens, pigs--all will disappear. It's like cutting down a big tree-there's nothing left of it. It's gone."They have a lot of doubts about things, and so sometimes they hold to eternalism and other times they switch to annihilationism. The two views are directly opposed to one another which puts these people into quite a paradoxical situation, but they continue to run back and forth between the two extremes. They never stop in the middle, at the Middle Way. They just go from one extreme to the other. It's like someone trying to go from the West Coast to Chicago and ending up in New York instead. Or perhaps they want to go to the East Coast and think about it all the time but never take a single step in that direction. They never get there. Those attached to eternalism or annihilationism are like that. They go back and forth, and this is like having their hair all tousled, sticking out here and there.

THEY WERE HARMFUL, CRUEL, AND DANGEROUS/ Their hair was a mess, and this means they didn't clearly understand the principles the Buddha taught about impermanence and conditional arisal. When they assumed their views of eternalism, they did so to try to destroy the Buddha's true principle of impermanence. The Buddha taught that everything in this world is suffering, empty, and impermanent. When they assumed their views of annihilationism, they did so to try try to destroy the Buddha's true teaching of all things arising from conditions. The Buddha taught that everything comes about through cause and effect. Their view of annihilationism tossed them into the pit of annihilationism, and their view of eternalism tossed them into the pit of eternalism. This is what is meant by the phrase "They were harmful, cruel, and dangerous." Once you have fallen into these pits, it's hard to get out again. In other words, it's hard to understand genuine principle, to become a Buddha. So it is extremely dangerous.

OPPRESSED BY HUNGER AND THIRST/ THEY RAN ABOUT SHOUTING AND CRYING OUT/ Hunger means they had no food. Thirst means--no tea! Is that misery or not? The more they ran the hungrier and thirstier they got. Hunger is a bit easier to bear than thirst. Thirst is terribly hard to bear.

In China during the wars of the Three Kingdoms, there was a famous general named *Ts'ao-ts'ao* who was remarkably clever. He and *Chu Ke-liang* were enemies. One time *Ts'ao-ts'ao* was marching his troops, over a hundred men, through the desert. For a hundred miles, there was no water at all. They hadn't had any water to drink for several days. All the men were, besides, being hungry, so thirsty they couldn't even walk. They just lay down, as if sick, to rest. *Ts'ao-ts'ao* asked them, "Why are you lying down?" They told him they were just too thirsty to go on. He said, "Oh, is that all? Don't worry about that. About ten or twenty miles up ahead I happen to know that there is an orchard of sour plums. When we get there we can eat them and quench our thirst." As soon as he said the word "plums," the soldiers' mouths started watering. Since their mouths were watering, they weren't thirsty anymore, and they started marching again. They marched about twenty miles, and kept right on and walked right out of the desert. But there was no plum orchard at all. He made the whole thing up because he knew his "white lie" would enable his men to get out safely. He "cheated" them into forgetting about their thirst and into getting out of the desert. So if you are thirsty, think about sour plums!

When people are really hungry, they like to eat oil cakes. But to make oil cakes you have to have flour. If you haven't any flour or oil, what are you going to do? Well, you might get a piece of paper and draw a sketch of an oil cake. Still, since you know it's just a drawing, it's not going to satisfy your hunger. In China we have a saying,

> Thinking of sour plums can quench your thirst,
> But a drawing of an oil cake won't
> satisfy your hunger.

Hunger and thirst can be extremely fierce.The hunger and thirst referred to in the text here is the lack of the food of wisdom. Those who cultivate the Way must eat the food of wisdom. Without it, one goes hungry. Cultivators need to drink the water of Dhyana samadhi. This means you need to meditate. When you sit in meditation, quite naturally you will be filled with sweet dew. Then you will no longer be thirsty. Cultivating the way you need wisdom food and Dhyana samadhi drink. But here, there is neither one. Why not? Because they do not cultivate the Way. They don't come to listen to Sutra lectures. Lectures on the Sutras are wisdom food. Having listened to the lectures and understood the principles, you should return and take the time from your busy life to meditate and investigate Dhyana. That's drinking Dhyana samadhi. If you don't listen to Sutra lectures, you'll get no wisdom food; if you fail to sit in Dhyana samadhi, you have no Dhyana to drink and you will be oppressed by hunger and thirst.

Starving and dying of thirst, they ran about shouting. They were screaming: "Arghhhhhhhhhh! I'm staaaaarrving to death!" They ran about like lunatics. Their shouting and crying out represents broad proclamations of eternalism and/or annihilationism, sort of like that Bob Dylan song where he shouts:

> "God said to Abraham, kill me a son.
> Abe said, 'Man, you must be puttin' me on.'"

They shout, "It's all annihilated; there is nothing eternal! My principles are totally correct!" Or they scream at the top of their lungs, "You're wrong!! It's not annihilated! It's all eternal!" They cry out one or the other of their deviant doctrines, with their deviant understanding and their deviant views. These twisted, deviant doctrines are represented in the text by "shouting and crying out."

When they are done yelling, they run around. Where do they run to? Right into the six path wheel of birth and death. The phrase "they ran about" represents continuous birth and death in the six paths. They never stop turning in the wheel of birth and death. No matter how hard they run, they never get off the wheel.

THERE WERE YAKSHAS, HUNGRY GHOSTS/ AND ALL SORTS OF EVIL BIRDS AND BEASTS/ FRANTIC WITH HUNGER FACING THE FOUR DIRECTIONS/ PEEKING OUT THE WINDOWS/ SUCH WERE THE TROUBLES/ AND TERRORS BEYOND MEASURE THERE/ This section represents the appearance of afflictions created by the Five Dull and Five Quick Servants for living beings in the realm of desire.

Living beings in the realm of desire have outflows. Because they have outflows, they cannot obtain the flavor of cultivation of the Way, the flavor of Dhyana. Because they have not attained to the state of non-outflows or to the fruit of the Way or to the flavor of Dhyana's bliss, they are said to be "frantic with hunger." They are terribly hungry. The hungry ghosts and evil birds and animals are starving and they "faced the four directions." What is meant by "four directions?" Those non-Buddhist religions cultivate deviant contemplations, but they cannot awaken to true principle. They very much long for the fruit of the Way, for the gains of Dhyana, and this longing is like a hunger in them which causes them to look outside, to look in the four directions. They don't realize that all one needs is proper understanding and proper views and the ability to be unmoved by the Five Dull and Five Quick Servants in order to attain the fruit of the Way and the flavor of Dhyana. Because they can't attain it, they face the four directions "peeking out the windows." "Peeking" is a sneaky way of looking at things. It is not in accord with the rules. Even though these evil things try to peek out the windows, they can't see anything clearly. Those of non-Buddhist religions have many attached thoughts which obstruct their understanding and prevent them from knowing genuine principle. There are panes of glass in the window, but one's vision through a window cannot be unobstructed; there's always some degree of distortion.

The various difficulties and disasters were frightening to the extreme, to the point that you couldn't even measure it.

Sutra: T.14a18

THIS OLD, DECAYING HOUSE
BELONGED TO A MAN
WHO HAD GONE BUT A SHORT DISTANCE
WHEN, BEFORE VERY LONG,
THE REAR ROOMS OF THE HOUSE
SUDDENLY CAUGHT FIRE.

Outline:

N2. The cause of the fire.

Commentary:

THIS OLD, DECAYING HOUSE/ The house is in terrible condition. It's about ready to cave in altogether. This decaying house represents the three realms as without peace; everywhere you turn it is very dangerous. It is said to be old because it wasn't made just recently. The three realms had no beginning and so it is "old." BELONGED TO A MAN/ The three realms, the desire, form, and formless realms, are where the Buddha, in his Response body, teaches and transforms living beings. The Buddha, from the time he brought forth the thought of enlightenment up until the time he became a Buddha, passed through three great asankhyeya aeons. He made vows, great vows. His vows were limitless and measureless. These great vows were to save all living beings, to take them from suffering to bliss, to help them end birth and death.

For this reason, Buddhist disciples should follow the Buddha's example in making vows to save all living beings. If you are going to save them, where do you start? You start with the people close to you. If your relatives don't understand the Buddhadharma, you should exhaust your effects to lead them to believe in the Buddha. Since you believe in the Buddha and you know that the Buddhadharma is a good thing, you should first cross over your father and mother and lead them to believe in the Buddhadharma. It is said,

> When one's parents have left defilement,
> The child has then accomplished the Way.

If you can bring your parents to believe in genuine principle, then you are truly being filial. Then cross over your brothers and sisters so that they have a proper path to walk down. After you have saved your family, you should save your friends. Work from "near" to "far," from your inner family circle out to your friends, and then out to all living beings. In this way you should teach and transform living beings. Liberate them. In this way you are following the example of the Buddha's great vows. After he became a Buddha, Shakyamuni Buddha went up to the Heaven of the Thirty-three to speak the Dharma to his mother. He spoke *The Earth Store Bodhisattva Sutra* on her behalf. The three realms is where the Buddha appears in his Response body to teach and transform living beings and so the text says it "belonged to a man." This man is the great elder, the Buddha. Now, if the elder had been at home in the three realms, he could have told the children not to fool around and play with fire. But he had to go out on business, and the children were left there alone. They were actually pretty stupid. They had no genuine wisdom; they didn't know what was safe and what was dangerous. They started playing with fire and, sure enough, the house caught on fire.

WHO HAD GONE BUT A SHORT DISTANCE/ WHEN, BEFORE VERY LONG/ The elder had just left. This line refers to Shakyamuni Buddha who, during the time of the Buddha called Great Penetration, was teaching all living beings how to subdue the Five Turbidities. When the karmic influences of those living beings came to an end, Shakyamuni Buddha also entered Nirvana. After the Buddha entered Nirvana, living beings, having lost their "crutch," fell over. The Five Turbidities arose once again: the turbidity of the aeon, the turbidity of views, the turbidity of affliction, the turbidity of living beings, and the turbidity of life.

Although the Buddha had entered Nirvana in that world system, in another world system the causes and conditions for teaching living beings had ripened and he went there to teach them. But he couldn't stay in that world system forever. So the Buddha had "gone but a short distance." He appeared again, not very far away.

You could also explain these lines saying that the Buddha had already attained to the patience of unproduced dharmas; that is to say:

> He has done what he had to do;
> He has established his pure conduct;
> He will undergo no further becoming.

He will not again be born in the three realms. He has "gone out." Although in becoming a Buddha he has transcended the three realms, still, after a short period of time, he comes back. So he has gone but a little ways. In the "Lifespan Chapter" of this Sutra it says that the Buddha has appeared to enter Nirvana many, many times. Many times he has appeared in the world and many times he has entered Nirvana. This means that he has gone out of the burning house of the three realms.

WHEN, BEFORE VERY LONG/ THE REAR ROOMS OF THE HOUSE/ The house is the three realms. The "rooms" are the Five Skandhas--form, feeling, perception, impulse, and consciousness. He hadn't been gone for very long when the back part of the house SUDDENLY CAUGHT ON FIRE/ A fire broke out. How did it happen? The kids were playing with fire, and they were careless. What do you think will happen to the children? Will they burn to death? What about us here in the burning house of the three realms where there is no peace, no safety? What about us caught in the fire of the five skandhas?

Sutra: T.14a20

> ALL AT ONCE, ALL FOUR SIDES
> WERE ENVELOPED BY RAGING FLAMES.
> THE BEAMS, RIDGEPOLES, RAFTERS, AND PILLARS
> SHOOK AND SPLIT WITH THE SOUND OF EXPLOSION,
> SNAPPED APART AND FELL,
> AS THE WALLS AND PARTITIONS COLLAPSED
> AND FELL IN.

Outline:

N3. The force with which the fire breaks out.

Commentary:

ALL AT ONCE, ALL FOUR SIDES/ The four sides represent the Four Applications of Mindfulness. The Four Applications of Mindfulness were given by the Buddha as a dwelling place for the Bhikshus after his departure into Nirvana. They are mindfulness with regard to the body, feelings, thoughts, and dharmas.

First of all one must contemplate the body as impure. One should also contemplate feelings, thoughts and dharmas as impure as well. Since the body is impure, one's feelings are likewise impure and so are thoughts and dharmas.

Secondly, one must contemplate feelings as suffering. All the feelings we experience are involved with suffering. One should also contemplate the body as involved with suffering, and thoughts and dharmas likewise.

Thirdly, one should contemplate thoughts as impermanent. Our thoughts shift and change constantly, like waves on the water. When one thought goes, another takes its place; when that thought goes, yet another takes its place. Likewise one should contemplate the body, feelings, and dharmas as impermanent.

Fourthly, one should contemplate dharmas as without a self. One should also contemplate the body, feelings, and thoughts as without self. The body, feelings, thoughts, and dharmas should each be regarded in these four ways, making sixteen applications.

One begins cultivating the Four Applications of Mindfulness by cultivating the contemplation of impurity. The contemplation of impurity breaks one's attachment to self. Why are you attached to your body and always trying to help it out? It's because you think it is a good thing. You want to help out that "good thing." You feel, "My body is so loveable. I really can't bear to let it get cold or overheated. I don't want it to be hungry or thirst either. In general, I'm always looking out for it." This is because you don't realize that it is actually impure. If you knew how unclean the body really is, when you put on those fine clothes, eat that fine food, you'd know it was unclean. No matter how pretty the clothes you put on, it's still just like dressing up a toilet! I mean, you can put the most elegant clothing and accessories on the toilet, but no matter how fine you dress it up, it's still dirty. Our bodies are just the same. No matter how nice your clothes, it's just like dressing up a toilet. No matter how fine the food you eat, you are still doing nothing more than making a little more excrement. It's no great use. So you should contemplate the body as impure in order to get rid of your attachment to self. Don't see your body as so precious.

If you follow your body's insatiable greed and create offenses, then the body is a bad thing, an impure thing. If, on the other hand, you cultivate the Way, then the body is pure and it can help you to become a Buddha. It's the same body; it just depends on how you use it.

How is the body impure? It is a combination of the mother's ovum and the father's sperm. Therefore, it is basically impure. We should not look upon it as so very important. If, for example, you don't bathe for a week, the body starts to smell and collects all kinds of unclean matter. From nine orifices the body constantly excretes impure substances. There are tears and matter always coming from the eyes. Earwax is always coming out of one's ears. That makes four orifices. The mouth has saliva and phlegm which is also unclean. That makes seven orifices. Then you add the eliminatory orifices and that makes nine. You may think of your body as being very precious, but actually when you get right down to it, it is filled with all manner of unclean substances. Our bodies are nothing more than garbage cans. If you insist on slaving away like mad for the body, what good is it? You work so hard to give it a nice place to live in, a lot of fine clothes, and the best food. You are so good to it, but it shows you no courtesy at all. When the time comes, it's still going to get old. No matter how well you treat it, when it gets old, it gets old. That's all there is to it. No matter how you pamper it, when it gets sick, it just gets sick. When the time comes for it to die, it goes right ahead and dies. It would be hard to discuss fully the impurity of the body as it flows with impurities from nine orifices. The body is impure. Having contemplated the impurity of the body, you should contemplate as impure the feelings, thoughts, and dharmas as well.

What does it mean to contemplate feelings as suffering? Feelings means what one experiences. One usually tries to have good feelings and experiences, and yet all our feelings are involved with some form of suffering. There are three, eight, and limitless sufferings. One should also contemplate the body, thoughts, and dharmas as suffering.

One should contemplate thoughts as impermanent. Our thoughts keep changing, thought after thought. One should also contemplate the body feelings, and dharmas as impermanent.

One should contemplate dharmas as without a self. Contemplate likewise, the body, feelings, and thoughts as without a self.

"All at once" is also an analogy. It stands for the sudden arisal of the Four Inverted Views, the Five Turbidities, and the Eight Sufferings. Those of non-Buddhist religions and inverted living beings reverse the Four Virtues of Nirvana, applying them to conditioned existence. They say:

1. What is not permanent is permanent.

2. What is not happiness is happiness.

3. What is not self is self.

4. What is not pure is pure.

Their views are in direct opposition to that of cultivation, so they are called the Four Inverted Views. Then the Five Turbidities arise. Add the Eight Sufferings: birth, old age, sickness, death, being separated from what you love, being together with what you hate, not getting what you want, and the raging blaze of the Five Skandhas. All this suffering arises and so the text says "all at once."

WERE ENVELOPED BY RAGING FLAMES/ The ridgepole is the main support of the building. The beams support the roof. The rafters and pillars all support the house, too. They represent the four limbs, our bones and various other parts of our bodies.

SHOOK AND SPLIT WITH THE SOUND OF EXPLOSION/ What is meant by "the sound of explosion?" When life is cut off, that is like an explosion. "Split" refers to the force of the wind cutting through the body like a knife. When life is over, energy is cut off and the bones separate from the flesh. This is represented by the line SNAPPED APART AND FELL/

AS THE WALLS AND PARTITIONS COLLAPSED AND FELL IN/ The walls and partitions referred to here are just the body. The body is a combination of the four elements. At death, the four elements separate and each one--

earth, air, fire, and water--returns to where it came from. When the four elements scatter that is like the walls and partitions falling apart and caving in. When the four elements in the body scatter, the body disintegrates.

Sutra: T.14a22

ALL THE GHOSTS AND SPIRITS
SCREAMED LOUDLY,
WHILE THE HAWKS, VULTURES, AND OTHER BIRDS,
THE KUMBHANDAS, AND SO FORTH,
RAN ABOUT IN A PANIC,
UNABLE TO GET THEMSELVES OUT.

Outline:

N4. The appearance of the blaze.

Commentary:

ALL THE GHOSTS AND SPIRITS/ meaning those ghosts and spirits mentioned before. They represent the Five Quick Servants and the Five Dull Servants. SCREAMED LOUDLY/ They raised their voices in a great, loud bellow. Why did they scream? They saw the walls falling in on them, and so they were all scared. WHILE THE HAWKS, VULTURES, AND OTHER BIRDS/ Hawks can eat deer. The vultures like to eat unclean things. The birds represent the Five Dull Servants. THE KUMBHANDAS, AND SO FORTH/ Kumbhandas represent the most powerful, the most evil of the Five Quick Servants. By "most evil" and "most powerful" we mean whichever Servant is the most dominant in any particular personality. Basically, the Servants themselves are of equal power, but an individual personality may be more afflicted with one of them than another and so, for that person, that Servant is the most powerful. For example, if you are a person with a great deal of greed, then greed is the most powerful servant on your list. Another person may not be bothered by greed, but may have an uncontrollable temper, and so hatred is the most powerful servant for him. The same applies to all the other Servants.

RAN ABOUT IN A PANIC/ UNABLE TO GET THEMSELVES OUT/ They couldn't get out of the three realms. If it weren't for the Triple Jewel, the Buddha, Dharma, and Sangha, and the Four Truths, and the Four Applications of Mindfulness, they would never be able to get out of the three realms.

Students of the Buddhadharma should not allow themselves to be controlled by the Five Quick or Five Dull Servants. Do not be turned by them. You should transform them and then they can become Dharma Protectors.

What has just been discussed represents the difficulty of escaping the realm of desire. One must rely upon the power of the Buddha, Dharma, and Sangha in order to escape the three realms.

Sutra: T.14a24

EVIL BEASTS AND POISONOUS INSECTS
HID AWAY IN THE HOLES AND CREVICES,
WHILE THE PISHACHA GHOSTS
ALSO DWELT THEREIN.

Outline:

M2. Verses about the events in the cave as likened to the form realm.
N1. Those creatures being burned.

Commentary:

This passage of text talks about the form realm. EVIL BEASTS AND POISONOUS INSECTS/ HID AWAY IN THE HOLES AND CREVICES/ When they saw the house catch on fire, they ran to hide away in the crevices and crannies. The holes and crevices represent the realm of form. WHILE THE PISHACHA GHOSTS/ Pishacha ghosts are the ghosts that eat essence and energy. They were also hiding in the holes, in the form realm, that is. This represents people who attain the Four Dhyanas and are born in the form realm heavens. The form realm heavens are like the holes and crevices. ALSO DWELT THEREIN/ there in the realm of form.

Sutra: T.14a26

THEIR BLESSINGS AND VIRTUE SCANTY,
THEY WERE HARD PRESSED BY THE FIRE;
THEY WROUGHT HARM ON ONE ANOTHER,
DRINKING BLOOD AND EATING FLESH.

Outline:

N2. Cause of the fire.

Commentary:

Why did the fire start? Why do people get angry? It was because THEIR BLESSINGS AND VIRTUE SCANTY/ THEY WERE HARD PRESSED BY THE FIRE/ Because they had no blessings, in turn they had no virtue, and so they liked to get angry. In China they say,

> "Lacking virtue, one wears a smokestack on one's head."

Why do people get angry? It's because they don't have enough virtue. People with virtuous conduct do not get angry. Even if they do get angry, it's not for real. They may pretend to get angry sometimes at people, but they are just using this kind of Dharma-door to subdue that person. This is their way of teaching people. Some living beings, unless you get a bit upset with them, will think you are joking and they won't take you very seriously. Bodhisattvas may sometimes use this kind of supressing dharma. When ordinary people get angry it's because they don't have enough virtue. Since they don't have enough virtue, they catch on fire with anger. They had no blessings or virtue and so when the fire started, they were hard pressed by it. This represents the fact that in the three realms there is no peaceful place. The Four Inversions, the Five Turbidities, the Eight Sufferings, and the Five Skandhas press in from all sides like a raging fire.

THEY WROUGHT HARM ON ONE ANOTHER/ Because they are in the form realm, they dislike the realm below, the realm of desire; they like the realm above, the formless realm. They forcefully apply the realms above to the realms below, they suppress the subtle afflictions in the lower realms. This is what is meant by "They wrought harm on one another"/ DRINKING BLOOD AND EATING FLESH/

Drinking blood refers to the attachments of those in the form realm. What attachments do they have? They are attached to not talking. They think that not talking is a form of cultivation. Those, for example, in the Fourth Dhyana are not beset with the evil dharmas found in the realm of desire. They do, however, crave the "flavor of Dhyana" and this is a subtle form of suffering. They are also attached to their merit and virtue, to the good deeds they have done. This is like eating flesh.

Sutra: T.14a27

AS THE PACKS OF YEH KAN
WERE ALREADY DEAD,
MONSTROUS EVIL BEASTS
RACED TO DEVOUR THEM,
WHILE BILLOWS OF STINKING SMOKE
PERMEATED ALL FOUR SIDES.

Outline:

N3. The appearance of the blaze.

Commentary:

AS THE PACKS OF YEH KAN/ These are animals like foxes, but they live out in the wilds and roam at night in packs, wailing with a strange and terrifying sound. They are kind of like foxes, but trickier. They represent greed in the desire realm.

WERE ALREADY DEAD/ This means that greed in the realm of desire was already dead. But MONSTROUS EVIL BEASTS/ representing greed in the form realm which can swallow the greed of the desire realm: RACED TO DEVOUR THEM/ The greed in the form realm can eat up the greed in the desire realm. So the fire has been subdued to a small "burn." This is a subtle form of suffering. They haven't as much suffering as the desire realm. The suffering is still there in a subtler form. They still have love. If people can get rid of love, they can go to the formless realm. In the form realm one still has thoughts of love and the flavor of states of Dhyana.

In the realm of desire, the Four Inversions and Eight Sufferings are like a blazing fire. In the form realm, they are like BILLOWS OF STINKING SMOKE/ This love attachment is like billows of stinking smoke. It PERMEATED ALL FOUR SIDES/ This represents the Four Inversions and the Eight Sufferings penetrating the four elements and the body, feelings, thoughts, and dharmas, the Four Applications of Mindfulness.

This ends the verses on the affairs in the holes and crevices representing the form realm.

Sutra: T.14a29

CENTIPEDES AND MILLIPEDES,
AND VARIOUS KINDS OF POISONOUS SNAKES,
BURNT BY THE FIRE,
FOUGHT TO ESCAPE THEIR HOLES.
KUMBHANDA GHOSTS
GRABBED AND ATE THEM.

Outline:

M3. Verses on events outside the cave as likened to the formless realm.
N1. Those creatures being burned.

Commentary:

These verses represent the affairs in the formless realm. The formless realm is one level higher than the form realm. Cultivators who attain to the form realm heavens grow to dislike them because in the form realm heavens there is still the mark of form which can be seen. They grow weary of the cage of form. In the form realm living beings are not free at all. Form keeps them locked up, so they decide that they want to go up to the formless realm, like birds flying out of their birdcages. People in the form realm heavens suffer;

they have coarse obstacles. They hope to be born in the formless realm where there is no form only emptiness. This is represented by the line of text BURNT BY THE FIRE/

CENTIPEDES AND MILLIPEDES/ AND VARIOUS KINDS OF POISONOUS SNAKES/ Being burned by the Four Inversions, the Five Skandhas, and the Eight Sufferings is like being burned in a fire. FOUGHT TO ESCAPE THEIR HOLES/ They fought. None wanted to fall behind. They all tried to get in front of each other. The holes represent the form realm heavens. They are trying to get out and get into the formless realm. The samadhi in the formless realm is one level higher than that in the form realm. Having attained the formless samadhis, they have extinguished the causes and conditions in the form realm. Having seized the samadhis in the upper realms and extinguished conditions in the lower realm, the text says KUMBHANDA GHOSTS/ The conditions in the lower realms have been extinguished just like being eaten by kumbhands ghosts. The ghosts also represent the Five Dull Servants and the Five Quick Servants. Basically, if one were to explain in detail, the Five Dull Servants and Five Quick Servants can all attain the formless samadhis. But here in this passage we are only referring to the Five Dull Servants which detest the lower realms and want to attain to the formless relam. The Five Quick Servants have already attained to the formless realm. They have extinguished the lower form realm.

Sutra: T.14b2

FURTHER, ALL THE HUNGRY GHOSTS,
THE TOPS OF THEIR HEADS AFLAME,
TORMENTED BY HUNGER, THIRST, AND HEAT,
RAN ABOUT IN TERROR AND DISTRESS.

Outline:

N2. The appearance of the blaze.

Commentary:

FURTHER, ALL THE HUNGRY GHOSTS/ Hungry ghosts have nothing to eat. Their throats are as thin as needles, and their stomachs are as large as bass drums. They eat all day long but never get full. Hungry ghosts represent the living beings in the heavens of the Four Stations of Emptiness: 1) the station of emptiness without limit, 2) the station of consciousness without limit, 3) the station of nothing whatsoever, 4) the station of neither perception nor non-perception. Although beings in these heavens have reached emptiness, they still have consciousness, and they have not ended birth and death. They have not obtained the food and drink of non-outflows and so they are said to be like hungry ghosts. They haven't eaten of the food and drink of no-outflows.

Although they are at the top of the three realms, in the formless realm, in the highest of the heavens, they still haven't ended birth and death. They still can't avoid impermanence, and eventually they are burned by it. Thus, the text says THE TOPS OF THEIR HEADS AFLAME/ When they have used up all their heavenly blessings, they will fall again into other destinies. In the heaven of neither perception nor non-perception, beings live for eighty-thousand great aeons, enjoying their heavenly blessings, but then they fall--burned by the fire of impermanence.

TORMENTED BY HUNGER, THIRST, AND HEAT/ Hunger represents their inability to aquire the Proper Path. The Proper Path means cultivating the genuine Way. Because they don't find the path of cultivation which leads to the end of birth and death, they are hungry. They are said to be thirsty because they have not gained the drink of the aids to the Path. They haven't obtained the causes and conditions which aid one in cultivation of the Path, and so they are thirsty.

Although they are at the top of the three realms, they are still vexed by subtle forms of the Eight Sufferings--not a lot, just a little. These sufferings remain in their eighth consciousness and that is what is meant by "heat."

They are also tormented by subtle forms of delusions which manifest. The delusions are very few and very fine, but they are still present because they have not severed the root of the delusions. In the future when they fall, they will have more delusions.

There are various categories of delusions:

1. View delusions. This refers to giving rise to greed and love for externals.

2. Thought delusions. This refers to being confused about a principle and giving rise to discrimination.

3. Delusions of ignorance. This refers to being stupid about things. For example, one may clearly know that a given action is wrong, but do it anyway. One may know that something is bad, but do it anyway. Why? Because one doesn't really know that it is bad! One has no true understanding of things.

These delusions tormented them and they RAN ABOUT IN TERROR AND DISTRESS/ The beings in the formless heavens are still on the wheel of birth and death, but they give no thought to escaping it. They don't look for a method to escape the three realms, to transcend the turning wheel of rebirth. They run about confusedly all over the place in terror and distress. This has been a discussion of the affairs in the formless realm.

Sutra: T.14b3

SO IT WAS IN THAT HOUSE:
TERRIFYING TO THE EXTREME,
WITH DANGERS AND CONFLAGRATIONS--
A HOST OF TROUBLES, NOT JUST ONE.

Outline:

M4. General conclusion: many kinds of difficulties.

Commentary:

SO IT WAS IN THAT HOUSE/ The burning house, as stated above, was a dangerous place. This means that there is no place of peace in the three realms. It is TERRIFYING TO THE EXTREME/ WITH DANGERS AND CONFLAGRATIONS/ A HOST OF TROUBLES, NOT JUST ONE/ Not just one kind of trouble beset them. This represents the fact that when you are in the burning house of the three realms if you don't cultivate the Way and find a way to get out of the burning house, you remain in great danger. It is filled with danger. If you don't run into one kind of disaster, you encounter another. There's not one single happy day. Now, we in this world should think it over. Where is there peace in the world? No place. Everywhere you go, you see a lot of problems. You might say that several thousand years ago the Buddha was addressing us here in the world today where there are a host of troubles, not just one.

Sutra: T.14b5

AT THAT TIME THE OWNER OF THE HOUSE
WAS STANDING OUTSIDE THE DOOR
WHEN HE HEARD SOMEONE SAY,
"ALL OF YOUR CHILDREN
AWHILE AGO, IN PLAY,
WENT INTO THIS HOUSE.
BEING YOUNG AND IGNORANT,
THEY DELIGHT IN PLAY AND CLING TO AMUSEMENTS."
HAVING HEARD THIS, THE ELDER
ENTERED THE BURNING HOUSE, IN ALARM.

Outline:

K2. Specific verses about the parable.
L1. Elder sees the fire start.

Commentary:

AT THAT TIME, THE OWNER OF THE HOUSE/ WAS STANDING OUTSIDE THE DOOR/ The Buddha was standing outside the door. What does this mean? "Outside the door" refers to the Buddha as having already certified to the ground of the Dharma body. "Standing" means that the Buddha always keeps a heart of compassion. In his great compassion and kindness he always wishes to rescue living beings. He never forgets living beings; he always works to save them. He does not dwell in the emptiness of the primary principle because he wants to teach and transform living beings. WHEN HE HEARD SOMEONE

SAY/ In the previous prose section the text said, "When he sees..." and this points to the non-duality of hearing and seeing. "Says" refers to samadhi. The Buddha takes the Dharma as his teacher, the Dharma of samadhi. When you obtain the Dharma of samadhi, you can observe the potentials of the beings and dispense the proper teaching to them. Thus, the Buddha's entering samadhi enables him to view the potential of beings. His samadhi enables him to see those potentialities. Therefore the text says, "When he heard someone say/" representing samadhi.

ALL OF YOUR CHILDREN/ This refers to all the living beings in the five destinies. AWHILE AGO IN PLAY/ WENT INTO THIS HOUSE/ This refers to living beings who have first brought forth the resolve for Bodhi. At this time it is as if they had already gotten out. But before they have ascended to the level of no-retreat, they can still give rise to the view delusions and thought delusions and thus "in play" run back into the burning house. You can also interpret this line thus: All living beings, speaking in terms of principle, are basically pure. In this sense, then, there is no burning house and there are no three realms. The basic nature of living beings is pure of itself, but because of ignorance, they falsely give rise to attachments leading to a continuous round of birth and death. This is like entering the house in play.

BEING YOUNG AND IGNORANT/ This refers to that time in their cultivation when their merit and virtue is not yet perfected and has not manifested. One is then young, not having enough virtue, being, as was said above "Of scanty merit and virtue." "Ignorant" means they are stupid. Being stupid, they are bound up by delusions, view delusions, thought delusions, and delusions of ignorance.

THEY DELIGHT IN PLAY AND CLING TO AMUSEMENTS/ Hah! There they are! They imagine that they are having a real good time. Who would have guessed that it was really so terrifying?

HAVING HEARD THIS, THE ELDER/ ENTERED THE BURNING HOUSE IN ALARM/ The Buddha, seeing living beings undergoing just too much suffering, gives rise to great compassion and comes to teach and transform living beings, to rescue them, and get them all safely out of the burning house.

Sutra: T.14b8

INTENDING TO SAVE THEM
FROM BEING BURNED
HE WARNED HIS CHILDREN
OF THE HOST OF DISASTERS:
"THE EVIL GHOSTS, THE POISONOUS INSECTS
AND THE SPREADING CONFLAGRATION,
A HOST OF SUFFERINGS, IN SUCCESSION
ARE CONTINUOUS, WITHOUT INTERRUPTION.
THE POISONOUS SNAKES AND VIPERS
AND ALL THE YAKSHAS,
AND KUMBHANDA GHOSTS,
YEH KAN, FOXES, AND DOGS,
HAWKS, VULTURES, KITES, AND OWLS,
AND VARIETIES OF CENTIPEDES
ARE FRANTIC WITH HUNGER AND THIRST,
AND TERRIFYING TO THE EXTREME.
THERE ARE SO MANY SUFFERINGS AND TROUBLES,
SO MUCH INCREASED BY THIS GREAT FIRE!"
BUT ALL THE CHILDREN, WITHOUT KNOWLEDGE,
ALTHOUGH THEY HEARD THEIR FATHER'S WARNINGS,
STILL CLUNG TO THEIR AMUSEMENTS
AND SPORTED WITHOUT CEASE.

Outline:

L2. Casting aside the table to use the carts.
M1. Casting aside the table.

Commentary:

INTENDING TO SAVE THEM/ Just at that time the elder, the Buddha, was preparing to use the Great Vehicle Dharma-door to rescue all living beings. He was intending to save them FROM BEING BURNED/ He wanted to keep all living beings from being burned in the house of the three realms, from being burned by the blaze of the five skandhas. HE WARNED HIS CHILDREN/ OF THE HOST OF DISASTERS/ He said, "This burning house is filled with many terrifying things. There is no peace in the three realms. It is like a burning house."

THE EVIL GHOSTS, THE POISONOUS INSECTS/ These represent the Five Dull Servants and the Five Quick Servants which are always playing tricks. AND THE SPREADING CONFLAGRATION/ The raging blaze of the five skandhas is spreading everywhere. The more it burns, the brighter it gets and the more territory it spreads across, burning through the three realms. A HOST OF SUFFERINGS, IN SUCCESSION/ These manifold troubles arise in succession, and ARE CONTINUOUS,WITHOUT INTERRUPTION/ They arise one after another without stopping. The fire is out of control; it cannot be stopped. THE POISONOUS SNAKES AND VIPERS/ Various snakes and venomous creatures again represent the Five Dull and Five Quick Servants. AND ALL THE YAKSHAS/ AND KUMBHANDA GHOSTS/ These ghosts are terrifying! Kumbhandas are the ghosts that look like watermelons. They may sit down on you when you are asleep so that you cannot move. YEH KAN, FOXES, AND DOGS/ HAWKS, VULTURES, KITES, AND OWLS/ AND VARIETIES OF CENTIPEDES/ ARE FRANTIC WITH HUNGER AND THIRST/ They lack the food of the proper Path and the drink of the Aids to the Path, and so they are hungry and thirsty AND TERRIFYING TO THE EXTREME/

THERE ARE SO MANY SUFFERINGS AND TROUBLES/ SO MUCH INCREASED BY THIS GREAT FIRE!"/ So many strange creatures and this big fire! Hurry and find a way out!

BUT ALL THE CHILDREN, WITHOUT KNOWLEDGE/ All the living beings lack any understanding of what is going on. They lack the disposition or the potential for the Great Vehicle Buddhadharma. ALTHOUGH THEY HEARD THEIR FATHER'S WARNINGS/ Even though they heard their father tell them of the danger and the fearsome creatures, they STILL CLUNG TO THEIR AMUSEMENTS/ They continued to play, imagining the place to be very amusing. AND SPORTED WITHOUT CEASE/ They jumped around having a good time and not listening to their father at all.

Sutra: T.14b15

AT THAT TIME, THE ELDER
FURTHER HAD THIS THOUGHT:
"BEING LIKE THIS, MY CHILDREN
ADD TO MY WORRY AND DISTRESS;
NOW, IN THIS HOUSE, THERE IS NOT
A SINGLE THING IN WHICH TO TAKE PLEASURE,
AND YET ALL THESE CHILDREN
ARE INTOXICATED BY THEIR PLAY.
NOT HEEDING MY INSTRUCTIONS,
THEY WILL BE INJURED IN THE FIRE."
JUST THEN HE THOUGHT
TO DEVISE EXPEDIENTS.

Outline:

M2. Using the carts.
N1. Suitability of the three carts.

Commentary:

AT THAT TIME, THE ELDER/ the Buddha, FURTHER HAD THIS THOUGHT/ "BEING LIKE THIS, MY CHILDREN/ They are not very bright, playing here. They ADD TO MY WORRY AND DISTRESS/ Why are the Buddha's worries and troubles intensified? Because the Buddha's vows are to save living beings, and when he fails to save them, his heart is unhappy.

"NOW IN THIS HOUSE, THERE IS NOT/ A SINGLE THING IN WHICH TO TAKE PLEASURE/ In the burning house of the three realms, there's not a single thing to be happy about. AND YET ALL THESE CHILDREN/ ARE INTOXICATED BY THEIR PLAY/ They are greedy for good times and don't worry about anything at all. Bound by ignorance, we people in the three realms have forgotten everything. We have forgotten to bring forth the Bodhi mind and forgotten to cultivate the Bodhi Path. NOT HEEDING MY INSTRUCTIONS/ THEY WILL BE INJURED IN THE FIRE/ They won't listen to the Buddha's teaching.There are people in the world who do not cultivate the Way at all, and who don't believe in the

Buddha at all. Today, one of my disciples told me that his parents came to San Francisco. They were very upset when they saw him. They told him he was really confused. Now, look at that! Basically, studying the Buddhadharma is a good thing, but they were upset by it. I said, "Before, when you were really doing bad things, they didn't pay that much attention to you. Now, you are doing the best kinds of things and they think you are confused. Just what do people base their judements on? When their son wants to cultivate the Way, they think it's terrible.

One of my disciple has recently had the experience of seeing everything as moving. This is true. Everything is, in fact, moving, just like the dust motes. When the sunlight streams in the window, you can see the motes of dust dancing in the air. Why can he see everything in motion? The light of his wisdom is unfolding, and so he can see that everything is alive, even the tables, chairs, the whole room is in motion, moving in frames. This is like seeing the dust motes in the sunlight. This experience happens to people just before they are about to open their five eyes. Not only may one have this experience, but it may happen that you can't see anything at all. You may be as if totally blind. Just before the opening of the five eyes, a special "chemical" or biological transformation takes place. When this transformation takes place, if you get attached to marks and become happy or unhappy or wish to attain the five eyes or wish not to attain them, it is easy to become possessed by a demon. Once the eyes have opened, it's not for sure they will always remain open. You must still continue to be good and remain in control of yourself. If you fail to do a good job at your cultivation, you can lose the vision in your five eyes. When the five eyes open they can shut again as well, if you start looking at things you shouldn't be looking at, unprincipled things, things that are none of your business. If you start looking at unprincipled things, you can lose those eyes again. If you do wrong things, you can lose them. So this state is one in which you must put your feet firmly on the ground and go forward. Don't start minding other people's business, taking a look at this and that. You can't do that. If you open the five eyes that doesn't mean you can look into other people's business, peeping in to see what your neighbors are doing and so on. It's easy to lose those eyes if you do that. Sometimes people open their five eyes, and in the beginning they can see very clearly with them. Later on they can't see so well with them, or they can't see anything at all with them. I have seen this happen many times. So take special care. If you have this experience, the most important thing is to maintain your samadhi power. If you have samadhi power and it becomes perfected, then you can give rise to wisdom power. Having genuine wisdom really counts for something.

THEY WILL BE INJURED IN THE FIRE/ In the future I am afraid they will all be burned in the great fire."

JUST THEN HE THOUGHT/ TO DEVISE EXPEDIENTS/ The Buddha decided to think of a way that they could cultivate expedient Dharma-doors. What is an expedient? It is a clever device. Since it won't work to try to teach them with the Great Vehicle Buddhadharma, there's nothing else to do but use the Small Vehicle dharmas to teach living beings.

Sutra: T.14c19

HE SAID TO THE CHILDREN,
I HAVE ALL KINDS
OF PRECIOUS PLAYTHINGS:
FINE CARRIAGES, WONDERFUL, BEJEWELLED
SHEEP CARTS, AND DEER CARTS,
AND GREAT OX CARTS,
NOW, RIGHT OUTSIDE THE DOOR.
SO COME OUT, ALL OF YOU,
FOR I HAVE, JUST FOR YOU,
HAD THESE CARTS MADE.
JUST AS YOU WISH,
YOU CAN PLAY WITH THEM."

Outline:

N2. Praising the three carts as rare.

Commentary:

These twelve lines of verse represent the Three

Turnings of the Dharma Wheel of the Four Holy Truths. The first four lines, HE SAID TO THE CHILDREN/ I HAVE ALL KINDS/ OF PRECIOUS PLAYTHINGS/ FINE CARRIAGES, WONDERFUL, BEJEWELLED/ represent the Exhortation Turning. The next three lines, SHEEP CARTS, AND DEER CARTS/ AND GREAT OX CARTS/ NOW, RIGHT OUTSIDE THE DOOR/ represent the Demonstration Turning. The following line, SO COME OUT, ALL OF YOU/ is again the Exhortation Turning. The last four lines are the Certification Turning: FOR I HAVE, JUST FOR YOU/ HAD THESE CARTS MADE/ JUST AS YOU WISH/ YOU CAN PLAY WITH THEM. For I have, just for you/ had these carts made/ points to the fact that the Buddha has already certified to the fruition of Buddhahood. Thus, we have the Three Turnings of the Dharma Wheel of the Four Holy Truths.

The Buddha told all living beings, all the children, "You are having so much fun now, but I have some toys that are a lot more fun than the ones you are playing with now. Hurry up and come out. They are the finest toys. What are they? They are the best carts you could imagine. Some are drawn by sheep and others are drawn by deer. Isn't that great? You've really never seen such neat toys. There's even some great ox carts. They are outside the door right now! So hurry up and come out. Don't hang around in that house. It's not that much fun anyway. I've got the best toys. I've got the carts! I had them made just for you. They are so much fun. You can sit in them and go wherever you like!!"

When the children heard this, they came scrambling out of the house.

Sutra: T.14b23

> WHEN THE CHILDREN HEARD HIM SPEAK
> OF CARRIAGES SUCH AS THESE,
> THEY IMMEDIATELY RACED
> OUT IN A SCRAMBLE,
> TO A CLEARING WHERE
> THEY WERE THEN SAFE FROM HARM.

Outline:

N3. Granting the children their wishes.

Commentary:

WHEN THE CHILDREN HEARD HIM SPEAK/ "Children" just means all living beings. "Heard" represents the wisdom of hearing. OF CARRIAGES SUCH AS THESE/ Good dharmas. Children like to play. If you give them fun toys, they won't cry. THEY IMMEDIATELY RACED/ They started running right away to go get the carts. "Raced" represents the two wisdoms of thinking and cultivating. Thus we have the three types of wisdom: Hearing, thinking, and cultivating. OUT IN A SCRAMBLE/ This shows their vigor in cultivating the methods of the three types of wisdom. TO A CLEARING WHERE/ The clearing represents the position beyond study, that is, fourth stage Arhatship. THEY WERE THEN SAFE FROM HARM/ At the position beyond study one has ended share section birth and death. Change birth and death remains, however. Once they arrived at the clearing, they were safe from sufferings and difficulties. This represents certification to the fourth fruit of Arhatship. This ends the section concerning the casting aside of the table to use the carts.

Sutra: T.14b25

THE ELDER, SEEING THAT HIS CHILDREN
HAD ESCAPED THE BURNING HOUSE,
AND WERE STANDING AT THE CROSSROADS,
SAT ON HIS LION'S THRONE
AND REJOICED TO HIMSELF, SAYING,
"NOW, I AM HAPPY!
ALL OF THESE CHILDREN
WERE HARD TO BRING INTO THE WORLD AND RAISE;
STUPID, YOUNG, AND WITHOUT KNOWLEDGE,
THEY WENT INTO THIS DANGEROUS HOUSE,

SWARMING WITH POISONOUS INSECTS
AND FEARFUL LI MEI GHOSTS,
ABLAZE WITH A GREAT FIRE,
RAGING ON ALL SIDES.
BUT ALL THESE CHILDREN
STILL CLUNG TO THEIR AMUSEMENTS.
I HAVE NOW RESCUED THEM
AND SAVED THEM FROM DISASTER.
THEREFORE, OF ALL PEOPLE,
I AM THE HAPPIEST!"

Outline:

L3. Granting all a great cart.
M1. Father sees children avoid disaster and rejoices.

Commentary:

THE ELDER, SEEING THAT HIS CHILDREN/ The elder is the Buddha. He has ten kinds of virtuous conduct. When he saw all living beings HAD ESCAPED THE BURNING HOUSE/ had run out of the burning house of the three realms AND WERE STANDING AT THE CROSSROADS/ What do the crossroads represent? The Four Holy Truths. Now, the living beings in the five paths and the thirty sons and five hundred people, since they have escaped the burning house and arrived at the stage beyond study, clearly understand the Dharma of the Four Holy Truths: suffering, origination, stopping, and the Way. SAT ON HIS LION'S THRONE/ The elder had been standing outside the door, not sitting. Now, he sits on his lion's throne. Why had he been standing outside the door? Because all living beings had not yet been saved. He was worried about them, afraid for them. What was he afraid of? He was afraid that living beings would be burned in the house. He was concerned because he can't put living beings down. He couldn't not try to save them, because the Buddha is like a greatly compassionate father, and all living beings are like his children. He can't not save them. He can't let them go. He was afraid that, unless he tried to save them, they would fall. Now, seeing that all the children had escaped disaster and gotten out of the burning house, he no longer worries; he has no more concern.

Since he is no longer afraid, he can sit down on his lion's throne. In the previous chapter the text said, "Now I am happy and without fears." Now the Buddha is really happy. He has nothing to fear. In other words, he can sit down and take it easy.

There is another meaning, here. Previously, the Buddha had not encountered beings disposed to the Great Vehicle, and so he was standing. Now, he has finished teaching and transforming living beings of the Small Vehicle. He has finished his work in that regard. He is just about to save Great Vehicle living beings, and so the Buddha can sit down on his lion's throne.

AND REJOICED TO HIMSELF, SAYING/ Why did he rejoice? Because he has encountered the beings with the Great Vehicle potential, the beings he is to teach and save. Since they have now been saved, he rejoices. Living being's have ripened for the Great Vehicle.

"ALL OF THESE CHILDREN/ WERE HARD TO BRING INTO THE WORLD AND RAISE/ It's not easy to raise children. Teaching living beings is also very hard. It's hard for the Buddha to teach and transform living beings. Here, we study the Buddhadharma, and I lecture the Sutras to you every day so that you can understand true principle. You are immersed in it, as it were. This work is by no means easy. In the beginning you didn't understand any Buddhadharma at all. Now, soon it will have been a year that I have been "raising" you in the Dharma and you understand it to some degree. Even so, you still waver between faith and doubt. See how difficult it is?

During the time of the twenty thousand million Buddhas mentioned previously, Shakyamuni Buddha taught living beings with the Great Vehicle Dharma. The text represents this by the phrase, "bring into the world." These children who had the Great Vehicle disposition sent down their seeds during the time of the twenty thousand millions Buddhas. Now they have grown.

Would you say this was hard or not? During the time of twenty thousand million Buddhas how much heart's blood was spent to teach living beings? You shouldn't think that lecturing on the Sutras and teaching the Dharma is an easy thing to do. If you lecture on a Sutra incorrectly, you can fall into the hells! You can't think that you can say whatever you please. You can't be casual about it, for if you make a mistake speaking the Dharma you are responsible for it. You will have to take on the burden of cause and effect involved. If you lecture incorrectly on the Sutras, you are in effect "blinding the eyes of people and gods." If you lecture unclearly, you will put people on the wrong track. People may start out intending to become a Buddha, but you lecture them into the hells! Not only that, but people who wind up there can drag you there as well. Once they get there, King Yama will ask them what they have come for and they will say, "I listened to the Sutras and was told I didn't need to cultivate. I was told all I had to do was take certain drugs and in this way I could obtain emptiness. So I didn't cultivate. Now, I know I was wrong. But the mistake was his, not mine, and you really should get him down here too." When Yama hears this, he can't help but agree and sends for the lecturer as well, and drags him into hell. It's not at all easy to lecture on the Sutras. However, during the time of twenty thousand million Buddhas, Shakyamuni Buddha taught living beings with the Great Vehicle nature and in such a long, long time he brought them to maturity. This is represented in the text by the phrase "and raise." How much time do you think it took to teach these living beings? A long, long time, indeed. In all this time, Shakyamuni Buddha expended so much energy, so much toil to nurture those seeds of the Great Vehicle. It wasn't easy. It was a lot of hard work. It's like planting a tree, carefully placing the soil around its roots, watering and fertilizing it. It's also like planting a flower. It's a lot of work to take care of it. In today's Chinese lesson we learned the sentence, "Red lotuses fill the pond." Do you know how much work it takes to cultivate all those lotuses in the pond? We can imagine how much work the Buddha has to do to teach and transform living beings so that they can leave suffering and attain bliss. Really hard!

STUPID, YOUNG, AND WITHOUT KNOWLEDGE/ Stupid means that they aren't very bright. Young means that they are quite immature. This represents those whose good roots are weak and not very deep. Their virtue is thin and their blessings are few. They don't have much virtue and so they are stupid and young. Without knowledge means that they are covered by false delusions. Because they have no wisdom, the five turbidities arise. Once the five turbidities arise, they must undergo retribution. Their undergoing retribution is what is meant by the line of text THEY WENT INTO THIS DANGEROUS HOUSE/ They went into the dangerous house to suffer retribution. SWARMING WITH POISONOUS INSECTS/ AND FEARFUL LI MEI GHOSTS/ The three realms are marked by the Five Quick Servants and the Five Dull Servants. The three realms are very dangerous, filled with such toxic substances.

ABLAZE WITH A GREAT FIRE/ RAGING ON ALL SIDES/ The fire is an analogy for the eight sufferings and the four inversions which are in the burning house of the three realms.

BUT ALL THESE CHILDREN/ all living beings STILL CLUNG TO THEIR AMUSEMENTS/ Some of them give rise to view delusions; others give rise to love's delusions. They can't get free of them. They have no way to separate from the delusions of love and views because they are so attached to them. They cling to their amusements. BUT NOW I HAVE RESCUED THEM/ AND SAVED THEM FROM DISASTER/ All living beings in the three realms, as attached to love and views as they are, have been saved. I have rescued them from their suffering and difficulty. THEREFORE, OF ALL PEOPLE/ I AM THE HAPPIEST/ The elder says that he is the happiest person there is.

Sutra: T.14c3

THEN, ALL THE CHILDREN,
KNOWING THEIR FATHER WAS SITTING AT EASE,
ALL WENT BEFORE HIM
AND ADDRESSED HIM SAYING,
"PLEASE GIVE TO US
THE THREE JEWELLED CARTS
THAT YOU PROMISED TO US, SAYING,
'IF YOU CHILDREN COME OUT
I WILL GIVE YOU THREE CARTS
JUST LIKE YOU WANTED.'
NOW THE TIME HAS COME,
PLEASE GIVE THEM TO US!"

Outline:

M2. The children demand the carts.

Commentary:

The children had escaped the burning house. Once

they had run out, they didn't even toss a look over their shoulders to see how high the flames were raging. The first thing on their minds was to go straight to their father and ask for those carts. Their father had told them that the carts were outside. Once they got outside, they didn't see the carts, and so they decided to ask. THEN, ALL THE CHILDREN/ KNOWING THEIR FATHER WAS SITTING AT EASE/ They saw him just sitting there on his lion's throne, upright and proper and very happy. They knew it was a good time to ask for the carts. This represents the time when *The Dharma Flower Sutra*, the Great Vehicle Dharma, was about to be spoken. All living beings had a hope of attaining the Great Vehicle Dharma.

ALL WENT BEFORE HIM/ Previously in the text it said, "All, with reverent hearts/ went before the Buddha." There were all very respectful as they went to the Buddha. AND ADDRESSED HIM SAYING/ PLEASE GIVE TO US/ THE THREE JEWELLED CARTS/ You told us awhile ago that you had small, medium, and large carts to give to us. Now, we have come out and want them. THAT YOU PROMISED TO US/ They still had some attachments that they had not broken off. They were attached to the Small and Middle Vehicle Dharma which the Buddha had previously spoken. They had doubts about the Great Vehicle Dharma now being spoken. They clung to the past and had doubts about the present. See? The Buddha had dwelt in the world teaching Dharma for so long. And yet, when, at the very end he spoke *The Dharma Flower Sutra*, all the disciples gave rise to doubts. They didn't show them on the outside, of course; but they still had doubts. Small wonder, then, that now as I speak this Sutra you don't believe. It's all very muddled for you although you do admit to it's having some meaning, and so you listen. Basically, you aren't sure whether the Buddhadharma is true or false, but there's so much to be said about it that you half believe and half disbelieve. The reason that you don't obtain a response in the Dharma is just because of this doubt which prevents you from entering it deeply, from giving rise to genuine faith. Genuine faith means that you have to reform all your previous views about things. If you continue to have deviant knowledge and views, it doesn't matter whether you study for one life, or repeatedly through lifetime after lifetime, you still won't understand it. Studying the Buddhadharma means that you must bring forth genuine faith.

'IF YOU CHILDREN COME OUT/ I WILL GIVE YOU THREE CARTS/ I will give you the Three Vehicle Dharma FOR YOU TO TAKE AS YOU WISH/ The Buddha has said they could choose whatever vehicle they wished according to which fruit they wanted to certify to--Sound Hearer, Pratyeka Buddha, or Bodhisattva. Now, in the Dharma Flower Assembly, the Three Vehicle Dharma is said to be expedient. That means there must be some other Great Vehicle Dharma to be given to living beings.

NOW THE TIME HAS COME/ PLEASE GIVE THEM TO US/ It's just the right time because we want to study the Great Vehicle Dharma; so all of us living beings pray that the Buddha will use the Great Vehicle Dharma to teach and transform us.

Sutra: 14c7

THE ELDER, HAVING GREAT WEALTH,
AND STOREHOUSES CONTAINING MUCH
GOLD, SILVER, AND LAPIS LAZULI,
MOTHER-OF-PEARL AND CARNELIAN,
USED THESE PRECIOUS THINGS
TO MAKE SEVERAL GREAT CARTS.
THEY WERE DECORATED AND ADORNED,
SURROUNDED BY RAILINGS,
HUNG WITH BELLS ON ALL FOUR SIDES,
WITH GOLDEN CORDS STRUNG ABOUT THEM,
AND GEM-STUDDED NETS
SPREAD ABOVE THEM.
THERE WERE GOLDEN FLOWERED TASSELS
HANGING FROM THEM EVERYWHERE,
AND VARIOUS MULTI-COLORED ORNAMENTS
ENCIRCLING THEM.
SOFT SILK AND COTTON
MADE UP THE CUSHIONS,
AND FINE COVERINGS,

VALUED IN THE THOUSANDS OF MILLIONS,
PURE WHITE AND SPARKLING CLEAN
WERE SPREAD ATOP THEM.
GREAT WHITE OXEN,
PLUMP, STRONG, AND POWERFUL,
OF FINE APPEARANCE,
WERE YOKED TO THE PRECIOUS CARTS.
THEY WERE SURROUNDED BY MANY FOOTMEN
WHO WERE ATTENDING TO THEM.
SUCH FINE CARRIAGES AS THESE
WERE GIVEN EQUALLY TO ALL THE CHILDREN.

Outline:

M3. Giving to all the children a great cart.

Commentary:

THE ELDER, HAVING GREAT WEALTH/ In all the worlds, the Buddha is the most honored, the most noble, the most "wealthy." He has the nobility of a king and the wealth of the four seas. He stood to inherit the throne in India. In transcendental terms he has cultivated and attained self-enlightenment, the enlightenment of others, and the perfection of enlightened practice.

> Having perfected the three kinds
> of enlightenment,
> And complete with the ten thousand virtues,
> He is therefore called the Buddha.

AND STOREHOUSES CONTAINING MUCH/ Storehouses are places to put valuable things. The storehouses represent our six sense organs. Within the six sense organs the nature of the Thus Come One's Storehouse is hidden. The Buddhanature manifests as a precious enlightenment nature at the gateways of our six sense organs. They also represent the ten thousand conducts which comprise a precious storehouse. You could also say that they represent the six perfections. Using the dharma of the six perfections one adorns the virtuous fruition of the ten thousand conducts. Each one of the six perfections contains the ten thousand conducts. Each one of the ten thousand conducts contains the six perfections. Therefore, the six perfections and ten thousand conducts are interrelated. All dharmas contain all conducts, and all the conducts contain all dharmas. This is the limitlessness of both the dharmas and the conducts. Limitless conducts are used to cultivate limitless dharmas; limitless dharmas are used to realize the limitless conducts. The six perfections and ten thousand conducts are represented by this line of text.

GOLD, SILVER, LAPIS LAZULI/ MOTHER-OF-PEARL AND CARNELIAN/ If you consider gold and silver a kind of gem, then there are four types of gems represented here. They stand for the Buddha's Four Kinds of Wisdom which are priceless jewels:

1. The great perfect mirror wisdom.

2. The equality wisdom.

3. The wonderful observing wisdom.

4. The perfecting wisdom.

USED THESE PRECIOUS THINGS/ TO MAKE SEVERAL GREAT CARTS/ There are more than just four kinds of precious gems in the world, and likewise among all the Buddha's Dharmas there are not just four kinds of wisdom. There are also five roots, five powers, seven Bodhi shares, the eight-fold path, the four applications of mindfulness, the four right efforts, and the four bases of psychic power--a great many dharmas. Using these various Dharma-doors, he creates a Great Vehicle Dharma. The Great Vehicle Buddhadharma, the Buddha Vehicle, is comprised of all these dharmas.

THEY WERE DECORATED AND ADORNED/ SURROUNDED BY RAILINGS/ They were adorned with intertwining decorations, very beautiful, representing the Buddha's Great Vehicle Dharma which illuminates heaven and earth. It is extremely beautiful in the world. The carts were surrounded by railings, another kind of adornment. HUNG WITH BELLS ON ALL FOUR SIDES/ The bells represent the four kinds of unlimited eloquence. WITH GOLDEN CORDS STRUNG ABOUT THEM/ AND GEM-STUDDED NETS/ The jewelled cords were strung about the cart in the form of a net or macrame. Would you imagine that such a netting would be expensive? This represents the

Buddha's compassion. The methods of compassion used by the Buddha are as many as the holes in the netting. He has compassion like a network, like the net in the Heaven of the Great Brahma King in which there is a jewel in every hole in the net. Each jewel reflects the light of all the other jewels, as they shine upon each other infinitely. Such light represents wisdom. The Buddha has many methods of using compassion and just as many methods of using wisdom. Thus the lines of text here represent the Buddha's compassion and wisdom.

The line "surrounded by railings"/ also represents Dharani. Dharani, a Sanskrit word which means "uniting and holding," unites all dharmas and holds limitless meanings. Dharani unites all dharmas, both the Great and Small Vehicle. Dharani holds limitless meanings, all the limitless meanings in all the dharmas. Through the Dharani, one can offer up all good conduct and supress all evil.

"Hung with bells on all four sides"/ also represents the four kinds of unlimited eloquence. "With golden cords strung about them"/ represents the Four Vast Vows:

I vow to save the boundless number of beings.

I vow to cut off the endless afflictions.

I vow to study the limitless Dharma-doors.

I vow to attain the supreme Buddha Way.

All the Buddhas, Bodhisattvas, Sound Hearers, and Condition-enlightened Ones are included within these Four Vast Vows. Therefore, it's not enough just to recite them. You have to return the light and think it over: The vow says that I will save the boundless number of beings. Have I done so? If I have, it should still be the same as if I had not saved them. Why? It is said that the Thus Come One saves all living beings, and yet not a single living being has been saved.

"Well," you say, "if my saving them is the same as not saving them, then is my not saving them the same as saving them?"

No. You can say that you save them, and yet are not attached to them; not attached means that you are not attached to the mark of saving living beings. But you can't fail to save them and claim to have saved them. It doesn't work that way. You can say that you save them without saving them because you are not attached to them. But you can't say that you have saved them when you have not saved them.

The Buddha leads all beings to Nirvana, and yet not a single being is led to Nirvana. We have not yet become Buddhas or saved living beings, and so it is not all right for us to say that we have done so.

"Then just what are living beings?" you ask.

Living beings are born from a combination of causal conditions.

"How many?"

Twelve. Twelve causal conditions lead to the production of a living being. They are: Ignorance, which conditions action, action which conditions consciousness, consciousness which conditions name and form, name and form which condition the six senses, the six senses which condition contact, contact which conditions feeling, feeling which conditions craving, craving which conditions grasping, grasping which conditions becoming, becoming which conditions birth, birth which conditions old age and death.

This is not to say that only people are living beings. Why, even the smallest of ants are also living beings. The tiniest mosquito, too, is a living being. Even to all the tiny germs and so forth, all are living beings. Since this is the case, we should not look outwardly in our search to save living beings. Right within our self-nature can be found living beings, limitless in number, for us to save. Right inside our bodies there are limitless living beings. Recent progress in the science of medicine gives proof to the fact that human beings are all like big bugs and within our bodies live countless smaller bugs. How many? No scientific method can count them accurately. Why? Because they are countless! Who knows how many living beings are inside our blood, our flesh, and our internal organs? Why are there so many living beings? Some people even eat living beings! They eat the flesh of pigs, cows, sheep, fish, chicken, and ducks. When you eat the flesh of living beings, inside it are hidden the germs particular to that living being. When you eat it, that kind of living being's organisms go into you. Whichever kind of meat you eat the most of, you have a majority of that kind of living being's germs. That makes it very easy to become a member of the family of the kind of living being. You turn into one of his clansmen; because you have causal conditions with him that are just too deep, you can't get away from him. If you eat mostly pig meat, you have an opportunity to turn into a pig. If you eat mostly beef, you may turn into a cow.

"Gees, I eat rice. Will I turn into a plant?" you ask.

No, because rice is not generally considered sentient in the way that animals are. If you eat sentient beings you can turn into that kind of living being. If you eat insentient things, you will not turn into plants or grass or anything, but you will be truly helping the wisdom-life of your Dharma body. So don't worry about turning into a rice plant if you eat rice.

Sentient beings have blood and breath, and when you eat them their blood and breath mixes with yours. If you eat a lot of them, you turn into that kind of living being. You could even say that by not eating a particular kind of living being, you are saving that living being! If you do not eat beef, you are saving cows. If you don't eat sheep, you are saving the sheep. By not eating pigs, you are saving pigs.

What is meant by "save?" It means stopping the revolution of the wheel of birth and death by taking a being across the sea of suffering to the other shore of Nirvana.

You say, "Dharma Master, I really don't believe this. How can it be that by not eating something I am saving it? If I don't eat it, someone else will. So how can you consider it saved?"

Well, you should just look after yourself. The other people don't understand the principle, but you do. Those who don't understand will do confused things; those who do understand should not do confused things. You shouldn't look after other people.

While we are on the subject: There once was a meat-eater who died and was sent before King Yama. When he got there, all the pigs, sheep, and cows he had eaten when he was alive came to get even. One pig said, "When he was alive he ate a pound of my flesh." A sheep said, "He ate two pounds of me!" A chicken said, "Two pounds? He ate three pounds of me--my whole body!! Now, I want to eat him!!" The meat-eater tried to "reason" with Kind Yama by saying, "I didn't really want to eat their meat, you know. If was for sale in the store, and I figured if they were selling it, I could buy it and eat it. The offense should be with the person who sold it. It shouldn't be my offense just for eating it."

Then King Yama brought the meat-seller before him and said, "You sell meat? That's an offense, you know." The meat-seller objected, saying, "Yes, I sell meat, but only because people want to buy it. If no one wanted it, how could I sell it? The reason I sell meat is because people want to buy it."

The meat-eater piped up saying, "But if he didn't sell it, how could I buy it?"

The meat-seller said, "Then it's not my fault and it's not your fault. I sell it because you buy it and you buy it because I sell it, but neither one of us killed the pig. The offense lies with the butcher who killed the animal!"

Then the one who killed the pig was called in.

"Are you the one who kills the pigs?" King Yama asked him. "That's a grave offense."

The pig-killer said, "Right, I killed those pigs. But if he didn't eat them, why would I kill them?"

So, in the final analysis, who do you blame?

If the person didn't eat the pig, the pig-killer would not have killed it. If the seller didn't sell the meat, the buyer would not have bought it. The pig-eater said, "I bought it because you sold it!"

The pig-killer said, "I killed it because you wanted to eat it!"

The pig-eater said, "If you hadn't killed it, I couldn't have eaten it!"

What a confusing case! There was no way King Yama could render a judgement. They each presented their testimony quite well, but they had all committed offenses. King Yama said, "Okay, if you ate a pound of pig's flesh, you have to be reborn as a pig to repay that pound of meat. Since you ate two pounds of sheep meat, you can then be reborn as a sheep to repay that two pounds of meat. Since you ate a whole chicken, you can be reborn as a chicken to pay back your debt." That's how the case was settled.

You can see then that you establish affinities with whatever type of living being you eat. There's a verse which goes:

There are two people in the word for meat:
The one inside pushes the other out.
Living beings return to eat living beings.
Isn't this just people eating people?

肉
jou

In *The Shurangama Sutra*, we read, "Sheep return to become people." So can pigs and cows. But before you have gained the use of the heavenly eye you can't see clearly and so you think that sheep are just sheep and cows are just cows. In a short time, many changes take place, and, like a magical transformation, your life force moves on. Hah! From the body of a person, it may move to the body of a pig and from the body of a pig to the body of a cow. One moves around and around without knowing where one will ultimately end up. Would you say that this was dangerous or not? If you expect to save living beings, you must put an end to such an eaten/eating relationship. Whatever type of living being you do not eat, you can consider yourself as having saved it.

The beings in our self-nature are limitless and boundless. In order to save the beings on the outside, you must first save the beings within your self-nature. If you can't cross over the beings within you, you won't be able to cross over those on the outside. Although you save living beings, you should not become attached to the mark of saving living beings.

The second of the Four Vast Vows is to cut off the endless afflictions. Without intending to, one gives rise to afflictions; without thinking, one gives rise to afflictions. Without realizing how it happens, ignorance manifests. In *The Heart Sutra* I explained a list of twenty following afflictions. Without reason or cause, afflictions arise. One vows to sever these afflictions, but they are endless. We'd be well-off indeed if we had as much money as we had afflictions. We'd always have money; no need to go to work for it. Afflictions are endless. Money is not. Use money, and it's gone. But some people think afflictions are the best thing going. They get angry and think it's more fun that eating bread and butter. Is this not weird? Once they give rise to afflictions, they burn off all the Dharma wealth of their merit and virtue. The Buddha taught all living beings to cut off afflictions.

The third vow is to study the limitless Dharma-doors. Last year, you studied *The Shurangama Sutra*. This year, you are studying *The Lotus Sutra*, *The Heart Sutra*, and the *The Earth Store Bodhisattva Sutra*. So many Sutras! And now-- *The Avatamsaka Sutra!!* And each Sutra has its own doctrines. How many doctrines would you say there are? There are as many as the grains of sand in the Ganges River, as many as motes of dust. Today we learned that *The Avatamsaka Sutra* has as many chapters as motes of dust in an entire world! "How many is that?" you ask. It's as many as those dust motes. If you can count them, then you know how many there are. If you can't well, don't ask me, because I am just like you.

There are so many Dharmas! There are Great Vehicle Dharmas and Small Vehicle Dharmas. There are the Dharmas of the Six Perfections and the Four Truths, the Twelve Causes and Conditions, and the Thirty-seven Wings of Enlightenment. A lot of Dharmas! There are eighty-four thousand Dharma-doors. If we were to study one Dharma-door every day, we would need eighty-four thousand days. How many days are there in our lives? There are 365 days in a year, 3,650 days in ten years, and 36,500 days in a hundred years. Before we finished, we would die. National Master Ch'ing Liang lived to be 101 years old.

How can one ever finish studying something? One can never finish studying. Then should we quit altogether? No. You have to keep on studying. As the vow says, "I vow to study the limitless Dharma-doors." If you don't study, you won't ever understand even one of them.

By way of elaboration, how many different languages are there in this world? Each country has it's own language and literature. You may claim that some person has gotten his doctorate at such and such a university, but how many languages does that mean he has mastered? At the most, perhaps thirty or forty or even fifty. But that is by no means all of them. Is there anyone who has been able to learn all the languages in the world? No. To say nothing of other subjects of study, you can see how hard it is just to learn languages. To say nothing of the literature of each land and it's various styles. They are not easy to learn. It was the Chinese sage *Chuang-tzu* who said,

> "My life has a limit, but knowledge has no limit. To pursue the unlimited with that which is limited is dangerous indeed."

Here he is referring to ordinary knowledge, not to real wisdom. There's no way to attain your aim. It's dangerous.

We now study the Buddhadharma, and as we learn a bit, still a lot remains to be learned. Why do we meditate? We meditate in order to learn about those Sutras which are originally within each one of us, to learn about our inherent wisdom. Within the self-nature of each one of us are limtless Sutras, limitless wisdom, limitless Dharma-doors. The eighty-four thousand

Dharma-doors are all included within our own self-natures. However, you are unable to make use of your self-nature and so you just search outwardly, not realizing that you have to return the light and reverse the illumination. So, when I lectured on *The Heart Sutra,* I said, "Turn the light to shine within and contemplate in comfort." Take a look at yourself to see whether you are in comfort or not. If you are, then you can give rise to profound Prajna wisdom and illuminate the five skandhas all as empty. Once you have seen the five skandhas as empty, you have also exhausted all other Dharmas as well. So you should meditate quietly for a time each day. That is the process of returning the light to shine within. You must diligently study and cultivate the Dharma-doors. You have to cultivate them. You can't just learn them and then put them away somewhere and pay no attention to them. As you learn the Dharma-doors, you must put them into practice by cultivating them.Cultivate according to the Dharmas. That is what is meant by, "I vow to study the limitless Dharma-doors."

The fourth vow is "I vow to realize the supreme Buddha Way." In this world, there is nothing higher than the accomplishment of Buddhahood. Becoming a Buddha is the highest and most noble of accomplishments in and beyond this world. That is why the Buddha is also called the World Honored One. He is honored both in and beyond the world. To become a Buddha is the ultimate perfection, the final accomplishment. Before one has become a Buddha, one is simply a confused person in the nine realms. Only after you have become a Buddha are you one who really understands. Therefore, one should vow to realize the supreme Buddha Way. You must make a vow that you are absolutely determined to become a Buddha yourself, and to save all living beings as well so that you all become Buddhas together.

Do you see how broad these four vows are? They are truly heroic!

You can't run around just telling other people that they should cut off their afflictions. You can't walk up to someone and say, "See how many years you have studied the Buddhadharma, and you still have a terrible temper! Just what meaning does all your study have?" You are not supposed to be looking after other people. You are supposed to watch over yourself. People who study the Buddhadharma are supposed to take care of themselves and not mind other people's business. There is a saying,

Other's wrongs and other's obsessions,
are their offenses and their transgressions!

Don't take out stocks in his "Wrong Company." If you know he is not solvent, why insist on taking a loss? Why insist on doing business in the red? If you see other people getting afflicted, you should stop a minute and think, "Oh, affliction is really no good. I should sever it." Don't inspect other people's clothing and find their spots and stains and yet refuse to see that your own clothing is even filthier. Don't wash other people's clothes for them and forget about washing your own. The Buddha Way is supreme; you should accomplish it. You should launder your minds and hearts. Wash your hearts and purify your thoughts. Sweep out all that false thinking. Don't allow it to run around in your minds.

What is false thinking? Negative thoughts, thoughts about things you don't like, things that upset you. That's all just affliction and false thinking. However, the things that you are are "happy" false thinking. It's all false thinking, and when you are caught up in it, if you aren't liking something, you're disliking it. Liking is false thinking and not liking is also false thinking.

What's to be done?
What's to be done?

PUT IT DOWN, HEY!

Just let it go, and then there won't be any more liking or not liking. That's the ultimate meaning of the Middle Way. You don't give rise to afflictions or worries, and you don't go insane and run off to dances and whatnot. That's insane happiness; it's not in accord with the Middle Way. Every day you should be very calm and even-minded and keep ahold of the Middle Way. Eventually, the day will come when you become enlightened. Enlightened, you can become a Buddha. In this way you will have fulfilled the vow, "I vow to realize the supreme Buddha Way."

The Four Vast Vows are very important. So they are represented in the text by the phrase "With golden cords strung about them"/ Don't ever forget these Four Vast Vows. Cultivate in accord with them always.

THERE WERE GOLDEN FLOWERED TASSELS/ These represent the Four Methods of Conversion, which are four kinds of forces. The more sincere you are, the more power you have. If you are not entirely sincere, the force won't be as great.

The four are: Giving, kind words, beneficial conduct, and cooperation.

The power of giving comes through sincerity. It cannot be forced. Why should one practice giving? Because all living beings are greedy to a degree. You have to give them something that they like, and so Bodhisattvas practice giving. What do they give? They give everything. If someone wants your head, you give them your head. If someone wants your hands, you give them your hands. If someone wants your eye, brains, and marrow, you give them away. In giving this way, one must first be free of having a "self." If you have no self then you can give. Once there is a "you," you'll start thinking, "Gosh, if I give this away, then I won't have it anymore. What will I do?" And you won't be able to give. You must forget about yourself. Forget about others and a self. Think, "Giving is my job."

Kind words means speaking in such a way that eveyone loves to listen to you and feels really happy. It isn't to say a single sentence and have the effect of setting off a bomb or slicing through people's bodies with a sharp knife. You shouldn't make people hurt all over. Kind words means you make everyone happy. Take care not to say things that will cause people to become afflicted. Those are not kind words. They are harmful words If you say hurtful things people will point at you and say, "He really doesn't know how to talk." Then you won't be able to be a Bodhisattva. Bodhisattvas make people happy and everyone is overjoyed to see them. Those who walk the Bodhisattva Path have affinities with everyone.

Beneficial practice means helping other people Cooperation means that you first become good friends with whoever it is you want to save. You make them happy, as you work beside them. Bit by bit, you take them across.

HANGING FROM THEM EVERYWHERE/ means that there are none who are not saved. The Bodhisattvas go everywhere to practice these Four Methods and practice the Bodhisattva Path.

AND VARIOUS MULTI-COLORED ORNAMENTS/ ENCIRCLING THEM/ The adornments on the cart were extremely wonderful. SOFT SILK AND COTTON/ MADE UP THE CUSHIONS/ AND FINE COVERINGS/ VALUED IN THE THOUSANDS OF MILLIONS/ This represents the use of contemplative wisdom in cultivation to attain all the Dhyanas. PURE WHITE AND SPARKLING CLEAN/ WERE SPREAD ATOP THEM/ Pure and white means that they are without evil. This is the cultivation of good on a vast scale. "Sparkling clean" means keeping the precepts. One who breaks the precepts cannot be said to be white and sparkling clean. First, you must keep the precepts. If your precepts are strictly held and you don't break them, they are like a covering for your cultivation. In cultivation, keeping the precepts is always the most important thing.

GREAT WHITE OXEN/ represent no-outlfows, the no-outflow wisdom. Whoever can be without outflows has a great white ox, the wisdom, that is, which the white ox represents. PLUMP, STRONG, AND POWERFUL/ OF FINE APPEARANCE/ This represents the mind, because the mind is complete with all the ten thousand dharmas. WERE YOKED TO THE PRECIOUS CARTS/ This represents the use of non-outflow wisdom in the cultivation of the Great Vehicle Buddhadharma. THEY WERE SURROUNDED BY MANY FOOTMEN/ Although one uses the non-outflow wisdom to cultivate the Great Vehicle Dharma, one employs the paramita of expedients. Expedient dharmas aid the Great Vehicle Dharma. Although you cultivate using the non-outflow wisdom, you still must employ many other methods to help it out. What other methods?

If you wish to cultivate the non-outflow wisdom, you must rid yourself of all greed, hatred, stupidity, arrogance, and doubt, for they are all outflows. Deviant views are also outflows. Through the application of expedient methods, one gets rid of all one's faults and afterwards one can attain the non-outflow wisdom.

Non-Buddhist religions and those of the Two Vehicles use the expedient dharmas. "Footmen" also represent the spiritual powers gained on the result ground. When one certifies to the fruit, one attains spiritual powers. They have a miraculous kind of functioning that allows one to do whatever one wishes to do. WHO WERE ATTENDING TO THEM/ They were protecting and helping them, as the expedients aid one in the cultivation of the Great Vehicle Dharma.

SUCH FINE CARRIAGES AS THESE/ WERE GIVEN EQUALLY TO ALL THE CHILDREN/ The elder gave these valuable carts to all the children. The Buddha gave the Great Vehicle Dharma as a teaching to all living beings because he wanted to lead them to cultivate according to it and in the future certify to the Buddha fruit.

Sutra: T.14c17

THEN ALL THE CHILDREN
DANCED FOR JOY;
THEY MOUNTED THEIR JEWELED CARTS
AND RODE OFF INTO THE FOUR DIRECTIONS,
HAPPILY AMUSING THEMSELVES
IN UNOBSTRUCTED COMFORT.

Outline:

M4. The children obtain the carts and rejoice.

Commentary:

THEN ALL THE CHILDREN/ When the children got their precious carts they DANCED FOR JOY/ They were very happy indeed, so happy that they jumped up and started dancing around. THEY MOUNTED THEIR JEWELED CARTS/ AND RODE OFF INTO THE FOUR DIRECTIONS/ They rode off in all directions to teach and transform living beings. HAPPILY AMUSING THEMSELVES/ IN UNOBSTRUCTED COMFORT/ They were in a state of total freedom. When one attains the Great Vehicle Dharma and understands the realm of the Great Vehicle, one wishes to dance for joy. It is inconceivably and ineffably wonderful. Relying on the Great Vehicle Dharma in cultivation, "mounting their jeweled carts" they rode into the four directions, into all the Buddhadharmas, understanding them all: The Four Truths, the Six Perfections, the Twelve Causes and Conditions, the various Buddhadharmas. They cultivated as well the Four Unlimited minds, the Four Unobstructed Eloquences, the Four Applications of Mindfulness, the Four Right Efforts. They perfected and understood all these Dharmas, because all dharmas are included in the Great Vehicle Dharma. They are having a great deal of fun here in the Great Vehicle Dharma, happily amusing themselves, and taking these dharmas as provisions for their spirit. "In unobstructed comfort" means they were feeling especially happy and very, very free.

Sutra: T.14c19

I TELL YOU, SHARIPUTRA,
I AM LIKE THIS, TOO,
THE HONORED AMONG MANY SAGES,
THE FATHER OF THE WORLDS.

Outline:

J2. Correlating the parable with the Dharma.
K1. Correlating the parable in general.
L1. Correlating the elder.

Commentary:

I TELL YOU, SHARIPUTRA/ The Buddha says to Shariputra, I AM LIKE THIS, TOO/ The Buddha, the World Honored One is like the elder in the parable of the burning house I have just spoken. THE HONORED AMONG MANY SAGES/ Of all the sagely ones, I am the most revered, the most lofty. THE FATHER OF THE WORLDS/ I am the father of all living beings in the world.

Sutra: T.14c20

ALL LIVING BEINGS
ARE MY CHILDREN;
DEEPLY ATTACHED TO WORLDLY PLEASURES,
THEY HAVE NO WISE THOUGHTS AT ALL.

Outline:

L2. Correlating the five hundred people and the thirty sons.

Commentary:

ALL LIVING BEINGS/ ARE MY CHILDREN/ DEEPLY ATTACHED TO WORLDLY PLEASURES/ to the joys of the world, they take suffering to be bliss. THEY HAVE NO WISE THOUGHTS AT ALL/ They lack wisdom.

Sutra: T.14c22

IN THE THREE REALMS THERE IS NO PEACE;
THEY ARE LIKE A BURNING HOUSE...

Outline:

L3. Correlating the house· and the meaning of obtaining the one door.

Commentary:

IN THE THREE REALMS THERE IS NO PEACE/ They don't know that in the realm of desire, the realm of form, and in the formless realms, there is not a single place where there is any kind of security. THEY ARE LIKE A BURNING HOUSE/ like the burning house described above.

Sutra: T.14c22

FILLED WITH MANY SUFFERINGS,
AND FRIGHTENING INDEED.
EVER PRESENT ARE THE WOES
OF BIRTH, OLD AGE, SICKNESS, DEATH,
FIRES SUCH AS THESE,
RAGING WITHOUT CEASE.

Outline:

L4. Correlating the fire breaking out.

Commentary:

FILLED WITH MANY SUFFERINGS/ The three, eight, and limitless sufferings fill the three realms entirely. This is FRIGHTENING INDEED/ What is there to be afraid of? It is very easy to fall into the three evil paths.

EVER PRESENT ARE THE WOES/ OF BIRTH, OLD AGE, SICKNESS, DEATH/ Let us not imagine that it is such a happy thing to be born as a person. When you are born it is a lot of suffering. As soon as a baby is born, it starts to cry. Yes, it is suffering, but who told you to come into this world in the first place? You created the karma all by yourself which brought you here. In fact, being born is as painful as ripping the shell off a live turtle. Death is as painful as flaying a live cow. When you get old, your eyes and ears will refuse to help you out. Even a good doctor can't keep you from dying eventually. Doctors can cure illnesses on a superficial level, but they can't do anything about your growing older; when the time comes for you to die, they have no medicines that will keep you from dying.

"Then what do we have all these doctors for?" you ask.

Doctors can cure illnesses which are not fatal. But fatal illnesses, no doctor can cure. If they could, then nobody in the world would die. But people still keep growing old and dying.

"If people are going to die eventually anyway, then why keep all the doctors?" you ask.

Well, that's just the way the world works:

There's the

true & the false
& the false & the true--
true, true
false, false,
false, false, true...

Things are all mixed up together. If you expect things to be a certain way, the unexpected is sure to pop up. If you prepare for the unexpected then everything goes just as expected! That's just the way it is. So someone who is going to die for sure can't be cured by a doctor. Even though we can transplant hearts and so forth, you can transplant all you want, but at some point, the person is still going to die. Nobody lives forever. If you found a way to keep everyone from dying, then the world would disappear entirely. Why? There would be so many people on the earth that there wouldn't be any place to put them. We could colonize outer space, but that is not easy. It seems to me that if no one died, it would be the same as if everyone died.

FIRES SUCH AS THESE/ The sufferings of birth, old age, sickness, death, being separated from what you love, being joined to what you hate, not getting what you want, and the fire of the five skandhas, are RAGING WITHOUT CEASE/ The more they burn, the higher the flames rise and the bigger the fire gets. The karma of living beings grows greater everyday, and so the fire of the three realms burns higher everyday, raging without cease. It never stops.

The principles I have just spoken are really true. Think about it: Which person can never die? No one.

Sutra: T.14c24

> THE THUS COME ONE HAS ALREADY LEFT
> THE THREE REALMS' BURNING HOUSE BEHIND.
> QUIETLY I DWELL AT EASE,
> IN FOREST AND FIELD AT PEACE.
> AND NOW IT IS, THAT THE THREE REALMS,
> ENTIRELY BELONG TO ME,
> AND IN THEM ALL THE LIVING BEINGS
> ARE CHILDREN OF MINE.
> BUT NOW, THIS PLACE
> IS FILLED WITH CALAMITIES,
> AND I AM THE ONLY ONE
> ABLE TO RESCUE THEM.

Outline:

K2. Correlating the specific analogies.

L1. Correlating the seeing of the fire.

Commentary:

THE THUS COME ONE HAS ALREADY LEFT/ THE THREE REALMS' BURNING HOUSE BEHIND/ The Buddha has already left the burning house of the three realms. QUIETLY I DWELL AT EASE/ IN FOREST AND FIELD AT PEACE/ The Buddha is at ease; he doesn't need to work. He is quiet and very still. In the forests and fields he cultivates in a "peace garden" far away from the world, in a pure and happy place. AND NOW IT IS, THAT THE THREE REALMS/ Although the Buddha has escaped the three realms, the burning house, still they ENTIRELY

BELONG TO ME/ They are mine. The text said above, "It belonged to one person," and that means that it is the Buddha's. AND IN THEM ALL THE LIVING BEINGS/ ARE CHILDREN OF MINE/ They are all like my own children.

BUT NOW, THIS PLACE/ IS FILLED WITH CALAMITIES/ In the three realms there are so many calamities, so much danger, poisonous insects, and savage beasts. AND I AM THE ONLY ONE/ ABLE TO RESCUE THEM/ Only the World Honored One, can rescue these living beings. The Buddha says that all living beings are his children, but there are some living beings who don't even recognize their own father! Hah! They slander the Buddha, the Dharma, and the Sangha. Would you say they were unfilial or not?

You say, "Well, the Buddha might say he is our father, but that is not necessarily the case."

I ask you, "If the Buddha is not your father, ultimately , who is?"

"I already have a father!" you protest. "I don't need another one."

That father is your worldly father who is related to you through the principle of karmic retribution. The Buddha is your transcendental father, a pure, greatly compassionate father. He is pure and undefiled. If you can recognize your father, then in the future you too, can obtained purity and non-defilement, and get rid of all filth. So don't run outside and fail to recognize your own father. Later on in the Sutra, it speaks about the poor son who ran away from home and no longer recognized his own father. We are like that poor son. Our father tells us to come home, but we don't recognize him as our father.

Sutra: T.14c28

ALTHOUGH I INSTRUCT THEM,
THEY DO NOT BELIEVE OR ACCEPT,
BECAUSE OF THEIR DEEP ATTACHMENT AND GREED
TO ALL THE DEFILING DESIRES.

Outline:

L2. Correlating casting aside table to use carts.

M1. Casting aside the table.

Commentary:

ALTHOUGH I INSTRUCT THEM/ Although the Buddha teaches living beings, using various methods to instruct them, nevertheless, living beings still do not believe. THEY DO NOT BELIEVE OR ACCEPT/ They continue to act as if they had never heard them. Why don't they believe? BECAUSE OF THEIR DEEP ATTACHMENT AND GREED/ TO ALL THE DEFILING DESIRES/ There are many kinds of desires. Some people are greedy for wealth; they desire more and more money. Other people are greedy for sex. Still others are greedy for fame and want a good reputation. They want to be famous. This, too, is a form of desire. Some people are attached to eating good food. This is also a desire. Some people want to be leaders of the world; they have the desire for leadership. Other people want to be heads of state, emperors or presidents. Have you noticed how many people run for office? They all desire to be leaders. The various desires smother one's wisdom. In every thought, one thinks only of how one can fulfill one's desire. In every thought one never forgets. They are called "defiling" desires because they cover up one's wisdom. Because one has all these desires, one cannot have genuine wisdom. One does confused things. One is constantly doing stupid things. Why? Because one is attached to one's desires So the text says, "Because of their deep attachment and greed." They are attached to fame, profit, sex, food, power--all these things. Their desires control their minds to the point that they become extremely dull-headed. So, although the Buddha speaks the Dharma to them, they don't believe it.

This is a bit like all the young people today who are taking drugs. This is a form of desire, too. When they take drugs, their powers of reason and all their genuine wisdom gets lost. They live drunkenly and die in a dream; such is their "lifestyle." They have no idea what they are doing. They have been covered by the defilements of their desires, and so their wisdom fails to manifest.

Sutra: T.15a1

USING THESE EXPEDIENTS,
I SPEAK TO THEM OF THREE VEHICLES,
CAUSING ALL LIVING BEINGS
TO UNDERSTAND THE PAIN OF THE THREE REALMS.
I REVEAL AND EXTENSIVELY PROCLAIM
THE PATH WHICH TRANSCENDS THE WORLD.
ALL OF THESE CHILDREN,
IF THEY FIX THEIR MINDS,
CAN PERFECT THE THREE CLARITIES
AND THE SIX SPIRITUAL POWERS.

Outline:

M2. Using the carts.

Commentary:

USING THESE EXPEDIENTS/ I SPEAK TO THEM OF THREE VEHICLES/ Because living beings become attached to the defiling desires and because their greed for them is so deep, the Buddha puts away the genuine Dharma and teaches the expedient, clever dharmas. He speaks to them of the Sound Hearer Vehicle, the Vehicle of the Conditioned-enlightened Ones, and the Bodhisattva Vehicle. This is called casting aside the permanent and using the provisional. One sets aside the eternal teaching and uses provisional dharmas, provisional wisdom, not real wisdom.

I mentioned earlier that young people were taking drugs nowadays. They take them and think, "Ah! I have gone to empty space!" Some people have come here and told me that they have gone into emptiness. Would you say that was stupid or not? They even claim that a teacher has certified to their attainment of empty space. This is truly a case of:

> One confused teaches others to be confused.
> With one teaching, both misunderstand.
> The teacher plummets to the hells
> And the disciples follow with their
> hats in their hands.

To get to empty space, you certainly don't need to take any certain kind of drug. If, in order to get to this "emptiness" you have to ingest a drug, and if you can't get there without it, then ultimately, what kind of emptiness is it? You are just cheating yourself. You are being simply too stupid. People like this, as I have said before, won't believe you if you tell them that they haven't made it to emptiness. When the confused teacher tells them that they have, indeed, gone to emptiness, they believe him. Isn't this pitiful? It is just as if they were holding onto a big turd and refusing to let it go when you offer them some fine pastry. They insist that the excrement is more tasty than anything. Would you say such a person was intelligent or confused? And this isn't an exaggeration. The situation is actually worse than that! Why? Because one is losing control of one's own humanity altogether. They don't know that, in order to be human, you have to have genuine wisdom. In believing such illusive and false states, they are much to be pitied. The Buddha had no way to deal with such people. All he could say was, "Ah! The 'drug' I am taking is even more wonderful than the one you are taking. Not only can you go to emptiness when you take it and come down when you quit taking it, but, if you believe in my Dharma, you can stay in space forever; you don't have to come down at all." Those living beings, with their greedy attachments, believed the Buddha. They believed in the Four Truths, the Twelve Causes and Conditions, the Six Perfections, and the Ten Thousand Conducts. The Buddha taught the Three Vehicles TO CAUSE ALL LIVING BEINGS TO UNDERSTAND THE PAIN OF THE THREE REALMS/ In the desire realm, the form realm, and the formless realm, there is nothing but suffering; there's not a single good place among them.

I REVEAL AND EXTENSIVELY PROCLAIM/ I instruct living being, speaking to them of THE PATH WHICH TRANSCENDS THE WORLD/ There are three aspects to the world. There is

1. the world of living beings,

2. the material world, and

3. the world of proper enlightenment.

What is the world of living beings? This is also called the world of proper retribution. It is the world of all of us living beings. The material world is also called the world of dependent retribution. The world of proper enlightenment is the world of the Buddha.

The Buddha has transcended the world. There are worldly dharmas, transcendental dharmas and dharmas which are both worldly and transcendental. ALL OF THESE CHILDREN/ IF THEY FIX THEIR MINDS/ CAN PERFECT THE THREE CLARITIES/ AND THE SIX SPIRITUAL PENETRATIONS/ The three clarities are:

1. The clarity of the past (the penetration of former lives),

2. The clarity of the present (the penetration of the extinction of outflows),

2. And the clarity of the future (the heavenly eye).

The clarity of the past refers to the penetration of past lives, knowing the affairs of former lives. "Ah, last life I was a student. I got my Ph.D. but was so exhausted I spit blood and died. What a pity. I just got my Ph.D. and then I got sick and died. Just as I was dying I had an enlightened thought: This is too bitter! In my next life I am going to study the Buddhadharma and cultivate. And so in this life I have met a Dharma Master and I listen to the Sutras. That's how this happened! When I understood the Sutra, I decided to leave home."

Someone else gains the clarity of former lives and thinks, "I was a shepherd on the mountains. I felt that my life wasn't too interesting and it would be better to study the Buddhadharma. But I never met up with the Buddhadharma. As I died, I made a vow that in my next life, when I was still young, I would encounter the Buddhadharma, listen to the Sutras, and cultivate. And so, this life, I have."

These are just examples. Perhaps someone was a man who liked women and so this life he became a woman. Or perhaps someone was a woman in his last life, but now has become a man. These are examples of the clarity of knowing former lives. You know about yourself and about others. It is also called the clarity of the past.

The clarity of the present is also called the clarity of the exhaustion of outflows. This means that one attains the state of no outflows. Those who have listened to the Sutras will know what this means, but others might wonder, so I will give you a simple analogy: It is like a teacup with a leak in it. Whatever you pour in flows right back out. If there is no leak, then it has no "outflows." People who don't know how to cultivate the Way all have outflows. If you cultivate and attain the Way, then you will have no outflows. When you have no outflows, that is the clarity of the present. This refers to the attainment of genuine wisdom. How can you gain the state of no outflows? You must have genuine wisdom in order to do this. The reason one has outflows is because one is stupid.

What are outflows? Do you like to eat? That is an outflow. Do you like to drink coffee? That is an outflow. Women like men; that is an outflow. Men like women; that is an outflow.

"Well, what isn't an outflow?" you ask.

Cultivation!! That's simply all there is to it. Number one, you have to cultivate. If you cultivate you can be without outflows. If you do not cultivate you cannot be without outflows. There's simply no way around it.

"I'd rather have outflows than cultivate!" you say.

If that's what you like, go ahead. If it suits you to have outflows, then go ahead and "outflow." Let's just see where you "flow" to. You could flow out and turn into a pig, or a horse, or an ox, or flow out into the hells, into the path of animals, or hungry ghosts. You pick your own path.

"You mean it's that dangerous?" you say.

You just figured that out? It's still not too late. You can still turn around and cultivate. Then you won't go to those evil places. You will go to the position of Buddhahood, Bodhisattvahood, or to the Vehicle of Sound Hearers or Conditioned-enlightened Ones. There's nothing difficult about it. All you have to do is cultivate and then you can attain the state of no outflows. That's the clarity of the present.

The third clarity is the clarity of the future, also called the clarity of the heavenly eye. With the heavenly eye, you can see the things inside the room you are in and also what is outside of it.

"Dharma Master," you ask, "do you have the heavenly eye?"

I don't know. You ask me, but who do I ask? I'm not asking you if you have it. Why do you ask me if I have it? With the heavenly eye not only can you see what is going on beyond the walls which enclose you, but you can even see right into the heavens. You can see things in other worlds.

The first of the Six Spritual Penetrations is that of the heavenly eye. With it you can see what is inside your own body, all the living beings within you that you must vow to save. Although scientists can't count the number of living beings inside the human body, if you have the heavenly eye you can see them, and count them, and take them across.

Most people explain the heavenly eye by saying that you can see into the heavens with it. It is also true that you can see all the beings inside yourself. You can even count up the grains of rice you eat. You can see how your meal is digesting in your stomach, just what's going on. You can know for sure just how good your digestion is.

The second of the Six Spiritual Penetrations is that of the heavenly ear. With the heavenly ear, not only can you hear what the gods are saying, but you can hear all the little bugs inside of you calling out. You can hear the germs talking, the flowers talking, and the trees talking. Didn't someone say recently that when you go to pick a flower it is afraid and lets out a scream. That's right. "Oh no! This is it!! It's all over. I'm going to die!!!" When you start hearing all these sounds, though, you shouldn't dislike it. You can choose not to listen to them, too. It's up to you. The heavenly eye sees more clearly than an x-ray machine and the heavenly ear hears more clearly than sonar equipment.

The third is the penetration of other's thoughts. With this penetration you can know exactly what someone is thinking before they have expressed their thoughts in words. While their ideas are still just thoughts in their minds, you can know just what they are. With this penetration one can know the thoughts in another's mind, thoughts which flow like the waves on the sea, one after another.

Long ago there was an Arhat who had the Six Penetrations and could read other's thoughts. One time he and his disciple went out on a pilgrimage carrying their belongings with them. They bowed to the different monasteries and shrines. The disciple carried the luggage. As they walked along, the disciple thought, "In the future I am definitely going to practice the Great Vehicle Dharma and cultivate the Bodhisattva Path, the Six Perfections and the Ten Thousand Conducts. I will save all living beings." When the Master saw that his disciple had resolved to practice the Great Vehicle path of a Bodhisattva while he himself was still just an Arhat, he knew that his disciple's vows surpassed his own, and so he made his disciple give him the baggage. Then, despite his disciple's protestations, he carried it on his own back.

After they had walked for a while, the disciple thought, "Gosh. The Bodhisattva Path is very hard to practice. Why, even Shariputra couldn't do it. How much the less will I be able to do it. It would be better to forget it." As soon as he had the thought to retreat from his Great Vehicle Bodhisattva vows, his master came up to him and handed the baggage to him saying, "Here, you carry this." The disciple had no idea why he did this. The luggage went back and forth like this several times until the disciple finally asked, "Why do you keep switching the luggage like that? What's going on, anyway?"

"Do you really want to know?" said the Arhat. "When you resolved to practice the Bodhisattva Path, since I am still just one of the Small Vehicle, it was my duty to carry the luggage. After awhile you retreated from your Great Vehicle vows, feeling that if it was too hard for Shariputra, it would certainly be too hard for you. Then I gave the bags back to you."

How do we know it was too hard for Shariputra?

Shariputra was a Sound Hearer. Once he resolved to cultivate the Dharma of the Great Vehicle Bodhisattva. Now, it so happens that as long as you don't bring forth a resolve for Bodhi, no one will test you. However, as soon as you bring forth the Bodhi mind, especially if you are quite sincere about it, then the gods and dragons and the eight-fold division or the Bodhisattvas will come to test you out. It's sort of like university entrance exams. If you pass, you get in. If you don't, you have to start over again. Shariputra decided to practice the Bodhisattva Path and Bodhisattvas must practice giving. If someone wants something, they have to give it to them. Otherwise, they can't be called Bodhisattvas. As he was busy practicing the Bodhisattva Path, Shariputra ran into a man who was sitting beside the road, crying. He was sobbing violently, and Shariputra's compassionate heart--Bodhisattvas must have sympathy and pity for all living beings--was moved. Since Bodhisattvas must find a way to ease the grief and distress of living beings, he asked the man, "Layman, why are you crying?"

"My mother is sick," said the man, "and in order to cure her illness, I have to find the eye of a living person. Where can I go to find a living person's eye? Yet without it, my mother won't get well. There's no druggist anywhere who can fill my prescription. What else is there for me to do but cry?"

When Shariputra heard this he thought, "Ah, his mother is sick. He needs a live eye. He is very filial but there's obviously no pharmacy anywhere that's going to have a live eye. I'll give him one of mine." Then, filled with compassion, he reached up and plucked out his own eye with his hand. "Here," he said, "take this eye and go cure your mother. I've helped you out; now don't cry."

The man took the eye, looked at it, and suddenly threw it down on the ground in disgust and stomped it to bits."

"Gees, why did you do that?" asked Shariputra.

The man said, "Your old eye is stinky and smelly and just plain useless, you know? Besides, what I need is a LEFT EYE! You gave me a RIGHT EYE!! You didn't even ask me which eye, but just gave me the WRONG ONE!!! It's useless, utterly useless. If you really want to help me, then give me your other eye!"

Shariputra's left eye-socket was hurting quite a bit by this time. If he ripped out his other eye, he'd be totally blind. "That sinks it!" he said. "You're not getting any more eyes from me. Go look somewhere else. See you later, man. Have a nice day."

"Ah hah!" said the man, "So your Bodhisattva resolve was just half a resolve, eh? It wasn't total. You could only give one eye. You couldn't give them both. Okay. So much for that. We'll just have to wait awhile, won't we?" and the man suddenly flew up into the air. He was actually a god who had come to test Shariputra. He flunked of course, so he'd just have to wait a few years and try again.

So the Arhat said to his disciple, "When you remembered the story of Shariputra, you didn't dare to bring forth the Bodhisattva resolve. I gave the bags back to you, then, because we both were Small Vehicle people at that time. Being the teacher, it wasn't right for me to carry the luggage. If there's work to do, the disciples should do it. If there's good food and drink, the teacher should get it first!"

"In the future," the disicple thought, "I am certainly going to bring forth the Great Vehicle resolve.

To continue the discussion of the Six Spritual Penetrations, the fourth is the penetration of past lives. This means that one knows what one did in one's past lives. You know if you were good or evil. You know if you were Chinese or not. "Ah! Last life I was Chinese, but I got born in America. What for? Last life I made a vow. 'There's no Buddhadharma in America. I am going to go there and be reborn so that I won't have to learn English later. I can pick up Chinese real quickly then.'"

So now you have met a Chinese Dharma Master and this is all because of conditions set up in former lives. Bit by bit, you learn the Buddhadharma. Some learn real fast. Some learn very slowly. Some can only listen to it, they can't practice it. They think, "The Buddhadharma is the Buddhadharma and I am me."Others can actually practice it, really cultivate. They aren't afraid of suffering or hardships in their cultivation.

Perhaps in one's last life one was an Indian who knew that is was time for Buddhism to move west and so was reborn in America. In general, that's what the knowledge of past lives is like. It just means to know what went on in one's past lifetimes.

The next penetration is that of spiritual fulfillment, also called the realm of the spiritual, also called the as-you-will penetration. This means that however you think you'd like it to be, that's the way it is. If you want to eat an apple--zip!--there's an apple! If you want to eat an orange--zip!--there's an orange. The same applies to pastries and everything! In general, whatever you think you want, there it is. It's as-you-will and auspicious. You can even think, "I'd like to have a lot of money," and a lot of money appears. With this penetration you can go into the water and not drown. You can go into the fire and not be burned. That's really as-you-will. This doesn't mean just walking on a few coals, either. You can sit right in the middle of the flames and meditate and they won't burn you. Why not? Because you have the penetration of the realm of the spirit. This doesn't mean you can just pick up a dharma in Japan and then be able to walk on some coals. That isn't so special. If you can sit right in the fire and have a lotus appear beneath you, that's really something. What's the use of just being able to walk across some coals? It's of no great use, really. The world isn't covered with burning coals, you know. If it was and you were the only person who could walk on them, that would be pretty meaningful. But this isn't the time of Hsüan-tsang in the T'ang Dynasty. He went to India to get Sutras and had to pass through the flaming mountains. If you can get through the flaming mountains, then you've got some talent. People who have the penetration of spiritual fulfillment are not afraid of water or fire.

Some people are not affected by cold, but this isn't any great use either. When I was in Manchuria, I could walk around outside in the freezing weather without a coat on. I could walk barefoot in the snow. The snow didn't hurt my feet at all. But this is just a minor state, a tiny bit of skill. It's certainly not the penetration of spiritual fulfillment. Anybody can bear the cold. All you have to do is be able to bear it and not be afraid. People are like that. If it's cold and you bear it, and get through it, then after awhile you won't feel cold anymore. Take a look at the birds. They don't wear shoes or socks, but they walk around in the snow. That doesn't mean they have spiritual powers, does it? They all can do it. Being able to bear the cold just means you have entered a bit into the realm of no outflows.

If you have the penetration of spiritual fulfillment, you can walk right through walls. You can go right down into the earth and you can appear and disappear at will.

"I don't believe that," you say.

Of course you don't believe it. If you did believe it you could do it,too.

"You believe it," you say. "Can you do it?"

Don't ask me. I am lecturing to you. You aren't lecturing to me. You don't understand the principle and so I am explaining it to you, but don't ask me. I don't need anyone to give me tests. I don't want into any university and so I am not up for any university exams or any tests of my capacity to practice the Bodhisattva Path. The penetration of spiritual fulfillment is miraculous and ineffably wonderful. I have just described it superficially to you because there isn't any way to describe it fully. It's too profound and wonderful. With it you can rise right up into empty space, and, from the top of your body emit fire and from the lower half emit water. Or you can emit water from the top of your body and fire from the lower part. You can manifest the eighteen changes in empty space.

Finally, the sixth penetration is that of the extinction of outflows. This means that there are no outflows into the three realms. The ghosts and spirits have the other five spiritual penetrations, but they do not have the penetration of the extinction of outflows. They all have outflows and they have not certified to the fruit. In order to be without outflows one must have certified to the fruit of Arhatship. One then obtains the penetration of the extinction of outflows. Only when one has the six penetrations is one an Arhat. You can't say that, with one or two of them, you are an Arhat. Arhatship isn't that easy to come by. You can't just open your heavenly eye or obtain some small measure of wisdom and be an Arhat. If you can't be without outflows, then you are very far away from being an Arhat. However, you should be aware of this point: Even if you obtain the five eyes and the six spiritual penetrations, you can't use them carelessly and waste them.

"But if I don't use them, then what's the use of having them?" you ask.

I'm not telling you not to use them. I'm just telling you to use them in a big way, not for petty affairs. For example, if you're being small-minded with them, you might see someone and think, "I'll just show off a few spiritual powers for this person." Then you say to him, "You were just at home and I know what you had to eat and who you made telephone calls to."

"Strange, indeed," says the person as he hears you enumerate his lunch and phone calls. "He really does have spiritual powers."

You musn't use spiritual powers for such petty purposes. If you do, your state will be just that small.

How does one use spiritual powers in a big way? Take a look and when you see a place where a great disaster is due, for example an earthquake that will kill hundreds of thousands of people, then think of a way to make the ground undergo a transformation so that it won't quake. That's a big use. Don't use your spiritual powers to determine how many cookies a child ate in one day or how many times the child cried. What's the use of knowing things like that? If you see a disaster due in a certain place and use your powers to save the people there, without their even knowing it, then that's using them in a big way. They will be saved, but they won't even know that a certain Arhat saved them. You shouldn't let people know or encourage them to give you thanks. If people know and start thanking you, then your state once again is very small. There is a saying,

> The good which is done for others to see
> is not truly good.
> The evil which is done fearing others will
> know, is truly great evil.
> When one of great goodness falls
> he becomes one of great evil;
> When one of great evil reforms,
> he becomes one of great goodness.

In the future, when you obtain the five eyes and the six spiritual penetrations, don't use them to satisfy your curiosity. Don't go minding other people's business, either, checking out what the neighbors are having for lunch or what's on sale at the supermarket. That's not what they are for. When you obtain them you must save them for great, important matters, not small, petty ones. Use them when you have no other recourse. If you can handle the problem without using them, then don't use them. They are like jewels. If you leave a pearl on the doorstep, sooner or later someone is going to come along and steal it. If you leave your precious gems out in view and fail to put them in a safe place, they are going to get stolen. Spiritual powers are like gems, too, and you must take good care of them. Put them away in your Thus Come One's treasury.

Sutra: T.15a4

SOME SHALL BECOME CONDITIONED-ENLIGHTENED ONES, AND OTHERS IRREVERSIBLE BODHISATTVAS.

Commentary:

Continuing the last passage on using the carts, the Buddha says that, having gained the three clarities and the six spiritual penetrations SOME SHALL BECOME CONDITIONED-ENLIGHTENED ONES/ AND OTHERS IRREVERSIBLE BODHISATTVAS/ The term "Conditioned-enlightened Ones" here includes Sound Hearers. Sound Hearers are those who awaken to the Way upon hearing the Buddha's voice. Conditioned-enlightened Ones attain the Way through cultivation of the Twelve Causes and Conditions. Those of the Sound Hearer Vehicle cultivate the Dharma of the Four Holy Truths; Suffering, origination, extinction and the Path. The Conditioned-enlightened Ones cultivate the Dharmas of the Twelve Causes and Conditions, the first of which is ignorance. They observe ignorance. Because of ignorance, there is an improper activity. This false activity gives rise to a false consciousness. With this false consciousness false name and form arise. The false name and form turn into the false six entrances. With the false six entrances there comes contact. With contact comes feeling. With feeling there is love. Why do you have love? Because you wish to experience certain feelings.

Love conditions grasping. With love, there is selfishness. One selfishly wishes to obtains one's love-object. You want to appropriate it for your very own. This is all selfish activity. When you get what you were grasping after, then that is the cause of becoming. With becoming there is future birth. Future birth means old age and death as well. Conditioned-enlightened Ones cultivate these twelve. They observe them all the way from ignorance up to old age and death, step by step. "Oh! So all along I was just being turned upside-down by ignorance." If one breaks through ignorance, the Dharma nature manifests. Suddenly, they break through ignorance. "Why should I run along after ignorance?" they think, and they refuse to follow it. Not following along with ignorance means not following along with living beings. Instead, living beings follow you. You manifest the Dharma nature, your true, inherent Buddha nature. If you don't break through ignorance, although you have not lost your Dharma nature, still, you can't use it. Conditioned-enlightened Ones work on these twelve from #1 right up to #12. Then they take them back down the line like this:

When ignorance is extinguished then activity is extinguished.

When activity is extinguished, then consciousness is extinguished.

When consciousness is extinguished, then name and form are extinguished.

When name and form are extinguished, then the six senses are extinguished.

When the six senses are extinguished, then contact is extinguished.

When contact is extinguished, then feeling is extinguished.

When feeling is extinguished, then love is extinguished.

When love is extinguished, then grasping is extinguished.

When grasping is extinguished, then becoming is extinguished.

When becoming is extinguished, then birth is extinguished.

When birth is extinguished, then old age and death are extinguished.

They look into these coming and going and get enlightened all by themselves. They are called those of the Conditioned-enlightened Vehicle.

The text also mentions irreversible Bodhisattvas. Some Bodhisattvas retreat, you know. For example, Shariputra: He brought forth the Bodhisattva heart, made Bodhisattvas vows, and practiced the Bodhisattva conduct. But he met someone who wanted an eye and he gave him the wrong eye. When the man refused to take the eye, he retreated from the Bodhisattva Path. "Ah! It is difficult indeed to practice the Bodhisattva Path. I quit!" he said, and turned back. The Bodhisattvas mentioned in the text here do not retreat.

Technically, there are three types of irreversibility: Irreversible practice, irreversible position, and irreversible thought.

If you want to practice as a Bodhisattva, you'd better think it over first. Why? The Buddhadharma is extremely difficult to practice. When you don't understand the Buddhadharma, you may think it's very simple to study. Who would have guessed that it is just the hardest thing there is to do! To study the Buddhadharma, you have to be patient. Firmness, sincerity, and perseverence are three qualities necessary in your study.

Firmness: You must think, "My wish to study the Dharma is more solid than a diamond. Diamonds may be the hardest things there are, but I am even firmer in my resolve than a diamond." It shouldn't be the case that today you wish to study the Dharma, but tomorrow you give it up, and by the third day you have forgotten it entirely. That's not being firm at all. Sincerity: You must also be sincere. If you are sincere, you won't be afraid of any kind of difficulty, suffering, or hardship. Perseverence: You can't give up as soon as the going gets a bit rough. You can't ever quit. That's being irreversible. In your cultivation you should only go forward vigorously and never turn back and retreat.

The second kind of irreversibility is that of position. The Bodhisattvas give rise to the Great Vehicle Bodhisattva heart and would never retreat to the Two Vehicles. Even if they have to chop up their bodies and grind their bones and give their head, eyes, brains and marrow, they will do so and never regret it.

They would never retreat to the Two Vehicles. The third kind of irreversibility is that of thought. Their Great Vehicle Bodhisattva hearts never change. They are constantly giving rise to the Bodhisattva heart. Bodhisattvas benefit all living beings. You must be good to all living beings.

There are several people here who have already left home; there are some who would like to leave home, but have not yet done so. Others are still thinking it over; they haven't decided for sure yet. They want to leave home, but are afraid to commit themselves. They want to stay at home but are afraid they will fall. They can't make up their minds, and so they haven't reached the state of a Bodhisattva. Bodhisattvas only care about others. They don't care about themselves. They only care to help others. They don't care about helping themselves. Bodhisattvas help others, but they don't hold on to the thought of having helped them. They do it and forget it. They feel that helping others is just helping themselves. They don't go around bragging about it. It's enough that the Buddhas and Bodhisattvas know what they did. It doesn't matter if other people know. Further, if you practice the Bodhisattva Path, take special care not to disturb other living beings. If you want to cultivate, don't cause other living beings to have affliction. If you cause one person to have affliction, then towards that person you have not perfectly walked the Bodhisattva Path. If you cause two living beings to have affliction, then towards both of them you have not walked the Bodhisattva Path. You must not cause others to become afflicted. Do not hurt other poeple with your words or deeds. In general, in every move and word, don't cause others to be unhappy with you. In this way your cultivation will be successful. If you think, "I can ignore other people and do whatever I like, say whatever I please...If you get angry--well, the more the better!" If you think like that you won't be able to cultivate the Way, and if you try you will run into a lot of demon-obstacles. If you cause others to have affliction, they will certainly cause you to have affliction so that in the future a lot of demonic obstructions will arise for you. People who wish to leave the home-life and cultivate must take care not to obstruct others. You must always keep a close watch over your body and mind to see if you are doing things wrong, saying improper things, or hurting others and causing them affliction. You should always look within yourself like this. Don't hurt other people. That's the Bodhisattva heart. Bodhisattvas are irreversible in position, thought, and practice. They never retreat from the Bodhi mind.

Sutra: 15a5

SHARIPUTRA,
I, FOR LIVING BEINGS,
SPEAK THIS PARABLE
OF THE ONE BUDDHA VEHICLE.
IF ALL OF YOU ARE ABLE
TO BELIEVE AND ACCEPT THESE WORDS,
YOU SHALL, IN THE FUTURE,
REALIZE THE BUDDHA WAY.
THIS VEHICLE IS SUBTLE AND WONDERFUL,
PURE AND FOREMOST.
IN ALL OF THE WORLDS
IT IS THE MOST SUPREME.
THE BUDDHAS REJOICE IN IT,
AND ALL LIVING BEINGS
SHOULD PRAISE IT AS WELL.
MAKE OFFERINGS AND BOW BEFORE IT.
LIMITLESS THOUSANDS OF MILLIONS
OF POWERS AND LIBERATIONS,
DHYANA SAMADHIS AND WISDOM,
AND THE BUDDHAS' OTHER DHARMAS
ARE OBTAINED IN A VEHICLE SUCH AS THIS.

Outline:

L3. Correlating giving all a great cart.
M1. Corr. "giving to all"

Commentary:

SHARIPUTRA/ I, FOR LIVING BEINGS/ Shakyamuni Buddha

says,"Shariputra, for the sake of all living beings, I now SPEAK THIS PARABLE/ OF THE ONE BUDDHA VEHICLE/ IF ALL OF YOU ARE ABLE/ TO BELIEVE AND ACCEPT THESE WORDS/ YOU SHALL, IN THE FUTURE/ REALIZE THE BUDDHA WAY/ Previously, you were taught the Three Vehicles, but that was only provisional Dharma, provisional wisdom. This, now, is real. Don't think that what you heard before was correct and have doubts about the real wisdom you heard just now. You should listen to what I say, believe and accept it. Then, you can all become Buddhas.

THIS VEHICLE IS SUBTLE AND WONDERFUL/ The Buddha Vehicle is especially fine and miraculous. All you have to do is have faith, and you can become a Buddha. You don't neceesarily have to do a certain amount of merit and virtue or cultivate like I did in the past for three great asankhyeya aeons in order to become a Buddha. Now, I have taught you the Dharma-door of the One Buddha Vehicle and all you have to do is believe and you have a chance to become a Buddha. PURE AND FOREMOST/ This is the foremost of pure Dharmas. IN ALL OF THE WORLDS/ IT IS THE MOST SUPREME/ There is nothing higher than the Buddha Vehicle. It is the unsurpassed Dharma-door. THE BUDDHAS REJOICE IN IT/ AND ALL LIVING BEINGS/ SHOULD PRAISE IT AS WELL/ MAKE OFFERINGS AND BOW BEFORE IT/ The Great Vehicle's *Wonderful Dharma Lotus Flower Sutra* is the pure and perfect teaching. You should all revere and worship this Great Vehicle Buddhadharma. LIMITLESS THOUSANDS OF MILLIONS/ OF POWERS AND LIBERATIONS/ DHYANA SAMADHIS AND WISDOM/ AND THE BUDDHAS OTHER DHARMAS ARE OBTAINED IN A VEHICLE SUCH AS THIS/ You have no idea how many offerings you must have made in the past in order to meet up with this Dharma-door now and obtain the Buddha Vehicle. This is a very rare affinity. Don't think it's easy to meet up with.

Sutra: T.15a12

I CAUSE ALL MY CHILDREN,
NIGHT AND DAY FOR MANY AEONS,
EVER TO AMUSE THEMSELVES
IN THE COMPANY OF THE BODHISATTVAS
AND THE HOST OF SOUND HEARERS,
RIDING THIS PRECIOUS VEHICLE

STRAIGHT TO THE FIELD OF THE WAY.
FOR THESE REASONS,
THOUGH THEY SEEK IN THE TEN DIRECTIONS,
THERE IS NO OTHER VEHICLE,
EXCEPT FOR THE BUDDHAS' EXPEDIENTS.

Outline:

M2. Correlating their rejoicing.

Commentary:

All living beings have been given the Great Vehicle Buddhadharma; it has been spoken equally for all living beings. Now, in this passage, the Buddha tells all living beings they should be happy. I CAUSE ALL MY CHILDREN/ NIGHT AND DAY, FOR MANY AEONS/ What is meant by "day?" When all living beings obtain the Buddha's real wisdom that is like the day. When all living beings have not exhausted their ignorance, that is like the night. Ignorance is the night and wisdom is the day. "Many aeons" refers to a long stretch of time. EVER TO AMUSE THEMSELVES/ IN THE COMPANY OF THE BODHISATTVAS/ Many aeons is a long of time, and it points to the time of the Buddha Sun-Moon-Lamp and the living beings who were transformed by that Buddha. Since then, they have amused themselves by cultivating the Great Vehicle Dharma. AND THE HOST OF SOUND HEARERS/ RIDING THIS PRECIOUS VEHICLE/ STRAIGHT TO THE FIELD OF THE WAY/ to the stage of the Buddha's enlightened fruition, to the realization of Buddhahood. FOR THESE REASONS/ THOUGH THEY SEEK IN THE TEN DIRECTIONS/ THERE IS NO OTHER VEHICLE/ EXCEPT FOR THE BUDDHAS' EXPEDIENTS/ If you found some other vehicle, it would simply be one of the Buddhas' expedient dharmas set up to teach and transform living beings.

Sutra: T.15a15

I TELL YOU, SHARIPUTRA,
THAT ALL OF YOU
ARE MY CHILDREN,

AND I AM YOUR FATHER.
FOR MANY AEONS, YOU
HAVE BEEN BURNED BY MANY MISERIES,
AND I HAVE SAVED YOU ALL,
LEADING YOU OUT OF THE TRIPLE REALM.
ALTHOUGH EARLIER I SAID
THAT YOU HAD PASSED INTO EXTINCTION,
IT WAS ONLY AN END TO BIRTH AND DEATH
AND NOT REAL EXTINCTION.
WHAT YOU SHOULD ACCOMPLISH NOW,
IS NOTHING BUT THE BUDDHAS' WISDOM.
IF THERE ARE BODHISATTVAS
WITHIN THIS ASSEMBLY,
THEY CAN SINGLEMINDEDLY LISTEN TO
THE BUDDHA'S REAL DHARMA.
ALTHOUGH THE BUDDHAS, WORLD HONORED ONES,
EMPLOY EXPEDIENT DEVICES,
THE LIVING BEINGS THEY TRANSFORM
ALL ARE BODHISATTVAS.

Outline:

L4. Correlating the absence of falsehood.

Commentary:

I TELL YOU, SHARIPUTRA/ THAT ALL OF YOU/ ARE MY CHILDREN/ Shakyamuni Buddha continues speaking to Shariputra saying, "All of you living beings, Bodhisattvas, Sound Hearers, Conditioned Enlightened Ones, Bhikshus, Bhikshunis, you study the Buddhadharma and have brought forth the Bodhi heart. You are all my children. AND I AM YOUR FATHER/ Since you are the Buddha's children, then I am your father. FOR MANY AEONS YOU/ HAVE BEEN BURNED BY MANY MISERIES/ The three, eight, and limitless sufferings have scorched you. AND I HAVE SAVED YOU ALL/ LEADING YOU OUT OF THE

TRIPLE REALM/ the desire, form, and formless realms. ALTHOUGH EARLIER I SAID/ THAT YOU HAD PASSED INTO EXTINCTION/ IT WAS ONLY AN END TO BIRTH AND DEATH/ AND NOT REAL EXTINCTION/ You have only ended share-section birth and death. You have by no means ended change birth and death. Speaking in terms of real wisdom, real Dharma, you have not gained extinction.

WHAT YOU SHOULD ACCOMPLISH NOW/ IS NOTHING BUT THE BUDDHAS' WISDOM/ Your job now is to study the Buddha's wisdom and practice the genuine Dharma.

IF THERE ARE BODHISATTVAS/ WITHIN THIS ASSEMBLY/ THEY CAN SINGLEMINDEDLY LISTEN TO/ THE BUDDHAS' REAL DHARMA/ the genuine Dharma-door which I am speaking. This is the real wisdom; it is not provisional dharma.

ALTHOUGH THE BUDDHAS, WORLD HONORED ONES/ EMPLOY EXPEDIENT DEVICES/ THE LIVING BEINGS THEY TRANSFORM/ ALL ARE BODHISATTVAS/ They bestow the provisional for the sake of the real and set forth the dharma of Three Vehicles. The expedient dharma-doors are taught for the sake of the real Dharma. So all the beings they teach are in reality Bodhisattvas. They should turn away from the small and go towards the great, cultivating the Bodhisattva conduct.

Sutra: T.15a23

IF THERE ARE THOSE OF LITTLE WISDOM,
DEEPLY ATTACHED TO LOVE AND DESIRE,
FOR THEIR SAKES
I TEACH THE TRUTH OF SUFFERING.
LIVING BEINGS THEN REJOICE
GAINING WHAT THEY NEVER HAD,
FOR THE BUDDHA'S TEACHING OF SUFFERING'S TRUTH
IS TRUE, REAL, AND NOT FALSE.
IF THERE ARE LIVING BEINGS,
WHO DO NOT KNOW THE ORIGIN OF SUFFERING,
WHO ARE DEEPLY ATTACHED TO THE CAUSE OF SUFFERING,
UNABLE TO LEAVE IT FOR EVEN A MOMENT,
FOR THEIR SAKES

I EXPEDIENTLY SPEAK OF THE PATH.
THE CAUSE OF ALL SUFFERING
IS ROOTED IN DESIRE.
IF ONE EXTINGUISHES GREED AND DESIRE,
SUFFERING HAS NOTHING TO REST UPON.
THE EXTINCTION OF ALL SUFFERING
IS CALLED THE THIRD TRUTH.
FOR THE SAKE OF THE TRUTH OF EXTINCTION,
ONE CULTIVATES THE PATH;
LEAVING ALL SUFFERING'S BONDS
IS CALLED THE ATTAINMENT OF LIBERATION.
FROM WHAT IS IT
THAT THESE PEOPLE HAVE BEEN LIBERATED?
THE MERE SEPARATION FROM THE FALSE
IS CALLED LIBERATION.
IN REALITY THEY HAVE NOT YET
ATTAINED TOTAL LIBERATION.
THE BUDDHA SAYS THAT THESE PEOPLE
HAVE NOT YET TRULY REACHED EXTINCTION,
BECAUSE THEY HAVE NOT YET ATTAINED
THE UNSURPASSED PATH.
IT IS NOT MY WISH
TO LEAD THEM TO EXTINCTION.
I AM THE DHARMA KING,
AT EASE WITHIN ALL THE DHARMAS.
I MANIFEST WITHIN THIS WORLD
TO BRING PEACE AND TRANQUILITY TO LIVING BEINGS.

Commentary:

This passage is a continuation of the previous one, bearing the outline title "L4. Correlating the absence of falseness." IF THERE ARE THOSE OF LITTLE WISDOM/ If there are those living beings who do not have any great wisdom, in fact, who don't have any "small" wisdom, either. DEEPLY ATTACHED TO LOVE AND DESIRE/ They are profoundly addicted to love and lust. Here we are referring to the delusions of views and the delusions of thought. View delusions means that when something happens you don't understand it and get confused by it. Thought delusions means that you can't figure out clearly in your mind what is true and what is false, what is right and what is wrong. Although you can't tell the difference, you still keep trying to; you keep thinking it over, but you lack the wisdom to decide properly. FOR THEIR SAKES/ I TEACH THE TRUTH OF SUFFERING/ I teach the first of the Four Holy Truths, the Truth of Suffering. LIVING BEINGS THEN REJOICE/ Before, living beings thought that suffering was bliss. Although they were in a state of suffering, they didn't realize that they were suffering. Now that I have taught them about the Truth of Suffering, they are extremely happy, GAINING WHAT THEY NEVER HAD/ FOR THE BUDDHAS' TEACHING OF SUFFERING'S TRUTH/ IS TRUE, REAL, AND NOT FALSE/ They had never heard such a wonderful Dharma. It's real! It's not false. It is really, really true Dharma.

IF THERE ARE LIVING BEINGS/ WHO DO NOT KNOW THE ORIGIN OF SUFFERING/ What is the origin of suffering? It is the Second of the Four Holy Truths, the Truth of Origination. WHO ARE DEEPLY ATTACHED TO THE CAUSE OF SUFFERING/ Origination is the cause of suffering. Suffering is the fruit. Origination is just affliction. Their are six kinds of basic afflictions, ten minor following afflictions, two middle following afflictions, and eight great following afflictions. These twenty-six kinds of afflictions cause suffering.

UNABLE TO LEAVE IT FOR EVEN A MOMENT/ They don't want to separate from these afflictions for any length of time. FOR THEIR SAKES/ I EXPEDIENTLY SPEAK OF THE PATH/ For living beings like this I speak of the Path which is to be cultivated.

THE CAUSE OF ALL SUFFERING/ IS ROOTED IN DESIRE/ Suffering comes from origination. The most important factors in origination are greed and desire.

What is greed? It means never being satisfied. No matter how much one gets, one always wants more. Say, to begin with you didn't even have a hundred dollars. In your greed you think of a way to get a hundred dollars. But once you get that hundred dollars you feel it's still not enough. "I need a thousand," you think. When you've got a thousand you still aren't satisfied. "I want some clothes. I really need a house and a piece of land. So this is not enough. If I had ten thousand dollars I'd really be satisfied. In fact, I'd retire. I'd never want anything again or be greedy for anything else. That would do it, really." But then when you get ten thousand dollars, what with inflation and all... "Everything's going up, you know," you say."I'd like to retire, but I've got to have a hundred thousand first." So you greedily go after a hundred thousand and it's still not enough! Suddenly your greed gets entirely out of hand, and you go after a million. But, before you get it, it comes time to die. As you die, you think, "I wanted a million dollars, but I never did reach my aim. I'll try again next life for sure." However, in your next life, you turn into a horse or a cow.

So what advantages does greed have anyway? Greed always brings misery, for greed is the root of suffering.

IF ONE EXTINGUISHES GREED AND DESIRE/ SUFFERING HAS NOTHING TO REST UPON/ If you have no greed or desire, then there will be no suffering. If you wish to get rid of suffering, first of all you must get rid of greed and desire. If you have no greed or desire, then suffering has no root, nothing to rest on, no place to stay.

THE EXTINCTION OF ALL SUFFERING/ IS CALLED THE THIRD TRUTH/ The third of the Four Holy Truths. FOR THE SAKE OF THE TRUTH OF EXTINCTION/ ONE CULTIVATES THE PATH/ If you want to attain the Truth of Extinction, you must first cultivate the Way.

LEAVING ALL SUFFERING'S BONDS/ IS CALLED THE ATTAINMENT OF LIBERATION/ Leaving all those things which bind us in suffering is called liberation from the world. Why is one not liberated? Because one can't see through the affairs of the world, can't put them down. Until one can see through everything and put it all down, one cannot be liberated. When you can see through it all and put it all down, that is freedom, that is release.

People are greedy for this and greedy for that. Why? Because they can't put it down. If, while alive, you can look upon yourself as already dead, then, you won't bother to be a slave for your body. If you can be a "living dead person" you won't be attached to anything. You'll see through everything. That's just the attainment of liberation.

FROM WHAT IS IT/ THAT THESE PEOPLE HAVE BEEN LIBERATED/ THE MERE SEPARATION FROM THE FALSE/ IS CALLED LIBERATION/ Those who have cultivated and put and end to the delusions of views and thought thus ending share-section birth and death may call this liberation. IN REALITY THEY HAVE NOT YET/ ATTAINED TOTAL LIBERATION/ They have not attained ultimate liberation. In order to do this you must see through everything and put it down. I often say to you, "With me, everything is okay." This may seem very shallow, but its meaning is quite profound. As long as something is a problem for you, then you have not been liberated. When there are no more problems, then you have been freed. You are just like empty space. Who can bind up empty space? Who can tie it down? When you are no longer greedy for fame, you are liberated from fame. When you no longer seek profit, you are liberated from profit. Freed from fame and profit, what else is there to keep you down? Nothing.

Although the Buddha taught that the Four Holy Truths led to liberation, this is not, in reality, liberation. Why not? Because one only ends share-section birth and death. Change birth and death still persists. As long as you have change birth and death you are still not free because you still haven't put it all down.

THE BUDDHA SAYS THAT THESE PEOPLE/ HAVE NOT YET TRULY REACHED EXTINCTION/ They are not yet truly extinct; they haven't been completely liberated.

IT IS NOT MY WISH/ TO LEAD THEM TO EXTINCTION/ It is not my intention, before they have any real attainment, to lead them to extinction.

I AM THE DHARMA KING/ AT EASE WITHIN ALL THE DHARMAS/ Among all the dharmas, I am the king. Speaking coming and going, it's the Dharma, broadly and minutely, it's the Dharma. Coming and going, I am at ease within all the dharmas. However I explain it, it is correct. I MANIFEST WITHIN THIS WORLD/ TO BRING PEACE AND TRANQUILITY TO LIVING BEINGS/ Why do I appear in the world? I want living beings to be at peace, to attain ultimate happiness and ultimate liberation. That is why the Buddha appears in the world.

a god (cover detail)

Sutra: T.15b7

SHARIPUTRA!
THIS DHARMA SEAL OF MINE
IS SPOKEN BECAUSE I WISH
TO BENEFIT THE WORLD.
WHEREVER YOU ROAM,
DO NOT PROPAGATE IT WRONGLY.

Outline:

H3. The exhortation to faith.
I1. Advice to Shariputra.

Commentary:

SHARIPUTRA/ Shakyamuni Buddha here is speaking to Shariputra. He is also speaking to you and me and all the living beings of the present. He was then speaking to Shariputra, but he is also speaking to all of us Buddhist disciples right now, all those who propagate this Dharma, Dharma Masters who lecture on the Sutras and speak the Dharma.

THIS DHARMA SEAL OF MINE/ IS SPOKEN BECAUSE I WISH/ TO BENEFIT THE WORLD/ The Dharma seal of the reality mark, that is, the Dharma seal of the real mark which is unmarked, is what I use to certify all living beings as potentiallly able to realize the Buddha Path. It is, therefore, most honorable and noble. It is not something to be used casually. I am speaking it now because I want to benefit all living beings.

What is meant by "benefit?" It refers to self-benefit and benefitting others. This Dharma seal is used to help all living beings.

There are three types of worlds, the world of living beings, the world of material objects, and the world of proper enlightenment. The benefit here is to the world of living beings. The Buddha says, "I speak *The Dharma Flower Sutra* in order to benefit living beings in the world."

WHEREVER YOU ROAM/ DO NOT PROPAGATE IT WRONGLY/ However, this Dharma is the most venerable and noble. Don't propagate it casually. Wherever you go, take care not to speak *The Dharma Flower Sutra* casually. If you speak the Dharma to those who are not ready to hear it, they will slander it. Then, not only will you have failed to save them, you will have caused them to fall into the hells. Why should you take care not to speak the Sutra recklessly? It's because if you do so people might fall. Hearing the Sutra, most people would slander it, saying, "How can this be? How can it be that, without doing any merit and virtue, we can still become Buddha? That's just too good to be true. People are just people. How can they become Buddhas? The Sutras just cheat people." By uttering that single sentence, "The Sutras just cheat people," that person falls into the avichi hells. This principle will be discussed in more detail later. So it was out of fear that people might slander the Sutra and fall into the hells that the Buddha warned Shariputra not to speak the Sutra casually, not to propagate it wrongly. Those with the disposition of the Great Vehicle who hear it once and give rise to unlimited belief--you can speak it for people like that.

Sutra: T.15c9

IF THERE BE THOSE WHO HEAR IT,
AND REJOICE, RECEIVING IT ATOP THEIR CROWNS,
YOU SHOULD KNOW THAT SUCH PEOPLE
ARE AVAIVARTIKA.
THOSE WHO BELIEVE AND ACCEPT
THE DHARMA OF THIS SUTRA,
THESE PEOPLE HAVE ALREADY SEEN
THE BUDDHAS OF THE PAST,
REVERENTLY MAKING OFFERINGS,
AND HEARING THIS DHARMA AS WELL.
THOSE WHO ARE ABLE
TO BELIEVE WHAT YOU SAY,
THEY THEN SEE ME,
AND THEY SEE YOU,
AND ALSO THE BHIKSHUSANGHA,

AS WELL AS ALL THE BODHISATTVAS.
THIS SUTRA OF THE DHARMA FLOWER
IS SPOKEN FOR THOSE OF PROFOUND WISDOM;
WHEN THOSE OF SHALLOW UNDERSTANDING HEAR IT,
CONFUSED AND DELUDED, THEY FAIL TO UNDERSTAND IT.
THE SOUND HEARERS, EVERY ONE,
AND THE PRATYEKA BUDDHAS,
FIND THE CONTENTS OF THIS SUTRA
FAR BEYOND THEIR POWERS.
YOU, SHARIPUTRA,
GAINED ENTRY TO THIS SUTRA
BY MEANS OF FAITH.
HOW MUCH THE MORE SO OTHER SOUND HEARERS.
THOSE SOUND HEARERS,
BECAUSE OF THEIR FAITH IN THE BUDDHA'S WORDS,
COMPLY WITH THIS SUTRA.
BUT IT'S BEYOND THE RANGE OF THEIR OWN WISDOM.

Outline:

I2. The explanation.
J1. Explaining the effable and ineffable.

Commentary:

IF THERE BE THOSE WHO HEAR IT/ AND REJOICE, RECEIVING IT ATOP THEIR CROWNS/ Shakyamuni Buddha says, "If there should be those who hear *The Dharma Flower Sutra*, and who rejoice, praise, and receive it with great respect, YOU SHOULD KNOW THAT SUCH PEOPLE/ ARE AVAIVARTIKA/ Avaivartika means "non-retreating." Those who believe in this Sutra have the resolve of a Bodhisattva and attain to the non-retreating position. They do not retreat to the Two Vehicles. They attain to non-retreating practice; they do not retreat to the status of a common person. They also attain to non-retreating thought, because their thought to cultivate the Great Vehicle never retreats.

THOSE WHO BELIEVE AND ACCEPT/ THE DHARMA OF THIS SUTRA/ THESE PEOPLE HAVE ALREADY SEEN/ THE BUDDHAS OF OF THE PAST/ Those who believe and accept the Great Vehicle Dharma of *The Dharma Flower Sutra* have in past lives seen limitless Buddhas. Who are "these people?" If you believe in this Sutra, it is you. If I believe in it, it is me.

REVERENTLY MAKING OFFERINGS/ AND HEARING THIS DHARMA AS WELL/ This is like those of you who now hear this Sutra. In former lives you planted good roots. Consequently, now you can hear the Sutra. Take a look at how many people there are in the world. How many of them have heard *The Dharma Flower Sutra?* Are the number of those who have heard this Sutra in the majority, or are the number of those who have not heard it in the majority? You don't have to be a mathematician to figure it out. Those of you who have graduated from college should certainly have no trouble with such calculations, right?

THOSE WHO ARE ABLE/ TO BELIEVE WHAT YOU SAY/ If poeple can believe in the doctrines of *The Dharma Flower Sutra* that you preach, THEY THEN SEE ME/ AND THEY SEE YOU/ This is Shakyamuni Buddha speaking of himself. "If you can believe in *The Dharma Flower Sutra,* then you see my complete body." When Great Master *Chih-che* was reciting the twenty-third chapter of this Sutra, "The Events of the Past of Medicine King Bodhisattva," he came to this line:

"This is called true vigor.
This is a true Dharma offering."[1]

As he read this line, he entered samadhi. In samadhi he saw Vulture Peak and the Dharma assembly there which had not yet dispersed. He then obtained the "Dharani of a single revolution," and entered the Dharma Flower Samadhi, opening limitless, boundless wisdom. So you see, *The Dharma Flower Sutra* is especially wonderful. Shakyamuni Buddha says, "IF you can believe and accept this Sutra, you are seeing me. And they see you, too, Shariputra."

AND ALSO THE BHIKSHUSANGHA/ the assembly of great

---

[1] *T.* 262, 53b11.

Bhikshus.

AS WELL AS ALL THE BODHISATTVAS/ Not only do they see the Bhikshus, but they see all the great Bodhisattvas in the Dharma Flower Assembly.

THIS SUTRA OF THE DHARMA FLOWER/ IS SPOKEN FOR THOSE OF PROFOUND WISDOM/ Only for those with genuine, profound Prajna wisdom. WHEN THOSE OF SHALLOW UNDERSTANDING HEAR IT/ CONFUSED AND DELUDED, THEY FAIL TO UNDERSTAND IT/ If stupid people hear it, they don't understand it. What qualifies one as "stupid?" People with big tempers are stupid. People with big tempers have the most ignorance. People with great ignorance are on fire all day long. If such people hear *The Dharma Flower Sutra,* they get angry! "What is this, anyway? What's this *Dharma Flower Sutra?* If you don't eat, will it make you full? Huh? You lecture on the Sutras all day long. Well, don't eat for a couple of days and we'll see how hungry you get, okay?" Very wise, very wise...

THE SOUND HEARERS, EVERY ONE/ AND THE PRATYEKA BUDDHAS/ FIND THE CONTENTS OF THIS SUTRA/ FAR BEYOND THEIR POWERS/ Those of the Two Vehicles are incapable of propagating *The Dharma Flower Sutra*. They don't have that much power.

YOU, SHARIPUTRA, GAINED ENTRY TO THIS SUTRA/ BY MEANS OF FAITH/ You, the greatly wise Shariputra, you have the most lofty wisdom of all the Sound Hearer disciples. You had to think about it. "I should believe this Sutra. I shouldn't fail to believe in it." Since you gained entry to this Sutra by means of faith, that implies that, in the beginning, you had doubts about it. If you hadn't had some doubts, you would not claim to have entered it by means of faith. You finally decided to believe it. Why? Because you have great wisdom. You truly believed the Sutra, without any doubt.

HOW MUCH THE MORE SO OTHER SOUND HEARERS/ who don't have as much wisdom as you do.

THOSE SOUND HEARERS/BECAUSE OF THEIR FAITH IN THE BUDDHA'S WORDS/ COMPLY WITH THIS SUTRA/ BUT IT'S FAR BEYOND THE RANGE OF THEIR OWN WISDOM/ It's not that they can understand it with their own wisdom. They basically don't have the wisdom to understand the doctrines of this Sutra. But because the Buddha spoke it, even though they don't understand it, they don't dare not believe it. They've got to believe it. The wisdomless Sound Hearers don't dare doubt this Sutra. After all, the Buddha spoke it. Even though they don't understand it, they insist on believing it. This is a kind of mixed-up belief. Mixed-up as their belief may be, in the future they will come to understand. You should know that one is "mixed-up" because of ignorance. After one studies the Buddhadharma and comes to believe in it, then one won't be mixed-up anymore, one will give rise to wisdom.

Sutra: T.15b20

FURTHER, SHARIPUTRA
TO THE ARROGANT AND LAZY
AND THOSE WHO RECKON THE VIEW OF SELF,
DO NOT SPEAK THIS SUTRA.
COMMON FOLK OF SHALLOW UNDERSTANDING,
DEEPLY ATTACHED TO THE FIVE DESIRES,
HEARING IT, WILL FAIL TO UNDERSTAND;
DO NOT SPEAK IT TO THEM, EITHER.
IF THERE BE THOSE WHO DON'T BELIEVE,
AND WHO SLANDER THIS SUTRA,
THEY THEREBY SEVER ALL
WORLDLY BUDDHA SEEDS.
OR IF, WITH A SCOWL,
THEY HARBOR DOUBTS AND DELUSIONS
YOU SHOULD LISTEN NOW,
AS I SPEAK OF THEIR OFFENSE-RETRIBUTION:
WHETHER A BUDDHA IS IN THE WORLD,
OR HAS ENTERED INTO EXTINCTION.
IF THERE BE THOSE WHO SLANDER
A SUTRA SUCH AS THIS ONE,
WHO, SEEING OTHERS READ OR RECITE IT,
COPY IT OUT OR UPHOLD IT,
SCORN, DESPISE, HATE AND ENVY THEM,
AND HARBOR GRUDGES AGAINST THEM,

AS TO THEIR OFFENSE RETRIBUTION,
LISTEN NOW, ONCE AGAIN:
THESE PEOPLE AT LIFE'S END
WILL ENTER THE AVICHI HELL
FOR AN ENTIRE AEON.
AT THE AEON'S END, BORN THERE AGAIN,
IN THIS WAY THEY WILL REVOLVE,
THROUGH UNCOUNTABLE AEONS.
WHEN THEY ESCAPE FROM THE HELLS,
THEY SHALL TAKE THE BODIES OF ANIMALS,
SUCH AS DOGS OR YEH KAN,
TALL AND EMACIATED,
MOTTLED, BLACK, AND SCABBED,
REPULSIVE TO OTHERS.
FURTHER, BY HUMAN BEINGS,
THEY WILL BE HATED AND SCORNED;
ALWAYS SUFFERING FROM HUNGER AND THIRST,
THEIR BONES AND FLESH WILL BE WITHERED UP.
DURING THEIR LIVES THEY WILL BE PRICKED
BY POISONOUS THORNS;
WHEN DEAD THEY WILL BE BURIED
UNDER TILES AND STONES.
THEY SUFFER THIS OFFENSE RETRIBUTION,
BECAUSE THEY HAVE SEVERED THEIR BUDDHA SEEDS.
THEY MAY BECOME CAMELS
OR THEY MAY BE BORN AMONG ASSES,
ALWAYS CARRYING HEAVY BURDENS
AND BEATEN WITH STICKS AND WHIPS,
THINKING ONLY OF WATER AND GRASS,
AND KNOWING NOTHING ELSE.
THEY SUFFER RETRIBUTION SUCH AS THIS
BECAUSE OF SLANDERING THIS SUTRA.

SOME MAY BECOME YEH KAN,
ENTERING VILLAGES,
THEIR BODIES COVERED WITH SCABS AND SORES,
AND ALSO MISSING AN EYE,
BEATEN AND STONED
BY YOUNG CHILDREN,
UNDERGOING ALL THIS PAIN,
EVEN TO THE POINT OF DEATH.
HAVING DIED IN THIS MANNER
THEY ARE THEN REBORN AS HUGE SERPENTS,
THEIR BODIES AS LONG
AS FIVE HUNDRED YOJANAS.
DEAF AND STUPID, WITHOUT FEET,
THEY WRITHE ABOUT ON THEIR STOMACHS,
STUNG AND EATEN
BY MANY SMALL INSECTS.
UNDERGOING SUFFERING DAY AND NIGHT
WITHOUT RESPITE,
THEY SUFFER SUCH RETRIBUTION
FOR HAVING SLANDERED THIS SUTRA.
IF THEY BECOME HUMANS,
ALL THEIR FACULTIES ARE DIM AND DULL.
THEY ARE SQUAT, UGLY, PALSIED, LAME,
BLIND, DEAF, AND HUNCHBACKED.
WHATEVER THEY MAY SAY,
PEOPLE WILL NOT BELIEVE THEM.
THEIR BREATH EVER STINKING,
THEY WILL BE POSSESSED BY GHOSTS,
POOR AND LOWLY,
THE SERVANTS OF OTHERS,
ALWAYS SICK AND EMACIATED,
WITH NO ONE TO RELY UPON.

ALTHOUGH THEY MAY DRAW NEAR TO OTHERS,
OTHERS WILL NEVER THINK OF THEM.
IF THEY SHOULD GAIN SOMETHING
THEY WILL QUICKLY FORGET AND LOSE IT.
SHOULD THEY STUDY THE WAYS OF MEDICINE,
FOLLOWING THE PRESCRIPTION TO CURE ILLNESS,
THEY WILL ONLY MAKE OTHER'S ILLNESSES WORSE.
EVEN TO THE POINT OF DEATH.
IF THEY GET SICK THEMSELVES,
NO ONE WILL TRY TO SAVE OR CURE THEM.
ALTHOUGH THEY TAKE GOOD MEDICINE,
IT WILL ONLY INCREASE THEIR PAINS.
IF THEY MEET WITH REBELLION,
THEY WILL BE PLUNDERED AND ROBBED.
PEOPLE WITH SUCH OFFENSES,
WILL PERVERSELY BE SUBJECT TO SUCH MISFORTUNES.
OFFENDERS SUCH AS THESE
WILL NEVER SEE THE BUDDHA,
THE KING AMONG THE SAGELY HOSTS,
SPEAKING THE DHARMA, TEACHING AND TRANSFORMING.
OFFENDERS SUCH AS THESE
WILL ALWAYS BE BORN IN DIFFICULT CIRCUMSTANCES.
INSANE, DEAF, WITH MIND CONFUSED,
THEY WILL NEVER HEAR THE DHARMA.
THROUGHOUT AEONS AS COUNTLESS
AS THE GANGES RIVER'S SANDS,
THEY WILL BE BORN DEAF AND DUMB,
WITH ALL THEIR FACULTIES INCOMPLETE;
THEY WILL ALWAYS DWELL IN THE HELLS,
ROAMING THERE AS IF IN PLEASURE GARDENS,
OR BORN IN THE OTHER EVIL PATHS,
WHICH THEY WILL TAKE AS THEIR HOUSE AND HOME.

AMONG CAMELS, ASSES, PIGS, AND DOGS--
THESE ARE THE PLACES THEY WILL WALK.
THEY UNDERGO SUCH RETRIBUTION,
BECAUSE OF SLANDERING THIS SUTRA.
IF THEY BECOME HUMANS,
THEY WILL BE DEAF, BLIND, AND DUMB,
POOR AND DECREPIT,
YET ADORNING THEMSELVES THEREWITH.
SWOLLEN WITH WATER, OR ELSE DEHYDRATED,
WITH SCABS AND BOILS,
AND OTHER SUCH ILLNESSES,
THEY WILL CLOTHE THEMSELVES.
THEIR BODIES WILL ALWAYS STINK
OF FILTH AND IMPURITY.
DEEPLY ATTACHED TO THE VIEW OF SELF,
THEIR HATRED SHALL ONLY INCREASE.
ABLAZE WITH SEXUAL DESIRE,
THEY ARE NO DIFFERENT THAN BIRDS OR BEASTS.
THEY WILL SUFFER SUCH RETRIBUTION
FOR HAVING SLANDERED THIS SUTRA.

Outline:

J2. Explaining when and where not to propagate the Sutra.
K1. The need for great compassion. Do not speak it to evil people.

Commentary:

FURTHER, SHARIPUTRA/ TO THE ARROGANT AND LAZY/ As to arrogance, poor people are seldom afflicted with it. Rich people easily become arrogant. Prideful people think that no one is as good as they are. They treat everyone in a rude manner. Lazy people like to slack off. They are sloppy and indolent. They don't do any work at all, but feel that they are making great contributions and their hearts grow weary; they are not vigorous and they do not go forward. AND THOSE WHO RECKON THE VIEW OF SELF/ They are conceited and lazy because their attachment to self is so deeply rooted. DO NOT SPEAK THIS SUTRA/ to them. Don't speak *The Dharma Flower Sutra* to people like this. Why not? If you speak it to them, they won't cultivate according to the doctrines expressed within it.

COMMON FOLK OF SHALLOW UNDERSTANDING/ Ordinary people have no wisdom. They are simple-minded. DEEPLY ATTACHED TO THE FIVE DESIRES/ All they understand are wealth, sex, fame, food, and sleep. These five are the five locks on the gates of the hells. If you commit offenses involving any one of these five, it is easy to fall into hell. If you are greedy for wealth, you will commit offenses. The same is true for sex, fame, food, and sleep. If you sleep too much, you'll become stupid. You should just eat until you are full and then stop; don't overeat. Don't crave the good food and keep eating and eating it. You'll get sick if you do that. You can eat yourself into the hells, in fact. If you stuff yourself until there is no room, then the food will have to "move house." If it doesn't move down and give you the runs, it will move up and you'll vomit.

Now,if you fast for a few days, then when the fast is over, your desire for food may be extremely fierce. Everything looks delicious! Even the water is very sweet, to say nothing of the food. But you have to be careful then not to overeat, or drink more than you usually do. If you eat too much after a two or three week fast, it is very easy to ruin your intestines, to break them. Then you'll have to go to a doctor. If the doctor is good, he can sew you up again. If you meet a bad doctor, he may just give you up as a hopeless case. Even if you don't break your intestines, it's easy to get diarrhea because of the changes in your digestion that have taken place during the fast. This all happens because you aren't in control of your eating habits.

As to sleep: Young people like to sleep. When one reaches fifty or sixty, one isn't that interested in sleeping anymore. But when you are young you can't just let yourself sleep all you want to. If you do, you may sleep one day and still feel it's not enough, sleep for two days and it's still not enough...You can waste a lot of time that way. People who sleep too much get stupid. People are controlled by the five desires and turned upside-down by them. Therefore the text says, "deeply attached to the five desires."

One can also explain the five desires as being sights, sounds, smells, tastes, tangible objects, and dharmas. In general, do not be attached to the five desires.

HEARING IT WILL FAIL TO UNDERSTAND/ Because they are deeply attached to the five desires, when they hear *The Dharma Flower Sutra*, they won't understand it. "Hmmm..." they say, "wealth is really fine. How can you say it is not good? Sex isn't bad either; it's pretty wonderful, in fact. How can you explain the Sutra as saying that sex is no good?" They don't believe it. "Everybody likes fame," they say. "Everybody likes the simple pleasures of eating good things. Sleep isn't bad either. You say it's not right. I don't believe you." Because they like these things, they disagree. DO NOT SPEAK IT TO THEM, EITHER/ Don't speak the Sutra for people like that.

IF THERE BE THOSE WHO DON'T BELIEVE/ AND WHO SLANDER THIS SUTRA/ THEY THEREBY SEVER ALL/ WORLDLY BUDDHA SEEDS/ Severing one's Buddha seeds means that their karmic offenses are deep and heavy indeed. In cutting off one's Buddha seeds, the seeds of the hells arise. When the seeds of the hells arise, then one can fall into the hells. Why did I lecture *The Shurangama Sutra* before lecturing *The Dharma Flower Sutra?* The *Shurangama Sutra* is not as stern on this point. So whatever you do, take care not to slander *The Dharma Flower Sutra.*

OR IF, WITH A SCOWL/ THEY HARBOR DOUBTS AND DELUSIONS/ A scowl means that you knit your eyebrows together in a frown. As soon as they hear the Sutra being lectured, they frown. Their eyes and their noses move together on their face to form a corporation. Why do they scowl? Because they have doubts and delusions. Perhaps in their hearts they object to the doctrines beings spoken, thinking that they don't agree with them at all. "I really like these things and this person is saying that they are no good. This is just claptrap. What kind of Sutra lecturing is this, anyway? It's confused rubbish!" Their minds give rise to doubts.

YOU SHOULD LISTEN NOW/ AS I SPEAK OF THEIR OFFENSE RETRIBUTION/ Listen to what I tell you. As retribution for the offenses this person has committed, he is certain to fall into the hells, to undergo limitless and boundless suffering.

WHETHER A BUDDHA IS IN THE WORLD/ OR HAS ENTERED INTO EXTINCTION/ IF THERE BE THOSE WHO SLANDER/ A SUTRA SUCH AS THIS ONE/ WHO, SEEING OTHERS READ OR

RECITE IT/ COPY IT OUT OR UPHOLD IT/ SCORN, HATE, AND ENVY THEM/ Whether or not the Buddha has entered Nirvana, if people slander this Sutra or slander those who recite and uphold it, they will certainly fall into the hells. If they say, "That's too superstitious.What's the use of reciting Sutras, anyway? If reciting Sutras enables one to end birth and death, then way back in the old days, what Sutra did the very first Buddha recite?" They seem to have some principle in their words, but actually they are just ridiculing those who recite the Sutras out of malice. They ridicule those who bow to Sutras even more. "Up and down, up and down...What are they doing? Senseless!!" They heap scorn upon them, despise, hate, and envy them. Why? Because these people are different from them. They like to drink wine and take drugs. If you did that with them they would be happy. But they don't like to recite Sutras or cultivate. When people do that, they hate it. They get jealous. AND HARBOR GRUDGES AGAINST THEM/ For no reason at all, they hate you.

AS TO THEIR OFFENSE RETRIBUTION/ LISTEN NOW,ONCE AGAIN/ THESE PEOPLE AT LIFE'S END/ WILL ENTER THE AVICHI HELLS/ FOR AN ENTIRE AEON/ They are certain to fall into the unspaced hells and will be there for an entire aeon. AT THE AEON'S END, BORN THERE AGAIN/ IN THIS WAY THEY WILL REVOLVE/ THROUGH UNCOUNTABLE AEONS/ They will be there for one whole great aeon and when that aeon is over they will be ping-ponged to another avichi hell to do it again. They will spin from hell to hell in this way for countless aeons.

WHEN THEY ESCAPE FROM THE HELLS/ THEY SHALL TAKE THE BODIES OF ANIMALS/ One who slanders *The Dharma Flower Sutra* or who slanders those who read and recite it, will remain in the hells for countless kalpas. And what happens once they get out of the hells. They turn into animals! What kind of animals? Animals SUCH AS DOGS OR YEH KAN/ TALL AND EMACIATED/ MOTTLED, BLACK, AND SCABBED/ REPULSIVE TO OTHERS/ These animals live out in the wilds or atop tall trees. At night they roam in packs but during the day they hide. They have only one eye, too. Why are they born with only one eye? Because they looked down on the people who read, recited, and bowed to *The Dharma Flower Sutra*. They hated and envied them, so now they have only one eye. This is after they have escaped from the hells, mind you.

There is no flesh on the bodies of these dogs and *yeh kan*, and so they are as thin as sticks of firewood. They are spotted and black, covered with scabs that keep falling off and forming again without healing.

Nobody wants to get near them. Actually, no one wants to get close to them because they stink. People who cultivate the twelve ascetic practices and who truly cultivate will always emit a fragrance from their bodies. Even their clothes will smell fragrant. They may look bad, wearing rags, so that no one will fall in love with them, but it's not because they don't smell good!

If you stank before you started cultivating, you will become fragrant after you have cultivated for awhile.

"Sure," you say, "if you are in the Buddhahall all day where the incense is burning you will start to smell like the incense."

Well, maybe. But if you truly cultivate, you yourself will emit a precept fragrance, a samadhi fragrance, and a wisdom fragrance, as well as a liberation fragrance and a fragrance of the liberation of knowledge and vision. You will emit those five types of fragrance. If you truly practice the twelve ascetic practices, for sure you will emit a fragrant odor. You won't smell bad.

The animals mentioned here, on the other hand, had slandered the Triple Jewel and the Sutra and so they stink. Nobody wants to get near them.

FURTHER, BY HUMAN BEINGS/ THEY WILL BE HATED AND SCORNED/ Everybody will hate them. ALWAYS SUFFERING FROM HUNGER AND THIRST/ THEIR BONES AND FLESH WILL BE WITHERED UP/ DURING THEIR LIVES THEY WILL BE PRICKED BY POISONOUS THORNS/ WHEN DEAD THEY WILL BE BURIED UNDER TILES AND STONES/ Their lives are the epitome of suffering! Their deaths are filled with ignominy. THEY SUFFER THIS OFFENSE RETRIBUTION/ BECAUSE THEY HAVE SEVERED THEIR BUDDHA SEEDS/ Because they have cut off their Buddha seeds and let the seeds of the hells start growing, they must suffer this retribution.

THEY MAY BECOME CAMELS/ OR THEY MAY BE BORN AMONG ASSES/ ALWAYS CARRYING HEAVY BURDENS/on their backs, AND BEATEN WITH STICKS AND WHIPS/ by their owners. THINKING ONLY OF WATER AND GRASS/ All they think about is eating and drinking; they don't understand anything else. THEY SUFFER RETRIBUTION SUCH AS THIS/ BECAUSE OF SLANDERING THIS SUTRA/

SOME MAY BECOME YEH KAN/ They are even more cowardly than foxes. They have more doubts, too. In past lives, they looked down on those who read, recited, bowed to, and lectured on *The Dharma Flower Sutra*. ENTERING VILLAGES/ THEIR BODIES COVERED WITH SCABS AND SORES/ AND ALSO MISSING AN EYE/ BEATEN AND STONED/ BY YOUNG

CHILDREN/ Sometimes, when their karmic obstacles obstruct them, they go into human settlements. Why do they do this? Because they are sick and have nothing to eat. Because their brains get addled and they can't think clearly, they go into town. The scabs itch terribly. When the children see a sick animal coming into town, they beat it with sticks or throw rocks at it. UNDERGOING ALL THIS PAIN/ EVEN TO THE POINT OF DEATH/ They may hit it on the head with a large rock and kill it.

HAVING DIED IN THIS MANNER/ THEY ARE THEN REBORN AS HUGE SERPENTS/ THEIR BODIES AS LONG/ AS FIVE HUNDRED YOJANAS/ DEAF, STUPID, WITHOUT FEET/ THEY WRITHE ABOUT ON THEIR STOMACHS/ STUNG AND EATEN/ BY MANY SMALL INSECTS/ On the bodies of these huge snakes are many parasites. These bugs eat their flesh and blood so that they are UNDERGOING SUFFERING DAY AND NIGHT/ WITHOUT RESPITE/ The bugs eat them all day and all night too, to that they never get a break from their torment. Would you say that this was severe punishment or not? Why must they undergo it? THEY SUFFER SUCH RETRIBUTION/ FOR HAVING SLANDERED THIS SUTRA/ for slandering *The Wonderful Dharma Lotus Flower Sutra*.

IF THEY BECOME HUMANS/ ALL THEIR FACULTIES ARE DIM AND DULL/ If they should perhaps become human beings, their eyes, ears, noses, tongues, bodies and minds will all be dim and dull. Their arms and legs will be crippled. They won't be able to see or hear clearly. Their sense of taste will be blunted and their sense of touch inaccurate. Their minds will be extremely stupid. They may also be missing and arm or a leg. All their faculties do not listen to their instructions. They may tell their eyes to look at something, but it will be five minutes before they get around to looking at it. The same goes for the ears and nose. This is because they are dim and dull. "Dim" means stupid and lacking wisdom. "Dull" means that they are very slow.

THEY ARE SQUAT, UGLY, PALSIED, LAME/ BLIND, DEAF, AND HUNCHBACKED/ Squat means that they are very short, maybe three feet tall and three feet wide, sort of like kumbhanda ghosts. Ugly means they are hideous. Not only are they very short, but they are horrible looking. Instead of two lips, for example, they might have four! Their lips might be split in the middle. One eye might be as big as a ball and the other as small as a soybean. How could they ever focus them! Palsied means that they don't have control of their limbs. They can't stretch out their arms or legs or their back may be bent over like a bow ready to shoot an arrow. When you see people like this, you can know that limitless aeons in the past, they slandered *The Dharma Flower Sutra*. You should be able to recognize them. You won't need the penetration of other's thoughts, the heavenly eye or the knowledge of past lives. You just need to remember that it said very clearly in *The Dharma Flower Sutra* that people like this have slandered this Sutra.

WHATEVER THEY MAY SAY/ PEOPLE WILL NOT BELIEVE THEM/ No one will even listen to them! When they talk, there will be an edge on their voice. They may sound like a dog barking. THEIR BREATH EVER STINKING/ THEY WILL BE POSSESSED BY GHOSTS/ POOR AND LOWLY/ THE SERVANTS OF OTHERS/ ALWAYS SICK AND EMACIATED/ WITH NO ONE TO RELY UPON/ This bad breath comes, first of all, because they slandered the Sutra. Secondly, it is because they are always sick and their digestion is poor. Whatever they eat fails to nourish them. Sometimes people may have bad breath when they are sick with a cold or the flu. Some people may have a kind of metallic energy which smells like bad breath but which they actually use to subdue heavenly demons and control those outside the Way. They are cultivators of the Secret School. If you always recite *The Dharma Flower Sutra* your breath will smell like a blue lotus flower. This is discussed later in the Sutra.

They will be possessed by ghosts, such as the kumbhanda ghosts and others, who will cause them to be afraid. Not only will they have all the above-mentioned problems, but they will also always be poor and have no money. Lowly means they will always do the lowliest type of work. They will be used as servants of others, doing their bidding. They will continually be sick and therefore extremely thin. They will have no one to help or protect them. No one will take care of them at all. If they die, even, their corpse will just lay there in the street for the dogs to eat. No one will pay the slightest bit of attention to it.

ALTHOUGH THEY DRAW NEAR TO OTHERS/ OTHERS WILL NEVER THINK OF THEM/ They have no one to care for them, so they may look for someone. They may draw near to someone, being very flattering and buttering them up, but no matter how nice they are to them, the person will pay no attention to them at all.

IF THEY SHOULD GAIN SOMETHING/ THEY WILL QUICKLY FORGET AND LOSE IT/ If they study the Buddhadharma, and recite a Sutra, working very hard until they can remember it, as soon as they quit reciting it, they will forget it.

IF THEY STUDY THE WAY OF MEDICINE/ If they should learn to be doctors...

In Chinese medicine one speaks about the "four energies," chill, heat for fever, warmth, and coolness. There is also neutral, drugs that do not incline towards warmth or coolness.

Chinese medicine also speaks of diagnosis by means of 1) looking, 2) hearing or smelling (the Chinese term means both), 3) asking, and 4) taking the pulse.

Those who truly understand the science of medicine do not need to do any more than take a good look at the color of the patient's face to know where the sickness lies. It is said, "To be able to tell just by looking is called the spiritual method." Hearing is called the sagely method. Perhaps they will listen to the sound of the patient's voice or smell the patient's breath. This is the way the sage does it. Asking and knowing is called work. They may ask the patient for symptoms such as, "Do you have a headache?" "No," the patient may reply, "my stomach hurts." Then they will know. Feeling the pulse and knowing is called using one's craft. By feeling the pulse they can tell on which meridian the sickness is located. These are important principles in the study of medicine.

As to the pulse it may be 1) floating, 2) sinking, 3) slow, 4) fast, 5) slippery, 6) still, 7) hollow.

I have studied all the books on medicine, but I was afraid of "curing people to death" so I didn't become a doctor.

That reminds me, however, of a story: One day King Yama got sick and wanted to find a doctor to cure him. He sent on of his ghosts to find a doctor. "Which doctor shall I get?" said the ghost. King Yama said, "Well, you are a ghost, so you can see ghosts. Take a look at the doctors doors and whichever doorway has the fewest ghosts hanging around it, ask that doctor to come. He's probably the best doctor because he will have cured the fewest people to death."

The ghost went off and pounded the streets. At the door of every doctor there were many hateful ghosts shouting out things like, "You gave me the wrong prescription and cured me to death!" There were a lot of them. Finally, he reached one doctors' door and saw only two ghosts there. He invited that doctor to go cure King Yama. King Yama asked him, "How long have you been practicing medicine?"

"I just started today," he said.

King Yama groaned, "Oh, you started today and you

already have two ghosts at your door! Good grief, I can't use you for my doctor. I'd better go find someone else."

This goes to show you that, in China, doctors who use herbal medicines can cure non-fatal illnesses. If they are inept, then, even if the patient was supposed to get well, they would "cure them to death." If one uses the wrong medicine, it is very easy to take a person's life. This is especially true of Chinese herbal medicine. So the text says, "If they study the ways of medicine/" to cure someone's illness, they will cure one illness but another will take it's place, or other illnesses will arise before the first one is cured until, finally, the patient dies. FOLLOWING THE PRESCRIPTION TO CURE ILLNESS/ THEY WILL ONLY MAKE OTHER'S ILLNESSES WORSE/ EVEN TO THE POINT OF DEATH.

IF THEY GET SICK THEMSELVES/ NO ONE WILL TRY TO SAVE OR CURE THEM/ ALTHOUGH THEY TAKE GOOD MEDICINE/ IT WILL ONLY INCREASE THEIR PAINS/ If they get sick, no one will try to cure them. If they give themselves some kind of prescription, the sickness will get much worse.

IF THEY MEET WITH REBELLION/ THEY WILL BE PLUNDERED AND ROBBED/ If they encounter a time of social confusion and war, all these calamities will befall them. PEOPLE WITH SUCH OFFENSES/ WILL PERVERSELY BE SUBJECT TO SUCH MISFORTUNES/ OFFENDERS SUCH AS THESE/ WILL NEVER SEE THE BUDDHA/ THE KING AMONG THE SAGELY HOSTS/ SPEAKING THE DHARMA, TEACHING AND TRANSFORMING/ The Buddha is the king among all the sages. He speaks all dharmas to teach living beings.

OFFENDERS SUCH AS THESE/ WILL ALWAYS BE BORN IN DIFFICULT CIRCUMSTANCES/ Among the eight difficulties we find the difficulty of being born at a time when the Buddha is not in the world. Such offenders will not see the Buddha, hear the Dharma, or meet up with the Sangha.

INSANE, DEAF, WITH MINDS CONFUSED/ THEY WILL NEVER HEAR THE DHARMA/ THROUGHOUT AEONS AS COUNTLESS/ AS THE GANGES RIVER'S SANDS/ They are always plagued with insanity. They can't hear and they are continually subject to mental disorders. They never get to hear the Buddhadharma. One who slanders *The Dharma Flower Sutra* will have no opportunity to hear the Dharma. Even if he does get to hear it, his mind won't be reliable. For example, people may come here to listen to the Sutra. They hear three or five sentences, they listen for three, five, ten, or twenty minutes, and then they run off. Why do they run off? It's because their karmic obstacles are too weighty. Their offense karma is too deep. If you tell them to study something good, to investigate the

Buddhadharma, their karmic obstacles will immediately arise, and they will run off. Some people don't even understand Chinese, and, right after the Chinese, they run off without even waiting for the English translation. You have seen many of these people. They run off because they don't have sufficient good roots; their offense-karma is too heavy. There is a verse which says,

> If exhorted to do good, he says he has
> no money;
> He has it, but not for that.
> In an emergency, if he needs a hundred
> thousand,
> He might not have it, but he'll come
> up with it.

Perhaps there is a bank robbery and someone is kidnapped. Their ransom is five hundred thousand dollars. Then, even though they don't have the money, they come up with it. But if you try to get them to do something good, saying, "Let's go listen to a Sutra lecture," what do you think they will say?

"Ah, I'd really like to, but I'm just too busy." They don't have the time.

> When his life is over and he's buried
> in the Yellow Springs,
> As busy as he is, he has to go.

When the time comes to die and one is called before King Yama, no matter how busy one is, one has to go. Hah!

So it is not that easy to listen to the Sutra lectures. You must have planted good roots throughout limitless aeons. That you are able to come and listen now to *The Dharma Flower Sutra* means that you have conditions with the Dharma Flower Assembly. Didn't the Great Master *Huai-tzu* say that he was with Great Master *Chih-che* on Vulture Peak listening together to *The Dharma Flower Sutra?* So they met together in China. Now, we, too, were all together in the Vulture Peak Assembly listening to *The Dharma Flower Sutra*. Since you have all now forgotten I am lecturing it over again for you.

THEY WILL BE BORN DEAF AND DUMB/ WITH ALL THEIR FACULTIES INCOMPLETE/ If they get born as people they will be born dumb, unable to speak, or deaf. They may be missing an eye or an ear, or they may be missing their nose, or their lips won't look anything like lips.

THEY WILL ALWAYS DWELL IN THE HELLS/ ROAMING THERE AS IF IN PLEASURE GARDENS/ They are as happy in hell as one would be in a park. We like to go to the park and play. These people feel comfortable in the hells. They like being there.

OR BORN IN THE OTHER EVIL PATHS/ WHICH THEY WILL TAKE AS THEIR HOUSE AND HOME/ AMONG CAMELS, ASSES, PIGS, AND DOGS--/ THESE ARE THE PLACES THEY WILL WALK/ They will behave like camels, asses, pigs, and dogs, liking to be around them. In India there are those who keep to the morality of cows and dogs. In the past they slandered *The Dharma Flower Sutra*, and so now as people they still like to act like animals. THEY UNDERGO SUCH RETRIBUTION/ BECAUSE OF SLANDERING THIS SUTRA/ IF THEY BECOME HUMANS/ THEY WILL BE DEAF, BLIND, AND DUMB/ POOR AND DECREPIT/ YET ADORNING THEMSELVES THEREWITH/ If they get out of the hells or the animal realms they will be crippled and poor. Why are people poor? It's because in former lives they slandered this Sutra and slandered the Triple Jewel. They didn't believe in the Triple Jewel or make offerings to it. Even though they had money, they offered none of it to the Triple Jewel. If one doesn't seek blessings and plant blessings by making offerings to the Triple Jewel, one will always be poor. Decrepit means that nothing goes right for them.

There is a story about a person named *Chang T'ai-kung*. People said he was jinxed because his fate was no good. It wasn't because he slandered the Triple Jewel or anything like that. He was the Prime Minister for King Wen of Chou. During the Chou Dynasty he was an official. Later, he quit and took up selling salt instead. Then his salt got infested with bugs. Basically, salt can't get infested with bugs. However, his did. No one would buy it. Then he sold flour, taking it out all day on the streets to sell. No one bought any. One evening, a person came to buy a penny's worth. There was no inflation in those days, and so one could probably buy a lot of flour for a penny. Just has he was measuring out the flour, the general and his cavalry galloped by on their horses. The general's horse kicked over his flour container, spreading flour all over the street. They didn't have concrete in those days, and the flour got all mixed in with the dirt. He picked up what he could of the flour, but people were even less interested in buying it then. About eight or nine o'clock that night he went home. He called to his wife, but she didn't hear him. Just as he was going to knock on the door, a bee flew in between his hand and the door stinging him. He drew his hand back suddenly and slammed the back of it into a nail. Gosh! How unlucky can you get? Why did this happen? It was because in a former life had had been a bear. This bear saw an old cultivator called *Yü Hsü-kung*, and recognized that he was a high cultivator who had attained the Way. The bear knelt outside the cultivator's door, seeking the Way. He knelt there for five hundred years. During that five hundred years, he dropped his bear body; the flesh rotted away; the bones turned to dust. He was reborn as a person with a lot of merit. However, in the more remote past, he had slandered the Triple Jewel. Therefore, he had a lot of bad luck. He had bad luck because his wife was not a good person. He received her influence. So he couldn't sell his flour or anything. Nothing went right. He was very unlucky. That is what is meant by the line of text: "Poor and decrepit." Such people have a lot of bad luck.

They decorate themselves, as it were, with poverty and misfortune.

SWOLLEN WITH WATER, OR ELSE DEHYDRATED/ WITH SCABS AND BOILS/ AND OTHER SUCH ILLNESSES/ THEY WILL CLOTHE THEMSELVES/ Their bodies are always swollen up or else they are all dried out like a piece of kindling. Their scabs itch all the time. Although the itching is on the skin, their minds find it unbearable. Boils are big sores. Some may be as big as a teacup or a wineglass, or a rice bowl. They hurt unbearably. Don't be afraid of boils which are large, red, and swollen or "raised." Just be afraid of black or purple boils which sink into the skin. They cannot be cured.

They will have these sicknesses on their body and THEIR BODIES WILL ALWAYS STINK/ OF FILTH AND IMPURITY/ The scabs and sores will stink.

DEEPLY ATTACHED TO THE VIEW OF SELF/ THEIR HATRED SHALL ONLY INCREASE/ They have terrible tempers that grow worse everyday. Everyday they have more afflictions.

ABLAZE WITH SEXUAL DESIRE/ THEY ARE NO DIFFERENT FROM BIRDS OR BEASTS/ Thoughts of sexual desire are constantly on their minds. This is like the great general of the Ch'ing Dynasty, *Nien Kung-yao* who had to have twelve women to sleep with every night, and even sent out for cows, horses, donkeys...

THEY WILL SUFFER SUCH RETRIBUTION/ FOR HAVING SLANDERED THIS SUTRA/ Because they slandered *The Dharma Flower Sutra*, they bring this retribution upon themselves.

Sutra: T.16a8

I TELL YOU, SHARIPUTRA,
WERE I TO SPEAK OF THE OFFENSES
OF THOSE WHO SLANDER THIS SUTRA,
I WOULDN'T FINISH TO THE END OF AN AEON.
FOR THESE REASONS,
I EXPRESSLY TELL YOU,
DO NOT SPEAK THIS SUTRA
AMONG THOSE WHO HAVE NO WISDOM.

Commentary:

This concludes the outline section mentioned above: "Do not speak for evil people." I TELL YOU, SHARIPUTRA/ Shakyamuni Buddha is speaking of the retribution incurred by THOSE WHO SLANDER THE SUTRA/ WERE I TO SPEAK OF THE OFFENSES/ I WOULDN'T FINISH TO THE END OF AN AEON/ I could speak for several great aeons but wouldn't finish.

FOR THESE REASONS/ I EXPRESSLY TELL YOU/ DO NOT SPEAK THIS SUTRA/ AMONG THOSE WHO HAVE NO WISDOM/ Speak this Sutra only to those who have wisdom. You should not speak a Sutra like this to those who have no wisdom, because it will only cause them to slander it, creating offenses for which they must suffer retribution. So now the people here in the Buddhist Lecture Hall are listening to the Sutra being spoken because they all have a bit of wisdom. If you were stupid, I wouldn't even speak it. If I did, you would run far away This is like one person who said that listening to the Sutras was boring. She went off to find a Good Knowing Advisor. Now, I believe that in this world, if you don't listen to the Sutras or study the Buddhadharma, you can travel the entire world around, but you won't find a Good Knowing Advisor. Why not? Because a Good Knowing Advisor will start out by teaching you the doctrines in the Sutras. Then he will teach you to cultivate and investigate Dhyana and sit in meditation. There are various preparatory steps to learning to sit in meditation. You can't just sit in meditation and not have the slightest idea what you are doing. If you do, you may enter a demonic state. You may claim to have certified to that which you have not yet certified; you may claim to have attained that which you have not yet attained. To say that you have certified to the fruit of Arhatship when you have not is telling a monstrous lie. One who does this will fall into the hells. Such a person might claim, "I am enlightened. I am a Patriarch. I am an Arhat. I am a Bodhisattva. I am a Buddha," claiming to have attained the genuine Buddhadharma when they haven't. What kind of a "Buddha" are they?

Someone says, "The Buddha really knows how to hurt people. If he hadn't spoken *The Lotus Sutra*, then how could people have fallen into hell? He spoke the Sutra and as a consequence a lot of people have fallen into hell. Why? Because they slandered it! Now, if the Buddha had never spoken it, for sure no one would have slandered it. If no one had slandered it, then no one would have fallen into hell. So it more or less amounts to Shakyamuni Buddha sending people to hell!"

Do you think this person is speaking reasonably? Let's figure it out. This person is arguing his case in favor of living beings and against Shakyamuni Buddha, or so it seems. But the Buddha's side must be presented as well, so I'll dare to do it:

You say that if Shakyamuni Buddha hadn't spoken this Sutra no one would have fallen into the hells. On the other hand, if Shakyamuni Buddha hadn't spoken the Sutra, no one would have become a Buddha. If people have fallen into the hells, you can't blame it on the Buddha because he very clearly warned us that to slander the Sutra is to commit a serious offense. Since you know already that it is an offense, you shouldn't slander the Sutra. If you don't slander the Sutra, you won't fall into the hells.

The Buddha said a slanderer would fall into the hells, so if you insist on going ahead and slandering it even more, just to spite him, you will then fall even deeper. There's not the slightest doubt about it. He warned us that one who slanders the Sutra would fall into the hells or turn into a hungry ghost or an animal for boundless aeons. So why do you still want to slander the Sutra? If you do, you are just deliberately pitting yourself against the Buddha. If nobody slanders it, nobody is going to fall into the hells. Ah...so you can't say that people fall into the hells because the Buddha spoke the Sutra. By speaking the Sutra, just think of how many people were caused to bring forth the Bodhi heart and who will in the future become Buddhas. More will become Buddhas than will fall into the hells. Those who fall into the hells are the stupidest ones; they don't believe in anything at all. They know very well that the Buddha said it was an offense to slander the Sutra. They insist on doing it. Now, who can save a person like this? Well, there is someone. It's Earth Store Bodhisattva. When they have fallen into the hells and suffered enough to learn their lesson, Earth Store Bodhisattva will go there to speak the Dharma for them and wipe away their offense karma so they can be born in the heavens or among human beings. Don't worry about the people who slander the Sutra and fall into. the hells. Just pick out a good future for yourself and go forward and make progress. Don't fret about the offenders and get upset about those in hell.

Sutra: T.a10

IF THERE ARE THOSE WITH KEEN FACULTIES,
AND WISDOM WHICH CLEARLY COMPREHENDS,
WITH MUCH LEARNING AND A STRONG MEMORY,
WHO SEEK THE BUDDHA'S PATH,
FOR PEOPLE SUCH AS THESE,
YOU MAY SPEAK IT.
IF THERE ARE THOSE WHO HAVE SEEN IN THE PAST
HUNDREDS OF THOUSANDS OF MILLIONS OF BUDDHAS,
WHO HAVE PLANTED WHOLESOME ROOTS,
WHO HAVE DEEP AND FIRM MINDS,
FOR PEOPLE SUCH AS THESE,
YOU MAY SPEAK IT.
IF THERE ARE THOSE WHO ARE VIGOROUS,
EVER CULTIVATING MINDS OF COMPASSION,
NOT SPARING BODY OR LIFE,
FOR THEM YOU MAY SPEAK IT.
IF THERE ARE THOSE WHO ARE REVERENT,
WITHOUT ANY OTHER THOUGHTS,
WHO HAVE LEFT THE COMMON STUPID FOLK,
WHO DWELL ALONE IN MOUNTAINS AND MARSHES,

FOR PEOPLE SUCH AS THESE
YOU MAY SPEAK IT.
FURTHER, SHARIPUTRA,
IF YOU SEE PEOPLE
WHO HAVE CAST ASIDE BAD KNOWING ADVISORS,
AND DRAWN NEAR TO GOOD FRIENDS,
FOR PEOPLE SUCH AS THESE,
YOU MAY SPEAK IT.
IF YOU SEE DISCIPLES OF THE BUDDHA,
HOLDING PRECEPTS AS PURELY,
AS PURE, BRIGHT JEWELS,
FOR PEOPLE SUCH AS THESE,
YOU MAY SPEAK IT.
IF THERE ARE THOSE WHO HAVE NO HATRED
WHO ARE STRAIGHTFOWARD AND GENTLE,
ALWAYS MERCIFUL TO ALL BEINGS,
AND REVERENT OF ALL BUDDHAS,
FOR PEOPLE SUCH AS THESE,
YOU MAY SPEAK IT.
FURTHER, IF THERE ARE BUDDHA'S DISCIPLES,
WHO IN THE GREAT ASSEMBLY,
WITH MINDS CLEAR AND PURE,
USE VARIOUS CAUSAL CONDITIONS,
PARABLES AND PHRASES,
TO SPEAK THE DHARMA WITHOUT OBSTRUCTION,
FOR PEOPLE SUCH AS THESE,
YOU MAY SPEAK IT.
IF THERE ARE BHIKSHUS,
WHO, FOR THE SAKE OF ALL-WISDOM,
SEEK THE DHARMA IN THE FOUR DIRECTIONS,
WITH PALMS TOGETHER, RECEIVING IT ATOP
THE CROWN,

WHO DELIGHT ONLY IN RECEIVING AND UPHOLDING
THE CANON OF GREAT VEHICLE SUTRAS,
REFUSING TO ACCEPT SO MUCH
AS A SINGLE LINE FROM ANOTHER SCRIPTURE,
FOR PEOPLE SUCH AS THESE,
YOU MAY SPEAK IT.
IF THERE BE THOSE WHO, WITH MIND INTENT,
SEEK THE BUDDHA'S SHARIRA,
OR WHO LIKEWISE SEEK THE SUTRAS,
AND ATTAINING THEM HOLD THEM ATOP THEIR CROWNS,
SUCH PEOPLE WILL NEVER AGAIN
RESOLVE TO SEEK OTHER SUTRAS
NOR EVER HAVE THE THOUGHT
TO SEEK THE WRITINGS OF OUTSIDE WAYS,
FOR PEOPLE SUCH AS THESE,
YOU MAY SPEAK IT.

Outline:

K2. The need for the great kindness heart: Speak the Sutra to good people.
L1. Five pairs of good people to whom the Sutra may be spoken.

Commentary:

The previous verses warned people not to slander the Sutra. This was a case of the Buddha opening the door of his great compassion. Fearing that people might slander the Sutra, the Buddha warned them that if they did so they would fall into the hells. This is not a case of the Buddha trying to scare people, either, because it is true. This is the Sutra spoken for the sake of becoming a Buddha. To say nothing of slandering it outright, you should not even have doubts about it in your mind. The Buddha is being extremely compassionate in warning living beings of this fact. If you clearly know that you will fall into the hells, but insist on slandering it anyway, it must just be that you want to fall into the hells. If you are having trouble getting into the hells, just slander this Sutra, and you will go there on an express. But don't think it's a lot of fun and games. When you get to hell you will be crying. It's no daycare center, that's for sure. You'll be crying your eyes out.

The verses just read are the Buddha opening the great kindness door telling people to cultivate in accord with the Dharma. For example, those people who come to listen to the Sutra being lectured all have good roots. People without good roots might come to listen, but they will immediately want to run away. They won't come back. They'll fly away like birds. They won't even wait for the translation!

In the above passage of text, ten kinds of good people for whom the Sutra may be spoken are listed. They divide into five pairs:

1. The pair of the present and the past: IF THERE ARE THOSE WITH KEEN FACULTIES/ People with keen faculties are intelligent. They are not stupid. When you speak principle to them, they deeply believe it and have no doubts. WITH WISDOM WHICH CLEARLY COMPREHENDS/ They are wise and smart. They believe as soon as they hear it. WITH MUCH LEARNING AND A STRONG MEMORY/ They have read a lot of books and they understand and remember a great many things. WHO SEEK THE BUDDHA'S PATH/ They singlemindedly seek the Buddha Path, looking upon everything in human life as being involved with suffering. Even if a person lives to be a hundred, eventually he is going to die. There's no great meaning to all of it. Thus, they diligently seek the Buddha Path. FOR PEOPLE SUCH AS THESE/ YOU MAY SPEAK IT/ These lines refer to people in the present who have cultivated.

The following lines refer to people in the past who have cultivated: IF THERE ARE THOSE WHO HAVE SEEN IN THE PAST/ HUNDREDS OF THOUSANDS OF MILLIONS OF BUDDHAS/ WHO HAVE PLANTED WHOLESOME ROOTS/ I will tell you: If you want to make offerings to the Triple Jewel, don't make discriminations about it. You should just go ahead and make your offerings singlemindedly. The Buddha, Dharma, and Sangha are one substance. You shouldn't think, "I will give money. What will it be used for?" You shouldn't worry about what it will be used for, and you shouldn't pay attention to what the recipients do with it. That's being insincere. You shouldn't try to control the Triple Jewel with your money. That's not helping them out at all. They can't be controlled by you. If you try to control them then not only do you make no merit for yourself, but you create offenses.

As you plant good roots, just plant them. Don't worry about what the harvest is going to be like.

WHO HAVE DEEP AND FIRM MINDS/ FOR PEOPLE SUCH AS THESE/ YOU MAY SPEAK IT/ You should have deep wisdom, profound Prajna, and your mind should be firm and solid, not making a lot of discriminations. This concludes the pair of the present and past.

2. The pair of the cultivation of blessings and wisdom: IF THERE ARE THOSE WHO ARE VIGOROUS/ EVER CULTIVATING MINDS OF COMPASSION/ NOT SPARING BODY OR LIFE/ FOR THEM YOU MAY SPEAK IT/ These lines represent the cultivation of blessings. Compassion means that you don't see the faults of others. Even if they make mistakes, you still don't reject them. You think, "Oh, they are just children and they don't understand what they are doing. That's why they are creating offenses. I should teach them untiringly and distract them from their games. "Here, kids, don't play with that. I have a nice carriage for you. You can go anywhere you like in it." This is like Shakyamuni Buddha who did a lot of baby-sitting himself. That's being compassionate.

"Not sparing body or life" means that they never rest. Some people do a little something and then feel that it was too bitter. They want to rest. When Bodhisattvas decide to do something, they don't care about their bodies or their lives. They don't spare their bodies or lives to work for living beings.

The following lines represent the cultivation of wisdom: IF THERE ARE THOSE WHO ARE REVERENT/ WITHOUT ANY OTHER THOUGHTS/ They don't have "two hearts." Do you see how detailed the Buddha got in this line? There are some people who seem to be reverent on the outside, but inside they are thinking, "Is this right or not? The Dharma Master says one thing, but are things really this way? Probably not. He speaks the Dharma, but he's just like all of us. Nothing special about him. I better take a good look into it myself. I'm not going to let that Dharma Master cheat me." I'll tell you, now: People with wisdom can't be cheated, even if people try to cheat them. People without wisdom always end up getting cheated whether they are afraid of getting cheated or not. Whether or not you get cheated depends on whether you have genuine wisdom or not.

WHO HAVE LEFT THE COMMON STUPID FOLK/ WHO DWELL ALONE IN MOUNTAINS AND MARSHES/ FOR PEOPLE SUCH AS THESE/ YOU MAY SPEAK IT/ This concludes the pair of blessings and wisdom.

3. The pair of reform and repentance. The following lines represent the quality of reforming one's behavior, and external operation: FURTHER, SHARIPUTRA/ IF YOU SEE PEOPLE/ WHO HAVE CAST ASIDE BAD KNOWING ADVISORS/ What is a bad knowing advisor? One who teaches his disciples contrary to the moral precepts. AND DRAWN NEAR TO GOOD FRIENDS/ FOR PEOPLE SUCH AS THESE/ YOU MAY SPEAK IT/

The following lines refers to the quality of repentance, protecting one's internal cultivation through morality. IF YOU SEE DISCIPLES OF THE BUDDHA/ HOLDING PRECEPTS AS PURELY/ AS PURE, BRIGHT, JEWELS/ FOR PEOPLE SUCH AS THESE/ YOU MAY SPEAK IT/ you may speak *The Dharma Flower Sutra*. This concludes the pair of reform and repentance.

4. The pair of self and others. The following lines refer to cultivation of oneself: IF THERE ARE THOSE WHO HAVE NO HATRED/ WHO ARE STRAIGHTFORWARD AND GENTLE/ If you meet up with a person who has no hateful thoughts...Hate is one of the three poisons. The three poisons are greed, hatred, and stupidity. One without hatred is also without greed or stupidity. Their disposition is very straightforward; such people are incapable of being devious. Their minds are straight. Gentle means they are compliant towards living beings. They are not hard to get along with. ALWAYS MERCIFUL TO ALL BEINGS/ AND REVERENT OF ALL BUDDHAS/ Most people don't know how to be reverent of the Buddhas. When one sees the Buddhas, one should bow respectfully to them. Not to bow is to be irreverent. Why should we bow to the Buddhas? The Buddha is the father of all living beings in the world and we must be respectful to our father. When we see the Buddha, we should bow; when we see Buddha images, we should bow. When we see members of the Sangha who uphold the Buddhadharma, we should bow. We must revere the Triple Jewel. The phrase "to be reverent towards the Buddha" includes being reverent towards the Dharma and the Sangha as well. FOR PEOPLE SUCH AS THESE/ YOU MAY SPEAK IT/

The following lines refer to helping others in their cultivation: FURTHER, IF THERE ARE BUDDHA'S DISCIPLES/ WHO IN THE GREAT ASSEMBLY/ WITH MINDS CLEAR AND PURE/ USE VARIOUS CAUSAL CONDITIONS/ PARABLES AND PHRASES/ TO SPEAK THE DHARMA WITHOUT OBSTRUCTION/ FOR PEOPLE SUCH AS THESE/ YOU MAY SPEAK IT/ They might say, "No killing, no stealing, no sexual misconduct, no false speech, and no taking intoxicants. If you keep the five precepts you can be born in the heavens. If you plant good causes you will reap a good fruit; if you plant bad causes, you will reap an evil fruit. Whatever kind of cause you plant, you reap that fruit. So be very careful with respect to cause and effect.

This concludes the pair of self and others.

5. The following lines represent the pair of beginning and end, that is, beginning by seeking the benefits and ending by receiving the teaching respectfully atop the crown.

The following lines represent the beginning of the search: IF THERE ARE BHIKSHUS/ WHO, FOR THE SAKE OF ALL-WISDOM/ SEEK THE DHARMA IN THE FOUR DIRECTIONS/ WITH PALMS TOGETHER, RECEIVING IT ATOP THE CROWN/ Bhikshu is a Sanskrit word. It has three meanings: 1) a mendicant, 2) frightener of mara. Because they cultivate according to Dharma, they cause the demon kings to be afraid of them. 3) Destroyer of evil. They destroy all the evils of affliction. Because it has so many meanings, it is not translated.

The Bhikshus visit good knowing advisors in the four directions, seeking the Dharma. WHO DELIGHT ONLY IN RECEIVING AND UPHOLDING/ THE CANON OF GREAT VEHICLE SUTRAS/ *The Dharma Flower Sutra*, *The Avatamsaka Sutra*, *The Shurangama Sutra*-- in general they seek the Great Vehicle Sutras everywhere. REFUSING TO ACCEPT SO MUCH/ AS A SINGLE LINE FROM ANOTHER SCRIPTURE/ Having found a Great Vehicle Sutra, they keep it exclusively. They don't study other Sutras. FOR PEOPLE SUCH AS THESE/ YOU MAY SPEAK IT/ For people who are intent on their study, you can speak the Sutra.

The following lines refer to the end of the search: IF THERE BE THOSE WHO, WITH MIND INTENT/ SEEK THE BUDDHA'S SHARIRA/ OR WHO LIKEWISE SEEK THE SUTRAS/ AND ATTAINING THEM HOLD THEM ATOP THEIR CROWNS/ To receive them atop the crown means to hold them in the highest respect. SUCH PEOPLE WILL NEVER AGAIN/ RESOLVE TO SEEK OTHER SUTRAS/ NOR EVER HAVE THE THOUGHT/ TO SEEK THE WRITINGS OF OUTSIDE WAYS/ FOR PEOPLE SUCH AS THESE/ YOU MAY SPEAK IT/ They won't run off to the east or west looking for other texts.

This concludes the pair of beginning and end.

Sutra: T.16b4

I TELL YOU, SHARIPUTRA,
WERE I TO SPEAK OF THE CHARACTERISTICS
OF THOSE WHO SEEK THE BUDDHA'S PATH,
EXHAUSTING AEONS, I WOULD NOT FINISH.
PEOPLE SUCH AS THESE
CAN BELIEVE AND UNDERSTAND,
AND FOR THEIR SAKE'S YOU SHOULD SPEAK
THE WONDERFUL DHARMA LOTUS FLOWER SUTRA.

Outline:

L2. General conclusion.

Commentary:

I TELL YOU, SHARIPUTRA/ WERE I TO SPEAK OF THE CHARACTERISTICS/ of the ten kinds of good people for whom the Dharma may be spoken, OF THOSE WHO SEEK THE BUDDHA'S PATH/ EXHAUSTING AEONS, I WOULD NOT FINISH/ So in general, I have just mentioned the ten above. PEOPLE SUCH AS THESE/ CAN BELIEVE AND UNDERSTAND/ the Sutra, AND FOR THEIR SAKE'S YOU SHOULD SPEAK/ THE WONDERFUL DHARMA LOTUS FLOWER SUTRA.

Some people who study the Buddhadharma have come up with doubts about this passage. They recollect that *The Avatamsaka Sutra* says that if one claims that only one Sutra is correct and the others are wrong, that is the activity of a demon. Here, the Sutra seems to be telling us to cultivate one particular Sutra and not study the other Sutras. Isn't this a contradiction? In reality, to maintain one Sutra is to maintain them all. The one gives rise to the many, and the other Sutras are all included in the one Sutra. *The Lotus Sutra* does not tell you explicitly to cultivate only one Sutra. It's just that if you really exhaust all your efforts, you can only maintain one. If you are capable of maintaining more, that is fine. The more the better. So don't get attached and say that *The Lotus Sutra* tells you to maintain just one Sutra. Don't listen to the Sutras and get attached to them. You have to be flexible.

END OF CHAPTER THREE--*THE DHARMA FLOWER SUTRA*

INDEX

THE BUDDHIST TEXT TRANSLATION SOCIETY

Chairperson: The Venerable Master Hua, Abbot of Gold Mountain Monastery, Professor of the Tripitaka and the Dhyanas

PRIMARY TRANSLATION COMMITTEE:

Chairpersons: Bhikshuni Heng Yin, Lecturer in Buddhism
Bhikshuni Heng Ch'ih, Lecturer in Buddhism

Members: Bhikshu Wei Sung, Lecturer in Buddhism
Bhikshu Heng Kuan, Lecturer in Buddhism
Bhikshu Heng Sure, Lecturer in Buddhism
Bhikshuni Heng Hsien, Lecturer in Buddhism
Bhikshuni Heng Ch'ing, Lecturer in Buddhism
Shramanerika Kuo Ching
Upasaka Huang Kuo-jen, Kung-fu Master, B.A.
Upasaka I Kuo-jung, Ph.D., U.C. Berkeley

REVISION COMMITTEE:

Chairperson: Upasaka I Kuo-jung

Members: Bhikshu Heng Kuan
Bhikshu Heng Sure
Bhikshuni Heng Yin
Bhikshuni Heng Hsien
Professor Lewis Lancaster, U.C. Berkeley
Professor M. Tseng, San Francisco State University
Upasaka Hsieh Ping-ying,author, professor, editor
Upasika Phoung Kuo-wu
Upasaka Lee Kuo-ch'ien, B.A.
Upasaka Li Kuo-wi, M.A.
Upasika I Kuo-han, B.A.
Upasika Kuo-ts'an Epstein
Upasika Kuo-chin Vickers

EDITORIAL COMMITTEE:

Chairperson: Bhikshu Heng Kuan

Members: Bhikshu Heng Sure
Bhikshu Heng Shun
Bhikshuni Heng Yin
Bhikshuni Heng Ch'ih
Bhikshuni Heng hsien
Bhikshuni Heng Chü
Bhikshuni Heng Ch'ing
Professor Irving Lo, University of Indiana

Upasaka I Kuo-jung
Upasaka Kuo K'uei Bach
Upasaka Kuo Chou Rounds, B.A., Harvard
Upasika Kuo Chin Vickers
Upasika Kuo Tsong Bach
Upasaka Kuo T'ang Yager, Ph.D., Columbia
Upasika Kuo Chao Eberle
Upasika Kuo Ts'u Smith
Upasika Kuo Ling Berger
Upasaka Kuo Tsun Dinwiddie, B.A. University of Washington
Upasika Kuo Hsun Nolan, B.A., San Franciso State University

CERTIFICATION COMMITTEE:

Chairperson: The Venerable Master Hua

Members: Bhikshu Heng Kuan
Bhikshuni Heng Yin
Bhikshuni Heng Ch'ih
Bhikshuni Heng Hsien

Upasaka Wong Kuo-chun
Upasaka I Kuo-jung
Upasika T'an Kuo-shih, B.A.
Upasika Kuo-chin Vickers

THE BUDDHIST TEXT TRANSLATION SOCIETY

The Buddhist Text Translation Society is dedicated to making the genuine principles of the Buddhadharma available to the Western reader in a form that can be put directly into practice. Since 1972, the Society has been publishing English translations of Sutras, instructional handbooks in meditation and moral conduct, biographies, poetry, and fiction. Each of the Society's translations is accompanied by a contemporary commentary spoken by the Venerable Master Hsüan Hua. The Venerable Master Hua is the founder of Gold Mountain Monastery and the Institute for the Translation of Buddhist Texts, both located in San Francisco, as well as Gold Wheel Temple in Los Angeles, and the new center of world Buddhism, the City of Ten Thousand Buddhas, near Ukiah, California.

The accurate and faithful translation of the Buddhist Canon into English and other Western languages is one of the most important objectives of the Sino-American Buddhist Association, the parent organization of the Buddhist Text Translation Society.

VII.

EIGHT REGULATIONS FOR TRANSLATION SOCIETY TRANSLATORS:

The translation of the Buddhist Tripitaka is a work of such magnitude that it could never be entrusted to a single person working on his own. Above all, translations of Sutras must be certified as the authentic transmission of the Buddha's proper Dharma. Translations done under the auspices of the Buddhist Text Translation Society, a body of more than thirty Sangha members and scholars, bear such authority. The following eight regulations govern the conduct of Buddhist Text Translation Society Translators:

1. A translator must free himself from motives of personal gain and reputation.
2. A translator must cultivate an attitude free from arrogance and conceit.
3. A translator must refrain from advertising himself and denigrating others.
4. A translator must not establish himself as the standard of correctness and supress the work of others with his fault-finding.
5. A translator must take the Buddha-mind as his own mind.
6. A translator must use the wisdom of the selective Dharma-eye to determine true principles.
7. A translator must request the Virtuous Elders from the ten directions to certify his translations.
8. A translator must endeavor to propagate the teachings by printing Sutras, Shastras, and Vinaya texts when his translations have been certified.

VIII.

A BRIGHT STAR IN A TROUBLED WORLD:

THE CITY OF TEN THOUSAND BUDDHAS

Located at Talmage, California, just south of Ukiah and about two hours north of San Francisco, is Wonderful Enlightenment Mountain. Situated at the base is the 237 acre area holding 60 buildings which is called the City of Ten Thousand Buddhas which is fast becoming a center for religious, educational, and social programs for world Buddhism.

At present, the complex houses Tathagata Monastery and the Great Compassion House for men, Great Joyous Giving House for women, the campus of Dharma Realm Buddhist University, and a large auditorium. Plans are underway to present many kinds of programs to benefit people in spirit, mind, and body--a home for the aged, a hospital emphasizing the utilization of both eastern and western healing techniques, an alternative mental health facility, and educational programs ranging from pre-school through Ph.D. Cottage industries, organic farming, and living in harmony with our environment will be stressed. The City is an ideal spot for conventions where people of all races and religions can exchange their ideas and unite their energies to

Buddha-recitation at the City of Ten Thousand Buddhas

A Dharma lecture in the Hall of Ten Thousand Buddhas

promote human welfare and world peace.

Religious cultivation will be foremost and the City will be instrumental in the transmission of the orthodox precepts of the Buddhas, thus developing Bhikshus and Bhikshunis to teach and maintain the Buddhadharma. Rigorous cultivation sessions are held regularly and the grounds of the monastery provide a pure and quiet setting to pursue the study of meditation. A number of facilities are available for those found qualified to retreat into contemplative seclusion. The spacious grounds have more than a hundred acres of pine groves, and a running stream.

At a time when the world is torn with strife, the City of Ten Thousand Buddhas appears as a guiding star for all of us to discover life's true meaning and pass it on to future generations.

The four-fold assembly of disciples: City of Ten Thousand Buddhas

X.

DHARMA REALM BUDDHIST UNIVERSITY

A SPECIAL APPROACH

Focus on Values: examining the moral foundations of ancient spiritual traditions, relating those traditions to space-age living, and finding what it takes to live in harmony with our social and natural environments.

Focus on change: a key to understanding ourselves, our relationships, and the crises of the modern world. What we seek is to be open to new ways of seeing ourselves, to new modes of relating to friend and stranger, and to new methods and technological aids that supplement and open up for us the limitless store of human wisdom, past and present.

Total environment education where teacher and student are partners in the educational process and share responsibility for it. Learning takes place both in and out of the classroom in a community which is concerned with the complex problems of society.

Personally tailored programs in which education need not be constricted by traditional department boundries. The emphasis will be on meaningful learning, not just the accumulation of facts and test-taking skills.

Education for young and old where the different generations come together to share in the experience of learning and thereby enrich that experience. The University also especially encourages those with valuable life experience to apply for special experimental learning credits.

GUIDING IDEALS

These are the ideals which will guide education at Dharma Realm University:

To explain and share the Buddha's teaching;
To develop straightforward minds and hearts;
To benefit society;
To encourage all beings to seek enlightenment.

CAMPUS

The main campus of Dharma Realm University is located at the foot of Cow Mountain National Recreation Area in the beautiful Ukiah valley. It is surrounded by the woods, meadows, and farmland of the City of Ten Thousand Buddhas.

The University will be housed in several large buildings set among trees and broad lawns. One classroom building has been newly refurbished for educational use.

The air is clean and fresh, and the climate is pleasant and temperate (av. min. temp. 43.2 deg; av. max. temp. 76 deg.) Rarely falling below freezing in the winter and usually dry in the summer, the area is very fertile with much grape and fruit tree cultivation. Close by are the Russian River, Lake Mendocino and Clear Lake, several hot springs, redwood and other national forest lands, and the scenic Pacific Coast.

PROGRAMS-Undergraduate and graduate, full-time and part-time

The University intends to provide quality education in a number of fields, with emphasis (wherever possible) on matching classroom theory with practical experience. The curriculum is divided into three main areas:

The Letters and Science Program: In addition to a regular curriculum of Humanities, Social, and Natural Sciences, special emphasis will be laid on East-West studies, with strong offerings in Asian languages, literature, philosophy, and religion. We expect pioneering interdisciplinary approaches in many of these areas, combining the best of Asian and Western approaches to education. Education for personal growth and the development of special competencies will be the twin aims of the program.

The Buddhist Studies Program will emphasize a combination of traditional and modern methods including actual practice of the Buddhadharma as well as scholarly investigation. Offerings will range from introductory fundamentals to advanced meditation and will include advanced seminars in both English and canonical languages.

The Arts Program: Practical Arts will concentrate on putting knowledge to work right away in workshops for building a living community ecology, energy, gardening and nutrition, community planning, management, etc. Creative Arts offerings will include the meeting of East and West in a whole panorama of studio arts. There will be special courses in Chinese calligraphy, in the creation of Buddha images, and in music. Individual Arts workshops will include t'ai-chi ch'üan, yoga, meditational techniques, wilderness survival, and much more.

THE INTERNATIONAL TRANSLATION CENTER

The Translation Center will sponsor courses, workshops, and special programs concerned with translation techniques for a wide range of languages and will coordinate a unique degree program in translation.

THE WORLD RELIGIONS CENTER

The world Religions Center will sponsor workshops, conferences, and other special programs to aid in mutual understanding and good will among those of different faiths.

SPECIAL INTERNATIONAL STUDENT PROGRAM

In the future, there will be special emphasis on welcoming students from Asian countries to complement the University's strong offerings in East-West studies. Areas of special interest to Asian students will be added to the curriculum as well as a strong English as a Second Language (ESL) Program.

DONATIONS

Dharma Realm University welcomes your help with donations. In addition to financial assistance, the University needs home and office furniture, books and scholarly journals, supplies and equipment, and the services of volunteers. *All donations are tax deductable.*

VERSE ON RETURNING THE LIGHT

Truly recognize your own faults
And don't discuss the faults of others.
Other's faults are just your own faults,
Being one with everyone
is called great compassion.

— Ven. Master Hsuan Hua

THE BUDDHIST TEXT TRANSLATION SOCIETY

The Buddhist Text Translation Society is dedi- ·d to making the genuine principles of the Bud- dharma available to the Western reader in a form can be put directly into practice. Since 1972, Society has been publishing English translations utras (the sayings of the Buddha), instructional dbooks in meditation and moral conduct, biogra- s, poetry, and fiction. Each of the Society's a translations is accompanied by a contempor- commentary spoken by the Venerable Master n Hua. The Venerable Master is the founder of Mountain Monastery and the International In- te for the Translation of Buddhist Texts, in San cisco, of the City of 10,000 Buddhas and Dhar- Realm Buddist University in Mendocino County, fornia, and of Gold Wheel Temple in Los eles. The Venerable Master's sublime commen- s on the wonderful Dharma, given in daily public res, have been heard by sincere cultivators in rica since 1962. For many years he has been ing tirelessly to establish the proper Dharma in Vest by providing clear explanations of the most rtant texts of the Buddhist Canon and by lead- housands of disciples-monks, nuns, laypeople, students-along the Buddha's path to enlighten- through moral practice and spiritual discipline.

BUDDHIST SUTRAS:

Dharma Flower (Lotus) Sutra, with commen- *"Those of slight widsom who delight in lesser nas do not believe that they can become Bud- . That is why we (the Buddhas) use expedient ods, discriminating and teaching the various es. Although three vehicles are taught, it is only e sake of instructing Bodhisattvas". The Lotus er of the Wondrous Dharma Sutra is the king of uddhist Sutras because it is the final teaching e Buddha in which he proclaimed the ultimate only vehicle- the Buddha-vehicle. Vol. 1, In- ction, 85 pgs. $3.95, Vol. II, 324 pgs. $7.95, Vol. 9.00, Fall '78. Further volumes forthcoming.*

The Flower Garland (Avatamsaka) Sutra:

Preface by T'ang Dynasty National Master Ch'ing Liang. *"Going and returning without any trace; Movement and stillness have one source. Embracing the multitude of wonders yet more remains; Transcending words and thought by far. This can only be the Dharmarealm!" The succint verse commentary to the Avatamsaka Sutra by the Venerable T'ang Dynasty Master present the Sutra's principles in concise and elegant form, explained for modern readers in the appended commentary by the Ven. Master Hua. $9.00*

The Ten Dwellings, Chapter Fifteen *with commentary. "All dharmas are apart from words and speech. Their nature is empty, still, extinct and uncreated. Desiring to understand this principle of reality, the Bodhisattva resolves to become enlightened." The major stages passed through by Bodhisattvas after an initial perfection of the Ten Faiths are: the Ten Dwellings, the Ten Practices, the Ten Transferences, the Ten Grounds, Equal Enlightenment and Wonderful Enlightenment. During the course of the Ten Dwellings the Bodhisattva truly brings forth the great thought for Bodhi, is reborn in the household of the Thus Come One, and receives Annointment of the Crown.*

The Ten Grounds, Chapter 26. *Part 1 with commentary. "As the traces of a bird as it wings its path though space are difficult to express, difficult to discern, so too are the principles of the Ten Grounds. From compassion, kindness, and the power of vows one can enter the practices of the Grounds and gradually the mind will become perfected." Part One gives an explanation of the Bodhisattva's First Ground called 'happiness' in which the perfection of giving is brought to completion. $9.00*

The Shurangama Sutra, with commentary. *"The Buddha said, 'Hey. Ananda that is not your mind'. Startled, Ananda leapt from his seat, stood and put his palms together, and said to the Buddha, 'If this is not my mind, what is it?' The Buddha said to Ananda, 'It is your perception of false appearances based on external objects, which deludes your true nature and has caused you from beginningless time to your present life to recognize a thief as your son, to lose your eternal source, and to undergo the wheel's turning.'" It is said, "With the Shurangama one develops wisdom; with the Dharma Flower one becomes a Buddha." Included in this Sutra is the Buddha's explanation of the 50 demonic states associated with the five skandhas. Vol. I 289 pgs., $8.50. vol. II $9.00, Summer '78. Vol. III $9.00, Fall '78. Further volumes forthcoming.*